Healing Fractures in Contemporary Theology

Healing Fractures
in Contemporary Theology

❧

EDITED BY
Peter John McGregor
and Tracey Rowland

CASCADE *Books* • Eugene, Oregon

HEALING FRACTURES IN CONTEMPORARY THEOLOGY

Copyright © 2022 Wipf and Stock Publishers. All rights reserved. Except for brief quotations in critical publications or reviews, no part of this book may be reproduced in any manner without prior written permission from the publisher. Write: Permissions, Wipf and Stock Publishers, 199 W. 8th Ave., Suite 3, Eugene, OR 97401.

Cascade Books
An Imprint of Wipf and Stock Publishers
199 W. 8th Ave., Suite 3
Eugene, OR 97401

www.wipfandstock.com

PAPERBACK ISBN: 978-1-7252-6608-7
HARDCOVER ISBN: 978-1-7252-6609-4
EBOOK ISBN: 978-1-7252-6610-0

Cataloging-in-Publication data:

Names: McGregor, Peter John, 1959, editor | Rowland, Tracey, 1963, editor.
Title: Healing fractures in contemporary theology / edited by Peter John McGregor and Tracey Rowland.
Description: Eugene, OR : Cascade Books, 2022 | Includes bibliographical references.
Identifiers: ISBN 978-1-7252-6608-7 (paperback) | ISBN 978-1-7252-6609-4 (hardcover) | ISBN 978-1-7252-6610-0 (ebook)
Subjects: LCSH: Catholic Church—Doctrines. | Theology—Study and teaching—Catholic Church. | Theology—Doctrinal.
Classification: LCC BX900 R69 2022 (print) | LCC E185.9.M6 (ebook)

Scripture quotations marked RSV are from the Revised Standard Version Bible, Ignatius Edition, copyright ©2006 Division of Christian Education of the National Council of the Churches of Christ in the United States of America. Used by permission. All rights reserved.

Table of Contents

Contributors vii

Introduction ix
—Peter John McGregor

1. Theology and Spirituality 1
—Peter John McGregor

2. What Is Philosophy? 41
—William C. Hackett

3. Theology and Philosophy 50
—D. C. Schindler

4. Theology and Liturgy 69
—David W. Fagerberg

5. The Literal and Spiritual Senses of Sacred Scripture 91
—Leroy A. Huizenga

6. Theology, Preaching, and Apologetics 118
—James Baxter, OP

7. Theology and Ethics 141
—Paul Morrissey

8. Theology and Social Theory 165
—Matthew John Paul Tan

9. Dogmatic and Pastoral Theology 189
—Tracey Rowland

10. Theology and the *Koinonial* Christian Life 206
—Kevin Wagner

11. Theologians and Non-Theologians 229
—John R. Cihak

12. The Generation Gap between Gen X
and Millennial/Post-Millennial Catholics 250
—Helenka Mannering

13. Theologians and the Magisterium 263
—Nigel Zimmermann

Contributors

Fr. James Baxter, OP, is a doctoral candidate at the University of Fribourg.

Mons. John R. Cihak, STD, is the pastor of Christ the King Parish and School in Oregon and has taught theology at Mount Angel Seminary in Oregon and the Pontifical Gregorian University in Rome.

David W. Fagerberg, PhD, is a professor of theology at the University of Notre Dame.

William C. Hackett, PhD, is an assistant professor of philosophy at Saint Meinrad Seminary and School of Theology in Indiana.

Leroy A. Huizenga, PhD, is the administrative chair of arts and letters and professor of theology at the University of Mary in North Dakota.

Helenka Mannering is a doctoral candidate at the Catholic Institute of Sydney.

Peter John McGregor, PhD, is a lecturer in dogmatic theology and spirituality at the Catholic Institute of Sydney.

Paul Morrissey, STD, is the president of Campion College, a liberal arts college in Sydney.

Tracey Rowland, PhD, STD, holds the St. John Paul II Chair of Theology at the University of Notre Dame Australia. She was a member of the IXth International Theological Commission and a recipient of the 2020 Ratzinger Prize.

D. C. Schindler, PhD, is a professor of metaphysics and anthropology at the Pontifical John Paul II Institute for Studies on Marriage and Family at the Catholic University of America in Washington, DC.

Matthew John Paul Tan, PhD, is the dean of studies at St. John Vianney College Seminary, Wagga Wagga, Australia, and an adjunct lecturer in theology at the University of Notre Dame Australia.

Kevin Wagner, PhD, is a lecturer in theology at the University of Notre Dame Australia.

Nigel Zimmermann, PhD, is a senior fellow with the PM Glynn Institute at Australian Catholic University and an adjunct lecturer with the Institute for Ethics and Society at the University of Notre Dame Australia.

Introduction

Peter John McGregor

When I first began to do post-graduate studies in theology, I kept coming across the word "methodology." I would be asked, "What is your methodology?" Frankly, this big word confused and worried me. It was something that my teachers seemed to regard as important, but what did it mean? Finally, I managed to translate it into plain English and realized that it just meant, "How are you going to theologize? How are you going to do what theologians do?" Well, I did no courses on methodology, yet somehow I managed to explain my "methodology" well enough to have my doctoral proposal approved. If I have a methodology, then I think I have acquired it through imitating great theologians, most especially, but not exclusively, Joseph Ratzinger. I have just tried to do what I saw him and others doing.

My doctoral thesis was on something called the Spiritual Christology of Joseph Ratzinger. It was from studying this Christology that I came to realize more concretely how one actually theologizes. I also came to see that many people who are called theologians have very different ideas about what theology is and how one should go about it. Eventually, I came to the conclusion that much contemporary theology is "fractured." There are things that should be integral elements of how one theologizes that have, to greater or lesser extents, become disintegrated. The extent of this disintegration varies from school to school and theologian to theologian.

The genesis of this book lies in a paper that I gave at an Australian Catholic Theological Association conference. The introduction to that paper read:

> Before Vatican II, theological arguments tended to revolve around various *quaestiones disputatae*, for example, the

relationship between nature and grace. However, since the Council, the key question that has developed in theology, often unstated or unrecognised, is much more fundamental. It is, "What is theology?" At present, some theologians regard what some other theologians do as not being theology at all, but something else, perhaps philosophy of religion, or history of religion, or sociology of religion, or psychology of religion, or religious linguistics. In this paper, the fundamental question I wish to address is, how should one theologise?

My starting point is that contemporary theologizing is fractured, and I wish to identify and discuss twelve fractures. These fractures are between 1) Theology and Spirituality 2) Theology and Philosophy 3) Theology and Liturgy 4) Theology and Sacred Scripture 5) the Literal and Spiritual Senses of Sacred Scripture 6) Theology and Christian Life 7) Theology and Doctrine 8) Theology and Preaching/Apologetics 9) various "Branches" of Theology and the related problem of Hyper-Specialisation 10) Theologians and the Magisterium 11) "Theologians" and "Non-Theologians" and 12) the Faculties of the Theologian; their senses, imagination, memory, passions, intellect, and will.

I choose the term "fracture" deliberately. Fractures vary in seriousness. It is one thing to fracture a femur, and another to fracture the distal phalanx bone in a little toe. It is one thing to have a fracture where the bone is shattering into pieces, and another to have a stress fracture that is only a crack. I will not be giving a detailed analysis of each fracture, but confine myself to some introductory analysis, and suggestions about how they could be healed.

To this, I would add that, in saying that fractures can vary in seriousness, I meant that they can vary in seriousness between theologians and that a particular theologian may suffer from some fractures but not others. In each case, an individual diagnosis is required. I would not consider my theologizing to be completely without fractures. I too need splints and bandages.

After giving the paper, two colleagues who heard it suggested independently that I should write a book on this subject. Although I felt completely inadequate for this task, it somehow came to pass that Tracey Rowland and I managed to gather some scholars whom we think have the ability needed to recognize these fractures and prescribe the proper ways in which they should be set. To the original list, three more fractures have been added: "Theology and Ethics," "Theology and Social Theory," and "Dogmatic and Pastoral Theology." These cover what was originally included under the heading of "Theology and Doctrine." Hyperspecialization in theology is addressed in the chapters on "Theology and Ethics" and "Theologians and Non-Theologians." "Theology and Sacred Scripture" is covered in the chapter on "The Literal and Spiritual Senses of Sacred Scripture." There are two additional chapters, one on "What Is Philosophy?" and the other on "The Generation Gap between Gen X and Millennial/Post-Millennial Catholics." There is no chapter on "The Faculties of the Theologian." It is my own conviction that at least a part of the cure for the disintegration of these faculties is the integration that can be achieved by pursuing a theological anthropology of the heart. This is touched upon in the last chapter on "Theologians and the Magisterium."

As for the chapters themselves, the first is on theology and spirituality. This was because the editors think that it is *the fundamental fracture* and that other fractures are manifestations or results of this ur-fracture. This also accounts for it being the longest chapter. Its argument is that we need to recapture and further develop an older understanding of theology, that is, the patristic understanding of *theologia*, if we wish to heal this fracture. This understanding was maintained with reasonable success down to the great scholastic theologians. While a hubristic human reason has always been a danger to true theology, it is argued that the key break between theology and spirituality occurred with William of Ockham. Paradoxically, it was Ockham's exultation of faith over reason that made a truly spiritualized theology impossible since, in a way, it made theology impossible. In Ockham's wake, neither Neo-Thomism, nor transcendental Thomism, nor the "orthopractic" theologies of Johann Baptist Metz, Edward Schillebeeckx, and the liberation theologians have been able to heal this breach. It is in the work of the *ressourcement* theologians that one finds the greatest awareness of the division and the most explicit attempts at reconciliation.

The second chapter, by Chris Hackett, does not deal with a fracture per se but seeks to define the nature of philosophy. This chapter is included because, like theology, currently there is some confusion about the nature of philosophy. To define philosophy, Hackett starts with its Presocratic beginnings. His method is to contrast philosophy with what it is not. Via this method, he concludes that authentic philosophy deals with God, the human, and the world. Moreover, rational *logos* is not set over against "irrational" *mythos*. This means that religion is not foreign to philosophy but is, in fact, the "water in which the philosopher swims." Even revelation is not out of bounds for the philosopher.

D. C. Schindler addresses the fracture between theology and philosophy. He begins by looking at the original unity between philosophy, theology, and the reality of life as displayed by the ancient Greeks. He then introduces the difference made to this unity by Christianity. Initially, Christianity was understood to be the definitive philosophy, the culmination of the theology/philosophy that had preceded it. Yet Christianity also introduced the first self-conscious distinction between theology and philosophy. In spite of this, a certain unity was still maintained into the Middle Ages. It was the rise of modernity that led to a radical breakdown between God and the world, and between faith and reason. Schindler proposes that the way to a restoration of unity lies in the recognition that philosophy and theology are both about "everything," albeit approached on the basis of radically different principles.

For David Fagerberg, the opposite of a fractured theology would be a theology with integrity. Such a theology must take account of liturgy. When it does, theology is not simply human reasoning; it arises from the mystery that liturgy celebrates. This liturgy is not simply human ritual behavior; it should be treated as the work of God. Liturgical theology would be more than talking about God. It would be our speech harmonizing with the word of God, liturgically presented. In that case, theology is Church-speech. Liturgy rests upon the Trinity's self-disclosure, which the theologian contemplates in liturgy. As Evagrius tells us, "If you are a theologian you truly pray. If you truly pray you are a theologian." So, according to Alexander Schmemann, liturgical theology needs to recover the unity of liturgy–theology–piety. For Fagerberg, that would be integral theology—theology with integrity.

In his contribution to healing the fracture between the literal and spiritual senses of Sacred Scripture, Leroy Huizenga also addresses the gulf between theology and biblical studies. He argues that the fractures between both biblical studies and theology on one hand and the letter and spirit on the other parallel each other, for the spiritual senses pertain to the metaphysical realm, where the truth of doctrine exists. According to him, these fractures were occasioned by the rise of nominalism and voluntarism, which influenced the Reformation, which in turn was a stage on the way to the Enlightenment and the so-called historical critical method. Nominalism and voluntarism occasioned major shifts in philosophy, theology, and ultimately cosmology, and so healing the fractures in these areas involves recovering classical conceptions of reality, God, and the cosmos that are plausible today.

As a Dominican, it is fitting that Fr. James Baxter address the fracture between theology on the one hand and preaching and apologetics on the other. He observes that much contemporary Catholic preaching is of a poor quality, not only in style but in theological content and depth. He argues not only that theology must be at the heart of good preaching but that much theology actually comes from preaching. His answer to this theological deficiency is to develop the confidence of preachers in their theological preaching through developing a culture of excellence. Then turning to apologetics, he examines how the previously close relationship between theology and apologetics has developed into a cultural gap. He suggests different ways in which this previously close relationship between theology and apologetics may be restored. These ways are a restoration of the internal unity of apologetics, a refocusing on the unity of apologetics and ecumenism, and the recognition that there is a substantial overlap between theology and apologetics.

In his approach to mending the breach between theology and ethics, Paul Morrissey begins with the problem of hyper-specialization that has affected theology per se. After recounting Avery Dulles's lament about the current fragmentation of theology and his prescription for its reintegration through a recovery of its sapiential dimension, as a guide for the reintegration of theology and ethics (moral theology), Morrissey proposes the moral theologian Servais-Théodore Pinckaers. After a brief introduction to Pinckaers's life and work, he looks at what he regards as the three keys to the reunification of theology and ethics. The first is the retrieval of Aquinas's unifying vision of ethics and the moral life. The second is the work of Pinckaers himself in seeking a renewal of moral theology. The third is the renewal of moral theology as exemplified in the most important magisterial teaching since Vatican II, John Paul II's *Veritatis splendor*, a work that seeks to incorporate a unitive rather than fragmented approach to moral theology.

Matthew Tan's contribution on theology and social theory is to seek to "navigate a path between the uncritical capitulation to social theory or condemnation of it, by analyzing both the promises and pitfalls" of the intersections between theology and social theory. Against the supposed immunity to transcendence present in social theory, he sees a growing openness of social theorists to incorporating a transcendent horizon within their analyses of social phenomena. Since theology is both "a transcendent and immanent mode of analysis and critique of the real," it can intersect with contemporary social theory. Since it is dedicated to "outlining the contours of revelation vis-à-vis creation," it is compelled to breach the borders of "pure secularity." Tan gives the background for this imperative, highlighting how it is not a recent trend but one that goes back at least to the Middle Ages. To meet the need for theology's reconciliation with social theory, he turns to Thomas Aquinas and *Gaudium et Spes*.

In seeking a restoration of unity between dogmatic and pastoral theology, Tracey Rowland argues that "the incarnation, the sacraments, the external order of the Church, and the internal working of sanctifying grace" are all parts of one organic unity that has been undermined by a quintet of "villains"—William of Ockham, Francisco Suárez, Martin Luther, Immanuel Kant, and Georg Hegel. She argues that they in particular are responsible for the severance of the relationship between dogmatic and pastoral theology. She also agrees with Livio Melina that the idea of using prudence, or practical reason, rather than revelation, as a foundation for social ethics, is an idea of Lutheran provenance. For her, the prescription for healing the fracture contains a number of ingredients. These are the Christocentric Trinitarian theological anthropology of John Paul II and Benedict XVI; a return to the priority of *logos* over *ethos* favored by Romano Guardini and Benedict XVI; the need to keep revealed truth, history, and kerygma together; and an eschatological understanding of "the signs of the times."

Kevin Wagner's chapter on theology and the *koinonial* Christian life addresses the relationship between the theologian and the Christian community. He begins with a practical example, his own experience of theologizing as a member of a "new ecclesial community." Then, after defining the terms theology, *koinonia*, and the *koinonial* Christian life, he proposes that the fracture between theology and the *koinonial* Christian life has grown more concerning in the years following Vatican II. He focuses on the secularization and corporatization of many theologates in the West, which now are often comprised primarily of lay theologians rather than priests and religious. Looking at the drawbacks for both the individual theologian and the *ecclesia* of theology done outside of communal life, he proffers some thoughts on how the theologian and the theologate might work to heal the fracture for the benefit of the individual theologian, the theologate, and the wider *ecclesia*.

After defining his terms—theology, theologian, and non-theologian—Mons. John Cihak diagnoses the causes of the rift between theologians and non-theologians as being some "fundamental problems in philosophical and cultural currents in western civilization since the Enlightenment." These currents have affected both theologians and non-theologians. For non-theologians they have resulted in widespread religious indifference and consequent religious ignorance; the attitude that faith, not being "scientific," is not something to be thought about; a distrust in authority; and a spiritual blindness caused by the "sexual revolution." From the side of the theologians, the results have been a lack of consensus about the nature of theology itself, suspicion of ecclesiastic authority, the adoption of philosophical approaches that are incompatible with the nature of divine revelation, the hyper-specialization of theology, and the failure to find formats that effectively connect with non-theologians. Cihak's prescription for this fracture includes a recovery of the sapiential dimension of theology, especially one that enables an encounter with beauty. This theological beauty would also be encountered in the liturgy and in works of charity.

As a budding "millennial" theologian, Helenka Mannering addresses another kind of fracture, the theological generation gap between some younger and older committed Catholics. In particular, she concentrates on that between Generation X Catholics on the one hand and millennial and post-millennial Catholics on the other. According to Mannering, both sides of this divide have experienced similar cultural changes, and in some ways, their resulting approaches to the Catholic faith are similar. However, whereas Gen X's are apt to seek "horizontal" community, Gen Y and Z are more likely to seek "vertical" community as well. While Gen Xers tend to reject metanarratives, their younger counterparts can be more amenable to a broader understanding of reason, operating according to an implicit theo-ontology. Liturgically, Gen Y/Zers are more "mystical" than Cartesian. Morally, they are more on board with *Humanae Vitae* and the theology of the body. They are interested in theology but desire clarity more than creativity. Finally, maturing in a world that is increasingly hostile to religion, they are more likely to hold that no compromise is possible when it comes to the truths of the faith.

In looking at the fracture that sometimes exists between theologians and the magisterium, Nigel Zimmermann sees St. John Henry Newman making a vital contribution to the healing of this relationship. Although the fractures we have encountered in the Church over the last century run deep, they are not insurmountable. In particular, he looks at Newman's fundamental attitude to the question of papal infallibility as an example of how a theologian can work fruitfully with the magisterium, whilst still retaining his or her integrity as a theologian. Taking Mary as the archetype for the development of doctrine and of the "realizing process" of the Church, Newman proposes that the two things necessary are to have a heart open to the divine message and its reality and to be rooted in sound principles. For Zimmermann, Newman's account of the place of the heart and affectivity, and his "thoughtful fidelity" in the theological task, provides a faithful and inspiring model.

The fragmentation of theology is a topic that has engaged many theologians in the twentieth and twenty-first centuries. This book is not the final word on all of the fractures addressed. Nor does it even try to answer all the questions that could be asked. Are these the only fractures in contemporary theology? Is the fracture between theology and spirituality the ur-fracture? What are the relationships between all of these fractures? Are there more remedies that could be applied? In the first chapter of this book, it will be proposed that there is, in fact, only one theologian—"You have one teacher, the Christ" (Matt 23:10)—and that one is a theologian only to the extent that one theologizes in Christ, and Christ theologizes in one. Furthermore, we could go "behind" this and ask ourselves, "Why does Christ teach us?" Certainly, it is so that we can be saved. It is also because it is the will of his Father. Yet Jesus has another motive, that his Father be glorified. Perhaps this is the master key to the healing of theology. Perhaps the answer is best summed up in the words of Yves Congar, OP, "I have given my whole life to theology. But I still consider the highest mode of theology to be doxology."[1]

---

1. Yves Congar, OP, *Word and Spirit* (San Francisco: Harper and Row, 1950), 5.

1

Theology and Spirituality

Peter John McGregor

If someone were a member of an Introduction to Theology class at a seminary or university, the most simple definition of theology that he or she would be likely to hear would almost certainly be St. Anselm's dictum *fides quaerens intellectum*, faith seeking understanding. Or a person might be told that, based on the etymology of the term, theology is the "word about" or the "study of" God. Or one might be directed to read the first question in St. Thomas Aquinas's *Summa Theologiae*, there discovering that *sacra doctrina* is a science that is based on principles revealed by God.[1] Or a more contemporary definition proposed might be something like that of Karl Rahner, that theology "is essentially the conscious effort of the Christian to hearken to the actual verbal revelation, which God has promulgated in history, to acquire a knowledge of it by the methods of scholarship and to reflect upon its implications."[2] Or another might be that of St. John Paul II, that theology "is a cognitive process through which the human mind, illuminated by faith and stimulated by love, advances in the immense territories that divine Revelation has thrown open before it" and is "a science through which the Christian's reason, which receives certitude from the light of faith, by reasoning strives to understand what it believes, that is, the revealed mysteries and their consequences."[3] Having said this, one thing that all of these definitions

---

1. Aquinas, *Summa Theologiae*, Ia, q. 1, a. 2.
2. Rahner and Vorgrimler, *Concise Theological Dictionary*, 456.
3. John Paul II, "Homily."

of theology have in common is that they can give the impression that theology, while it involves revelation and faith, is at its most fundamental level *an exercise in discursive reasoning*.

In contrast, Joseph Ratzinger has drawn attention to the ancient Greek use of the word θεολογία (*theologia*) to designate not a human science but the divine discourse itself. For this reason, the Greeks designated as theologians only those who could be regarded as instruments of the divine discourse. So, Aristotle drew a distinction between θεολογία and θεολογιχή (*theologiche*)—between theology and the study of theology, between the divine discourse and human effort to understand it. Pseudo-Dionysius used the word theology to designate Sacred Scripture—the discourse of God rendered into human words.[4] According to him, Scripture alone is theology in the fullest sense of the word. The writers of Sacred Scripture are *theologoi*, "through whom God as subject, as the word that speaks itself, enters into history."[5] Thus the Bible becomes the model of all theology, and the biblical writers the norm for the theologian. Because theology is ultimately the word that God speaks to us, it can never be a merely "positive" science, but rather a "spiritual" one. Even when studied in the academe, theology must be studied "in the context of a corresponding spiritual praxis and of a readiness to understand it, [and] at the same time, as a requirement that must be lived[;] . . . just as we cannot learn to swim without water, so we cannot learn theology without the spiritual praxis in which it lives."[6] It must include "the necessary self-transcendence of contemplation into the practice of the faith."[7]

Here Ratzinger is saying something more than that theologians need to be prayerful people. The spiritual praxis to which he refers is something more than being faithful to prayer, or even that it must be a theology "on one's knees."[8] It is a praxis within which theology "lives," and "a requirement that must be lived." One must understand this spiritual praxis, this "spirituality," as something more than one's prayer life, or a particular spirituality identified as Benedictine, Franciscan, Dominican,

---

4. Ratzinger, *Principles of Catholic Theology*, 320–21.

5. Ratzinger, *Principles of Catholic Theology*, 321.

6. Ratzinger, *Principles of Catholic Theology*, 322. See also Balthasar, "Spirituality," 1:211: "Spirituality is the subjective aspect of dogmatic theology."

7. Ratzinger, *Principles of Catholic Theology*, 321. Here Ratzinger is referring to the theology of St. Bonaventure.

8. Balthasar, "Theology and Sanctity," 1:206.

or Carmelite. It is contemplation that is put into practice, that is, it is *theoria* that is put into *praxis*.

It will be the contention of this chapter that a "fracture" is to be found in much contemporary theology between what Ratzinger calls the "positive" and the "spiritual" aspects of this theology. This could also be expressed by the statement that much contemporary theology is "despiritualized." This is not to say that the definitions, as given, of Anselm, Aquinas, Rahner, and John Paul II, are wrong. Rather, they are incomplete. Of all of them, it is John Paul II's that comes closest to a full definition, since he says that theology is "a cognitive process," not just "illuminated by faith" but also "stimulated by love." Herein, it will be proposed that we need a kind of *ressourcement*, not just one that is biblical, or liturgical, or patristic, or Thomistic, but *one that recovers the original nature of theology itself*.

The Patristic Understanding of Theologia

How was this contemplation, this spiritual praxis that Ratzinger speaks of and within which theology exists, understood in patristic times? The original meaning of the term theology, as used by Plato, was the presentation of the truth about God, regardless of the poetic, epic, lyric, or tragic form in which that truth was presented.[9] Given this association with pagan mythology, the earliest Christian "theologians" did not call themselves theologians, nor what they did "theology." Rather, for people such as St. Justin Martyr, Christianity was the "true philosophy." Origen called himself a philosopher. Even as late as St. Augustine, Christianity is referred to as "the true philosophy."[10]

It was not until the time of Eusebius of Caesarea that the term theology begins to be used in a Christian sense. Eusebius described St. John as the Theologian, since he saw his Gospel as concerned primarily with the divinity of Christ.[11] Furthermore, he said that the purpose of his Church history was to show the "theology and economy of salvation according to Christ."[12] However, we must be careful not to read back into the writings of the fathers a later concept of theology. As Balthasar states,

---

9. Plato, *Republic*, bk 2, 379a5.
10. Augustine, *Contra Iulianum*, 4.72.
11. Eusebius of Caesarea, *De eccl. theol.*, 1.20; 2.12. See also Spidlík, *Prayer*, 191.
12. Eusebius of Caesarea, *History of the Church*, 1.1.7; *prol.* 2.

> The subsequent separation of theology and spirituality was quite unknown to them. It would not only be idle but contrary to the very conceptions of the Fathers to attempt to divide their works into those dealing with doctrine and those concerned with the Christian life (spirituality).[13]

Thus, for St. Gregory Nazianzus, theology is "the contemplation of heavenly things."[14] It cannot be engaged in by the impure.[15] To be a theologian is to be a "herald of God," specifically in proclaiming the divinity of Christ.[16] For Maximos the Confessor, it is a "grace." Thus, "the intellect is granted the grace of theology when, carried on wings of love . . . it is taken up into God and with the help of the Holy Spirit discerns—as far as is possible for the human intellect—the qualities of God."[17]

For Evagrius of Pontus, *theologia* is the highest degree of contemplation. Thus, when he writes that, "If you are a theologian, you will pray truly. And if you pray truly, you are a theologian,"[18] what he means is, "If you are a contemplator of God, you will pray truly. And if you pray truly, you are a contemplator of God." For Evagrius, theology is the highest degree of *theoria*, that is, the contemplation of the Trinity.[19] Theology is not a direct vision of God, since that is possible for us only in the beatific vision. However, in patristic writings about theology, expressions such as "to see God" and "vision of God" were frequently used. It is spoken of as a beholding as "in a mirror."[20] "For now I see in a mirror dimly, but then face to face. Now I know in part, then I shall understand fully, even as I have been fully understood" (1 Cor 13:12). It is "not a vision of lower creatures, but an indirect vision of God in the soul itself, in the deified mind which is the image of God."[21]

The vision of God in the soul was also spoken of by Evagrius as the vision of God in "the place of God." He used the Septuagint text of Exodus

---

13. Balthasar, "Theology and Sanctity," 1:182–83.

14. Gregory Nazianzus, *Oratio 26: In seipsum*, 5; PG 35:1233B. See Spidlík, *Prayer*, 191.

15. Gregory Nazianzus, *Oratio 28: Theologica* 2.2ff, PG 36:29AB. See Spidlík, *Prayer*, 191.

16. Gregory Nazianzus, *Epistola*, 185; PG 37:153C. See Spidlík, *Prayer*, 191.

17. Maximos the Confessor, *Four Hundred Texts*, no. 26, in *Philokalia* 2, 69.

18. Evagrius, *De oratione*, 60.

19. Evagrius, *Praktikos*, prologue. See Spidlík, *Prayer*, 191.

20. Spidlík, *Spirituality of Christian East*, 338.

21. Spidlík, *Spirituality of Christian East*, 338.

24:11: "And of the chosen ones of Israel there was not even one missing, and they appeared in the place of God, and did eat and drink." This differs from the Masoretic text in speaking of the "place of God" rather than simply "God." Using this, Evagrius identified "the vision of one's appropriate state" with the vision of the Holy Trinity.[22] We are the "place of God." For most Eastern spiritual writers, the state of the human being is the heart. Therefore, the height of contemplation is the contemplation of God in one's heart.[23] Whereas speaking of the vision of God could imply a distance between the Creator and the creature, the expression "place of God" encourages movement toward a more direct encounter, but on the level of the soul and not "face to face."[24]

How does one obtain the necessary purity of heart to contemplate God in the place of God? The heart must be purified through *praxis*, which is the indispensable precondition for *theoria*. Yet the two are mutually dependent. Although it is through *praxis* that one ascends to *theoria*, there can be no *praxis* without *theoria*.[25] For Origen, the virtues lead to knowledge.[26] For Philoxenes of Mabbug, "mystical contemplation is revealed to the mind after the soul has recovered its health."[27] A traditional definition of prayer is that it is the ascent of the mind to God. However, as Evagrius says, "the mind will make no progress, will not safely complete this way of trials and will not enter the realm of the incorporeal, unless it sets right what is within."[28] Another way of saying this is that there is no true knowledge without love. According to Evagrius, "The first and the greatest of the commandments is charity, thanks to which the mind sees the first love, that is, God."[29] According to St. Ephrem, contemplation and charity, truth and love, are inseparable wings by which we rise to God.[30] As Tomaš Špidlík explains the fundamental patristic attitude, "without

22. Evagrius, "Letter 39." See Špidlík, *Spirituality of Christian East*, 338.

23. Špidlík, *Spirituality of Christian East*, 338.

24. Špidlík, *Spirituality of Christian East*, 338.

25. Špidlík, *Spirituality of Christian East*, 334.

26. Origen, *Commentarium in Matthaeam*, 12.14. See Špidlík, *Spirituality of Christian East*, 334.

27. Philoxenes of Mabbug, in Hausherr, *Hésychasme et prière*, 28. See Špidlík, *Spirituality of Christian East*, 334.

28. Evagrius, "Praktikos," 61. See Špidlík, *Spirituality of Christian East*, 334.

29. Evagrius, "Letter 56." See Špidlík, *Spirituality of Christian East*, 334.

30. Ephrem, *De fide*, 20.12. Špidlík quotes Ephrem in *Spirituality of Christian East*, 335.

love, the knowledge of God through 'connaturality' is not possible, because 'God is love' (1 Jn 4:8, 16)."³¹

One more element of the patristic practice of theology needs to be enunciated. *Theoria* and *praxis* are not to be conceived of as exclusively private pursuits but ultimately must be grounded in liturgical prayer. As Ratzinger has pointed out, it was the theology of the Cappadocian fathers that undergirded the reaffirmation of the Nicaean Creed at the first Council of Constantinople and, in the case of St. Basil of Caesarea, the source of that theology was the liturgy. "Basil developed his concept of the Holy Spirit, his concept of Christian monotheism, entirely from the liturgy of the Church; his book about the Holy Spirit is, at bottom, nothing other than a theology of the liturgy."³²

When Does the Fracture Take Place?

In 1946, Jean Daniélou wrote, "It is no longer possible to disassociate, as was done too much in times past, theology and spirituality. The first was placed upon a speculative and timeless plane; the second too often consisted only of practical counsels separated from the vision of man which justified it."³³ Here Daniélou is referring to the then contemporary neoscholastic way of theologizing. Some would blame the separation on what Marie-Dominique Chenu called Baroque Thomism, the Thomism of Thomas Cajetan and Francisco Suárez.³⁴ Yet, Balthasar would place the rupture earlier, with the movement of the *locus* of theologizing from the pastoral and monastic worlds to that of the university, so that "theology at prayer was superseded by theology at the desk."³⁵ According to Balthasar, this secession did not take place until after the time of St. Albert the Great, St. Bonaventure, St. Thomas Aquinas, and perhaps even Duns Scotus.³⁶ In Larry Chapp's explanation of Balthasar's position,

---

31. Spidlík, *Spirituality of Christian East*, 335.
32. Ratzinger, *Principles of Catholic Theology*, 120.
33. Daniélou, "Orientations présentes," 17. Although Daniélou here is referring to a separation that he perceived between neoscholastic theology on the one hand and spirituality on the other, it will be maintained that this split is also evident in some more historically aware theologies. See also Chenu, "Position de la théologie," 252; and Balthasar, "Theology and Sanctity."
34. Chenu, *École de théologie*, 155–57. See also Rowland, *Catholic Theology*, 46.
35. Balthasar, "Theology and Sanctity," 1:208.
36. Balthasar, "Theology and Sanctity," 1:187. See also Chapp, "Union," 229.

As practiced in the hands of its masters (such as Albertus Magnus, Aquinas, Anselm, and Bonaventure) the scholastic method was at once academic and deeply spiritual, holding in view the proper distinctions between faith and reason (or nature) and grace, all the while grounding those distinctions in a theological criterion. Following in their wake was an era of epigones who could not hold the synthesis together, and so theology began to degenerate into an arid, rationalistic formalism that viewed the task of theology as an exercise in the deductive application of the first principles of Revelation to a host of topical theological "issues." After the Reformation, the scientific revolution, and the Enlightenment, this hypertrophy of the deductive moment in theology was contaminated with the bacillus of a kind of Cartesianism that sought logical certitude above all things. It thus degenerated into a theology in full defensive, reactionary mode, intent on "proving" the truth of faith to the nonbelievers through the putatively "certain" philosophical propaedeutic, with an equally rationalistic rigor applied to theological debates with the Protestants.[37]

Balthasar is not the only one who posits the beginnings of a split during the Middle Ages. In two successive general audiences in 2009, Pope Benedict XVI spoke about two types of theology, which he called "monastic" and "scholastic."[38] He also called them, respectively, the "theology of the heart" and the "theology of reason."[39] According to him, during the twelfth century, Latin theology flourished in two milieux, monasteries and *scholae*, which followed two different theological models. The monks practiced what he calls a biblical theology, which entailed the devout listening to and reading of Sacred Scripture, that is to say, *lectio divina*, a prayed reading of the Bible. It was a biblical theology practiced in docility to the Holy Spirit. The aim was to read Sacred Scripture in the same spirit as that in which it was written. This praxis demanded a purification of the heart if it were to reach its ultimate goal, an encounter with the Lord, knowing and loving God. By it, "theology thus becomes meditation, prayer, a song of praise and impels us to sincere conversion."[40]

On the other hand, according to Benedict XVI, the aim of scholastic theology was "to train professionals of culture in a period in which

37. Chapp, "Union," 229.
38. Benedict XVI, "Monastic Theology."
39. Benedict XVI, "Two Theological Models."
40. Benedict XVI, "Monastic Theology."

the appreciation of knowledge was constantly growing." Central to the scholastic method was the *quaestio*, the questions that arise from Scripture and tradition and give rise to debate. Scholastic theology sought to achieve a synthesis between arguments based on authority and those based on reason "in order to reach a deeper understanding of the word of God." The aim of this kind of theology was to add "the dimension of reason to the word of God and thus [create] a faith that is deeper, more personal, hence also more concrete in the person's life."[41] The creation of syntheses led to the birth of "systematic" theology. The scholastic method sought to present the unity and harmony of Christian revelation through the use of human reason.

In looking at these two methods, Benedict XVI does not treat one as correct and the other as incorrect. Scholastic theology enables us to give an account of the hope that is in us (cf. 1 Pet 3:15). He agrees with St. John Paul II that "faith and reason are like two wings on which the human reason rises to the contemplation of the truth."[42] However, the essential insight of monastic theology concerns the ultimate goal of all theology. Both faith and reason must be "inspired by the search for intimate union with God."[43] Taking St. Bernard and Abelard as representatives of the two methods of theology, Benedict XVI states that, in pursuing the goal of *fides quaerens intellectum*, St. Bernard put the emphasis on faith, while Abelard put it on reason. Thus,

> for Bernard faith itself is endowed with deep certitude based on the testimony of Scripture and on the teaching of the Church Fathers. Faith, furthermore, is reinforced by the witness of the Saints and by the inspiration of the Holy Spirit in the individual believer's soul. In cases of doubt and ambiguity, faith is protected and illumined by the exercise of the Magisterium of the Church.[44]

The dangers that Bernard saw in Abelard's approach were an arrogant intellectualism, a relativization of truth, and even a questioning of the truths of the faith. He saw the danger of a lack of intellectual humility wherein the theologian could come to believe in the ability of reason to "grasp" the mystery of God. Monastic, that is to say, contemplative

---

41. Benedict XVI, "Monastic Theology."
42. Benedict XVI, "Monastic Theology." See John Paul II, *Fides et Ratio*, preface.
43. Benedict XVI, "Monastic Theology."
44. Benedict XVI, "Two Theological Models."

theology must form the basis of scholastic theology. As Benedict XVI says,

> [In] the theological field there must be a balance between what we may call the architectural principles given to us by Revelation, which therefore always retain their priority importance, and the principles for interpretation suggested by philosophy, that is, by reason, which have an important but exclusively practical role.[45]

For Benedict XVI, in theology, humble love must direct the intellect. Thus,

> when love enlivens the prayerful dimension of theology, knowledge, acquired by reason, is broadened. Truth is sought with humility, received with wonder and gratitude: in a word, knowledge only grows if one loves truth. Love becomes intelligence and authentic theology wisdom of heart, which directs and sustains the faith and life of believers.[46]

In the terms of the argument presented here, Abelard's theologizing suffered from a degree of despiritualization. In fact, Benedict makes the point that it was Abelard "who introduced the term 'theology' in the sense in which we understand it today."[47]

Are the Scholastics to Blame for the Despiritualization of Theology?

We have seen that Balthasar places the beginnings of the despiritualization of theology in the fourteenth century, while Ratzinger claims to see its beginnings as early as Abelard in the twelfth century. Let us examine this question by looking at the understanding of the nature of theology of the two greatest scholastic theologians, St. Thomas Aquinas and St. Bonaventure.

---

45. Benedict XVI, "Monastic Theology."
46. Benedict XVI, "Monastic Theology."
47. Benedict XVI, "Two Theological Models."

St. Thomas Aquinas

It was Thomas himself who explained the work of the Dominicans as *contemplare et contemplate aliis tradere* (contemplate and hand over to others the fruits of contemplation).[48]

The question is, what does Thomas mean by "contemplation"? At the very beginning of the *Summa Theologiae*, he writes,

> It was necessary for man's salvation that there should be a knowledge revealed by God besides philosophical science built up by human reason. Firstly, indeed, because man is directed to God as to an end that surpasses the grasp of his reason. . . . But the end must first be known by men who are to direct their thoughts and actions to the end. Hence it was necessary for the salvation of man that certain truths which exceed reason should be made known to him by divine revelation. . . . It was therefore necessary that besides philosophical science built up by reason, there should be a sacred science learned through revelation.[49]

Two points need to be made from this passage. First, the end for man is not knowledge about God but simply God. Second, it is necessary to understand that what Thomas means by sacred science, *sacra doctrina*, is more than what today would be encompassed by the term theology. It includes what is revealed through Sacred Scripture and all levels of Christian teaching. According to Matthew Levering, for Thomas, *sacra doctrina* is "wisdom." That is, it is "knowledge (*scientia*) of the things that have been divinely revealed (God and all things insofar as they are referred to God as their beginning and end)."[50] As Levering also points out, Thomas sometimes uses *sacra scriptura* interchangeably with *sacra doctrina*.[51] Theology is *sacra doctrina* in a scientifically developed form. Since it has to do with revelation, faith is necessary for the practice of theology. As a science, theology is subordinate to the knowledge that God has of himself. The mystery of the Trinity, and the providence of God towards the human beings he has created, is known only to God himself and can be made evident to the blessed by participation in the beatific vision. The theologian can have access to this knowledge only through faith.

48. Aquinas, *Summa Theologiae*, IIa–IIae, q. 188, a. 6.
49. Aquinas, *Summa Theologiae*, Ia, q. 1, a. 1.
50. Levering, *Scripture and Metaphysics*, 31.
51. Levering, *Scripture and Metaphysics*, 31.

God is the subject, not the object, of this science. God is the reality that this science seeks to know, but this reality can be known only through the mediation of concepts. It is these concepts that are the objects of this science. These concepts never exhaust the reality of the subject. The end of the theologian is not just objective concepts of God but *God*. For Thomas, the ultimate end of *sacra doctrina* is *contemplatio primae veritatis in patria*, the contemplation of the first truth in the fatherland.[52] The first truth is simply God.

For Thomas, theology is principally "speculative" rather than "practical." In this, Thomas differs from the scholastic theologians who proceeded him. For these theologians, although theology is speculative, it is primarily practical.[53] It is practical in that it should guide human action according to the gospel so as to reach beatitude. That is, charity is the end. For Thomas, to say that theology is principally speculative is to say that it is principally contemplative. Thus, "action is not what is ultimately pursued in this science, but rather the contemplation of the first truth in the fatherland, to which we will attain once we have been purified by our good works, according to Mt 5:8: 'Blessed are the pure in heart: they shall see God.' This is why it is more speculative than practical."[54] As Thomas also says, "All those who think rightly recognize that the end of human life is found in the contemplation of God."[55] As Jean-Pierre Torrell points out, "It is significant that this statement immediately precedes the discussion on the end of theological knowledge, a clear sign that the latter extends and further defines the former."[56] Torrell further points out that, for Thomas, theology is "the sole body of knowledge whose end as a science (*finis operis*) is identical with the end of the one who practices it (*finis operantis*)."[57]

Theologizing enables the theologian to pursue a contemplation that remains, in this life, incomplete. Since theology begins with what God reveals, even though it employs reason, its divine origin means that it is

---

52. Aquinas, *Sent.* I, prologue, a. 3. See Torrell, *Christ and Spirituality in St. Thomas Aquinas*, 6.

53. Aquinas, *Summa Theologiae* Ia, q. 1, a. 4; *Sent.* I, prologue, a. 3. See Torrell, *Christ and Spirituality*, 6.

54. Aquinas, *Sent.* I, prologue, a. 3. ad 1. See Torrell, *Christ and Spirituality*, 7.

55. Aquinas, *Sent.* I, prologue, a. 1. See Torrell, *Christ and Spirituality*, 7.

56. Torrell, *Christ and Spirituality*, 8.

57. Torrell, *Christ and Spirituality*, 8. See Aquinas, *Summa Theologiae*, IIa–IIae, q. 180, a. 4.

"like a certain imprint of the divine science," that is, the divine knowledge.[58] The faith of the theologian "ensures a continuity between the theologian's knowledge [*savoir*] and God's own knowledge of himself."[59] This continuity, established by faith, enables theological contemplation to procure "a foretaste of eternal beatitude, a *praelibatio quaedam* of the divine goods that we enjoy in the beatific vision."[60]

Thomas's understanding of contemplation is that it is "an act of the cognitive power directed by the will."[61] In the case of Christian contemplation, since it is an act that ends in its object, namely God, it is also an affective act that "proceeds from love of the object, for where love is found, there also is found the gaze; cf. Mt 6:21: 'Where your treasure is, there also is your heart.'"[62] Furthermore, "the end of contemplation is nothing else than truth; but when contemplation becomes a way of life it also takes account of affectivity and the good."[63] For Thomas, contemplation engages not just the intellect but also the will and affectivity.

Where does theological contemplation fit within this schema? As Levering points out, Thomas presents wisdom in four ways: "wisdom as a (natural) intellectual virtue, wisdom as a gift of the Holy Spirit, wisdom as *sacra doctrina*, and Wisdom as the Son of God."[64] Thomas says that theological science is the same as wisdom. Wisdom per se judges all things according to the highest causes. Theological wisdom judges the highest cause of all, which is God. So, it is the highest form of human wisdom. This theological wisdom is obtained through study. This could be called acquired wisdom. Yet there is another form of wisdom, the gift of wisdom given by the Holy Spirit by infusion.[65] Through the first, one is wise in a human way; through the second, by a connaturality with

---

58. Aquinas, *Summa Theologiae*, Ia, q. 1, a. 3, ad 2. See Torrell, *Christ and Spirituality*, 10.

59. Torrell, *Christ and Spirituality*, 10. See Aquinas, *In Boet. De Trin.* q. 3, a. 1, ad 4.

60. Torrell, *Christ and Spirituality*, 10. See Aquinas, *Compendium theol.* I, ch. 2; *Summa Theologiae* IIa–IIae, q. 4, a. 1.

61. Aquinas, *Sent.* III, d. 35, q. 1, a. 2, qla 1. See Torrell, *Christ and Spirituality*, 10–11.

62. Aquinas, *Sent.* III, d. 35, q. 1, a. 2, qla 1. See Torrell, *Christ and Spirituality*, 11.

63. Aquinas, *Sent.* III, d. 35, q. 1, a. 2, qla 1, ad 1. See Torrell, *Christ and Spirituality*, 11.

64. Levering, *Scripture and Metaphysics*, 27.

65. Aquinas, *Summa Theologiae*, IIa–IIae, q. 45, a. 2. See Torrell, *Christ and Spirituality*, 15–17.

what is known. So, "Hierotheus became wise not only by studying, but by experiencing the divine."[66] Theological wisdom is an intellectual virtue. Infused wisdom is the anointing of the Holy Spirit that will teach one all things (cf. 1 John 2:27). It is "an intuitive grasp of the realities of the faith which are at the origin of all Christian wisdom. The gift of wisdom thus culminates in a deiform and in a certain sense explicit contemplation, of the realities which faith holds implicitly in a human manner."[67] As Levering explains,

> *Sacra doctrina* remains wisdom according to a human mode: the transmission of *sacra doctrina* requires for its task of ordering the normal methods of the human mind. Aquinas points out that *sacra doctrina* "is acquired by study, though its principles are obtained by revelation" (ST 1, q.1, a.6, ad 3). Thus *sacra doctrina* as wisdom is not the same as the wisdom that is the gift of the Holy Spirit. In the interplay of grace and nature, the truths known by metaphysical reasoning are not displaced by the infusion of revealed knowledge. Yet the architectonic principle is not God known by natural reason, but God's own knowledge ... "in our frail minds."[68]

For Thomas, theologizing is a "wisdom-exercise" that is meant to enhance "the ability to participate more and more deeply in the dynamic presence, through faith and the gift of the Holy Spirit, of *God's own knowledge* in our frail minds.... By practicing theological wisdom, the believer is enabled to anticipate, and to live in accord with, the ultimate end of *deification* that marks the transition from grace to glory."[69] As Levering also points out, in his commentary on the Gospel of John, Thomas agrees with the patristic understanding of St. John the Evangelist as a contemplative who ascends to the knowledge of the Triune God.[70]

Although Thomas makes the above distinction between theological wisdom and infused wisdom, there is no reason why the theologian cannot experience both. Indeed, as Torrell points out,

---

66. Aquinas, *Summa Theologiae*, Ia q. 1, a. 3, a. 6. See Torrell, *Christ and Spirituality*, 15.

67. Aquinas, *Sent.* III, d. 35, q. 1, a. 2, qla 1, ad 1. See Torrell, *Christ and Spirituality*, 16.

68. Levering, *Scripture and Metaphysics*, 33.

69. Levering, *Scripture and Metaphysics*, 37–38.

70. Levering, *Scripture and Metaphysics*, 39–46.

the very demands of the wisdom that the theologian practices make it desirable for him not to remain a pure theorist. His knowledge could only become sharpened by this experience, and thus increase in penetration. Without extrapolating too much outside the limits of the texts, we may even say that this is what happened for St. Thomas himself.[71]

St. Bonaventure

If Thomas is not to blame for the fracture between theology and spirituality, should we blame the Franciscans? Was Thomas correct in holding that theology is a *scientia speculativa* and the Franciscans incorrect in holding that it was a *scientia practica*?[72] Let us attempt to answer this question by examining the nature of theology as held by Thomas's contemporary, and the greatest of the Franciscan theologians, St. Bonaventure.

As John Cihak has pointed out, "What is striking about the Seraphic Doctor's conception of theology . . . is the emphasis that Bonaventure gives to the formative and directive force that the unique 'object' of theology exerts upon the way theology proceeds. In other words, theology is guided not only by its *principles* . . . but most especially by its *relation* to its object.[73] Because of this, for Bonaventure, theology is an "affective science," a science of love. It "is located between speculative science, which perfects the intellect in itself (*in se*), and practical science, which perfects the intellect by extending it toward doing something (*ad opus*). In affective science, the intellect is perfected by being extended toward the *affectus* (*ad affectum*)."[74] It is "love seeking understanding."[75] One can see here a certain similarity with Thomas since, for him, Christian contemplation is both speculative and affective.

71. Torrell, *Christ and Spirituality*, 18.

72. For example, see Alexander of Hales, *Summa Theologica*, 1, tract. intro., cap 1, solutio: "Theology perfects the soul according to the will, by contrast, it is wisdom as far as it is wisdom." As Lydia Schumacher explains this assertion, "At the very start of the Summa, theology is defined as a 'practical' rather than a 'theoretical' science, the primary purpose of which is not to instruct the mind about God but to move the affections of the will towards what is good, on account of love for God" (Schumacher, "Divine Command Theory," 474).

73. Cihak, "How Faith Forges Reason," 145.

74. Cihak, "How Faith Forges Reason," 145.

75. Ratzinger, *Nature and Mission*, 27. See also Twomey, "Ratzinger on Theology," 54.

Since theology is an affective science, its end is not merely *scientia* (knowledge) but *sapientia* (wisdom). It is knowledge that has passed into love of its object, which is God.[76] What this means for the actual practice of theology is that while faith establishes this relationship with God, human reason must be transformed through grace in order for it to comprehend the object of theology, namely, God.[77] This transformation from knowledge to wisdom takes place through what Bonaventure calls holiness.[78] This holiness is a pure love that brings about a deiformity that enables the achievement of wisdom.[79]

Bonaventure explains how our deification through sanctifying grace (*gratia gratum faciens*) takes place in three stages. The first is the rectification and cleansing of the soul though the theological virtues of faith, hope, and charity. The second is the freeing of the soul so that the soul can move towards God through the gifts of the Holy Spirit. The third is the perfecting of the soul and uniting it to God through the beatitudes.[80] Bonaventure locates holiness in the second stage, after the virtues but before perfection. Holiness is the soul informed by the gifts of the Holy Spirit.[81] Yet all three stages—virtues, gifts, and beatitudes—function together. Each attains to its particular mode of theological knowing. The virtues correspond to symbolic or creedal theology, what we would call doctrine; the gifts of the Holy Spirit correspond to theology proper, that is, what we would call academic theology; and the beatitudes correspond to contemplative theology, both acquired and infused.[82]

Can we not say that those who call themselves academic theologians must strive to practice all three and integrate that practice into one? If we are to do so, then we must remember that, for Bonaventure, what we call academic theology is not the highest form of theology. For Bonaventure, St. Francis of Assisi was the greatest "modern" theologian. Continuing what Cihak says above,

---

76. LaNave, *Through Holiness to Wisdom*. See also Cihak, "How Faith Forges Reason," 145–46.

77. Cihak, "How Faith Forges Reason," 146.

78. Bonaventure, *Collationes in Hexaëmeron*, 19.3. See LaNave, *Through Holiness to Wisdom*, 11.

79. Cihak, "How Faith Forges Reason," 146.

80. Cihak, "How Faith Forges Reason," 146–47.

81. Cihak, "How Faith Forges Reason," 147.

82. Cihak, "How Faith Forges Reason," 146–47.

what is striking about the Seraphic Doctor's conception of theology . . . is the emphasis that Bonaventure gives to the formative and directive force that the unique "object" of theology exerts upon the way theology proceeds. In other words, theology is guided not only by its *principles* . . . but most especially by its *relation* to its object. This emphasis on the object comes as no surprise, considering the central event that serves as the irradiating nucleus driving and informing Bonaventure's theology: St. Francis's stigmatization on Mount La Verna. In this powerful mystical event, St. Francis, who for Bonaventure supplants the great Peter Lombard as "The Theologian," is not simply *thinking about* the things of faith; rather, something is happening to him. In soul and in body, he is being *conformed* into the likeness of the Crucified through love. In this event, Bonaventure sees an image and pattern of how the human soul comes to know the God of Revelation in Jesus Christ. This knowing involves the very transformation of the knower, leading him into loving union with the Blessed Trinity.[83]

After Thomas and Bonaventure

In the scholastic theologians who come after Thomas and Bonaventure, one phenomenon that we seem to find is a lack of substantial engagement with Sacred Scripture as the life blood of theology. Thomas wrote commentaries on Job, the Psalms, Isaiah, Jeremiah, the Song of Songs, Matthew, John, all the Pauline Epistles, and Hebrews, as well as the *Cantena Aurea*, and his engagement with Sacred Scripture in the *Summa Theologiae* and *Summa contra Gentiles* is foundational. Bonaventure wrote commentaries on Ecclesiastes, Luke, and John. However, later scholastics such as Duns Scotus, Petrus Aureolus, Gregory of Rimini, William of Ockham, Gabriel Biel, and Pierre d'Ailly wrote no biblical commentaries. Yet, before we categorize this as a post-Thomas and Bonaventure problem, we should also note that while Peter Abelard, St. Anselm, and St. Albert the Great did not write biblical commentaries, Peter Lombard did. Moreover, one cannot just divide the scholastics into "biblical" and "non-biblical" based on whether they wrote biblical commentaries. Rather, one would need to examine how a particular scholastic engaged with Sacred Scripture in his other works.

83. Cihak, "How Faith Forges Reason," 144–45.

While the growth of the universities may have made it easier to give in to the temptation to despiritualize theology, not only would the complementary immersion of scholastic theologians in Benedictine, Augustinian, Dominican, and Franciscan spiritualities have mitigated against such a despiritualization, but it seems that theologizing in the "schools" need not automatically lead to such a degeneration. Here we can call Thomas and Bonaventure as witnesses. Can we say that although some ages in the Church make it more difficult to maintain the spiritual nature of theology, in every age a thoroughly spiritualized theology is possible? Thus, a nineteenth-century theologian such as Matthias Scheeben can hold that the Holy Spirit has an important role to play in purifying and enlightening the theologian. He compares such a person to the "spiritual man" of St. Paul who judges all things. Through the moral disposition, purity of heart, and humility of such a person, the Holy Spirit is able to open the ear of the heart to surrender to God's revelation and the eyes of the heart to understand that revelation.[84]

Moreover, if we could return to patristic times and examine the theologizing of men such as Sabellius, Paul of Samosata, Arius, Apollinarius, Nestorius, and Eutyches, what would we make of it? Would we classify their theologizing as despiritualized? We cannot assume that nothing of this kind occurred in the first millennium of Christianity. The theology that we have from that time is the theology that has endured.

Yet, it is difficult to refute Balthasar's contention that in the later Middle Ages there was a widespread failure to hold the synthesis of theology and spirituality together. What came to be called "mystical theology" increasingly withdrew from the schools and, in people such as St. Gertrude, Bl. Angela of Foligno, Meister Eckhart, Bl. Richard Rolle, Johannes Tauler, Bl. Henry Suso, St. Catherine of Siena, Bl. John of Ruysbroeck, Bl. Julian of Norwich, Bl. Thomas a Kempis, and St. Catherine of Genoa, found its home in predicatory, cenobitic, or eremitic settings. As Balthasar says, "Alongside dogmatic theology, meaning always the central science which consists of the exposition of revealed truth, there came into being a new science of the 'Christian Life,' one derived from the mysticism of the Middle Ages and achieving independence in the *devotio moderna*."[85] He goes so far as to say that, eventually this mystical

---

84. Scheeben, *Die Mysterien des Christentums*, 648–55. See also Balthasar, "Theology and Sanctity," 1:202–3, and Rowland, *Catholic Theology*, 114. St. Paul concludes by saying to the Corinthians that "we have the mind of Christ" (1 Cor 2:16).

85. Balthasar, "Theology and Sanctity," 1:187.

theology became, to a certain extent, "de-theologized." He is even critical of St. Ignatius of Loyola, St. Teresa of Avila, St. John of the Cross, and St. Francis de Sales for not better integrating their spiritual teaching with the truths of revelation addressed in dogmatic theology.[86]

In the schools, the despiritualization of theology cannot be attributed to a single cause. As demonstrated by the debate between Bernard and Abelard, the glorification of human reason carried its own inherent hubristic danger. So did the substitution of theology practiced in the schools for theology with its roots in pastoral immediacy and biblically based prayer. Nor can any single theologian be blamed. Did Duns Scotus undermine the uniqueness of theology as a science by arguing for univocal predication of statements about God and creatures, as opposed to Thomas's upholding of its uniqueness by asserting analogical predication? Yet, in his fundamental understanding of what theology is, Duns Scotus seems to follow Bonaventure's path. For him, theology is the practical science of God, and the ultimate human goal is union with the Trinity through love. In other words, it could be described as an affective practical science. If any medieval scholastic theologian is to carry the lion's share of blame it should be William of Ockham, since he rejected the notion of theology as a science.[87] Paradoxically, by exalting faith over reason, he makes a truly spiritualized theology impossible, since the adjectives speculative, practical, and affective are all left to float in a noun-less void.

In the Twentieth and Twenty-First Centuries

In the last section of its 2012 *Theology Today: Perspectives, Principles, and Criteria*, "Science and Wisdom," the International Theological Commission makes a distinction between "theological wisdom" and "mystical wisdom." It says that there is a supernatural Christian wisdom, "what no eye has seen, nor ear heard, nor the human heart conceived" (1 Cor 2:9).[88] As the next verse tells us, God has revealed this wisdom to us through the Spirit (cf. 1 Cor 2:10).

> This supernatural Christian wisdom, which transcends the purely human wisdom of philosophy, takes two forms which

---

86. Balthasar, "Theology and Sanctity," 1:187–91.
87. Ockham, *Prologus et Distintio Prima*, q. 1, 205.
88. International Theological Commission, *Theology Today*, 91.

> sustain one another but should not be confused: theological wisdom and mystical wisdom. Theological wisdom is the work of reason enlightened by faith. It is therefore an acquired wisdom. . . . Mystical wisdom or "the knowledge of the saints" is a gift of the Holy Spirit which comes from union with God in love. Love, in fact creates an affective connaturality between the human being and God, who allows spiritual persons to know and even suffer divine things (*pati divina*), actually experiencing them in their lives.[89]

The ITC goes on to state that although these two kinds of wisdom are formally distinct and should not be confused, there are strong links between them in the person of the theologian and the community of the Church. They mutually strengthen each other. Thus, "an intense spiritual life striving for holiness is a requirement for authentic theology. . . . True theology presupposes faith and is animated by charity."[90] Yet, "the proper exercise of theology's task of giving a scientific understanding of the faith enables the authenticity of spiritual experience to be verified."[91] In this explanation, the ITC refers to not only Thomas's *Summa Theologiae* but also Pseudo-Dionysius's *De divinis nominibus*; Maximos the Confessor's *Four Hundred Texts on Love*; Richard of St. Victor's *De praeparatione animi ad contemplationem*; *Ubi amor, ibi oculus*; and *Tractatus de gradibus charitatis*; and St. Teresa of Avila's *The Way of Perfection*.[92] We can see that the ITC perspective is essentially the same as that of Thomas, Bonaventure, Balthasar, and Ratzinger. However, the ITC did not examine any particular theologians or schools of theology vis-à-vis their success or failure to achieve this integration of theological and mystical wisdom.

Numerous conflicts can be found in the theology of the twentieth and now twenty-first centuries, between being and history, nature and grace, faith and reason, *logos* and *ethos* (orthodoxy and orthopraxis),

---

89. International Theological Commission, *Theology Today*, 91.
90. International Theological Commission, *Theology Today*, 92.
91. International Theological Commission, *Theology Today*, 92.
92. International Theological Commission, *Theology Today*, 91–92. See Aquinas, *Summa Theologiae*, Ia, q. 1, a. 6; Ia q. 1, a. 6, ad 3; Pseudo-Dionysius, *De Divinis nominibus*, ch. 2, 9; Maximos the Confessor, *Four Hundred Texts*, no. 26; Richard of St. Victor, *De praeparatione animi ad contemplationem*, 13; *Ubi amor, ibi oculus* 3; *Tractatus de gradibus charitatis*, 23; and St. Teresa of Avila, *The Way of Perfection*, ch. 5. The ITC quotes Richard's saying "*amor oculus est, et amare videre est*" (love is the eye, to love is to see). In *Behold the Pierced One*, Ratzinger quotes Richard as saying that "love is the faculty of seeing" (77).

theology of the incarnation and theology of the cross, high Christology and low Christology, and so on. Is it possible that the fundamental reason for all of these conflicts is a fracture between theology and spirituality? We shall now attempt to assess the contemporary extent of this fracture.

Neo-Thomism

Neo-Thomism dominated Catholic theology from the time of Leo XIII to Paul VI. It has been criticized for being ahistorical, for separating the philosophical Thomas from the theological Thomas, for trying to find answers in Thomas to questions that he never asked, and for reducing theological education to the rote learning of dis-integrated philosophical and theological theses and propositions, collated and collected in manuals on various topics.[93] Yet, was this true in the case of the man who could be regarded as a great exemplar of Neo-Thomist theology, Reginald Garrigou-Lagrange?

Although François Mauriac called him *le monstre sacré* of Thomism, his formal title at the Angelicum was professor of dogmatic and mystical theology. His polemics against the *nouvelle théologie* and the fact that he wrote commentaries on the *Summa Theologiae* could lead people to categorize him as just another writer of manuals. Yet, not only do his commentaries far exceed any manualist caricature, his first professorship at the Angelicum was in ascetical and mystical theology, and his greatest work is generally recognized as *The Three Ages of the Interior Life*.

Granted that Garrigou-Lagrange was professor of both dogmatic and mystical theology, how did he understand the nature of theology? Were the two subjects he professed conceived of and taught in two parallel streams or in an integrated way? For the answer to the first question, he refers to the first question of the *Summa Theologiae* and says that

> [theology] is a science which proceeds under the light of divine revelation, and presupposes, therefore, infused faith in revealed truths and which has as its proper object God considered in his intimate life, as author of grace, God as revelation and faith make him known to us, accessible to the natural power of our reason.[94]

---

93. Rowland, *Catholic Theology*, 53–60.

94. Garrigou-Lagrange, "Thomisme," 848 (translated from French by Richard Peddicord).

As for the process of theologizing, Garrigou-Lagrange divides it into eight theological operations, the first being that "theology gathers together the various revealed truths contained in the deposit of faith, Scripture and Tradition, in the light of the magisterium of the Church that proposes to us these revealed truths."[95]

The answer to the second question is both yes and no. Garrigou-Lagrange saw dogma and mysticism as two separate streams, but he also saw Thomas as not just a master of dogmatic and moral theology but a master of ascetical and mystical theology as well. In his work *Christian Perfection and Contemplation According to St. Thomas and St. John of the Cross*, Garrigou-Lagrange treats of how Thomas's teaching about sanctifying grace, the theological virtues, the gifts of the Holy Spirit, infused faith, and the efficacy of grace can contribute to our understanding of Christian perfection and contemplation. Yet he does not address the question of whether the teaching of Thomas addresses the task of theologizing itself.[96]

Finally, there is a third question. How did Garrigou-Lagrange understand the nature of ascetical and mystical theology? He understood spirituality as an application of moral theology: "Moral theology ought to treat, not only of sins to be avoided, but of virtues to be practiced, and of docility in following the inspirations of the Holy Spirit. From this point of view, its applications are called ascetical and mystical theology."[97] This raises a question to which we must return. What is spirituality? According to Richard Peddicord, spirituality is a personal affair.

> Catholic spirituality is ultimately concerned with the interaction between the human person and God. As a branch of theology, it aims at understanding God's actions in the lives of human persons and the individual's call to respond to God's loving presence. Because of this, every Catholic spirituality implies a theology of grace, a more or less coherent explanation of how God comes to the individual to heal, forgive, justify, and sanctify.[98]

How does this definition compare with the spiritual praxis of which Ratzinger speaks, a requirement that must be lived?

95. Garrigou-Lagrange, "Thomisme," 849 (translated by Peddicord).

96. Garrigou-Lagrange, *Christian Perfection and Contemplation*, 48–94. For more on Garrigou-Lagrange's understanding of the nature of theology and spirituality, see Peddicord, *Sacred Monster of Thomism*, 136–210.

97. Garrigou-Lagrange, *Three Ages*, 1, 10.

98. Peddicord, *Sacred Monster of Thomism*, 179.

Transcendental Thomism

The two great transcendental Thomists of the twentieth century are Karl Rahner and Bernard Lonergan. Unlike the Neo-Thomists, both begin their theologizing from epistemic rather than metaphysic perspectives. Whereas the Neo-Thomists ignored the relationship between history and being, the transcendental Thomists tried to relate them epistemically. For Rahner, it is through our acts of knowing, which are immanent, that we ascend to God, who is transcendent. All our acts of knowing are made possible by an a priori apprehension of God as Absolute Being.[99] Rahner has been accused of naturalizing the supernatural and downplaying the significance of historical revelation. As Ratzinger says,

> Is it true that Christianity adds nothing to the universal but merely makes it known? Is the Christian really just man as he is? Is that what he is supposed to be? Is not man as he is that which is insufficient, that which must be mastered and transcended? Does not the whole dynamism of history stem from the pressure to rise above man as he is? Is not the main point of the faith of both testaments that man is what he ought to be by conversion, that is, when he ceases to be what he is? Does not Christianity become meaningless when it is reinstated in the universal, whereas what we really want is the new, the other, the saving trans-formation? Does not such a concept, which turns being into history but also history into being, result in a vast stagnation despite the talk of self-transcendence as the content of man's being?[100]

For our assessment of Rahner, the key term in this critique is conversion. To naturalize the supernatural means to despiritualize the supernatural. Our *theosis*, including the *theosis* of the theologian, takes place not from the starting point of Rahner's theologizing, which is human consciousness apprehending God in an unthematic way, but in the loving contemplation of God, and not just God as Absolute Being, but God as Father, Son, and Holy Spirit.

Sometimes a distinction is made between early Rahner and late Rahner. Perhaps a distinction also could be made between Rahner the fundamental theologian and Rahner the spiritual theologian. In 1954,

---

99. Vincelette, *Recent Catholic Philosophy*, 82.

100. Ratzinger, *Principles of Catholic Theology*, 166. See also Rowland, *Catholic Theology*, 63.

Rahner contributed to a symposium on devotion to the Sacred Heart with a paper entitled "Some Theses on the Theology of the Devotion." Like Ratzinger, Karl Rahner understands the heart as signifying an anthropological totality. For him, "[the heart] falls into the category of words for the whole man; that is, it signifies a human reality predicable of the whole man as a person of body and spirit, a reality which is therefore prior to any possible distinction between body and soul."[101] As he puts it,

> [The formal source of "heart"] is the original, concrete, ontological unity of body and soul. Since man in his entirety is a bodily being, the concept "heart" includes the idea of bodiliness, and therefore includes also a bodily heart. Not for its own sake is the bodily heart thus included; still less is it taken as a merely external symbol for something else, for what we really mean.... "Heart," taken in this primal sense, denotes that center which is the origin and kernel of everything else in the human person.... Here is the focal point of a man's primal and integral relations with others and above all with God; for God is concerned with the whole man, and in his divine actions it is to man's center, his heart, that he addresses his graces or his judgments.[102]

Rahner goes on to explain that every human person not only has innate, unalterable "qualities," but also "attitudes" towards themselves and others, attitudes that can be empirically "experienced" but not metaphysically deduced. According to him,

> [these attitudes] show a multiplicity, under which there exists, or ought to exist, a formal unity, joining together the attitudes of a person into an articulate, meaningful whole. This process of free, formative unification takes place in the concrete living person. His innate qualities, if we can imagine them prior to this process, are taken over by this free and formative act of self-understanding, they are "understood" (in one way or another), and actuated.[103]

The original, form-giving unity of a person's attitudes is the heart. The heart is not simply a piece of a person but the primal, unifying center of the whole. Ultimately, a person is indivisible. Thus, "in the person, the 'part,' because it is taken over and 'understood' by the personal center, can be seen correctly only in the whole, and the whole person can be judged

---

101. Rahner, "Some Theses," 132.
102. Rahner, "Some Theses," 133.
103. Rahner, "Some Theses," 135–36.

adequately only from his 'heart-center.'"[104] Rahner's understanding of the heart is very similar to that held by Ratzinger and the fathers.[105] Yet, despite the depth of Rahner's spirituality, he is not completely successful in integrating it with how he theologizes.

Whereas Rahner thought that all our acts of knowing are made possible by an a priori apprehension of God as Absolute Being, Lonergan held that an a priori desire for knowledge of the Absolute Being of God is the transcendental condition of all acts of knowledge.[106] Despite the fact that the above criticism of Rahner's theological epistemology might also be applied to Lonergan, Paul Michael Gallagher suggests that Lonergan's focus on conversion helps to overcome the separation of theology from spirituality.[107] It means that he "offers a map of the operations of theology, one that grounds them in both a coherent cognitional structure and the graced life of faith."[108] For Gallagher, Lonergan's religious, moral, and intellectual conversions form the basis of true theologizing. As Gallagher explains, "Without a real religious conversion—without being loved into love by God's love—the heart is not transformed and theology lacks its essential spiritual foundation."[109] As Lonergan says, through this religious conversion, "Christian experience" enjoys "the fruits of being in love with a mysterious, uncomprehended God."[110] Morally, this religious conversion pervades the imagination, enriches understanding, guides judgement, and reinforces decisions. Intellectually, it enables one to encounter the real world beyond the immediacy of the empirical world.[111]

Yet, an examination of Lonergan's understanding of conversion reveals a radical misunderstanding of its nature in three ways.[112] One element of this misunderstanding is summed up by the term "uncomprehended." For Lonergan, the experience of God's love flooding into our

---

104. Rahner, "Some Theses," 138.

105. McGregor, *Heart to Heart*, 279–80, 288–89, 306–10; Spidlík, *Spirituality of Christian East*, 103–6; Spidlík, *Prayer*, 254.

106. Vincelette, *Recent Catholic Philosophy*, 82.

107. Gallagher, "Realization of Wisdom," 134. For criticisms, see Nichols, *Scribe of the Kingdom*, 2:63, and Rahner himself in "Kritische Bermerkungen," 538.

108. Gallagher, "Realization of Wisdom," 132.

109. Gallagher, "Realization of Wisdom," 133.

110. Lonergan, *Method in Theology*, 242. For a critique of Lonergan's theological method, see McGregor, "Is Lonergan's Method Theological?"

111. Gallagher, "Realization of Wisdom," 133–34.

112. McGregor, "Is Lonergan's Method Theological?" 72–80.

hearts (cf. Rom 5:5), what he holds to be a state of being conscious of God without God being known, is the one exception to the Latin tag *nihil amatum nisi praecognoitum* (knowledge proceeds love).[113] Whereas Rahner proposes an unthematic consciousness, Lonergan proposes an unknowing love. The second element is the failure to adequately account for the nature of true conversion as including repentance. The third is his lack of attention to the biblical notion of the heart.

Lonergan's concept of conversion is radically at odds with anything found in the New Testament. There, conversion is never presented as uncomprehending. What we find there is not just conversion, "turning to" God, but also repentance, turning away from sin. Repentance involves a double revelation of the truth about God and his Christ and how one stands before God. It is the acceptance that Jesus is the Christ of God who, through his death and resurrection, has reconciled us with God. It includes the acknowledgment of one's sinfulness and a turning away from sin. Conversion involves a reorientation of one's life wherein one comes into the light and does what is right. One now lives for God. It depends on believing in the Lord Jesus and repentance for sins and results in forgiveness of sins and the gift of the Holy Spirit. To be authentic, it must produce deeds worthy of repentance.[114] Rather than being the experience of the love of an unknown God, it includes the revelation of God as our Abba (cf. Rom 8:15; Gal 4:6). To sum up the transcendental Thomists, Rahner presents us with a theologizing based on knowledge without love, and Lonergan with a theologizing based on love without knowledge.

Orthopractic Theology

The relationship between orthodoxy and orthopraxis, also called the relationship between *logos* and *ethos*, brings us back to the patristic question of the relationship between *theoria* and *praxis*. How are they related? Can they be integrated? Under the umbrella term "orthopractic theology" one can place the theologies of Johann Baptist Metz, Edward Schillebeeckx, and the liberation theologians.[115] For these theologians, orthopraxis

---

113. Lonergan, *Method in Theology*, 122.

114. McGregor, "Is Lonergan's Method Theological?" 67–82.

115. Feminist theology can be treated as a subset of liberation theology—liberation for women.

determines orthodoxy. As Rowland says, Metz, "in his appropriation of Jewish eschatological themes, . . . moved away from a theological interest in dogma to a theological interest in *praxis*."[116] According to Murray Hofmeyr, the Marxist Ernst Bloch "taught Metz to appropriate eschatology as belonging to the center of Christianity, to relate transcendence and the future, and to clarify the relationship between human praxis and the future as transcendence."[117] Under the influence of the critical theory of the Frankfurt School, both he and Schillebeeckx came to hold that the Church itself, especially the "institutional" Church, must be subjected to the critical scrutiny of Enlightenment reason in order to uncover hidden forms of repression and oppression.[118] For Schillebeeckx, this orthopraxis is contextual. As Erik Borgman explains, "what is normative, from the perspective of faith, are not Jesus' words and actions, but the relationship between the words and deeds of Jesus on the one hand and their context on the other. Believers here and now are not asked to imitate what Jesus said or did, rather they are to relate to their context as Jesus relates to his."[119] It is right experience rather than right doctrine that leads to right action.[120]

The significance of *praxis* in liberation theology is well known. In his seminal *A Theology of Liberation*, Gustavo Guitiérrez argued that the starting point for theology must be the questions raised by the realities revealed in the world and history, rather than just Scripture and tradition.[121] Zoë Bennett explains the priority of praxis over theory in liberation theology thus: "The commitment and practice of liberation theology requires three moments: the moment of *praxis*, the moment of reflexion on *praxis*, and the moment of return to a renewed *praxis*. It begins and ends in *praxis*."[122] As it happens, within liberation theology there has

116. Rowland, *Catholic Theology*, 146.

117. Hofmeyr, "Invloed van Ernst Bloch," 1199. See Rowland, *Catholic Theology*, 146.

118. Schillebeeckx, "Critical Theories," 49. See Rowland, *Catholic Theology*, 146, 150.

119. Borgman, "*Gaudium et Spes*," 54.

120. Schillebeekx calls these "experiences of contrast." As Borgman explains, "In concrete experiences of suffering or oppression, God's salvific presence is experienced as absent, but this experience itself is a redemptive experience of unexpected presence; salvation is anticipated in the struggle to change the situation" (Borgman, "Retrieving God's Contemporary Presence," 251).

121. Guitiérrez, *Theology of Liberation*, 12.

122. Bennett, "Action Is the Life," 39. See Boff, *Theology and Praxis*. See also

been some movement towards a reassessment of its *raison d'être*. Clodovis Boff has called for a reversal of the epistemological primacy of the poor over God.[123] Quoting the Puebla document, Guitiérrez has posited two errors, on the one hand, a "verticalism of a disembodied spiritual union with God or . . . a simple existential personalism," and on the other, "a socioeconomic-political horizontalism."[124] As Rowland explains, by this he means that "there are Catholics who focus on their personal spiritual lives caring little about the social (horizontal) dimensions of their faith, and Catholics who focus on social issues rather than their personal relationship to God (the vertical dimension), when the two dimensions should be integrated."[125]

Furthermore, Guitiérrez has said that the fate of liberation theology depends on spirituality. Acknowledging his debt to Chenu, he writes "that behind every faith-understanding is a way of following Jesus."[126] According to Guitiérrez,

> "spirituality" is the word we use today to designate what is known in the gospels as "following Jesus." This is what forms the backbone of faith discourse. This is what gives theology its deepest meaning and its breadth. This is one of the main points in construing theology as a reflection on practice, the very heart of discipleship. Its two great and interconnecting dimensions— prayer and commitment in history—make up what the Gospel of Matthew calls "doing the Father's will" in contrast to simply saying "Lord, Lord" (7:21). Thus the claim that "our methodology is our spirituality" (Guitiérrez, "The Historical Power of the Poor," 103–4) takes on meaning.[127]

The issue at stake here is deeper than the relationship between orthodoxy and orthopraxis, understood in terms of either right belief or right experience issuing forth in right action. What is needed is an older understanding of theory and praxis. We can see how removed the kind of praxis advocated by orthopractic theologians is from that which begins with a contemplative *theoria* of Jesus Christ and ends in the *praxis* of

---

Rowland, *Catholic Theology*, 173.

123. Boff, "Telogia da Libertação." See Rowland, *Catholic Theology*, 175–76.
124. Guitiérrez, "Theology: An Ecclesial Function," 8.
125. Rowland, *Catholic Theology*, 190.
126. Guitiérrez, "Situation and Tasks," 50–51. See Chenu, *École de théologie*.
127. Guitiérrez, "Situation and Tasks," 51.

personally and ecclesially becoming him and living as him. For *theoria* is not just theory but also experience.

Ressourcement Theology

What one finds in the work of the *ressourcement* theologians is at least the idea that there is an important relationship between theology and spirituality.[128] Daniélou laments the disassociation of theology and spirituality. In discussing theology as a science, Chenu states that, in the practice of theology,

> there follows not only the delivery of a datum, of a set of propositions accepted authoritatively by a legitimate intellectual "obedience" to a self-revealing God, but an organic, psychological and religious continuity wherein the light of faith—an emanation of the divine light in the mind of man—constitutes the indispensable *milieu* for the knowledge of what has been revealed.... And the very factor which makes theology scientific is the one which makes it "sacred"—we would be willing to say "mystical" if that venerable word had not become ambiguous.... And so ... in this continuity of light, in this communion of life, the theologian hears the Word of God. He converses with God, and this converse, indissolubly linked with faith, confers upon theology its divine "existence."[129]

Yves Congar, OP, says that the highest mode of theology is doxology.[130] Is it just serendipitous that one of the meanings of orthodoxy is right glory?

---

128. There is the question of exactly who qualifies as a *ressourcement* theologian. Strictly speaking, Romano Guardini is not. Balthasar is often classified as one, but equally he could be labeled *sui generis*. Ratzinger could be described as a second-generation *ressourcement* theologian.

129. Chenu, *Is Theology a Science*, 91–92.

130. Congar, *Word and Spirit*, 5. On the question of liturgical worship as theology par excellence, see Schmemann, *Introduction to Liturgical Theology* and *Liturgy and Tradition*; Kavanagh, *On Liturgical Theology*; and especially Fagerberg, *Theologia Prima*. Of particular interest is how Fagerberg links *askesis* with liturgy as theology.

Ratzinger as an Exemplar of a Different Praxis of Theologia

We have seen that, for Ratzinger, theology must be undertaken "in the context of a corresponding spiritual praxis and of a readiness to understand it, [and] at the same time, as a requirement that must be lived[;] . . . just as we cannot learn to swim without water, so we cannot learn theology without the spiritual praxis in which it lives."[131] It must include "the necessary self-transcendence of contemplation into the practice of the faith."[132] As it happens, Ratzinger both theorized about a spiritual praxis and put it into practice. The theory can be found in *Behold the Pierced One: An Approach to a Spiritual Christology*, and a report on the praxis can be found in *Jesus of Nazareth*. What Ratzinger calls a spiritual Christology *is* a spiritual praxis, that is, it is a *theoria* that leads to *praxis*.[133]

Ratzinger's spiritual Christology is composed of three elements: seven christological theses, a theology of the heart, and a eucharistic spirituality. The theses delineate his spiritual Christology. The first "filial" thesis is that the center of Jesus's life and person is his intimate communion with the Father, his prayer. The second "soteriological" thesis is that Jesus died praying. Who he *is* (Christology) and what he *does* (soteriology) come together in his sacrificial offering of himself on the cross. The third "personal" thesis is that since prayer is the center of the person of Jesus, "it is essential to participate in his prayer if we are to know and understand him."[134] The fourth "ecclesial" thesis is that "sharing in Jesus' praying requires communion with all his brethren."[135] The fifth "dogmatic" thesis is that the teaching of Chalcedon faithfully interprets the data of biblical Christology. The sixth "volitional" thesis is that it is only the teaching of the Constantinople III regarding the will of Jesus that enables the dogma of Chalcedon to yield its full meaning. The seventh "hermeneutical" thesis is that only a hermeneutic of faith is able to "hold fast [to] the entire testimony of the sources" and overcome the temporal, cultural,

---

131. Ratzinger, *Principles of Catholic Theology*, 322.

132. Ratzinger, *Principles of Catholic Theology*, 321.

133. What follows in this section is drawn substantially from McGregor, *Heart to Heart*.

134. Ratzinger, *Behold the Pierced One*, 25.

135. Ratzinger, *Behold the Pierced One*, 27.

and national differences between people.[136] Ratzinger's conclusion to his theses is that: "Christology is born of prayer or not at all."[137]

An analysis of these seven theses reveals that four of them—the filial, soteriological, dogmatic, and volitional—constitute the content of Ratzinger's spiritual Christology. The remaining personal, ecclesial, and hermeneutical theses are methodological.

The second element, a theology of the heart, also has its content and method. The contents are an anthropology of the human heart, a theology of the Father's heart, and a Christology and ecclesiology of the heart of Jesus.[138] Ratzinger's anthropology of the heart, rather than treating the heart as identical with the human person or as a particular faculty of the person, treats it as the integrating principle of the person. Ratzinger's theology of the Father's heart privileges the symbolic theology of images over the rational theology of concepts. This theology proposes that the bodily image of the heart gives us a greater insight into the nature of God's heart than do concepts. The method of this element is *theoria* (contemplation). This *theoria* is not just an activity of the mind but of the heart. It is a heart-to-heart beholding—the believer's heart beholding the pierced heart of Jesus who, since he is the one nearest to the Father's heart, reveals that heart in his own. Nor is this beholding an isolated one. It is a personal beholding in a corporate personality, the Body of Christ. The prerequisite for this beholding is a pure heart.

A key passage for understanding Ratzinger's concept of the heart is found in *Jesus of Nazareth*.

> "Blessed are the pure in heart, for they shall see God" (Matt 5:8). The organ for seeing God is the heart. The intellect alone is not enough. In order for man to become capable of perceiving God, the energies of his existence have to work in harmony. His will must be pure and so too must the underlying affective dimension of his soul, which gives intelligence and will their direction. Speaking of the *heart* in this way means precisely that man's perceptive powers play in concert, which also requires the proper interplay of body and soul, since this is essential for the totality of the creature we call "man." Man's fundamental affective disposition actually depends on just this unity of body and soul and on man's acceptance of being both body and spirit. This

---

136. The seven theses are presenting in Ratzinger, *Behold the Pierced One*, 15–46.
137. Ratzinger, *Behold the Pierced One*, 46.
138. Ratzinger, *Behold the Pierced One*, 47–69.

means he places the body under the discipline of the spirit, yet does not isolate intellect or will. Rather, he accepts himself as coming from God, and thereby also acknowledges and lives out the bodiliness of his existence as an enrichment for the spirit. The heart—the wholeness of man—must be pure, interiorly open and free, in order for man to be able to see God.[139]

How reminiscent is this of both Thomas and Bonaventure? Theologizing involves the intellect, will, and affections. It is speculative, practical, and affective, with the affective dimension "giving intelligence and will their direction."

The third element is a eucharistic one.[140] This too has its content and method. The content is that the core of eucharistic spirituality and ecclesial spirituality is to be found in the communion between the divine and the human found in the incarnate Word. In the Word, human nature has been assumed into the being of God. When one receives Jesus in the Eucharist, one enters into a community of being with him, a communion that is a precondition of communion between human beings. Grasping the spirituality of the Eucharist means grasping "the spiritual tension which marks the God-man: only in the context of a spiritual Christology will the spirituality of the sacrament reveal itself."[141] The method of this element is *koinonia*. It is participation in the celebration of the Eucharist and the continuation of the *koinonia* of the Eucharist through devotions such as adoration of the Blessed Sacrament and through continuing to love the brethren, especially the poor.[142]

Ratzinger's spiritual Christology is one of *koinonia*, of participation. Indeed, it is one of *theosis*. Through a personal and ecclesial participation in the prayer of Jesus, exercised in purity of heart and consummated in the eucharistic celebration, one comes into communion with Jesus Christ and all the members of his Body, so that eventually one can say truly: "It is no longer I who live, but Christ who lives in me" (Gal 2:20). In other words, it is a *lived* Christology. One could say that Ratzinger's starting point for theology is being a "Christologian." The theologian, that is to say, the one who prays, must begin by living the personal thesis—contemplating the Pierced One and then bearing the fruits of this

139. Ratzinger, *Jesus of Nazareth*, 92–93.
140. Ratzinger, *Behold the Pierced One*, 71–100.
141. Ratzinger, *Behold the Pierced One*, 90.
142. For Ratzinger's understanding of the relationship between eucharistic communion and communion with the poor, see *Behold the Pierced One*, 79–81.

contemplation. What Ratzinger has said of Christology could be applied by him to theology as a whole—it is born of prayer or not at all. This is reminiscent of Evagrius's definition of a theologian: "If you are a theologian, you will pray. And if you pray truly, you are a theologian." Ratzinger expresses the same thought in his commentary on *Gaudium et Spes* §22, when, in the article's final focus on adoration ("Christ has risen again, destroying death by his death, and has given life abundantly to us so that, becoming sons in the Son, we may cry out in the Spirit: Abba, Father!"), he says that the "culmination in adoration [is] theo-logy in the strictest sense of the term."[143] For Ratzinger, the starting point for Christology, indeed, for all theology, is a lived Christology. All who allow Christ to live in them are theologians. Every Christian is called to be a theologian in this fundamental sense.

However, theology is not just born from the individual believer. It is also born from the Church. Here, the ecclesial thesis must be lived. In *The Nature and Mission of Theology*, Ratzinger goes to the *apologia pro vita sua* of St. Paul, found in his Letter to the Galatians. There he sees St. Paul describing "the distinctive element of Christianity as a personal experience which revolutionizes everything and at the same time is as an objective reality: 'It is no longer I who live, but Christ who lives in me' (Gal 2:20)."[144] This conversion is a "death-event." That which in *Jesus of Nazareth* was viewed as an individual renewal of the mind and purification of the heart is here seen as an ecclesial event.[145] It is the exchange of the old subject for a new subject. The autonomous "I" now stands within a greater "I" and, in doing so, receives itself anew. Those who have been baptized into this new subject, Christ, have put on Christ (cf. Gal 3:27–29). The Christian has become "a new, singular subject together with Christ."[146] This exchange of subjects is not something that one can bring about by oneself. Rather,

> The exchange of subjects includes a passive element, which Paul rightly characterizes as death, in the sense of receiving a share in the event of the Cross. It can come to someone only from the outside, from another person. Because Christian conversion throws open the frontier between the "I" and the "not-I," it can be bestowed upon one only by the "not-I" and can never

---

143. Ratzinger, "Church and Man's Calling," 163.
144. Ratzinger, *Nature and Mission*, 50.
145. See Ratzinger, *Jesus of Nazareth*, 95.
146. Ratzinger, *Nature and Mission*, 52.

be achieved solely in the interiority of one's personal decision. It has a sacramental structure. The "I no longer live" does not describe a private mystical experience but rather defines the essence of baptism. What takes place is a sacramental event, an event involving the Church. The passive side of becoming a Christian calls for the acting Church, in which the unity of believers manifests itself in its bodily and historical dimensions.[147]

However, the new subject is not simply the Church by itself. It is "in no wise a separate subject, endowed with its own subsistence. The new subject is much rather 'Christ' himself, and the Church is nothing more but the space of this new unitary subject."[148]

According to Ratzinger, in the Gospel of John, this new subject is the place of right understanding. Rather than coming to know Jesus through retracing his history, the Christian comes to know him through being in him. John "affirms that only the Paraclete, the Spirit, who is the Spirit both of the Father and the Son himself, can make Jesus known. Someone can be understood only through himself."[149] The Holy Spirit works to bring the Church to understanding. How does the Spirit work?

> First of all, by bestowing remembrance, a remembrance in which the particular is joined to the whole, which in turn endows the particular, which hitherto had not been understood, with its genuine meaning. A further characteristic of the Spirit is listening: he does not speak in his own name, he listens and teaches how to listen. In other words, he does not add anything but rather acts as a guide into the heart of the Word, which becomes light in the act of listening. The Spirit does not employ violence; his method is simply to allow what stands before me as an other to express itself and enter into me. This already entails an additional element: the Spirit effects a space of listening and remembering, a "we," which in the Johannine writings defines the Church as the locus of knowledge. Understanding can only take place within this "we" constituted by participation in the origin. Indeed, all comprehension depends on participation.[150]

This reality does not lead into a private relationship with Jesus. It has a "we" character. Only when we enter this "we" can our obedience to the

---

147. Ratzinger, *Nature and Mission*, 52.
148. Ratzinger, *Nature and Mission*, 54.
149. Ratzinger, *Nature and Mission*, 54–55.
150. Ratzinger, *Nature and Mission*, 55.

truth become concrete. God must become "concrete" if we are to avoid making him a projection of our own selves. God has become concrete, has become flesh, in Jesus Christ. And Christ remains concrete, in the flesh, in the Church. Therefore, rather than following an autonomous "search for God" wherein the individual need obey only his or her own thoughts and judgments about God, "Obedience to the Church is the concreteness of our obedience. The Church is the new and greater subject in which past and present, subject and object come into contact. The Church is our contemporaneity with Christ: there is no other."[151] Consequently,

> [the] Church is not an authority which remains foreign to the scientific character of theology but rather is the ground of theology's existence and the condition which makes it possible.... This subject [the Church] is by nature greater than any individual person, indeed, than any single generation. Faith is always a participation in a totality and, precisely in this way, conducts the believer to a new breadth of freedom.[152]

Because the Church is the inner foundation and wellspring of theology, it must be competent to pass judgment on the work of individual theologians. This is a part of her pastoral office, wherein she preaches to the faithful, amongst whose number academic theologians are included. For all are believers. There is no special caste of theologians. Rather, *all* can be theologians. As Ratzinger says: "Through not all men can be professional theologians, access to the great fundamental cognitions is open to everyone."[153]

Concluding Thoughts on Ratzinger's Understanding of Theology

Another way of putting Ratzinger's understanding of the nature of theology is that there is, in fact, only one theologian, one doctor, one *magister*. "You have one teacher, the Christ" (Matt 23:10). One is a theologian only to the extent that one theologizes in Christ and Christ theologizes in one. It is no longer I who theologize but Christ who theologizes in me. What Ratzinger says about the nature of theology could be taken even further than this. If the Word of God is theology in the original, most

---

151. Ratzinger, *Nature and Mission*, 60.
152. Ratzinger, *Nature and Mission*, 61.
153. Ratzinger, *Nature and Mission*, 63.

fundamental sense, then *Jesus the Christ is theology incarnate*. And if the Church is the Body of Christ, the new subject who makes Christ contemporary, then the Church is *the Body of Theology*. It is the place where theology is made present in the present. To participate in the prayer, life, and mission of the Church is to participate in theology.

We can see that Ratzinger's understanding of theologizing has gone beyond a strictly personal dimension. It has also taken on Christic, ecclesial, Trinitarian, eucharistic, and pneumatic dimensions. It is these last two dimensions, in particular, that can help reconcile two fundamental contemporary divisions, that between orthodoxy and orthopraxis and that between ontology and history.

The eucharistic dimension helps overcome the division between orthopraxis and orthodoxy in two ways. First, the Eucharist is a liturgical praxis that glorifies Christ. Second, it is a liturgical praxis that must become a social praxis. *Kononia* means both participation and contribution. For our Eucharist to avoid becoming fragmented, we must love the brethren, especially the poor. The greatest way in which we love the poor who are not brethren is by seeking to draw them into our *koinonia* with God and each other. The Eucharist also helps us to overcome the division between history and ontology, since it makes the ontological Christ present in the historical now. The pneumatic dimension helps overcome the division between history and ontology, in that while Christ has assumed human *nature*, the Holy Spirit is given to each *person*.[154] The Holy Spirit makes the ontological Christ present in us in the historical now by making an ontological presence of Christ a relational abiding presence. The Holy Spirit is new each day and makes Christ present, the same yesterday, today, and forever (cf. Heb 13:8). The Spirit also helps overcome the division between orthopraxis and orthodoxy by bringing to remembrance what the ontological Christ has taught, so that we can put his teaching into practice.

To sum up, what we need to do in order to re-spiritualize our theologizing is that we need to theologize "in the Spirit," and such theologizing is a part of "living in the Spirit." Another way of expressing it is to say that we need to be "Christified." What is living in the Spirit? According to the New Testament, it involves the experience of God's love being poured into the hearts of Christians through the gift of the Holy Spirit (cf. Rom 5:5). The Spirit is the spirit of sonship, enabling us to cry out, "Abba,

---

154. Ratzinger, "Holy Spirit and Church," 69–70.

Father" (cf. Rom 8:10; Gal 4:6). The Spirit bears witness to us that they are children of God (cf. Rom 8:16). It is only through the Spirit that we can confess that "Jesus is Lord" (cf. 1 Cor 12:3). Our minds are renewed by the Spirit, giving us the mind of Christ (cf. Rom 8:5 and 12:2; 1 Cor 2:15–16; Eph 4:23). We are able to worship God in the Spirit (cf. Eph 6:18; Phil 3:3; Jude 1:20). The Spirit enables us to pray as we ought (cf. Rom 8:26–27). The Spirit is a guarantee in our hearts who convinces us of the truth of the gospel and enables us to know that God is dwelling in us (cf. 2 Cor 1:22 and 5:5; 1 Thess 1:5; 1 John 3:24; 4:13; and 5:7–8). The Spirit grants spiritual gifts to us so as to build up the Body of Christ (cf. 1 Cor 12:1–13). We are able to understand "spiritual truths" and the gifts that God has bestowed upon us (cf. 1 Cor 2:12–15; Eph 1:17; Heb 6:4). The Spirit works miracles among us (cf. 1 Cor 2:4; Gal 3:5; Heb 2:4). We are led by the Spirit and walk in the Spirit (cf. Gal 5:5–25). In the power of the Holy Spirit, we are able to put to death the deeds of the flesh (cf. Rom 8:2–15; Gal 5:5–25). If we do so, we will bear the fruit of the Spirit—love, joy, peace, patience, kindness, goodness, faithfulness, gentleness, and self-control (cf. Gal 6:22; Rom 12:11 and 15:13; 1 Thess 1:6; 2 Tim 1:7). This is what we need to do if we wish to become theologians.

Bibliography

Alexander of Hales. *Summa Theologica*. Quaracchi, It.: Collegii S. Bonaventurae, 1924.

Aquinas, Thomas. *Compendium of Theology* [*Compendium theol*]. Translated by Cyril Vollert. St. Louis: Herder, 1947.

———. *In Boet. De Trin*. Aquinas. https://aquinas.cc/la/la/~DeTrin.

———. *Sentences*. Aquinas. https://aquinas.cc/la/en/~Sent.I.

———. *The Summa Theologica of St. Thomas Aquinas*. Translated by the Fathers of the English Dominican Province. New York: Benziger Brothers, 1948.

Augustine. "Answer to Julian [*Contra Iulianum*]." In *Answer to the Pelagians II*, edited by John E. Rotelle, OSA, translated by Ronald J. Teske, SJ, 268–536. Works of Saint Augustine: A Translation for the Twenty-First Century 1.24. Hyde Park, NY: New City, 1998.

Balthasar, Hans Urs von. "Spirituality." In *Explorations in Theology*, 1:211–26. Translated by A. V. Littledale with Alexander Dru. San Francisco: Ignatius, 1989.

———. "Theology and Sanctity." In *Explorations in Theology*, 1:181–209. Translated by A. V. Littledale with Alexander Dru. San Francisco: Ignatius, 1989.

Benedict XVI, Pope. "Monastic Theology and Scholastic Theology." Vatican, 28 Oct. 2009. http.www.vatican.va/holy_father/benedict_xvi/audiences/2009/documents/hf_ben-xvi_aud_20091028_en.html.

———. "Two Theological Models in Comparison: Bernard and Abelard." Vatican, 4 Nov. 2009. http.www.vatican.va/holy_father/benedict_xvi/audiences/2009/documents /hf_ben-xvi_aud _ 20091104_en.html.

Bennett, Zoë. "Action Is the Life of All: The Praxis-Based Epistemology of Liberation Theology." In *The Cambridge Companion to Liberation Theology*, 2nd ed., edited by Christopher Rowland, 39–54. Cambridge, UK: Cambridge University Press, 2007.

Boff, Clodovis. "Teologia da Libertação e volta ao fundamento." *Revista Eclesiástica Brasileria* 67, no. 268 (2007) 1001–22.

———. *Theology and Praxis: Epistemological Foundations*. Translated by Robert R. Barr. Maryknoll, NY: Orbis, 1987.

Bonaventure. *Collations on the Six Days* [*Collationes in Hexaëmeron*]. Translated by José de Vinck. Patterson, NJ: St. Anthony Guild, 1970.

Borgman, Erik. "*Gaudium et Spes*: The Forgotten Future of a Revolutionary Document." *Concilium* 41.4 (2005) 48–56.

———. "Retrieving God's Contemporary Presence: The Future of Edward Schillebeeckx's Theology of Culture." In *Edward Schillebeeckx and Contemporary Theology*, edited by Lieven Boeve et al., 235–51. London: T&T Clark, 2010.

Chapp, Larry S. "The Union of Sanctity and Theology in the Thought of Hans Urs von Balthasar: Implications for Seminary Formation." In *Entering into the Mind of Christ: The True Nature of Theology*, edited by James Keating, 225–42. Omaha: Institute for Priestly Formation, 2014.

Chenu, Marie-Dominique. "Position de la théologie." *Revue des Sciences Philosophiques et Théologiques* 24 (1935) 232–57.

———. *Is Theology a Science* [*La théologie est-elle une science*]? Translated by A. H. N. Green Armytage. London: Burns & Oates, 1959.

———. *Une école de théologie: le Saulchoir: avec les études de Guiseppe Alberigo, Étienne Fouilloux, Jean Ladrière et Jean-Pierre Jossua*. 1937. Reprint, Paris: Cerf, 1985.

Cihak, John R. "How Faith Forges a Reason Suitable for Theology According to Saint Bonaventure." In *Entering the Mind of Christ: The True Nature of Theology*, edited by James Keating, 143–72. Omaha: Institute for Priestly Formation, 2014.

Congar, Yves, OP. *The Word and the Spirit*. Translated by David Smith. London: Chapman, 1986.

Daniélou, Jean. "Les orientations présentes de la pensée religieuse." *Études* 249 (1946) 1–21.

Eusebius of Caesarea. *De eccl. theol*. In *Eusebius' Werke*, edited by E. Klostermann, 4:59–182. Griechische christliche Schriftsteller 14 (1906).

———. *The History of the Church from Christ to Constantine* [*Ecclesiastical History*]. Revised and edited by Andrew Louth, translated by G. A. Williamson. London: Penguin, 1989.

Evagrius Ponticus. "De oratione." In *The Praktikos and Chapters on Prayer*. Translated by John Eudes Bamberger, OCSO, 52–80. Spencer, MA: Cistercian, 1970.

———. "Letter 39." In *Evagrius Ponticus*, edited by Wilhelm Frankenberg, 587. Göttingen, Germ.: Göttinger Akademie der Wissenschaften, 1912.

———. "Letter 56." In *Evagrius Ponticus*, edited by Wilhelm Frankenberg, 605. Göttingen, Germ.: Göttinger Akademie der Wissenschaften, 1912.

———. "Praktikos." In *The Praktikos and Chapters on Prayer*. Translated by John Eudes Bamberger, OCSO, 12–42. Spencer, MA: Cistercian, 1970.

Fagerberg, David W. *Theologia Prima: What Is Liturgical Theology?* 2nd ed. Chicago: Hillenbrand, 2004.

Gallagher, Michael Paul, SJ. "Realization of Wisdom: Fruits of Formation in the Light of Newman." In *Entering the Mind of Christ: The True Nature of Theology*, edited by James Keating, 121–39. Omaha: Institute for Priestly Formation, 2014.

Garrigou-Lagrange, Reginald. *Christian Perfection and Contemplation According to St. Thomas and St. John of the Cross*. Translated by Sr. M. Timothea Doyle, OP. London: Herder, 1937.

———. *The Three Ages of the Interior Life*. Translated by Sr. M. Timothea Doyle, OP. London: Herder, 1951.

———. "Thomisme." In *Dictionnaire de Théologie Catholique*, 15:1, 823–1023. Paris: Letourzey et Ané, 1946.

Gregory Nazianzus. *Epistola 185*. In *Patrologia Graeca*, edited by Jacques Paul Migne, 37:303–6. Paris: Apud Garnier Fratres, 1862.

———. *Oratio 26: In seipsum*. In *Patrologia Graeca*, edited by Jacques Paul Migne, 35:1227–51. Paris: Apud Garnier Fratres, 1886.

———. *Oratio 28: Theologica*. In *Patrologia Graeca*, edited by Jacques Paul Migne, 36:26–74. Paris: Apud Garnier Fratres, 1886.

Guitiérrez, Gustavo. *A Theology of Liberation: History, Politics, and Salvation*. 15th anniv. ed. Maryknoll, NY: Orbis, 1988.

———. "The Situation and Tasks of Liberation Theology Today." In *On the Side of the Poor: The Theology of Liberation*, edited by Gustavo Guitiérrez & Gerhard Ludwig Müller, translated by Robert A. Krieg and James B. Nickoloff, 32–53. Maryknoll, NY: Orbis, 2015.

———. "Theology: An Ecclesial Function." In *On the Side of the Poor: The Theology of Liberation*, edited by Gustavo Guitiérrez and Gerhard Ludwig Müller, translated by Robert A. Krieg and James B. Nickoloff, 1–10. Maryknoll, NY: Orbis, 2015.

Hausherr, Irénée. *Hésychasme et prière*. Orientalia Christiana Analecta 176. Rome: Pont. Institutum Studiorum, 1966.

Hofmeyr, Murray. "Die invloed van Ernst Bloch op die Politieke Teologie van Johann Baptist Metz." *HS Teologiese Studies* 59, no. 4 (2003) 1199–222.

International Theological Commission. *Theology Today: Perspectives, Principles, and Criteria*. Washington, DC: Catholic University of America Press, 2012.

John Paul II, Pope. *Fides et Ratio*. Australian ed. Strathfield, Aus.: St Pauls, 1998.

———. "Homily to the Roman Pontifical Universities." *L'Osservatore Romano*, Nov. 9, 1981.

Kavanagh, Aidan. *On Liturgical Theology: The Hale Memorial Lectures of Seabury-Western Theological Seminary, 1981*. New York: Pueblo, 1984.

Keating, Daniel A. "The Essential Interrelation between Theology and Spirituality." In *Entering the Mind of Christ: The True Nature of Theology*, edited by James Keating, 71–90. Omaha: Institute for Priestly Formation, 2014.

LaNave, Gregory. *Through Holiness to Wisdom: The Nature of Theology According to St. Bonaventure*. Rome: Istituto Storico dei Cappuccini, 2005.

Levering, Matthew. *Scripture and Metaphysics: Aquinas and the Renewal of Trinitarian Theology*. Malden, MA: Blackwell, 2004.

Lonergan, Bernard. *Method in Theology*. London: Darton, Longman & Todd, 1972.

Maximos the Confessor. *Four Hundred Texts on Divine Love*. In *The Philokalia* 2, edited and translated by G. E. H. Palmer et al., 48–305. London: Faber & Faber, 1981.

McGregor, Peter John. *Heart to Heart: The Spiritual Christology of Joseph Ratzinger*. Eugene, OR: Pickwick, 2016.

———. "Is Lonergan's Method Theological?" *Radical Orthodoxy: Theology, Philosophy, Politics* 5, no. 1 (2019) 61–99.
Nichols, Aidan. *Scribe of the Kingdom: Essays on Theology and Culture*. London: Sheed & Ward, 1994.
Origen. *Commentarium in Matthaeam*. In *Patrologia Graeca*, edited by Jacques Paul Migne, 13:829–1799. Paris: Apud Garnier Fratres, 1867.
Peddicord, Richard. *The Sacred Monster of Thomism: An Introduction to the Life and Legacy of Reginald Garrigou-Lagrange*. South Bend, IN: St. Augustine's, 2005.
Plato. *The Republic*. In *Plato, Great Books of the Western World*, 2nd ed., edited by Mortimer J. Adler et. al., 6:295–441. Chicago: Encyclopaedia Britannica, 1990.
Rahner, Karl. "Kritische Bermerkungen zu B. J. F. Lonergan's Aufsatz: 'Functional Specialities in Theology.'" *Gregorianum* 51 (1970) 537–40.
———. "Some Theses on the Theology of the Devotion." In *Heart of the Saviour*, edited by Joseph Stierli, translated by Paul Andrews, 131–55. New York: Herder & Herder, 1957.
Rahner, Karl, and Herbert Vorgrimler. *Concise Theological Dictionary*. Edited by Cornelius Ernst, OP, translated by R. Strachan. London: Burns & Oates, 1965.
Ratzinger, Joseph. *Behold the Pierced One: An Approach to a Spiritual Christology*. Translated by Graham Harrison. San Francisco: Ignatius, 1984.
———. "The Church and Man's Calling—Introductory Article and Chapter One—The Dignity of the Human Person—Pastoral Constitution on the Church in the Modern World." In *Commentary on the Documents of Vatican II*, edited by Herbert Vorgrimler, translated by J. W. O'Hara, 5:115–63. London: Burns & Oates, 1969.
———. "The Holy Spirit and the Church." In *Images of Hope: Mediations on Major Feasts*, translated by John Rock and Graham Harrison, 63–73. San Francisco: Ignatius, 2006.
———. *Jesus of Nazareth: From the Baptism in the Jordan to the Transfiguration*. Translated by Adrian J. Walker. New York: Doubleday, 2007.
———. *The Nature and Mission of Theology: Essays to Orient Theology in Today's Debates*. Translated by Adrian Walker. San Francisco: Ignatius, 1995.
———. *Principles of Catholic Theology: Building Stones for a Fundamental Theology*. Translated by Sr. Mary Frances McCarthy, SND. San Francisco: Ignatius, 1987.
Rowland, Tracey. *Catholic Theology*. London: Bloomsbury, 2017.
Scheeben, Matthias Joseph. *Die Mysterien des Christentums*. Freiburg: Herder, 1958.
Schillebeeckx, Edward, "Critical Theories and Christian Political Commitment." *Concilium* 4, no. 9 (1973) 48–61.
Schmemann, Alexander. *Introduction to Liturgical Theology*. Translated by Asheleigh E. Moorhouse. Crestwood, NY: St. Vladimir's Seminary Press, 1966.
———. *Liturgy and Tradition: Theological Reflections of Alexander Schmemann*. Edited by Thomas Fisch. Crestwood, NY: St. Vladimir's Seminary Press, 1990.
Schumacher, Lydia. "Divine Command Theory in Early Franciscan Thought: A Response to the Autonomy Objection." *Studies in Christian Ethics* 29, no. 4 (2016) 461–76.
Spidlík, Tomas. *Prayer*. Vol. 2 of *The Spirituality of the Christian East*. Translated by Anthony P. Gythiel. Kalamazoo, MI: Cistercian, 2005.
———. *The Spirituality of the Christian East: A Systematic Handbook*. Translated by Anthony P. Gythiel. Kalamazoo, MI: Cistercian, 1986.

Torrell, Jean-Pierre. *Christ and Spirituality in St. Thomas Aquinas*. Translated by Bernhard Blankenhorn, OP. Thomistic Ressourcement 2. Washington, DC: Catholic University of America Press, 2011.

Twomey, D. Vincent. "Ratzinger on Theology as a Spiritual Science." In *Entering the Mind of Christ: The True Nature of Theology*, edited by James Keating, 47–70. Omaha: Institute for Priestly Formation, 2014.

Vincelette, Alan. *Recent Catholic Philosophy: The Twentieth Century*. Milwaukee: Marquette University Press, 2011.

William of Ockham. *Guillelmi De Ockham: Scriptum in Librum Sententiarum Ordinatio 1: Prologus et Distintio Prima*. Edited by Gedeon Gál and Stephano Brown. New York: St. Bonaventure, 1967.

2

What Is Philosophy?

WILLIAM C. HACKETT

THINGS ARE KNOWN THROUGH contrasts. One implication of this is that things are never exhaustively known: our knowledge depends on the perspicacity of the contrasts we assume or propose. And our contrasts can be set beside others, or displaced by deeper ones, or even replaced altogether, if better ones appear. Jaspers's contrast between an archaic and axial era, set beside that between poetry and philosophy, set beside that between narrative and theoretical kinds of understanding, illumines, surely, the phenomenon of Presocratic philosophy more fully than the privileged nineteenth-century contrast between *mythos* and *logos* alone; and such a collection of contrasts surely replaces the facile understanding (traced back to Aristotle) of *mythos* as merely primitive *logos* understood in its defining sense as *episteme*, "science."[1]

If contrasts themselves become uniquely thematic in philosophy, philosophy itself, when it becomes the object of inquiry, is no exception: our knowledge of it is only as good as the contrasts we discern in order to name it. We know, for example, that philosophy trades in concepts. Though this is distinctive, it is not unique. Theology too is a primarily conceptual enterprise. And not only are there other academic disciplines that involve a high degree of conceptuality—and what *academic* discipline does not?—but conceptuality is a widely human thing, if not a distinctively human thing. And even if we recognize that concepts derive

---

1. Jaspers, *Vom Ursprung und Ziel*. For the *mythos-logos* dialectic, see Aristotle, *Metaphysics*, 982b21–23.

from the contrasts discerned, it does not help us understand philosophy to say that it somehow privileges contrasts and makes them thematic, for contrast discernment is common to animals and perhaps all living things. The amoeba discerns contrasts—light and dark, for example— and the dog many more, but (surely) neither philosophize. Even, as we just noted, *intellectual* contrasts are not enough to distinguish philosophy from other disciplines. Any discipline—modern physics, for example— has its moments when fundamental contrasts are interrogated, displaced, or replaced, and new concepts and formulae emerge to take account of its data in a simpler and more comprehensive way. Yet we must recognize that it is precisely the contrasts that philosophy makes, and makes thematic, that determine it over against other disciplines. Take being, for example, contrasted to beings, as in Heidegger, or to nothing, as in Eriugena.[2] This kind of contrast is different from that between Euclidian and non-Euclidian planes in mathematics as much as that between *scapigliatura* and *risorgimento* types of transcendence in modern Italian literature. But the case of Eriugena should already give us pause. Is he a theologian or philosopher? Like Hegel, whom we consider a philosopher, he speaks of God;[3] like Bonaventure, whom we consider a theologian, he speaks of being.[4] Is this contrast the best way of determining what philosophy is? Perhaps it is the inability to make a determinative contrast that sheds the best light on philosophy—by contrast to what it is not.

One contrast takes itself as more fundamental and more far reaching, more difficult and more implicative than any other, actual or possible: that between God and the world. If this is the case, then it is the defining contrast for philosophy, which only wants to reach, precisely, an all-defining or primary level of intellectual resolution. But here again, philosophy is not alone; theology, in its attempt to say divine things as divinely as possible, pondering divinely given words, is turning, with philosophy, around this same distinction. We have mentioned "theology and philosophy" twice now, and looking for defining contrasts just there is important. One may hope, however, that discerning where or how that contrast really lies will be a result of first examining the shared live content of both kinds of thinking, what we called the most difficult and most

---

2. On the difference between *Sein* and *Seiende*, see Heidegger, *Sein und Zeit*, §6.19–27. On *ea quae sunt* and *ea quae non sunt*, see Eriugena, *De divisione naturae* (*Periphyseon*), bk 1, 1, 20.

3. Hegel, *Encyclopaedia Logic*, 50, 95.

4. Bonaventure, *Itinerarium mentis in Deum*, 304a.

implicative contrast just above. The remainder of this chapter will try to take this difficulty and its implications head on, in the form, which is all that can be done here, of a programmatic statement.

Concepts and Disciplines

"God" is the *central* and *most perplexing* intellectual concept of the Western tradition. As the terminal reality beyond the world, the goal of religious striving, this concept possesses important points of contact with other "civilizational" religious traditions, even beyond the Abrahamic tree, Buddhism and Hinduism, for example, which are of particular interest for Christianity, primarily (though not exclusively) in their monotheistic forms.

"Religion" is the context within which the concept becomes (or rather, has always been) a *question* that appears in its sharpest crystallization (i.e., where it becomes most clearly central and most properly perplexing). Religion, involving, surely, the "practice of the Absolute," may at least initially be defined simply as that context within which this two-edged crystallization occurs.

The meaning of God in the Western tradition is reciprocally interlinked with two sister-concepts: the "human" and the "world." These three basic concepts occupy the center, equally, of theology and philosophy. (If some or other philosophy or theology did not help us understand more fully ourselves, our world, and God, then that philosophy or theology, equally, would be of no value to us.) And similar to the concept "God," the meaningfulness of these latter two basic concepts arises most acutely, again, in the context of religion, which is where the insoluble questions reach their proper pitch. The questions of "being as such" or, just as important, "nothing as such" are (crucial) supplementary questions to the primary questions of God, the world, the human, and the constellation of basic, perennial questions that pervade human experience in every time and place, organizing it *precisely in a human sense*. The primary concepts are most acutely lived through in religion and therefore, finally, most intensely contemplated from within that site. The question of being is only the gathering of a resource to aid us in the definitive pursuit of humankind's perennial questions that deepen when we properly pursue answers to them. It is too abstract to be sufficient for most.

If philosophy is the pursuit of the most fundamental truth regarding our humanity behind which there is nothing more fundamental (that is, at least insofar as this fundamental truth is accessible to us), and religion is the context within which the fundamental conditions of humanity are most dramatically manifest, then it follows that the philosophy of religion is central to the academic study of religion, which is central, in its turn, to the humanities.

"Theology," from this perspective, is only an acute modality of philosophy itself, whether as a final stage of philosophical inquiry wherein the definitive is finally reached or as a uniquely given body of data, a "wisdom from above" (to quote the New Testament) that alone gives humans the chance of realizing the fundamental philosophical ambition. In theology, the tradition(s) of human reason is/are "applied to" revelation, albeit drawing from the latter, subsequently, basic information about itself and its proper tasks. Although not "necessary" to philosophy (at least in the sense that "regional" philosophies can and likely ought to undertake their work without the thought of God and of what God reveals in "religion"), theology also engages in philosophy's most fundamental task: the thought of God, and from theology, philosophy learns that reason itself is essentially implicated in the theological itself. Any distinction, in order to be partially retained, is going to have to endure an eclipse.

"Revelation" may be the master-concept of theoretical rationality in its most acute form. Revelation is concerned with the intelligibility of God, but not apart from the mutual reciprocity of the intelligibilities of the human and the world: God cannot be known "in Godself" but only in "relation" with the world (of humanity). Extrapolation from our human context (the world) only leads our thinking to less and less satisfying abstractions, as we have noted with the concept of "being," which, when taken as the controlling part of theoretical reflection, displaces the fundamental triad (God-world-humanity) requiring elucidation.

Subsequently, revelation itself becomes a central concept of philosophy, inasmuch as revelation proposes to reason the most acutely intelligible field of phenomena possible and insofar as the human condition makes impossible the realization of its most fundamental aim, the unconditioned. Accepted onto the plane of rationality, revelation maximizes intelligence in a definitive way and must be prioritized for philosophy, whose requisite content is, precisely, the field of reason. Paradoxically, therefore, the singular intelligibility of revelation becomes paradigmatic for our account of intelligibility itself. Otherwise said, revelation is reason's own most pressing concept in the account of itself that it is perpetually required to make.

Revelation ultimately provides the means by which (1) the "unity of reason" is made possible and (2) the distinction between worldly and divine modes of intelligibility is retained, inasmuch as God exceeds the world in an absolute and not relative way: the paradigmatic phenomenon is ever in excess of any worldly mode of appearing—although the thinker is required to take the concrete particular of revelation as possessing an indestructible form that contains with a compact and dense intelligibility that which conceptuality may only unfold but never transcend.

The operational position of human intelligence primarily focuses on and unfolds from the concept of God.

Principle and Attitude: Ineffability, Apophasis, Mediation of Practice

It is the God of religion that must be conceptualized; this is impossible, but this impossibility is the major source of the fruitfulness of human intelligence. The principle, therefore, of *ineffability* is the starting and end point of all thought about God in the Western tradition. It has corollaries far beyond the West that must always be recognized, respected, and learned from. With the central religious concept therefore we have a fundamental problem as long as religious consciousness lives, an irresolvable problem, in other words, that is paradoxically the index of its life. This problem was expressed clearly by Augustine, for example: "If you can conceive it, it is not God."[5] On the one hand, God must be accessible to the faith of believers; God must be intelligible and close enough to hear and respond in order to be trusted; on the other hand, God must *not* be accessible, intelligible, controllable by human designs, in order to be worthy of worship. *Both* a fundamental yes and a fundamental no, with no possible compromise between them, are held together in the religious attitude. God, the most basic concept, exceeds from the beginning, the principle of contradiction.

Because God is "everywhere and nowhere" at once, stabilizing and unraveling any final grasp on all possible experience, the thread of contradiction runs through everything without exception; a general orientation to reality by religious faith's intellectual practice must be first

5. Augustine, "Sermons on Selected Lessons," Serm. 2, xvi.

an "apophatic attitude": like my knowledge of God, I know not "what" humans are nor "what" the world is. I cannot grasp the totality of things, and like my human identity itself, the world's ungraspable roots sink into divine oblivion, when thought in this ultimate sense.

At this point of joining between height and depth, the enterprise of intellectual inquiry itself, however variegated, is intrinsic to religion, intimately joined to the principle of ineffability.

Ineffability is not pure silence but rather a ceaseless rhythm of speech and silence, of finding the silence at the heart of speech and the word that speaks from within the depths of silence. "God is passage, not possession," said Stanislas Breton.[6]

Consequently, the "objective reality" that is the goal of metaphysics, though inexhaustibly transcendent, can be discovered knowable in a relative sense. Traditionally expressed, God is the "ground" of objective reality and therefore the central "object" of metaphysical inquiry. But there is therefore in the concept of God a restless bifocality: classically God was conceived as simultaneously the condition of being (*ipsum esse subsistens*) and as the "highest being" (*ens perfectissimum*). As the transcendent as such, God must be the term of the movement of transcending that defines the religious aspiration: for reason as much as faith, God must therefore be accessible *and* inaccessible, before me and wholly beyond me at the same time.

Revelation, the disclosure of God as transpersonal reality, a wholly free actor in and for the world (though appearing, *precisely*, as an "item" among others in the world, that is, *strictly*, not an item among others), paradoxically (since it appears as a reversion to a surpassed "anthropomorphism") gives the conditions of the truest knowledge of "objective reality" that is not yet, since God, on the one hand, reveals himself in an unfinished history, and on the other, unveils the deeper truths of the world and of the human.

The above leads to three unavoidable conclusions:

(1) Most importantly, these revealed conditions are not "directly" known by the searching intellect, for they are *given* first in narrative and practice, and, most profoundly, in the immediate narratives and practices of religion. These conditions are, in other words, *believed in* and *lived through* in order to be *thought about*.

---

6. Breton, "Examen Particulier," 17.

(2) Because the intellectual practice of ineffability, for which reason recognizes the permanent distance between itself and its goal, is contextualized within the order of the body, of the world of word and action, we must further affirm that the world contains the ever richer and ever denser intelligibility that the purifications of the intellect do not and cannot exceed. Instead, the intellect finds that its critical distance is the enactment of a passage completed by means of a deeper entrance *into* the originally given data of its contemplation.

(3) Philosophical practice, therefore, is a "spiritual exercise," but subordinate to the normative practices of communal faith: the pneumatically esoteric modes of the intellectual elite are *only*, *merely*, and *fully* an intensification of the traditional exoteric forms already given as the phenomenon of "religion."

This is, of course, a Christian point of view, thoroughly determined by the intelligible data of Christian revelation.

On Pilgrimage: History, Religion, Philosophy

The central, dominant philosophical interpretation of Western thought (the narrative, in other words, that philosophy tells itself in order to grasp the conditions of its own practice) sees the ancient Greek philosophical enlightenment as opposed to the cosmic religions and myths, a critical and free *logos* set over against an "irrational" *mythos* in search of causal explanation of the phenomena that dominate natural experience. This telling of the history of the "genius of the West" sets Greece firmly against Jerusalem and the West against the Rest as the origin of "philosophy," "reason," and "science." This view sees, for example, the "orientalisms" of late antique Neoplatonism, pagan and Christian, especially in their sacramental or theurgic "divinely-mad" strands, as dimming corruptions of the original philosophical light in an era of civilizational crisis (similar to the way the Romantic or postmodern movements have been seen by contemporaries).

Besides the fact that the philosophical revolution, from the beginning, was primarily a quest for a more adequate conception of divinity, a movement that reached its greatest intensification arguably in late antique Neoplatonic radicalizations of Plato, Guy Stroumsa convincingly argued in *The End of Sacrifice* that Jerusalem itself (through the nascent traditions of Rabbinic Judaism and Apostolic Christianity) intensified

Greco-Roman civilization's budding enlightenment, an act that serves as the crucial development of the axial revolution in the West, within the *telos* of which we still live (defining Western understandings of the dignity of the person, freedom, and the spiritualized character of religion, as well as of the cleavage between "church and state," are rooted here).[7] Understood as a "final cause," it will be seen that religion is the context, after all, that imparts life to these principles.

The main consequence of this historical revision, fundamental apparently, is that what used to be called the *"history of religions" is the context for the interpretation and practice of philosophy*. In the early decades of the twenty-first century, we find ourselves swimming in new waters.

Two complementary but far-reaching conclusions are drawn from this radical starting point:

(1) The time has come for a surpassing of the "conflict of the faculties" that has marked Western thought for over three hundred years: there is no *necessary* animosity between "faith and reason" in a post-foundationalist age, except for ideological reasons (even if these can, as they should, be argued for as *sensible* reasons, though they rarely are). The debate must continue to center around the question: what is human rationality?

(2) This "integrated" understanding of Western thought, precisely understood as a synthesis with its own distinctive tensions, opens dramatically onto the possibility of intercultural and (same thing, only made acute) interreligious exchange. If religion is indeed the water in which the (Western) philosopher swims (*even* if only as the shadowy origin of his basic concepts, being, truth, nothing, good, evil, etc.), then he shares something fundamental with many other great traditions of the world, whether alive (Hindu, Buddhist, Chinese, etc.) or dead (for example, the ancient Near Eastern civilizations, from Egypt to the Persian Empire) but which live on in us, their distant posterity. I will be liberated from my past only when I cease to exist—and even then? Perhaps not. In these traditions, speculative, critical, and scientific rationalities emerged within and became classically expressed in the religious context and therefore with a permanent debt to the religious origin.

A final conclusion demands to be stated:

(3) Philosophical practice attentive to the most pressing exigencies of the contemporary "secular age" is (however paradoxically) inseparably

---

7. Stroumsa, *End of Sacrifice*.

grounded in the scholarly study of religion: the history of religion, the philosophy of religion, the reflection on religion intrinsic to its practice (theology), and comparative religion, which, understood as the beating heart of the cultural-civilizational production of meanings, symbols, customs, and sociopolitical organization, may go by the name "comparative (or intercultural) philosophy," if understood as the endless task of learning new ways of understanding our humanity through the light of others with whom we share that which creates the possibility for a mutual understanding: the irrepressible enigma of the human condition, which we live in various ways, always human ways, ways that mutually challenge to deeper understandings, greater justifications of our most pressing and difficult contrasts that illumine this condition.

Bibliography

Aristotle. *Metaphysics*. Vol. 2 of *The Complete Works of Aristotle*. Edited by Jonathan Barnes. Princeton, NJ: Princeton University Press, 1984.

Augustine. "Sermons on Selected Lessons of the New Testament." In *Nicene and Post-Nicene Fathers of the Christian Church*, edited by Philip Schaff, translated by R. G. MacMullen, 1st ser., 6:237–545. Buffalo: Christian Literature, 1888.

Bonaventure. *Itinerarium mentis in Deum, Doctoris seraphici S. Bonaventurae opera omnia* V. Edited by the Fathers of the Collegium Bonaventurae. Quaracchi, It.: Collegii S. Bonaventurae, 1882–1902.

Breton, Stanislas. "Examen Particulier." In *Philosopher par passion et par raison: Stanislas Breton*, edited by Luce Giard, 7–17. Grenoble, Fr.: Millon, 1990.

Eriugena, John Scottus. *Periphyseon: On the Division of Nature [De divisione naturae]*. Translated by Myra L. Uhlfelder. Reprint, Eugene, OR: Wipf and Stock, 2011.

Hegel, G. W. F. *The Encyclopaedia Logic*. Edited by T. F. Garaets et al. Indianapolis: Hackett, 1991.

Heidegger, Martin. *Sein und Zeit*. Tübingen, Germ.: Niemeyer, 1967.

Jaspers, Karl. *Vom Ursprung und Ziel der Geschichte*. Edited by Kurt Salamun. Gesamtausgabe 10. Basel: Schwabe, 2016.

Stroumsa, Guy. *The End of Sacrifice: Religious Transformations in Late Antiquity*. Translated by Susan Emanuel. Chicago: University of Chicago Press, 2012.

3

Theology and Philosophy

D. C. Schindler

THAT THERE IS A crisis of the Christian faith in the West has been known for at least a century, and the fairly recent upsurge in reactionary movements seeking to restore the effective force of Christianity, far from testifying to a new initiative of the Holy Spirit, seems rather to confirm the fact that the living Church is no longer appreciated as the vine from which all the branches of culture spring. That there is a crisis of reason is something recognized now with ever greater urgency, as we discover that the phrase "post-truth civilization" has become apt to describe not only political discourse and the media that pretend to convey it but, increasingly, every dimension of human existence, both public and private: even our academic institutions have become self-consciously anti-intellectual as a matter of course. But that these two crises are so closely related as to be ultimately two sides of one and the same coin, while prophetically indicated in John Paul II's *Fides et Ratio*, is something we need still to fathom. Meditating on the profound interdependence between faith and reason, and therefore on the interdependence of theology and philosophy, though provoked by the condition of crisis, serves the salutary purpose of deepening our understanding of each and helps reveal the outlines of a positive response.

The Original Unity

In order to understand what it might mean to say that a fracture has occurred in the relation between philosophy and theology, we first must try to understand what they are and why they belong essentially together. The popular imagination tends to view philosophy and theology, today, as separate departments in the humanities, which are similar insofar as they are equally distant from the practical matters of life, but different insofar as one is essentially religious and the other is not. Whereas one is principally a matter of indoctrination and perhaps learning about one's faith and why it is important, the other is about learning to ask questions regarding things we would normally take for granted and training in argumentation. But this separation of philosophy and theology, both from each other and from the reality of life, represents a striking contrast to the original state of affairs. Philosophy arose under that name—*philosophia*, the "love of wisdom"—at the beginning of the classical period of ancient Greece.[1] It did not designate a specific academic discipline, for there were no such things; instead, as an expression of love, it comprehended the practical order as much as the theoretical.[2] Philosophy, moreover, was not a single set of practices set over against others, as for example the various activities comprising the *technē* of ship-building would be distinguished from those of other *technai* and of the general praxis of life, but involved the whole of one's existence. It did so because it consisted of a devotion of one's life, a resolve to pursue a single thing and to order one's existence around this pursuit.[3] The *unum necessarium* to which one devoted oneself was "wisdom," *sophia*, a general term that indicated a certain depth of understanding (as opposed to a mere breadth

---

[1]. The first preserved occurrence of the word "philosophy" appears to be in Heraclitus (see his reference to "lovers of wisdom," *philosophous*, in fr. 35, Kirk et al., *Presocratic Philosophers*, 218), who wrote around the fifth century BC. It came to represent not quite a technical term but a recognizable category in Plato's work, though the practice certainly predated Plato. What seems to be the first appearance of the word "theology" also can be found in Plato (*Rep.*, 379a), though it is used to define a science in Aristotle (*Metaph.*, VI.1.1026a18–20). Interestingly, Aristotle identifies theology not as something separate from philosophy but as its highest form.

[2]. Pierre Hadot is the one who has most fully recovered this dimension in the ancient world; see his *What Is Ancient Philosophy?* and *Philosophy as a Way of Life*.

[3]. In *Republic* 519c, Plato presents philosophers as having a "single goal (*skopon . . . hena*) in life, at which they . . . aim in doing everything they do."

of knowledge—"polymathy"—to which Heraclitus contrasted it)[4] and an expression of and fidelity to that understanding in one's manner of living. To become a philosopher, in ancient Greece, meant not just to settle on a certain field of study—for the schools of philosophy essentially included all fields of intellectual inquiry, organized according to some basic principle—but to adopt a way of life, presumably forever, a way of life that included a rule concerning eating and physical training, study and spiritual exercise. It often entailed wearing a certain style of dress. In short, to become a philosopher resembled best what we would today in the Catholic world call entering religious life.

The connection between philosophy and religious life was not only existential, in the sense that philosophy was a form of devoted existence. It was also intellectual: as a love specifically of *wisdom*, philosophy was a desire to understand, and indeed a desire to understand in the most complete way possible. This is not to say that the philosophers assumed that complete understanding was something that could be achieved once and for all; to the contrary, there were lively debates about the limits of knowledge, and all schools maintained a basic respect for mystery. But it was to completeness that philosophy aspired, and this way of life was capable of attracting the commitment of the whole of one's life precisely because it embodied a perfection, an ideal.[5] This pursuit of profound understanding was a seeking to know things in all the basic ways they could be known: their origin, their most basic essence, and their ultimate purpose. These fundamental lines of inquiry, guided by the whence, what, and why questions, eventually became Aristotle's efficient, formal, and final causes.[6] It was perfectly natural to trace all of these lines of understanding to the divine, to God—which is what all of the schools of thought then did in one way or another.[7] The original philosophers spontaneously recognized that coming to know things in their innermost reality coincided with an entry into the presence of God, and so

---

4. Heraclitus, fr. 40: "Polymathy does not teach understanding," in Kirk et al., *Presocratic Philosophers*, 181.

5. On the centrality of the *ideal* in Greek culture, see Jaeger, *Paideia*.

6. Aristotle, *A post.*, 71b9–11, *Phys.* 194b17–20; *Phys.*, II.3 and *Metaph.*, V.2.

7. Even the iconoclastic schools, such as that of the Cynics, or the "agnostic" schools in the varieties of Skepticism, understood themselves as adopting theological positions of some sort, rather than occupying some neutral, non-theological space. Diogenes the Dog reportedly whispered into the ear of the pious woman flopped down in front of a religious statue, with her derriere thrust up into the air, "Remember, God is also behind you."

the project of philosophy was inseparable from prayer, from liturgy, and from training in virtue (indeed from *theōsis*).[8] In this respect, philosophy and theology were originally identical.

This identity was largely forgotten in modern accounts of the ancient world. The positivist spirit of the nineteenth century, which has, in various figures, continued its hold in the main intellectual currents, canonized a certain story regarding early human development, whereby a primitive religious age was liberated from superstition by philosophy, which, by purifying thought, cleared the way for science.[9] Already in the early twentieth century, the classicist Werner Jaeger decisively corrected this misinterpretation. He showed that the first recognizable "philosophers" in ancient Greece, far from moving away from religion in their patterns of thought, moved decisively *towards* it: they are best interpreted as attempting to restore religion in the face of a civilization falling into cynicism and to bring theology in a new way into the center of thought.[10] To regard the early Greek thinkers as "proto-scientists" rather than, as it were, "pagan monks" is anachronistically to project back into the past the fragmentation of thought that characterizes the present. *Integration* is the most distinctive feature of this most decisive moment in the creation of Western civilization. The original philosophers were scientists and mathematicians as much as they were poets and mystics, because the reality they studied betrayed all of these dimensions at once to the mind disposed to receive them.[11]

---

8. Parmenides, for example, describes the path of philosophical inquiry as the "far-famed road of the god" (*hodon . . . polyphēmon . . . daimonos*), fr. 1, in Kirk et al., *Presocratic Philosophers*, 242–43; Heraclitus famously invites visitors, who have surprised him in a humble setting, to philosophical discussion by saying "for the gods are present here, too" (see Aristotle's account in *De partibus animalium*, I.5.645aff); Plato insists that philosophical discussion always begin with prayer (*Tim*, 27b) and says that the aim of philosophy is in fact to become like God (*Theaet.*, 176a–b); and Aristotle says that, if the divine is present anywhere, it is in the science of being (*Metaph.*, VI.1.1026a18–20).

9. The main figure associated with this interpretation of the evolution of thought is Auguste Comte (1798–1857), but there have been many variations. See Comte's *Introduction to Positive Philosophy*.

10. Jaeger, *Theology of Early Greek Philosophers*. This book is the publication of the Gifford Lectures he delivered in 1936.

11. This is not to say that they were *merely* any of these: the practice of philosophy added to each of these particular activities an effort to get intellectually to the foundations of things. In this way, the philosophers were different from the poets, or statesmen, or doctors, and so forth, even if they entered into their particular intellectual

The Christian Difference

By opening up a wholly new level of discourse in some sense discontinuous with everything that preceded, the advent of Christianity thus brought about a radical change. To be sure, in the Hellenistic period, there was already a clear differentiation of the "disciplines" according to subject matters and the methods suited to them, a process initiated in a basic way by the rigorous thinking of Aristotle. But God's self-revelation introduced the principle of a differentiation of an entirely different order. To put the matter somewhat simply, in the incarnation, in the life, passion, and resurrection of Christ, the terms of man's relation to God underwent a certain reversal:[12] if in the Greek wisdom, man sought God through a plumbing of the depths of things, following an itinerary that eventually took him into his innermost interior (*gnōthi seauton*), in Christ, interpreted above all as the dramatic fulfillment of the old covenant, God revealed that he was in search of man and that human desire, even as it was created ultimately for God, would not present the ultimate measure of the gift to be given. According to the Christian dispensation, man was created for full participation in God's own inner life, to be elevated to the status of adopted sons of the Father in the Spirit, through membership in the Church, the sacramental Spouse of the only-begotten Son. This invitation to a radically new gift is in some sense strictly discontinuous with the initial gift of creation, no matter how God-centered one interprets nature to be. In this respect, Christianity introduces a principle of thought and praxis that arrives from outside the horizon of the world and thus can be considered as light "from above," a light strictly unanticipatable (or to appropriate the idealist philosopher Schelling's word in a theological context, "*unvordenklich*," "unprethinkable")[13] from within that horizon taken on its own.[14]

---

arenas, as it were.

12. See Balthasar, "Movement toward God."

13. Balthasar uses Schelling's term to explicate the essential surprise of love; see Balthasar's *Theologic* 2, 135–37.

14. It is important to note that Christianity did not introduce a world-transcending principle simply "from out of the blue," but such a principle was already clearly recognized in some sense already by Plato, with Plato's affirmation of the good "beyond being," and in any event, in a systematic way, by the stream of Neoplatonism—perhaps above all Plotinus (see, for example, Plotinus, *Ennead*, V.5.6). The reason this is important is that a failure to recognize it will eventually lead to the very faith-reason dualism we are contesting in this essay, a dualism that would tend to present revelation as a

At the same time, however, the new principle does not simply displace the old one, and indeed it *cannot* do so without undermining the generosity that lies in the first gift, and so also informs the second; it cannot do so without fracturing the unity of God's activity *ad extra*, which means the simplicity that God *is* in an absolutely exemplary way. In this respect, however novel God's self-revelation may be in the order of redemption, it does not nullify the movement of understanding that begins from within the reception of being and so is in that sense a movement "from below."[15] As we have been suggesting, it actually *demands* this complementary movement and fulfills it in a transformative way that simultaneously deepens and intensifies the movement. This paradox of an asymmetrical reciprocity of the "from above" and "from below," all of the dimensions of which must be retained in full at every step, establishes the principle of a distinction-in-unity between philosophy, governed by reason, understood as having the form of the desire to attain to the deepest and most complete understanding, and theology, governed by faith, understood as a supernatural virtue, infused into the soul as an anticipatory participation in the self-knowledge of God, which is ultimately identical with his self-love and indeed with his inner life *tout court*. We will return to spell this out in more technical terms below.

To be sure, in spite of the radical novelty of Christ's revelation of the Father, the distinction between philosophy and theology took time to develop. Christianity was initially understood to be the definitive philosophy, which gave a decisive form to man's groping attempts at a unified vision and an integrated life.[16] In the patristic period, "philosophy" was considered not a specific subject of study, one of the seven liberal arts, but a succinct expression designating the monastic life; along

---

crude contradiction to philosophical reason. Nevertheless, having affirmed a certain continuity between faith and the culmination of reason, we must still see the radical transformation that the world-transcending principle undergoes in Christianity: for Plotinus, the principle is essentially a negative one, approached "apophatically," whereas in Christianity the principle, for all its transcendence, is *first* positive; the assumption of flesh means that theology has a positive object, even if that object exceeds itself in a certain respect so as to include everything outside of it within itself.

15. As *Gaudium et Spes* famously puts it, "Christ, the final Adam, by the revelation of the mystery of the Father and His love, fully reveals man to himself and makes his supreme calling clear" (Second Vatican Council, *Gaudium et Spes*, §22). In the person of Christ, we have a convergence of the orders of creation and redemption, nature and grace.

16. Wilken, *Spirit of Early Christian Thought*, 162–85.

the lines we have already indicated, to become a philosopher meant in the Christian world to forsake the world and to follow Christ.[17] A first self-conscious distinction between philosophy and theology began to emerge in the Middle Ages, due to a complex array of causes. The distinctiveness of the principle of Christian theology, and so its novelty with respect to philosophy, became clarified in the more direct engagement with non-Christian religions (Judaism and especially Islam) that also laid claim in a certain respect to philosophy. This distinction was, moreover, strengthened by the increasingly rigorous training in logic, with its thematic attention to the evidential bases of inference, by the development of scholastic methods in the critical reception of tradition, and perhaps above by all the "rediscovery" of Aristotle's substantial works, which were on the one hand "pre-Christian" in a straightforward sense and at the same time internally compelling as an interpretation of reality. In this new context, philosophy—now as "metaphysics"—was generally recognized, through Aristotle, as a kind of "architectonic" science, and it was distinguished from what was called "sacra doctrina," "sacred teaching," a vision of things received from revelation, and so from Scripture and tradition, rather than derived directly from the evident reality of things as they present themselves. We thus have Aquinas, for example, clearly dividing intellectual tasks between the philosophers and theologians:

> The consideration of creatures belongs to both theologians and philosophers, though in different ways. For philosophers consider creatures according to how they exist in their own natures, and so they inquire into the proper causes of things and what those things undergo (*proprias causas et passiones rerum*); while the theologian considers creatures according to how they proceed from their first principle, and how they are ordered to their final end, which is God. Thus, it is right that this should be called divine wisdom (*divina sapientia*), for it considers the highest cause, which is God.[18]

Whether this is an adequate formulation of the distinction is a matter we will discuss below, but we may nevertheless see in it a kind of echo of the distinction between a hermeneutics "from below," which proceeds from the inner constitution of things, and an approach "from above," which would make a principle that transcends things as the

---

17. See Leclerq, *L'Amour des lettres*, 99–100.
18. Aquinas, *Sent II*, prologue.

origin and end of their being the fundamental point of reference for our understanding.

While an initial distinction thus emerged between philosophy and theology, it is crucial to see that these two "sciences" were not crudely separated from each other in this period. To stay with Aquinas for a moment, his *Summa Theologiae* was just that, namely, a summation *of theology*, though it obviously includes what he had described in the *Sentence Commentary* as the work of philosophy, namely, an attention to the inner nature of things, in addition to their origin and end in God.[19] Moreover, Aquinas did not limit philosophy to the immanent end of interpreting natural things in themselves. In the *Summa*'s opening pages, he explains that "the philosophical science built up by human reason" is not simply ordered to understanding the world but aspires to union with God, because it most basically concerns man's *salvation*.[20] Similarly, while the "science of sacred doctrine" is principally about God, it is not *exclusively* about God; it is rather about *all things*, the whole of reality, but specifically under the aspect of "being divinely revealed."[21] To shift to the later Middle Ages, John Duns Scotus, who is often contrasted to Aquinas on the relation between philosophy and theology, may be more definitive about the limits of philosophy (which we will discuss further below) but yet recognized the perspective of faith as opening a new vision of the whole of reality, founded on the recognition in faith of the God who freely created and redeemed the world, down to the innermost principles of being.[22]

The Unity in Fragments

If philosophy and theology still enjoyed a unity in the Middle Ages in spite of their emergent distinction, their intrinsic connection began to disappear in the ages that follow. While we cannot enter into the complex debate about how, when, and why the final break occurred (if there was, indeed, a single "break"), there is a basic consensus that the principal

---

19. On theology as comprehending all other sciences in Aquinas, see Jordan, *Ordering Wisdom*.

20. Aquinas, *ST*, 1.1.

21. Aquinas, *ST*, 1.3.

22. See Gilson's nuanced account in the chapter "Duns Scotus and the Philosophers," in *John Duns Scotus*, 491–524.

founders of modernity took for granted a decisive extrinsicism between the two. This extrinsicism was the result of a certain evolution in Christian thought. In his controversial "Regensburg Address," delivered in 2006,[23] Benedict XVI described the radical impoverishment that arose in our conception of God through the de-Hellenization of Christianity, which he says occurred in three stages in history: first, with the Reformation in the sixteenth century; second, with the emergence of liberal theology in the nineteenth century; and finally, with contemporary cultural pluralism. "De-Hellenization" is the attempt to purify Christianity by extracting from it the Greek influence that entered in through the Church's engagement with the world. The Greek influence is precisely philosophy, the role given to reason in the reception of God's self-revelation and the following of Christ. A commentator on Benedict's lecture observed that Benedict's three stages of de-Hellenization correspond roughly to the three waves of modernity that the political philosopher Leo Strauss described in a well-known essay.[24] The comparison is apt, even if one might quibble with the details, since the clear separation between faith and reason, and by implication between God and the world, is one of the most defining features of the modern age. We see this basic division expressed in what are arguably the two most representative institutions of modernity: political liberalism and "empirical" science—that is, a politics founded on the clear separation between church and state, and a programmatic study of the natural world conceived in abstraction from its teleological ordering to God. In the modern period, knowledge of God and knowledge of reality had little to do with each other.

As a result of this separation, the nature of philosophy and theology was transformed. Now that God and the world occupied different places, so to speak, these two intellectual disciplines—for that is what they have become in the new context—are henceforth defined by objects that are only extrinsically related to each other, if they encounter one another at all. Theology is no longer concerned with the world as manifest in the light of faith but is simply about God, or even just religious matters. Philosophy is now about the world *rather than* God, and so the world is posited as a reality that has an intelligibility of its own, independent of any relation to God. The world may still be identified in some sense as an expression of divine glory, but this expressiveness is no longer received as

23. Benedict XVI, "Faith, Reason and University."

24. See Schall, *Regensburg Lecture*, 90–112; Strauss, "Three Waves of Modernity," in *Introduction to Political Philosophy*, 81–90.

constitutive of the very being of the world and so as indispensable to our interpretation of it and disposition toward it. We saw that Aquinas distinguished between philosophy and theology by saying that philosophy investigated the inner nature of things, and theology investigated things in terms of their origin and end. But, truth be told, this distinction is not adequate either to philosophy or to theology. Is philosophy *not* in fact concerned with the origin and end of things—the whence and the why questions? As we observed at the outset, these questions were *essential* to the early Greek thinkers. Aquinas's formulation leaves open this dimension to a certain extent, even if in the background,[25] but it seems true to say that Scotus more clearly closes it off by positing a *definitive answer* to the question given in faith, which eliminates any reason for philosophy to pursue it.[26] Moreover, is reference to the origin and end of things what is most distinctive about theology? Is the principle that makes theology radically unique not, rather, the self-disclosure of that origin and end as a Trinity of Persons in one God, who has become incarnate in Christ and whose mission was extended in the Church through the Spirit? Insofar as this mission is *to* the world, a penetrative understanding of the inner nature of things is clearly essential to it. We saw that the distinction Aquinas made was relativized in his practice; Scotus, for his part, may not have separated God from the world in his all-comprehending sense of theology, but he arguably began a separation of the world from God in his interpretation of philosophy. However that may be, it is clear that whatever "cracks" began to appear in the late Middle Ages became a full-fledged fracture in the modern age.

But if philosophy and theology are thus transformed in their separation, so too, by implication, are the nature of faith and reason, along with the realities on which these are set, at least insofar as they enter into human experience at all. In this context of fragmentation, the reason that defines the human being becomes an apparatus of control and

---

25. Specifically, he claims that the philosopher seeks the "proper causes" of things, and of course the First Principle and Final End of things (which is God, the starting point of theology) belongs in this category, so to speak. This means that the reason that is directed *to* things is at the same time directed *beyond* them to their ultimate source.

26. See Emmanuel Perrier's excellent essay, "Duns Scotus Facing Reality," 638. Note that there is no opposition between having a definitive answer and continuing the inquiry: properly understood, which is to say, interpreted in the light of the ultimacy of gift, a recognition of the *that* does not preclude, but rather provokes, a wondering about the what, why, and how. For a more in-depth argument in defense of this statement, see my "Giving Cause to Wonder," in Schindler, *Catholicity of Reason*, 163–228.

mastery over the self-enclosed sphere of nature, rather than a principle of transcendence rooted in the deepest depths of man's being, which carries man beyond himself into the heart of the world and, through the world (which is itself moving from and toward its divine source in its very nature), all the way to God. Similarly, in its isolation from the world that is accessible to reason, faith ceases to be an ontological transformation that elevates man to participation in a greater reality and becomes instead a purely subjective belief about a reality set apart from the world. Faith, in this case, turns into little more than an insufficiently grounded intellectual operation, something roughly equivalent to opinion (*pistis*). In short, if the relationship between philosophy and theology is fractured, what is at stake is the nature of man, the nature of the world or reality, and the nature of God. It is important to keep these deep implications in mind when reflecting on what may seem like a merely academic problem, the relation between two branches of the humanities, two wings of the College of Arts and Letters building.

Restoring Unity

John Paul II elaborated the general cultural implications of the fracturing of philosophy and theology in his great encyclical *Fides et Ratio* (1998). According to John Paul II, properly understood, philosophy and theology are intrinsically related to each other. They form together, he says, a kind of circle, with each leading to the other as it follows its own natural course.[27] Another image he offers, which is even more profound and adequate to the reality, but less susceptible to geometric modeling unless one happens to have the ingenuity of M. C. Escher,[28] is that of a co-inherence and in some sense co-comprehension: "each contains the other," which is another way of saying that each emerges from the center of the other.[29]

---

27. John Paul II, *Fides et Ratio*, §73. Note that this is already different from the typical hierarchy of the sciences, which would have philosophy lead to theology, the "queen of the sciences," but would not clearly recognize any way that theology, which lies at the top of the pyramid, so to speak, and so is that science upon which all others in some sense depend, would lead to philosophy, in its turn.

28. M. C. Escher is well known for his mind-bending drawings, in which, for example, a hand makes a pencil-sketch of another hand, which becomes so realistic and lifelike, it turns out to be itself sketching a hand, and the hand *it* sketches is so realistic it turns out to be in fact the first, and so on.

29. John Paul II, *Fides et Ratio*, §17.

This is the proper way to describe an intrinsic relation and is strikingly different from the extrinsic relation one would illustrate by drawing two spheres juxtaposed to each other. Two separate spheres may approach one another for one reason or another in a given case, but, if they do, it is only at the circumference or outer region, where each is most distant from its own center.

The geometrical modeling is thus far a formal and abstract presentation of the relation. As we make it concrete, it becomes clear that the problem concerning the relation between philosophy and theology cannot be resolved in a purely formal manner, in which we would lay out the interaction between a generic philosophy and a generic theology. Content matters absolutely in this case: if philosophy opens up to theology at its center, it is both because it aims at achieving as fundamental, original, and complete an understanding of the world as possible, and because the world it seeks to understand is intrinsically related to God in its constitutive principles. The world has not only been actually, and in truth, created by God but indeed created by a radically generous God who communicates himself in his acts, and so, in this paradigmatically divine act of creation, reveals himself in and through the world he brought into being.[30] Given that the world is constituted in this way, philosophy opens up right at the heart of its ownmost task to God, and indeed to the very nature of God as he has revealed himself. Theology thus comes forth right from the heart of the philosophical task. Theology, in turn, is not simply the study of God in general (which would arguably be a theology no different, finally, from metaphysics) but the study, enabled by the gift of faith, of the God who has revealed himself both through the creation of the world and, more profoundly and intimately, in and through the incarnation, in the Son's and Spirit's complementary missions to redeem the world. This revelation is not only a display of the innermost life of God but is at the same time the most ultimate meaning of the world, which has become in some sense the object of the love between the Father and the Son: "For God so loved the world he sent his only Son . . ." Through the incarnation, God enters into the world, unto its darkest depths, and takes the world

---

30. Of course, a larger discussion would be necessary to determine whether, to what extent, and in what manner philosophy can *begin* within a recognition of this generosity as its founding assumption. But it is not our purpose here to resolve the problem of "Christian philosophy." It remains the case that, from the Christian perspective, this generosity characterizes the nature of things in the world irrespective of philosophy's capacity or incapacity to acknowledge it in an explicit way.

into himself in the assumption of the flesh: the intrinsic meaning of the world thus presents itself as a concern for theology, not when theology strays from its central task but right at the heart of this task, at the place wherein this task reaches its culmination. The holy effort (*sacra doctrina, sapientia divina*) to understand God through God's own self-revelation can remain faithful to itself only if it follows God into the world.

If we interpret the two thus concretely, from within the Christian vision of the world,[31] we see a new model that can preserve the unity between philosophy and theology without compromising the difference between them. Indeed, the boundless generosity at the heart of this model radicalizes the difference, even as it deepens the unity. The key to maintaining both a genuine distinction and a genuine unity is resisting any a priori limitation (in the modern sense) on either of them. Instead, both the philosopher and the theologian must respond in kind to the generosity at the origin of all things and so surrender to the truth of the reality each studies precisely as that reality presents itself, remaining faithful to its own movement. Thus, on the one hand, the absolutely unrestricted object of philosophy is not a pure "givenness," as Jean-Luc Marion has proposed,[32] since this remains formal, in spite of Marion's protests, and so still a matter of a priori method rather than actual "material" object; instead, the actual object that defines philosophy is the quite traditional "being qua being," the study of being in itself and its ultimate causes.[33] Because of the actual nature of reality—that is, because reality has been brought into being by the God of Jesus Christ and *not* because of the essence of philosophy as such—this study opens up spontaneously to the theological dimension, even as this dimension remains discontinuous with it. On the other hand, theology, the study of God, considered

---

31. It may be objected that it already denatures philosophy to be interpreted, thus, from within a Christian vision (Thomas Joseph White, for example, makes this argument with respect to Etienne Gilson: see his *Wisdom in the Face of Modernity*, and my response to White in "Discovering What Has Already Been Given: On a Recent Defense of Thomistic Natural Theology," in Schindler, *Catholicity of Reason*, 262–304). As Ferdinand Ulrich has shown with great insight, this objection itself presupposes a theological datum and so cannot be made without surreptitiously introducing theologoumena into one's philosophy (which can be shown to have occurred historically wherever post-Christian philosophy claims to operate in a state of purity). See Ulrich, *Homo Abyssus*, and my *Companion*, 89–112.

32. Marion, *Being Given*; see my critique of this argument in "The First First Philosophy." Marion's stress on the disciplined readiness to allow the object to reveal itself on its own terms is indispensable.

33. Aristotle, *Metaph.*, IV.1.

concretely, is an endeavor to understand the living God, the very God who has revealed himself, precisely *as* he has revealed himself, without the restrictions placed on this revelation in both form and content by virtue of one's a priori assumptions, and so as the Creator and Redeemer of the world. In this case, both philosophy and theology are concerned *with everything*, without remainder, though each approaches the whole on the basis of a radically different principle. In this way, philosophy and theology show themselves to be inseparable from each other in reality, even as they remain, from first to last, irreducibly different from each other. Difference belongs just as essentially to generosity as does unity, and both philosophy and theology have their basis in the generosity of God.[34]

Implications for Faith and Reason

If philosophy and theology are indeed intrinsically related to each other in this manner, which becomes visible in a unique way in the Christian tradition, or in other words, if it is natural to each to emerge from the center of the other, it follows that to separate them from each other is to denature them both. John Paul II sets forth a variety of cultural phenomena that result from, and give expression to, this denaturing. On the side of faith, the pope mentions the related impoverishments of fideism, radical traditionalism, and "biblicism," or as we might put it, biblical positivism.[35] If theology has refused to open up to philosophy at its center, it will lose the capacity to receive God's self-disclosure as meaningful, as capable of being unfolded and sounded in its depths through reflection, and therefore as a genuine truth to be contemplated. Instead, it will tend to degenerate into a matter of feeling, of mere assertion, or of purely technical study with the modern means of historical critical methods. We might add to the pope's list of distortions the fact that, when theology abandons philosophy as her traditional "handmaid," she will inevitably replace her with something less adequate: positivistic science, superficial historical methods, and perhaps most commonly now sociology and politics. Instead of theology as a meditative reception of the world-directed Word of God, we now have theology principally as political statement.

34. For a fuller exposition of the relationship between the two disciplines along these lines, see my essay "Philosophy and Theology," in Schindler, *Catholicity of Reason*, 305–33.

35. John Paul II, *Fides et Ratio*, §§52 and 55.

On the side of reason, John Paul II has even more to say. To separate itself from faith, reason has to retreat from its own center and recast itself in a more marginalized, compartmentalized, and indeed instrumentalized form. Reason is no longer what defines the human being as a dynamism that emerges from man's innermost reality in a life-comprehending way. Instead, it becomes a function, juxtaposed to others, a juxtaposition that tends to be to reason's disadvantage since abstract thought pales in comparison to more obviously vital functions. And reason no longer aspires to sound out the depths of things. Instead, it contents itself with an analysis of parts, a calculation of relations and an optimizing of processes, always with respect to ends that are themselves by definition nonrational. In contrast to all this, the pope describes reason in its healthy, natural state as displaying three characteristics:[36] first, it possesses a "sapiential" dimension, which is to say it is ordered to the asking of fundamental questions of meaning and seeking to conform one's existence to the same inquiry; second, it exhibits a confidence in its ability to grasp real truth, even if the truth it grasps is not all-comprehending and so without need for ever further inquiry; and, finally, it has a "genuinely metaphysical range," which is to say it culminates in a philosophy of being, an interpretation of the whole of reality without any a priori artificial restrictions. When philosophy actively dissociates itself from theology, it can no longer come to rest in its own natural center. It no longer has the form of self-transcendence, from the human spirit out into being and ultimately into God, and tends instead to restrict itself to the immanent and the positive. As John Paul II puts it, philosophy thus tends to become "phenomenalist," trapped inside the self-enclosed bubble of consciousness, occupied above all with analyzing the structures of consciousness, of the acts of knowing, of language, and methods—rather than reality in itself.[37] As a result, the human endeavor to know withers into trivialities; it fragments and gives in to despair. The list of problems that John Paul II elaborates in this regard are too familiar as cultural phenomena to require much explanation.[38] To mention a few: we have rationalism, a reduction of intellect to the instrumental power to calculate; scientism, the replacement of metaphysics as the paradigm of knowing by empirical science; relativism, the rejection of truth as a transcendent measure of culture;

---

36. John Paul II, *Fides et Ratio*, §§81–83.
37. John Paul II, *Fides et Ratio*, §§82–83.
38. John Paul II, *Fides et Ratio*, §§86.

eclecticism, the loss of an integrated vision of reality, compensated for by a collection of disjointed ideas *ad libitum*; and finally, nihlism, the abandonment of meaning altogether.

Contemporary Tasks

Given this diagnosis, what is the best response to the fracture between philosophy and theology, which is a fissure that passes through the core of human existence? There is an oft-encountered temptation to overcome the separation between philosophy and theology by reimposing theology onto philosophy so to speak. The most common strategy in this regard is to emphasize philosophy's need for theology, reason's essential inadequacy on its own, and so its need for faith. One might also complement this with an emphasis on theology's inadequacy in isolation from philosophy. Logos, one says, has its home only inside mythos; reason cannot ground itself and so has a ground only inside some kind of belief, some "leap" of faith; the autonomy or neutrality that reason claims for itself, at least since the Enlightenment, is ultimately a self-delusion, because reason is always conditioned by culture, history, tradition, and religious belief. In the end, reason is not capable, on its own, of grasping ultimate truth—or, ultimately, any truth at all—but must allow itself to be chastened by its failure and accept epistemic humility, modestly acknowledging a final, impenetrable mystery. Those who opt for this strategy—the effort to overcome reason's overweening claims by humiliating it in one way or another—tend to see allies in the more skeptically oriented figures of the postmodern age or of the modern age, such as David Hume who aimed at a deflation of the modern soul; they tend to see the ever-new varieties of a "hermeneutic of suspicion" in the postmodern age as a sign of hope. The "weak thought" promoted by Gianni Vattimo, for instance, which he understands as the proper instrument of nihilism, would thus appear to strengthen the case for faith and the position of believers.[39]

But this alliance takes for granted, however unwittingly, the very opposition between philosophy and theology, reason and faith, it seeks to overcome. It envisions these in a power struggle, in a zero-sum game, which would open reason to faith only by defeating it and would render

---

39. See Vattimo, "Dialectics, Difference, Weak Thought." John Paul II seems to have Vattimo's project in view when he writes, "It is an illusion to think that faith, tied to weak reasoning (*ragione debole*), might be more penetrating; on the contrary, faith then runs the grave risk of withering into myth and superstition" (*Fides et Ratio*, §48).

it transparent to the theological order only by thinning it out to the point of effacement, so to speak, or violently breaking it open. The problem is that a dialectical conception of interdependence is perfectly compatible with, indeed precisely expressive of, a fundamentally fractured relationship. The account of the relation between faith and reason that John Paul II offers in his encyclical implies the exact opposite approach in the endeavor to heal the fracture between philosophy and theology. If the two are in fact intrinsically related, then they stand or fall together. Each can be restored only in conjunction with the other, and to promote either one in a genuine sense is implicitly to promote the other at the same time.

Our discussion of the matter suggests three tasks in particular that must belong to an effort to heal the fracture between philosophy and theology. First, instead of seeking an artificial way to limit reason or weaken thought, or to appeal too quickly to faith or theology and so to absorb logos into mythos, we ought to restore the grandeur of reason, to broaden its scope so as to be fully adequate, both subjectively and objectively, to its original essence and ambition. In other words, we need to recover the wisdom dimension of reason and the philosophy of being at the foundation of all other knowing. Postmodern hermeneutics of suspicion, no matter how sympathetic they may appear to the mysteries of faith, must be criticized for the sake of a more ample recollection of the tradition. Second, as an objective grounding for the restoration of "the grandeur of reason,"[40] we need to restore a positively disposed openness to the truth of God's radical generosity, which implies that the created world is not just some *thing*, somehow fabricated or collocated apart from a purely transcendent God, but is a revelation of God's very being. God makes himself known in and through the being of the world, which means that philosophy will forever mediate theology in some respect, even as it is transcended into a more direct reception of the personal God. At the heart of this recollection is of course a recovery of the centrality of a Christian Neoplatonic participatory metaphysics, and so of what is often referred to as a "sacramental sense of reality." Finally, following the lead, again, of God's radical generosity, we need to relocate the center of theology in the place and manner of God's own self-disclosure, beyond either the mystification of apophaticism or the rationalism of modern critical methods: God *revealed himself* in his sending of the Son into the world and in his carrying of the world, thus redeemed, into his inner life of

---

40. The phrase comes from the closing lines of Benedict XVI's "Faith, Reason and University."

love. It is finally a systematically and existentially generous recognition of God's own generosity that will enable a healing of the fracture between philosophy and theology that is more than skin deep.

Bibliography

Aquinas, Thomas. *Scriptum super libros Sententarium II* [= *Sent II*]. Edited by M. Moos. Paris: Lethielleux, 1929–1933.

———. *Summa Theologiae* [= *ST*], vols. 4–12. Rome: Leonine Commission, 1888–1906.

Aristotle. *The Basic Works*. Edited by Richard McKeon. New York: Random House, 1941. (This collection includes *Posterior Analytics* [= *A post.*], *The Parts of Animals* [= *De partibus animalium*], *Metaphysics* [= *Metaph.*], and *Physics* [= *Phys.*].)

Balthasar, Hans Urs von. "Movement toward God." In *Explorations in Theology* 3:15–55. San Francisco: Ignatius, 1993.

———. *Theologic 2: The Truth of God*. San Francisco: Ignatius, 2004.

Benedict XVI, Pope. "Faith, Reason and the University: Memories and Reflections." Vatican, 12 Sept. 2006. http://www.vatican.va/content/benedict-xvi/en/speeches/2006/september/documents/hf_ben-xvi_spe_20060912_university-regensburg.html.

Comte, Auguste. *Introduction to Positive Philosophy*. Indianapolis: Hackett, 1988.

Gilson, Étienne. *John Duns Scotus: An Introduction to His Fundamental Positions*. London: T&T Clark, 2019.

Hadot, Pierre. *Philosophy as a Way of Life*. Hoboken, NJ: Wiley-Blackwell, 1995.

———. *What Is Ancient Philosophy?* 2nd ed. Cambridge, MA: Harvard University Press, 2004.

Jaeger, Werner. *Paideia: The Ideals of Greek Culture*. Oxford, UK: Oxford University Press, 1945.

———. *The Theology of the Early Greek Philosophers*. Oxford, UK: Clarendon, 1947.

John Paul II, Pope. "On the Relationship between Faith and Reason [*Fides et Ratio*]." Vatican, 14 Sept. 1998. http://www.vatican.va/content/john-paul-ii/en/encyclicals/documents/hf_jp-ii_enc_14091998_fides-et-ratio.html.

Jordan, Mark D. *Ordering Wisdom: The Hierarchy of Philosophical Discourses in Aquinas*. Notre Dame, IN: University of Notre Dame Press, 1986.

Kirk, G. S., et al., eds. *The Presocratic Philosophers*. 2nd ed. Cambridge, UK: Cambridge University Press, 1983.

Leclerq, Jean. *L'Amour des lettres et le désir de Dieu*. Paris: Cerf, 1957.

Marion, Jean-Luc. *Being Given: Toward a Phenomenology of Givenness*. Stanford, CA: Stanford University Press, 2002.

Perrier, Emmanuel. "Duns Scotus Facing Reality: Between Absolute Contingency and Unquestionable Consistency." *Modern Theology* 21, no. 4 (2005) 619–43.

Plato. *The Complete Works*. Edited by John Cooper. Indianapolis: Hackett, 1997. (This volume includes the *Republic* [= *Rep.*], the *Theaetetus* [= *Theaet.*], and the *Timaeus* [= *Tim.*].)

Plotinus. *Ennead* V. Edited by A. H. Armstrong. Cambridge, MA: Harvard University Press, 1984.

Schall, James. *The Regensburg Lecture*. South Bend, IN: St. Augustine's, 2007.

Schindler, D. C. *The Catholicity of Reason*. Grand Rapids: Eerdmans, 2013.

———. *Companion to Ferdinand Ulrich's Homo Abyssus.* Washington, DC: Humanum Academic Press, 2019.

———. "The First First Philosophy." *Recherches philosophiques* 6 (2018) 101–16.

Second Vatican Council. "Pastoral Constitution on the Church in the Modern World [*Gaudium et Spes*]." Vatican, 7 Dec. 1965. http://www.vatican.va/archive/hist_councils/ii_vatican_council/documents/vat-ii_const_19651207_gaudium-et-spes_en.html.

Strauss, Leo. *An Introduction to Political Philosophy: Ten Essays.* Detroit: Wayne State University Press, 1989.

Ulrich, Ferdinand. *Homo Abyssus: The Drama of the Question of Being.* Washington, DC: Humanum Academic, 2018.

Vattimo, Gianni. "Dialectics, Difference, Weak Thought." In *Weak Thought*, edited by Pier Aldo Rovatti, 39–52. Albany: SUNY Press, 2012.

White, Thomas Joseph. *Wisdom in the Face of Modernity: A Study in Thomistic Natural Theology.* Ave Maria, FL: Sapientia, 2009.

Wilken, Robert Louis. *The Spirit of Early Christian Thought.* New Haven, CT: Yale University Press, 2003.

4

Theology and Liturgy

DAVID W. FAGERBERG

DR. MCGREGOR HAS GIFTED us with a metaphor, for which we are grateful. He chose the metaphor, he says, because he wants to generate an ongoing discussion about certain fractures in the body theologic. The idea of a fracture communicates a concept, but the word itself communicates a sensation. The idea of a fracture is a separation of parts, but the word itself gives the sensation of limping, which I think is one of the reasons he chose it. When one suffers a fracture one can get along, but not well; one might make progress, but painfully; one could walk, but only by favoring the injured foot or leg. A theology that suffers fractures could limp down the path, but could not run. It certainly could not caper. A fracture is a separation that occurs under the action of a force, and these essays seek to discover what those forces have been, where the fractures are, what they are, and, most importantly, how they can be healed. As a body is more than the sum of its organs, theology would benefit from being understood as more than the sum of its specializations, and in order for that understanding to take root in our minds, theology must overcome its fragmentary character. An appetite for the whole is not satisfied with a sample taste of a portion.

We might say that what this collection of essays wishes to inspire is *theology with integrity*. I am not referring to the moral character of theologians as they go about their business, I am rather referring to the business the ordinary theologians go about. *Integritas* means a soundness or wholeness, a complete unit. An integer is a whole number, in contradistinction to a fraction; *integral theology* would be a theology of the whole, wholesome theology, in contradistinction to a fragment. However, such integrity requires more than artificial integration. A forced and temporary alliance between the parts is inadequate to the task. Therefore, the reader should not be sidetracked to think only about the reconciliations being sought within each chapter (although blessed are the peacemakers); the reader must also come away with a holistic grasp of theology at the end. The ultimate goal of this book is the health of the whole body, not merely the mending of one bone. In this light, I pause to remember that the medieval definition of beauty involved three constituents: *integritas* (completeness, perfection, wholeness), *consonantia* (harmony, due proportion), and *claritas* (splendor). Ultimately, integral theology is one constituent of the beauty required to save the world, as Dostoyevsky hoped for.

The mention of beauty is an appropriate transition to my assigned task, which is to consider the rapprochement of theology and liturgy. I wonder if this is the biggest breach among all those being considered. The reader might be tempted to suppose in other chapters at least some kind of connection between theology and spirituality, philosophy, Scripture, ethics, life, doctrine, preaching, and the magisterium, but still wonder what connection theology has to smells and bells. If liturgy is pious ceremony done by uneducated believers, and theology is clear analysis done by educated scholars, then trying to link the two is like trying to discover what splitting the atom has to do with flying a kite. Or, in the words of Aidan Kavanagh when he described a summer course named Creative Worship that promised to teach participants how to creatively use liturgy, liturgical robes, banners and stoles, "The relationship of embroidery to the driving of a diesel locomotive seems easier to demonstrate than the connection between stoles and proclaiming the Gospel. Something here seems to have been enthusiastically trivialized."[1] Spirituality, philosophy, Scripture, and the rest, are at least thought not trivial, so the healing of those fractures might be able to be done more readily and under a different therapy than the one required to heal the fracture between theology and liturgy. In the case of liturgical theology, this therapy may need to change both partners in the covenant, opening theology to mystery, and liturgy to the work of God.

1. Kavanagh, *On Liturgical Theology*, 47.

The Fault Line

For a brief review in how liturgy and theology bypassed each other we can turn to such an astute observer as Benedict XVI. He describes their relationship in the West by beginning with medieval theology, which "had already detached the theological study of the sacraments to a large extent from their administration and divine worship and treated it separately, under the headings of *institution, sign, effect, minister, and recipient*."[2] Here we find the familiar scholastic treatment of sacraments, and when the manuals of theology treated liturgical ceremony, it was at the close of sacramental theology, almost as an appendix. A fence was run through the field, distinguishing the essential from the nonessential, whereafter dogmatics and liturgics each had their own (unrelated) fields of interest. "Thus divine worship and theology diverged more and more; dogmatic theology expounded, not on divine worship itself, but rather on its abstract theological contents, so that the liturgy necessarily seemed almost like a collection of ceremonies that clothed the essentials . . . and hence might also be replaceable."[3] Liturgy might be nice, for people who like that sort of thing, but it is not absolutely necessary to dogmatic theology, even when it expounds on divine worship.[4]

In the origins of liturgical studies, history took the lead and theology followed along afterward. Martimort observes their relationship by noting that "scientific liturgical history, which was a seventeenth-century creation, showed the clergy and faithful the value and riches of the liturgy, its importance in the Church's Tradition, the precise meaning of rites and prayers."[5] Then after that, he says, came the theological step. "The results gained by historians must then become an object of theological study."[6] Liturgiology comes first, and theology comes second. This is the way their relationship has generally been framed.

The pope emeritus sees a temporary improvement in relations when the liturgical movement came on the scene. At that time liturgics was

---

2. Benedict XVI, *On the Way*, 153.

3. Benedict XVI, *On the Way*, 153–54.

4. I often begin my course on liturgical theology with an anecdote of the time I was dressed in cap and gown, waiting in line with my faculty colleagues to process into the end-of-year commencement exercises, and the colleague behind me, knowing that my field was liturgical studies, commented, "You must like this sort of thing."

5. Martimort, *Church at Prayer*, 16.

6. Martimort, *Church at Prayer*, 17.

little more than juridical positivism, and the liturgical movement sought to have people think of liturgy "not just as a more or less accidental collection of ceremonies, but rather as the organically developed and suitable expression of the sacraments in the worship celebration."[7] When the pioneers of the liturgical movement spoke about symbol, it had a tenor that was more theological than anthropological. Benedict XVI judges the "Constitution on the Sacred Liturgy" from the Second Vatican Council as a much better synthesis of liturgy and theology than what had gone before. One can think of statements like these from section 7.

> To accomplish so great a work, Christ is always present in His Church, especially in her liturgical celebrations. . . . Rightly, then, the liturgy is considered as an exercise of the priestly office of Jesus Christ. In the liturgy the sanctification of the man is signified by signs perceptible to the senses. . . . From this it follows that every liturgical celebration, because it is an action of Christ the priest and of His Body which is the Church, is a sacred action surpassing all others; no other action of the Church can equal its efficacy by the same title and to the same degree.[8]

We notice that the *Constitution* acknowledges liturgy to be an activity of the Church, and one that involves signs perceptible to the senses, but it also affirms the theological description of liturgy as an activity of sanctifying human beings. Unfortunately, liturgical studies later seems to have taken a turn in a different direction, in Benedict XVI's opinion, and now liturgical studies have again "tended to detach themselves from dogmatic theology and to set themselves up as a sort of technique for worship celebrations. Conversely, dogmatic theology has not yet convincingly taken up the subject of its liturgical dimension, either."[9]

Liturgy and theology may have drifted nearer to each other, but they did not dock. And in my opinion, they will not be able to until our understanding of each undergoes a change. The healing will come about neither by requiring theologians to quote examples from some historical liturgy of the past nor by requiring liturgists to note some dogmatic justification for a move they have already conceived. Rather, a more profound definition of *leitourgia* is required, one that will result in an appreciation for the mystical heart of theology.

---

7. Benedict XVI, *On the Way*, 154.
8. Second Vatican Council, *Sacrosanctum Concilium*, §7.
9. Benedict XVI, *On the Way*, 154.

What Shall the Liturgical Theologian Say?

Separated from liturgy, what would theology say? I am not asking what theology could talk about: I do not worry that, if separated, theology would suffer a dearth of PhD dissertation proposals or conference topics. We can rely upon the garrulousness of theologians to spare us that worry! But what a person says is different from what a person talks about. The former is a judgment, the latter is a topic; the former asserts, the latter discourses. I can listen to you cover the field and still ask, at the end, "But what do *you* say?" or "What have you *said*?" What one says comes from a deeply personal place. We say prayers, profess truths, declare love. We can describe God's revelation, we can talk about it, explain it, detail it, report it, define and outline it, but in order to do any of that, we must be able to say what God has said to us in that revelation, and God's Word continues to reverberate off the stone altar. Theology says out loud the apophatic and cataphatic revelations that give life to Christ's mystical body. Liturgy gives to theology what it is supposed to say. For theology to be theology, and not religious studies, it must harmonize with the Word of God liturgically presented. Theology is Church-speech.

Therefore, the motivation for healing the fracture between liturgy and theology is not for the sake of giving theology one more topic to talk about (theologians have plenty to talk about); the motivation is so theology has something to *say* when these other subjects are talked about.

All theology is liturgical, but that does not mean the liturgy is all theology talks about. All theology should be eucharistic, but that does not mean the eucharist is the only focus of theology. It does mean that theology has a eucharistic, ecclesial, eschatological pronouncement to make in all conversations. Theology's fundament, its footing, is the eucharistic liturgy of the Church making present the eschaton, so that theology can say what the kingdom of God means for mankind's relationship to God almighty. In liturgy, the theologian is taught theology's grammar. Theology learns this liturgical grammar not in order to talk about liturgy—that would be like only reading grammar books—but to say something true about everything. Liturgical theology trains us in God's speech about himself, about us, about the cosmos, about the Alpha and the Omega, about the condition of sin, about the economy of salvation, about the mystery to which God is directing creation and mankind with surety of hand. In liturgy, this condition of reality is experienced; and experiencing it, we may know it; knowing it, we love it;

loving it, we want to say it. Experimental knowledge of God in liturgical encounter lets theology truthfully say that God is God, creation is good, sin is idolatry, man is sinner, Christ is Savior, the Spirit is life, Church is mystery, asceticism is hard, the kingdom is coming, and the kingdom is here. Theology speaks the truth to the world that it encountered in liturgy. If separated from that wellspring, what could theology say? Its speech would be crippled—a fracture of the mouth, as it were. Theology says what *leitourgia* epiphanizes.

Becoming a Theologian

This claim depends upon a more profound understanding of liturgy, and I will present two such understandings. One is my own, the other comes from the man who influenced it, Alexander Schmemann.

The definition of liturgy needs to be thickened to the point that it means more than rubrics and ritual performance. My attempt to do so is to define liturgy as *the perichoresis of the Trinity kenotically extended to invite our synergistic ascent into deification.*[10] The Trinity's circulation of love extends itself in an outgoing that is creative, redemptive, and providential, which is what Dionysus was trying to explain with his neologism of "hierarchy," according to Alexander Golitzin.

> If the creature may only encounter God as the latter is in his transcendence through "passing out" of its proper being, then conversely God may enter into relationship, including the act of creation, only through a kind of "self-transcendence." Moved to create... God "leaves" in a sense that state of being, or "superbeing," proper to him. He goes "outside" his hidden essence. It is this divine "out-passing" that is the foundation or subject of the *Divine Names* and, in so far as they are the mirrors of God, of the Celestial and Ecclesiastical Hierarchies as well. God as he is known in his names and in his creation is God "outside," as it were, of his essence.[11]

The perichoresis of the Trinity goes beyond its three-person limit, and in humility the Son and Spirit work the Father's good pleasure for all creation, which is to invite our ascent to participate in the very life of God. This cannot be forced; it must be done with our cooperation.

---

10. Fagerberg, *On Liturgical Asceticism*, 9.
11. Golitzin, *Et Introibo ad Altare Dei*, 48–49.

In the midst of all the horizontal circulations of conversation (human sciences), there is a vertical one (theology) that recognizes the liturgical ground of creation. Louis Bouyer explains the ground of that being with the metaphor of a beating heart.

> Across this continuous chain of creation, in which the triune fellowship of the divine persons has, as it were, extended and propagated itself, moves the ebb and flow of the creating *Agape* and of the created *eucharistia*. Descending further and further towards the final limits of the abyss of nothingness, the creating love of God reveals its full power in the response it evokes, in the joy of gratitude in which, from the very dawn of their existence creatures freely return to him who has given them all. Thus this immense choir of which we have spoken, basing ourselves on the Fathers, finally seems like an infinitely generous heart, beating with an unceasing diastole and systole, first diffusing the divine glory in paternal love, then continually gathering it up again to its immutable source in filial love.[12]

So it turns out that being is liturgy in action. Liturgy is at the ontological ground of conversation because being is liturgical. The cosmos has its side of a liturgical exchange to uphold. Liturgical theology can speak to all subjects because liturgy is an ontological condition of the world. Healing the fracture between liturgy and theology will make it possible for liturgical theology to say the truth about all reality.

Why liturgy? Because here the Spirit moves through our throat to pronounce the Word that the Father has spoken. Because here is pneumatic respiration: we inhale liturgy and exhale theology when the Holy Spirit moves the diaphragm of the mystical body, and the Church inhales the Word of God so it may exhale theology. Because the Church must inhale Christ's truth, Christ's desires, Christ's charity (I have just named the theological virtues of faith, hope, love) before it exhales theology. Because if we talk without that Spirit and outside of that Word, then we are making human speech, not theology. Even if the conversation is about transcendent things, it would still be speech spoken under the rule of a human grammar instead of saying something under the rule of divine grammar. Theology emerges from the liturgical respiration of a body in mystical communion with the perichoresis of the Trinity.

The fractured relationship theology has with liturgy must be healed so that theology can catch its breath. Liturgy gives speech lessons. Liturgy

---

12. Bouyer, *Meaning of Monastic Life*, 28–29.

is a place for contemplating God himself, not as a rational exercise, but as noetic experience. It is experiential knowledge, made possible by the Son's revelation of the Father accomplished by the Holy Spirit's indwelling in us as God's temple. The theologian goes into the temple to conduct his theology because in that place the theologian will become a temple. In the words of Archimandrite Vasileios, "True theology is always living, a form of hierurgy, something that changes our life and 'assumes' us into itself: we are to become theology. Understood in this way, theology is not a matter for specialists but a universal vocation; each is called to become a 'theologian soul.'"[13] This experiential knowledge is the highest form of prayer, giving us a glimpse of what Evagrius means when he says, "If you are a theologian you truly pray. If you truly pray you are a theologian."[14] To speak theologically, theologians must have become living prayer: have become by grace what Christ is by nature. That is the ascent to which we are kenotically invited and to which we must synergistically agree. To be theology, an eternal word must be spoken, a word that does not generate from human genius even if it is spoken in human speech, in the same way that liturgy does not generate from human genius even if it is conducted in human cult. It says a word that is of God, and not merely about God; a word mothered by the Church when she does her work of *leitourgia*.

Thus *leitourgia* gives the theologian something to say. In each of its parts, the liturgy is transformed by the Holy Spirit into a real symbol of what it manifests, planted in our minds and even our senses, our hearts and affections, our imagination and sensibility, thereby fulfilling a theologian's desire to have something to say to God, to the world, to the Church, to himself or herself. I would be happy if theologians also want to discuss liturgy, but this will not heal the fracture. The corporate procession through the Paschal gates opened by Jesus, perpetuated under the in-breathing of the Holy Spirit, served by apostles and hierarchs, witnessed by Mary and saints, uniting the Church militant and the Church triumphant, gives the theologian something to say when he or she talks about various subjects inside and outside of the theological discipline. To speak theology, one must become a theologian; and creating theologians is a liturgical enterprise. Liturgy creates a liturgical theologian even out of Mrs. Murphy as it forms her as liturgical ascetic and liturgical mystic. For

---

13. Vasileios, *Hymn of Entry*, 27.
14. Evagrius, *Chapters on Prayer*, 60.

theology is not given by human knowledge and zeal, writes Metropolitan Hierotheos,

> but by the work of the Holy Spirit which dwells in the pure heart. The nous which has been purified "becomes for the soul a sky full of the stars of radiant and glorious thoughts, with the sun of righteousness shining in it, sending the beaming rays of theology out into the world" [Nicetas Stethatos].... Real theology is not a fruit of material concentration but a manifestation of the Holy Spirit. When a man's nous is purified then he is illuminated and if his nous has the capacity, that is, wisdom, he can theologise. Therefore we say that his whole life, even his body itself, is theology. The purified man is wholly a theology.[15]

Ordinary, academic theology is ordinary, human speech about a Supreme Being. Supernatural, Christian theology is Christ's speech about his Father, shared in a state of prayer imbued by the Holy Spirit. Tomas Spidlik makes the etymology plain: "The ancient Christian East understood the practice of theology only as a personal communion with *Theos*, the Father, through the *Logos*, Christ, in the Holy Spirit—an experience lived in a state of prayer."[16] Theology is not just talk *about* God, it is talk *of* God. More. It is dialogue *with* God: prayer.

Theology is the breath of the Spirit rising from our lungs. Theology is the Word-made-flesh now forming words on our lips. And this respiration-plus-speech, trained upon our bodies by liturgy, teaches us what to say about theological topics. Pope Benedict XVI saw the combination of this cosmic dimension of liturgy with the cultic dimension of liturgy in the fifteenth chapter of Paul's Letter to the Romans.

> In this verse alone does Paul use the word *"hierourgein"*—to administer as a priest—together with *"leitourgos"*—liturgy: he speaks of the cosmic liturgy in which the human world itself must become worship of God, an oblation in the Holy Spirit. When the world in all its parts has become a liturgy of God, when, in its reality, it has become adoration, then it will have reached its goal and will be safe and sound. This is the ultimate goal of St Paul's apostolic mission as well as of our own mission. The Lord calls us to this ministry. Let us pray at this time that

---

15. Hierotheos, *Orthodoxy Psychotherapy*, 147.
16. Spidlik, *Spirituality of Christian East*, 1.

he may help us to carry it out properly, to become true liturgists of Jesus Christ.[17]

Now there is nothing in theology irrelevant to liturgy, nothing in liturgy irrelevant to theology, because liturgical theology is a piety through which the whole world becomes worship of God. No topic, no subject, no theme, no science is immaterial to theology, because all the world is destined for a state revealed by liturgy, namely, the status of *logike latreia* that Paul mentions in Romans 12:1. Theological integrity is attained in liturgical logic.

Alexander Schmemann

Schmemann expressed this foundational quality of liturgy by calling liturgy the ontological condition for theology, and with that claim it can be justifiably said that he revamped the understanding of liturgical theology at that time. Schmemann awakened a memory from the Tradition wherein liturgy was a point of origin. He writes, "Liturgical theology . . . is based upon the recognition that the liturgy in its totality is not only an 'object' of theology, but above all its *source*, and this by virtue of the liturgy's essential ecclesial function: i.e., that of revealing by the means which are proper to it (and which belong only to it) the faith of the Church; in other words, of being that *lex orandi* in which the *lex credendi* finds its principal criterion and standard."[18] If theology is faith seeking understanding, as its simplest and most frequent description says, then to find the source and origin of theology one should go to the point where faith is mystically originated and fed on mystical food. This means going to the faith of the Church, to the place where the Church celebrates (accomplishes, manifests, epiphanizes, symbolizes, does) her faith by the proper means, means that were laid down by Christ himself in his founding of the Church and in his gifting her with sacramental endowments. It is true that individual theologians will hold this faith personally, that schools of theology will excavate the consequences of this faith, that historians will observe the unfolding and development of this faith, but none of these is the maternal home of faith to which theology should go when it wants to pick up the precious pearl that it seeks to understand.

---

17. Benedict XVI, "Homilies of His Holiness."
18. Schmemann, "Liturgical Theology: Remarks on Method," 137–38.

Schmemann was ordained in 1946 in Paris, where his family had relocated as Russian émigrés. After teaching at the St. Sergius seminary in Paris, he came to the United States in 1951 to join the faculty of St. Vladimir's Orthodox Theological Seminary in New York, in which he also served as dean from 1962 until his death in 1983. These were the years of liturgical renewal—the liturgical movement as it was known in the West—and because Schmemann thought and wrote about the liturgy, he garnered the reputation of being "a liturgical theologian." At least, this is what members in the guild of liturgical studies assumed; after all, in 1961, he had published *Introduction to Liturgical Theology* in French. But they were bringing their own understanding of the term when they used it of him, and Schmemann thought they were missing the mark.

In a published exchange of articles, Schmemann describes the view he thought other scholars held of his project. He describes them as thinking his goal for liturgical theology is to have it "relegate the 'accessories' to their place" or to "prepare grounds for liturgical reform that would restore the 'essence' of the liturgy."[19] In other words, they assumed he believed liturgical theology was the effort to tighten up liturgy under reforms exercised by historical and theological talent. Schmemann responds by saying, "The fact, however, is that such is *not* my concept of liturgical theology."[20] In fact, "In the approach which I advocate by every line I ever wrote, the question addressed by liturgical theology to liturgy and to the entire liturgical tradition is not about liturgy but about 'theology,' i.e. about the faith of the Church as expressed, communicated, and preserved in the liturgy."[21] Sensing the probable exasperation of his readers, he makes himself clear:

> Finally one may ask: but what do you propose, what do you want? To this I will answer without much hope, I confess, of being heard and understood: we need liturgical theology, viewed not as a theology of worship and not as a reduction of theology to liturgy, but as a slow and patient bringing together of that which was for too long a time and because of many factors broken and isolated—liturgy, theology, and piety, their reintegration within one fundamental vision. In this sense liturgical theology is an illegitimate child of a broken family. It exists, or maybe I should say it ought to exist, only because theology ceased to seek in

---

19. Schmemann, "Liturgical Theology, Theology of Liturgy," 38.
20. Schmemann, "Liturgical Theology, Theology of Liturgy," 38.
21. Schmemann, "Liturgical Theology, Theology of Liturgy," 40.

the *lex orandi* its source and food, because liturgy ceased to be conducive to theology.[22]

For Schmemann, liturgical theology is neither an addition nor a reduction, but the recovery of a union. Often he characterizes the problem as "scholastic" or "Western," but this is not a geographic reference; it is rather a methodological one. It is the temptation "to split theology into a number of virtually autonomous and self-sufficient 'departments' or 'disciplines'—Biblical Theology, Systematic Theology, Patristics, Liturgy, Canon Law."[23] It is the temptation to distort the theological work itself by imposing questions in categories that are alien to the mind of the Church.

What McGregor calls fractures, Schmemann calls a divorce. Things that were once connected are now separated and disunited, and Schmemann adds one more dimension so that he may treat the three together. Perhaps we should refer to it as a "trivorce."

> The goal of liturgical theology, as its very name indicates, is to overcome the fateful divorce between theology, liturgy and piety—a divorce which, as we have already tried to show elsewhere, has had disastrous consequences for theology as well as for liturgy and piety. It deprived liturgy of its proper understanding by the people, who began to see in it beautiful and mysterious ceremonies in which, while attending them, they take no real part. It deprived theology of its living source and made it into an intellectual exercise for intellectuals. It deprived piety of its living content and term of reference.[24]

There are numerous examples where he uses the language of divorce to describe the problem. Here are a handful. "The tragedy of all these debates on the liturgy is that they remain locked within the categories of a 'liturgical piety' which is itself the outcome of the divorce between liturgy, theology and piety."[25] And, "Theology did not care about the liturgy,

---

22. Schmemann, "Liturgical Theology, Theology of Liturgy," 46.

23. Schmemann, "Liturgical Theology, Theology of Liturgy," 47.

24. Schmemann, *Of Water and Spirit*, 12. By "liturgical piety," Schmemann does not mean "piety about the liturgy." He does not want to reduce piety's range of concerns to a simple call for more prayer. Rather, we may say liturgy is the source of the Church's piety because we experience the kingdom-to-come in the liturgy, and liturgical piety is that mystery showing up in our lives. Liturgy is the root; piety is the stalk, flower, and fruit that grows from it, for the sake of the world.

25. Schmemann, "Liturgical Theology, Theology of Liturgy," 46.

and the liturgy did not care about theology. There was a real divorce."[26] And, "Not only has theology been divorced from liturgy as 'source,' but it paid very little attention to it even as to one of its 'objects.'"[27] And, liturgical theology "means, above everything else, the overcoming of the tragical divorce between the thought of the Church and the experience of the Kingdom of God, which is the only source, guide, and fulfillment of that thought, and the only ultimate motivation of all Christian action."[28] And, the basic defect about theology is "its almost total divorce from the real life of the Church and from her *practical* needs."[29] And, Orthodox theological schools "remained for a long time an 'alienated' body within the ecclesiastical organism—alienated because of that divorce of 'theology' from 'piety.'"[30] And, finally,

> this double crisis—of theology and liturgy—is, I submit, the real source of the general crisis which faces our Church today, and which must shape our agenda, if theology is for us more than a quiet "academic" activity. . . . A crisis is always a divorce, a discrepancy, between the foundations and the life which is opposed to be based on these foundations; it is life drifting away from its own foundations. . . . If today both theology and liturgy have ceased, at least to a substantial degree, to perform within the Church the function which is theirs thus provoking a deep crisis, it is because at first they have been divorced from one another; because the *lex credendi* has been alienated from the *lex orandi*.[31]

So here we come to the real fracture, namely, the estrangement of the law of prayer (*lex orandi*) and the law of belief (*lex credendi*).

Repairing the estrangement is not a matter of gluing the two together, however, willy-nilly. One of them is a foundation, the other is a house built upon the foundation, and they are not to be reversed. Schmemann expresses this by saying liturgy is the *ontological condition* of theology.

> The formula *lex orandi est lex credendi* means nothing else than that theology is *possible* only within the Church, i.e. as a fruit of this new life in Christ, granted in the sacramental *leitourgia*,

26. Schmemann, "Liturgical Movement," 181–82.
27. Schmemann, "Liturgy and Theology," 98–99.
28. Schmemann, "Liturgy and Theology," 98–99.
29. Schmemann, "Task of Orthodox Theology," 182.
30. Schmemann, "Thoughts for the Jubilee," 96.
31. Schmemann, "Liturgy and Theology," 88–89.

as a witness to the eschatological fullness of the Church, as in other terms, a participation in this *leitourgia*. The problem of the relationship between liturgy and theology is not for the Fathers a problem of priority or authority. Liturgical tradition is not an "authority" or a *locus theologicus*; it is the ontological condition of theology, of the proper understanding of kerygma, of the Word of God, because it is in the Church, of which the *leitourgia* is the expression and the life, that the sources of theology are functioning as precisely "sources."[32]

Consequences of the Divorce

What are the consequences of this fracture, this divorce, this trivorce, the drifting apart of liturgy, theology, and piety?

First, each of the three elements is affected in itself. Separated from the other two, each one loses something crucial to its identity and vitality. Separate *liturgy* from theology and piety, and believers will embrace it as a beautiful and mysterious ceremony in which they take no real part; separate *theology* from liturgy and piety, and it will become an intellectual exercise for a privileged group of academics; separate *piety* from liturgy and theology, and it will lose its living content and term of reference. The three atoms change when they no longer serve the one molecule. Second, the three elements together are now so weakened that they cannot make an impact upon the world in which the Church lives. The molecule also changes when these three atoms isolate. "We seem to accept, without even noticing it, the brokenness of our Christian vision and experience into neat and unrelated compartments, to accept as normal a legalized and institutionalized divorce within which neither theology nor liturgy can truly be the victory which overcomes the world."[33] Schmemann calls the essence of that current spiritual crisis "secularism" and traces it to "the divorce from God of the whole of human life."[34] This is the tragic result of the divorce.

When liturgy does not unite with theology and piety, then liturgy loses its power of challenging our secularist assumptions. There will remain people who have a special interest in ritual activity and might

---

32. Schmemann, "Theology and Liturgical Tradition," 18.
33. Schmemann, "Liturgical Theology, Theology of Liturgy," 47.
34. Schmemann, "Confession and Communion."

remain attached to colorful liturgical rites as relics, but even those people will

> completely fail to see in them, in the totality of the Church's *leitourgia*, an all-embracing vision of life, a "philosophy of life" shaping and challenging all our ideas, attitudes and actions. As in the case of theology, one can speak of an alienation of liturgy from life, be it from the life of the Church or the life of the Christian individual. Liturgy is confined to the temple, but beyond its sacred enclave it has no impact, no power. . . . A liturgical pietism fed by sentimental and pseudo-symbolic explanations of liturgical rites results, in fact, in a growing and all-pervading secularism.[35]

Schmemann is not impressed by a liturgical pietism, if it leaves liturgy disconnected from life; he is not impressed by a liturgical theology, if it leaves theology blank-faced before the seductions of secularism; he is not impressed if the academy assigns liturgy and theology to be roommates, but they do not live in a conjugal relationship. Worldliness means taking the world without reference to God, and Christians can remain in this worldly condition even if they enjoy theological prattle, or receive a thrill from liturgical ceremony, or indulge in idiosyncratically formulated piety. Liturgy has no impact if confined to the temple, theology has no impact if confined to the academy, piety has no impact if confined to our private spiritualism.

Liturgy, theology, and piety dilute if they do not compound. They each become too thin to do any good. We can investigate each case.

First, if one begins with too thin a definition of liturgy, then it is impossible to defend liturgy as an ontological condition for theology. Why should theology turn to liturgy to commence its search for understanding if liturgy is nothing more than a human self-expression? Why should theology report to rubrics? Systematics to the sacraments? Metaphysics to the mass? Schmemann is aware of the problem. He knows that there are people who are enamored only of the surface of liturgy and acknowledges that this may be a particular problem for the East. He creates a name for it. "I realize how spiritually tired I am of all this 'Orthodoxism,' of all the fuss with Byzantium, Russia, way of life, spirituality, church affairs, piety, of all these rattles. I do not like any one of them, and the more I think about the meaning of Christianity, the more it all seems alien to

---

35. Schmemann, "Liturgy and Theology," 51–52.

me. It all literally obscures Christ, pushes Him into the background."[36] The ceremonial aspects of liturgy are important, but they are only the part of the liturgical iceberg we can see above the waterline; we should understand that it is connected to something much vaster below, namely, the economy Christ has let loose upon the world. If only specialists understand the intricacies of ritual performance, what has liturgy to do with our theological lives?

Second, if one begins with too thin a definition of theology, then it is impossible to defend theology's need for liturgy as its ontological foundation. Theology would need neither the Church nor her liturgical expression if theology is human conversation in the faculty lounge about transcendental topics. Such a discussion would issue from the humanly possible, even if the topic it is discussing is divine. If theology's business is to learn an academic vocabulary, why should it be constrained with liturgical grammar? What need would theology feel for prayer after it has ingested hermeneutics, metaphysics, historiography, anthropology, comparative religion, politics, and moral philosophy? Why would theology trouble itself with trivial ecclesiological matters? Schmemann is aware of the problem.

> [Theology] today constitutes within the Church a self-centered world, virtually isolated from the Church's life. It lives in itself and by itself in tranquil academic quarters, well defended against profane intrusions and curiosities by a highly technical language. Theologians avoid discussing the trivial reality of the Church's life, and do not even dream about influencing it in any way. In turn the Church, i.e., the bishops, priests and laity, are supremely indifferent to the writings of the theologians, even when they do not regard them with open suspicion.... Theology simply fails to reach anybody but professionals, to provoke anything but esoteric controversies in academic periodicals.[37]

If the fracture between theology and liturgy becomes a clean break, then theology floats free of the Church, like ocean plankton, without ecclesial root, and in some cases Schmemann believes this has come to pass. "Theology became a void, a mere intellectual status in the Church without any real reference to the liturgy.... What also happened was that theology became a professional occupation for theologians."[38] If only

36. Schmemann, *Journals*, 146.
37. Schmemann, "Theology and Eucharist," 70.
38. Schmemann, "Liturgical Movement," 181–82.

specialists understand the vocabulary of theology, what has theology to do with our liturgical lives?

Third, if one begins with too thin a definition of piety, then it is impossible to ground it in the twin roots of liturgy and theology. If piety is an activity one does only in Church, what concern is there for a theological perspective of the world? If piety is a theological activity done in one's mind, what concern is there for the ecclesial community? If devotion is private, and religion is spirituality, and reverence to God does not reach the public square, what connection has piety to life? A believer could enjoy the aesthetics without consequence. Schmemann is aware of the problem.

> What they are not aware of is that the Byzantine liturgy—which they dutifully and in faithfulness to their Orthodox heritage attend on Sunday—by its every word and rite challenges the culture in which they live and which they enthusiastically adopt as their "way of life" Monday through Saturday; that the Orthodox faith which they so proudly confess on the Sunday of Orthodoxy contains and posits a vision of man, world, nature, matter, entirely different from the one which in fact shapes not only their lives but their mental and psychological makeup as well.[39]

If piety is simply an enthusiasm for cult, ceremonial, and ritual (the external aspects), then "liturgical piety" is actually a "piety for the liturgy," and that is not the point. Liturgical piety is not a call for more prayer; it is a call for prayer to set fire to the world. When we liturgize God, we are saving the world.

It is clear, then, why Schmemann went in search of a more profound definition of *leitourgia*, and the first assertion he makes is that *leitourgia* cannot be expressed in terms of, or be reduced to, cult. "The ancient world knew a plethora of cultic religions or 'cults.' . . . But the Christian cult is *leitourgia*, and this means that it is *functional* in its essence, has a goal to achieve which transcends the categories of cult as such."[40] What goal is that? What possible goal could liturgy have beyond the Church walls? What possible function could liturgy have beyond the satisfaction it gives its participants? Schmemann answers:

> This goal is precisely the *Church* as the manifestation and presence of the "new eon," of the Kingdom of God. In a sense

---

39. Schmemann, *Church, World, Mission*, 206–7.
40. Schmemann, "Theology and Eucharist," 79.

> the Church is indeed a *liturgical institution*, i.e. an institution whose *leitourgia* is to fulfill itself as the Body of Christ and a new creation. Christian cult is, therefore, a radically new cult, unprecedented in both the Old Testament and paganism, and the deficiency of a certain theology, as well as of a certain liturgical piety, is that they not only overlook the radical newness of Christian *leitourgia* but rather define and experience it again in the old cultic categories.[41]

This means that *leitourgia* is not an entrance into cult; rather, *leitourgia* is entrance into the kingdom coming down to meet us, forward to encounter us, up to sustain us. The kingdom that the Church does in the liturgical cult is already present, though it is still coming.

This is the basis of Schmemann's notion of cultic antinomy: *leitourgia* is bigger than the liturgy that contains it (as C. S. Lewis imagines a Narnian stable having an inside bigger than its outside). "In this world, the *Eschaton*—the holy, the sacred, the 'otherness'—can be expressed and manifested only as 'cult.' Not only in relation to the world, but in relation to itself as dwelling in the world, the Church must use the forms and language of the cult, in order eternally to transcend the cult."[42] The liturgy is fundamentally antinomical because the Church does not gather in order to celebrate cult; she gathers to become, through cultic activity, what she really is. That's why Schmemann can say the whole life of the Church is a *leitourgia*, and that's why he can say *leitourgia* is the ontological condition for theology. In my Schmemann lecture at St. Vladimir's Seminary I could think to express this only with some neologistic novelty.

> If I can risk making my point clumsily, I will say that Schmemann is not talking about acts of liturgy, he is talking about liturgical acts of *leitourgia*. And if I may press my luck further, and create a verb, I will say that *leitourgia* is the action being performed when the Church "cults." By "culting" the Church becomes her true self, enjoys her true mystery, exercises her real *leitourgia*. The Church does not do cult, she uses cult to do *leitourgia*. And the *leitourgia* performed in her cult transforms the Church.[43]

This thicker definition of liturgy as *leitourgia* can be found scattered across the pages of Schmemann's corpus. *Leitourgia* is a "corporate

---

41. Schmemann, "Theology and Eucharist," 79.
42. Schmemann, "Theology and Liturgical Tradition," 17–18.
43. Fagerberg, "Anchor of Schmemann's Liturgical Theology," 406.

procession and passage of the Church toward her fulfillment";[44] its function is to "reveal and communicate that 'eschaton' without which the Church is but an institution among other human institutions";[45] it is "an effort toward and an experience of the Kingdom of God";[46] its true uniqueness "lies in its stemming from the faith in the Incarnation, from the great and all-embracing mystery of the 'Logos made flesh'";[47] it is cosmic; its original Greek meaning had to do with a public office and "service performed on behalf of a community and for its benefit;"[48] and the service the Church performs on behalf of the world, and for its benefit, is precisely to "manifest and to actualize in this world the *eschaton*, the ultimate reality of salvation and redemption. In and through the Church the Kingdom of God is made already present, is communicated to men."[49]

Conclusion: Theology's Home Address

Schmemann summarizes his position with words that apply fittingly to the therapy required for healing of the liturgy-theology fracture. First he says what benignly stops short and then takes it further to his conclusion. "What do I mean when I speak about this reunion or reconnecting together again of the liturgy and the theology? I mean not only that it is an invitation to theologians to pay more attention to liturgical data.... This would do no harm. [But] I am trying to go further than that and state, at least as my conviction, that in a very direct and real way, not only in a symbolical or educational way, but in a real way, the Eucharist, the sacraments, and the liturgy of the Church are the real sources of theology."[50] So what, in fact, does he hope for? The same thing I hope for: a theology that has something to say as a charismatic testimony.

> Now what do I mean? I mean that theology in the Church is a charisma, a gift of the Holy Spirit, not only a system of syllogisms and deductions, but a real power to bear testimony toward God's doing in the Church for the salvation of man....

---

44. Schmemann, "Prayer, Liturgy, and Renewal," 12.
45. Schmemann, "Prayer, Liturgy, and Renewal," 13.
46. Schmemann, "Prayer, Liturgy, and Renewal," 14.
47. Schmemann, "Worship in a Secular Age," 6–7.
48. Schmemann, "Theology and Eucharist," 79.
49. Schmemann, *Church, World, Mission*, 211–12.
50. Schmemann, "Liturgical Movement," 183–84.

> Where is that gift of the Holy Spirit given? Where does theology find its real and divine status if not in that sacrament of all sacraments in which the Church eternally becomes what she is, the temple of the Holy Spirit, the body of Christ, the eschaton, the anticipation of the world to come? . . . This is where the foundation of theology as a phenomenon *bene fundatum* is.[51]

If theology is faith seeking understanding, then before we follow faith downstream to all the plains of understanding it floods, we should travel upstream to the headwaters of that faith. This, of course, is not the liturgy. The source of faith is God, not rubrics. The home of theology is God. But the reason to heal the breach between theology and liturgy is the fact that liturgy is where God works. "Work" is in the etymological root of the word *leitourgia*.

Schmemann called the problem a divorce, and McGregor called the problem a fracture. Both are pointing out a dissolution between things that once were connected, that should be connected, and that suffer a distortion when they are not connected. Schmemann suggests that liturgical theology looks like an illegitimate child of a broken family, and I am going to end by upping the ante of that final metaphor. If separated from liturgy, then theology is *orphaned*.

I do not suggest that the parents of theology could ever die. The progenitors of theology are unending. Christ, the paterfamilias of the Church, is eternal, and his bride's liturgy is unfailing. Rather, in this case, "being orphaned" means losing one's home, being in want of family, being bereft of protection, support, and supervision. Theology has a domicile, a legal residence. Being orphaned means losing this home. This does not imply that theology should never leave the house! Theology is encouraged to explore nearby neighborhoods, but in doing so, it should never forget its address.

There will be some who will not understand. There will be some who think the cost of maturity is being orphaned. They will wonder how innovations can be made if one is submissive to the will of another. How there can be novelty of thought when there is compliancy of will? Some will think submission is servility, compliance is restriction, the episcopal *mandatum* conflicts with academic freedom. Theology will never grow up, some suppose, unless it feels a contempt for its home and, like the

---

51. Schmemann, "Liturgical Movement," 183–84.

prodigal son, asks for a portion of its inheritance to do with what it wants in far-off academic lands that seem to hold greater wealth and promise.

But surely this is a mistaken way of looking at things. We do not describe an orphan as "liberated from his parents." The orphan has less liberty, not more, when it is cut off from its heritage and inheritance; less perceptiveness, not more, when severed from tradition; a narrowed range of vision, not a broadened one, when fragmented. To have the Church as a home does not mean theology lacks either independence or maturity. Docility means quick to learn, teachable, an aptness for being taught the lessons that come from the heart of the Church,[52] and *leitourgia* is where the Church becomes what she is, becomes her true self. There, theology can be done with fullness, integrity, wholeness, because there, theology witnesses the full, integral, and whole revelation-in-action. Scripture records, and tradition hands on, but at the liturgy, God *constantly accomplishes* the Paschal Mystery within us (prayer for the fifth Sunday of Easter).

Bibliography

Benedict XVI, Pope. "Homilies of His Holiness Bartholomew I and His Holiness Pope Benedict XVI." Vatican, 29 June 2008. www.vatican.va/content/benedict-xvi/en/homilies/2008/documents/hf_ben-xvi_hom_20080629_pallio.html.

———. *On the Way to Jesus Christ*. San Francisco: Ignatius, 2005.

———. *The Spirit of the Liturgy*. San Francisco: Ignatius, 2000.

Bouyer, Louis. *The Meaning of the Monastic Life*. London: Burns & Oates, 1955.

Evagrius of Pontus. *Pratikos and Chapters on Prayer*. Kalamazoo, MI: Cistercian, 1981.

Fagerberg, David. "The Anchor of Schmemann's Liturgical Theology." *St. Vladimir's Theological Quarterly* 63, no. 4 (2019) 387–422.

———. *On Liturgical Asceticism*. Washington, DC: Catholic University Press, 2013.

Golitzin, Alexander. *Et Introibo ad Altare Dei: The Mystagogy of Dionysius Areopagita*. Thessalonica: Dedousis, 1994.

Hierotheos, Metropolitan. *Orthodoxy Psychotherapy: The Science of the Fathers*. Levadia, Gr.: Birth of the Theotokos Monastery, 1994.

Kavanagh, Aidan. *On Liturgical Theology*. New York: Pueblo, 1984.

Martimort, A. G. *The Church at Prayer* 1. Collegeville, MN: Liturgical, 1987.

Schmemann, Alexander. *Church, World, Mission: Reflections on Orthodoxy in the West*. Crestwood, NY: St. Vladimir's Seminary Press, 1979.

———. "Confession and Communion: Reports to the Holy Synod of Bishops of the Orthodox Church in America." Orthodox Church in America, 17 Feb., 1972. https://www.oca.org/holy-synod/encyclicals/on-confession-and-communion.

———. *Introduction to Liturgical Theology*. Crestwood, NY: St. Vladimir's Seminary Press, 1966.

52. Allusion to John Paul II, *Ex Corde Ecclesiae*.

———. *The Journals of Father Alexander Schmemann*. Crestwood, NY: St. Vladimir's Seminary Press, 2002.

———. "Liturgical Movement and Orthodox Ecumenical Feeling." *American Benedictine Review* 14, no. 2 (1963) 177–86.

———. "Liturgical Theology: Remarks on Method." In *Liturgy and Tradition: Theological Reflections of Alexander Schmemann*, edited by Thomas Fisch, 137–44. Crestwood, NY: St. Vladimir's Seminary Press, 1990.

———. "Liturgical Theology, Theology of Liturgy, and Liturgical Reform." In *Liturgy and Tradition: Theological Reflections of Alexander Schmemann*, edited by Thomas Fisch, 38–47. Crestwood, NY: St. Vladimir's Seminary Press, 1990.

———. "Liturgy and Theology." In *Liturgy and Tradition: Theological Reflections of Alexander Schmemann*, edited by Thomas Fisch, 49–68. Crestwood, NY: St. Vladimir's Seminary Press, 1990.

———. *Of Water and the Spirit*. Crestwood, NY: St. Vladimir Seminary Press, 1974.

———. "Prayer, Liturgy, and Renewal." *Greek Orthodox Theological Review* 14, no. 1 (1969) 7–16.

———. "The Task of Orthodox Theology in America Today." *St. Vladimir's Seminary Quarterly* 10, no. 4 (1966) 180–88.

———. "Theology and Eucharist." In *Liturgy and Tradition: Theological Reflections of Alexander Schmemann*, edited by Thomas Fisch, 69–88. Crestwood, NY: St. Vladimir's Seminary Press, 1990.

———. "Theology and Liturgical Tradition." In *Liturgy and Tradition: Theological Reflections of Alexander Schmemann*, edited by Thomas Fisch, 11–20. Crestwood, NY: St. Vladimir's Seminary Press, 1990.

———. "Thoughts for the Jubilee." *St. Vladimir's Theological Quarterly* 13, no. 1 (1969) 95–102.

———. "Worship in a Secular Age." *St. Vladimir's Theological Quarterly*, 16, no. 1 (1972) 3–16.

Second Vatican Council. "Constitution on the Sacred Liturgy [*Sacrosanctum Concilium*]." Vatican, 4 Dec. 1963. www.vatican.va/archive/hist_councils/ii_vatican_council/documents/vat-ii_const_19631204_sacrosanctum-concilium_en.html.

Spidlik, Tomas. *The Spirituality of the Christian East*. Kalamazoo, MI: Cistercian, 1986.

Vasileios, Archimandrite. *Hymn of Entry: Liturgy and Life in the Orthodox Church*. Crestwood, NY: St. Vladimir's Seminary Press, 1984.

5

The Literal and Spiritual Senses of Sacred Scripture

Leroy A. Huizenga

> While today's academic exegesis, including that of Catholic scholars, is highly competent in the field of historical-critical methodology and its latest developments, it must be said that comparable attention needs to be paid to the theological dimension of the biblical texts, so that they can be more deeply understood in accordance with the three elements indicated by the Dogmatic Constitution *Dei Verbum*.
> —POPE BENEDICT XVI, *VERBUM DOMINI*, 34

Introduction

Perhaps there never was a golden age when the Church, Scripture, and tradition functioned in perfect harmony, with every Christian, clergy or lay, a perfect saint on earth, clear in intellect and pure in body and heart. But prior ages, particularly the medieval, with its emphasis on the synthesis of all human knowledge and religious faith, did achieve a coherent, overarching vision in which everything was in perfect harmony, and Christian practice and belief (where and when exercised with fidelity) were in accord with Scripture, tradition, and magisterium, as well as with the entire cosmos. The harmony the Middle Ages achieved involved a robust metaphysics rooted first in St. Augustine's Neoplatonic vision and then synthesized masterfully by St. Thomas Aquinas. God, the uncreated Creator, was outside of all created being but also the source and ground of all being, with creation consisting of an invisible, metaphysical realm that grounded the nature of particular natural objects of the visible, physical realm.

Scriptural interpretation according to the fourfold sense relied on that structure, as Scripture and its meanings mapped that structure; Scripture's story told the truth of creation in both its invisible and visible aspects. The literal sense belonged below the line, so to speak, in the physical, visible realm, as words are human signs. But the spiritual sense (divided into three senses, the allegorical, moral or tropological, and anagogical) was above the line: it belonged to the metaphysical, invisible realm, while being rooted in the letter. The process is semiotic, semiotics being the science of signs: the signs (*signa*) of the words of Scripture signified its substance (*res*), first natural items and their concomitant forms, their signifieds; and then in a second step those signifieds (*res*) functioned also as *signa* in turn, new signs pointing to more realities, further signifieds (*res*), of spiritual realities: allegory, tropology, and anagogy.[1] So, historically, the fourfold sense of Scripture presumes and requires a serious metaphysical conception of reality.

While this chapter will focus on the fracture between the literal and spiritual senses of Scripture, there are other problems in the current relationship of theology and Sacred Scripture that stand in necessary parallel not only today but through the centuries, and so a few words on that broader split are in order.

The fracture between the literal and spiritual senses of Scripture runs parallel with the more extreme divorce between theology and Sacred Scripture (in our day, "biblical studies"). Which of the two fractures preceded and caused the other is difficult, if not impossible, to answer, both because of the challenges involved in teasing out intellectual and interpersonal influences in detail hundreds of years after the beginning of these splits but, more importantly, also because in many ways the spiritual senses of Scripture simply *were* theology itself. That is, the Church's fourfold way of reading Scripture was intrinsically bound up

---

1. Broadly conceived, semiotics concerns how signs, whether human words, human and other animal noises and gestures, natural objects, and human signs (from traffic lights to cinematic works), function to make meaning. Semiotics has a long history, as Plato and the Stoics and other ancient philosophers set the semiotic agenda for the West, and as St. Augustine was the greatest ancient semiotician.

with its theological doctrine (ultimately the realities of theology itself) and vice-versa: Scripture revealed the ultimate truth about God and his relation to the entire cosmos, and theology so understood determined the meaning of Scripture. Scripture could not mean other than what the Church officially taught, and what the Church officially taught was of necessity the faithful expression of Scripture. Theological realities were the ultimate conceptual referent of the spiritual senses, and while nature and reason could teach pagans, Muslims, Jews, and Christians true things about God, those truths were also taught by Sacred Scripture in both the literal and spiritual senses. In short, the ultimate referents of Scripture were theological truths on the level of the spiritual senses to which the literal pointed, so the separation of letter and spirit and the separation of biblical studies and theology simply had to parallel each other.

But the splits happened. They began long ago, and by the mid-twentieth century a situation obtained in which the fracture between serious biblical studies (as opposed to the sort of prooftexting one finds in hardcore confessional Protestantism today, with a theological grid and concomitant hermeneutical closure rooted in post-Reformation Protestant orthodoxy) and serious theology was all but total. Biblical scholars had effectively completed the task of liberating Scripture from dogma, while the academic theologians, ever inclined to bother with what their colleagues in biblical studies in ecclesially supported institutions were doing, found the results of historical-critical exegesis useless for their work. It was a situation of perceived reductionism against perceived eisegesis. Happily, since the 1960s and 1970s, many believing scholars and theologians have begun working on rapprochement, occasioned by growing dissatisfaction and disillusion with the promises of the historical-critical method. But why was a rapprochement between theology and biblical studies necessary? Whence the fracture?

The perfect conceptual unity among Scripture's letter and spirit and the Church's theology began to suffer the first tremors of fracture in the West over seven hundred years ago, when William of Ockham, a Franciscan priest who exercised great influence upon the Protestant Reformers, asserted philosophical nominalism and its theological concomitant, voluntarism.[2] Indeed, the real issue is philosophy, and indeed cosmology. (One might remember that at the origins of Western philosophy in Greece, philosophy and cosmology were not just intertwined

---

2. See McGrath, *Intellectual Origins*, 67–115.

but indistinguishable.) As Rudolf Bultmann famously argued, exegesis without presuppositions is impossible.[3] (Almost all nowadays have come to agree.) And those presuppositions are philosophical, and philosophy implies cosmology.

The fourfold sense—implicit in the Bible itself in its intra- or intertextual connections and codified through the ages by St. Augustine, St. John Cassian, and St. Thomas Aquinas—presumes a classical Christian cosmology, in which the uncreated triune Creator God superintends an invisible, stable, metaphysical realm of formal realities, and visible particular things are what they are by participation in those forms. (For our purposes here we need not delve into important questions concerning St. Augustine's relationship to Neoplatonism, St. Thomas's use of Aristotle, and to what extent and in what way St. Thomas should be read as an Augustinian.) So for the premodern Christian tradition, the visible signs of Scripture (the words) pointed to the metaphysical realities (that is, the formal realities), which was the ultimate signification of the literal sense. But then God was understood to be able to signify not only by signs but also by the formal, ideal signifieds, which then could function also as signs themselves that point to even higher, spiritual realities: this is the signification of the spiritual sense.

In short, the use of the classical fourfold sense presumes the uncreated Creator above and outside all and highest of all; then a created, invisible, stable realm; and below that a created, visible, dynamic realm. Particular things in the visible realm are signs that point to and participate in their forms in the invisible realm, and those metaphysical, formal things that signs signify can in turn be signs of higher, spiritual things.

St. Augustine turns to the example of St. Paul.[4] The *locus classicus* is 1 Corinthians 9:9-10. Paul writes, "For it is written in the Law of Moses: 'Do not muzzle an ox while it is treading out the grain.' Is it about oxen that God is concerned? Surely he says this for us, doesn't he? Yes, this was written for us, because whoever plows and threshes should be able to do so in the hope of sharing in the harvest."

The first step of literal signification is perceiving the sign (ox) as pointing to and participating in the formal ideal of "ox" (what we picture in our minds as an ox, because our minds can know both the oxen we have encountered in life or through description or pictures and also the

---

3. Bultmann, "Is Exegesis without Presuppositions Possible?"
4. Augustine, *De doctrina christiana*, II.16.

formal, ideal reality of "ox"). Put plainly, when Paul quoting Moses writes "ox," he means what we all understand to be an ox. But the second step Paul himself illustrates: the literal "ox" that is to be allowed to enjoy the grain it treads (so Deut 25:4) spiritually and thus ultimately means that ministers and missionaries deserve to enjoy their livelihood from their apostolic labors.

Another good example all but unexamined in contemporary literature is St. Paul's treatment of the Old Testament in 1 Corinthians 10:1–22. There Paul calls the wilderness generation of Israel "our fathers" (10:1) and speaks of them being "baptized" and eating "spiritual food" and drinking "spiritual drink" (10:2–4a), as if they were receiving Christian sacraments—Paul treats them as signs foreshadowing the Eucharist. Given that, Paul even dares to claim they drank from the rock that was Christ himself (10:4b). Here Paul is using the literal sense and the allegorical (typological) sense. Then he moves to the moral (tropological) sense, reminding his readers that most of that generation was destroyed in the wilderness (10:5), stating that "these things are warnings for us, not to desire evil as they did" (10:6), arguing shortly thereafter that their sin led God to punish them (10:7–10). His reminder to the Corinthians that these things about the wilderness generation "were written down for our instruction, upon whom the end of the ages has come" (10:5) involves the ramifications of the anagogical sense; just as that generation did not enter the promised land, neither will the Corinthians (and by extension all Christians) enter heaven if they engage in similar idolatry, immorality, testing of the Lord, and grumbling.

The fourfold sense developed and codified by the fathers and medievals is thus rooted in the apostolic witness in Scripture. But what happens when the cosmology undergirding the fourfold sense is overturned in early modernity?

The Symptoms: Fracture in the Wake of New Cosmologies

Until recently, most retellings of the rise of historical criticism have seen that criticism's beginnings in the nineteenth century, with some eighteenth-century antecedents (such as J. B. Koppe's *Marcus non epitomator Matthaei*,[5] which argued, against long tradition going back to Augustine, that St. Mark did not compose a summary of St. Matthew's Gospel but

---

5. Koppe, *Marcus non epitomator Matthaei*.

that St. Mark's Gospel was actually original). More recent treatments have sought the roots of historical criticism in not only Martin Luther and the sixteenth-century Catholic scholar Fr. Richard Simon but in the fourteenth century, with William of Ockham and other developments.[6]

Ockham, a Franciscan friar, was a proto-Protestant—indeed, what we call the Reformation is best seen theologically and sociologically as a major stage in reforming movements in Western Christendom begun well before the sixteenth century. Ockham's philosophical nominalism had the effect of undercutting metaphysics *in toto*—something that would influence the Protestant Reformers, who desired that Aristotle and philosophy should play little, if any, role in theology—while Ockham's theological voluntarism and advocacy of the primacy of the letter of Scripture would anticipate Protestant commitments. Ockham's nominalism held that true philosophical knowledge of things as metaphysical entities was both unneccesary—Ockham's razor holds that reality needs no metaphysical superstructure for its existence or perception—and fundamentally impossible. Thus, knowledge of the harmony of the cosmos was impossible, as the invisible, metaphysical realm did not exist—men and women could know particular things only in the realm of experience, and the names (*nomen*, hence nominalism) by which particular things that happened to resemble each other in the realm of experience (from trees to dogs to human persons) were called, were matters of mere social convention. For Ockham, that was no real issue, because Ockham also asserted voluntarism. God should not be thought of existing as a metaphysical substance, for that would constrain his absolute freedom (just as human nature constrains men and women—they cannot flap their wings and fly, for instance, since they have human and not avian nature). God is pure unconstrained will (*voluntas*, hence voluntarism). If things hold together or are a particular way (say, the nature of the human person or the means of salvation involving the sacrifice of God's Son as opposed to the exsanguination of some random donkey), it is because God wills it so. God, not metaphysics, guarantees the perceived stability of the created order—so long as God freely decides to restrain his *potentia absoluta* (absolute power) in favor of his *potentia ordinata* (ordained power).

Further, Ockham also asserted that Scripture alone was supreme in knowing God's will (thus anticipating the Protestant concept of *sola Scriptura*), and, as Ockham's nominalism and voluntarism had undercut

---

6. See Hahn and Wiker, *Politicizing the Bible*, and Hahn and Morrow, *Modern Biblical Criticism*.

the metaphysics of both things and persons, including the very person of God, he undercut the possibility of spiritual senses. Ockham was content with a way of reading Scripture according to the letter alone, and the readings of Scripture that model permitted showed that God was every bit as mercurial (in the Old Testament, at least) as Ockham's theological voluntarism required.

Ockham's nominalism thus destabilized medieval cosmology, and his voluntarism upended theology and longstanding ways of reading Scripture. His ideas also fueled later Protestant theories of grace and forensic justification. Without metaphysics, grace and justification are not real things infused into the real nature of a believer but can concern only God's attitude towards a sinner. For good measure, Ockham came into severe conflict with the pope of his day, John XXII, even coming to argue the pope was a heretic after John XXII excommunicated him for supporting Louis IV of Bavaria, an enemy of John XXII. Anticipating Protestant Erastianism, in which the prince (thus the state) is regarded as ruler and protector of the Church, Ockham had also argued that Louis as Holy Roman Emperor was supreme over Church and pope. Luther would also come into conflict with a pope of his day, Leo X, and support a functional Erastianism, calling in his "Address to the Christian Nobility of the German Nation" on the princes to drive his reformation of the Church forward in lands in which they held power. The long result of Ockham's program was the severing of the Bible from metaphysical order of the cosmos, since there was no robust, classical metaphysics in his system.

The Protestant Reformers in turn looked back to Ockham for inspiration. In October 1520, after his formal excommunication of 15 June 1519 and when Luther's theological and ecclesial opinions and options were fundamentally set, Luther said, "My master Occam was the greatest dialectitian."[7] It is no surprise, then, that Protestantism has largely been nominalist and voluntarist and focused on the letter of Scripture, rejecting "allegory," by which is meant the classic spiritual senses and the fourfold division *in toto*. Luther rejected "literal meaning" as a descriptor and insisted rather on the "grammatical, historical meaning" or (better, in his view) the publicly knowable "meaning of the tongue or of language," while allowing that the Spirit could disclose *mysteria* because

---

7. As quoted in Oberman, *Luther*, 11.

St. Paul himself finds *mysteria*: Paul sees further significance in certain Old Testament passages (particularly in Gal 4:21–31).[8]

This rejection of the spiritual senses (collectively referred to as "allegory" in a broad sense) in favor of the letter alone brings us to the separation of biblical studies and theology. The Reformation aided in ushering in the Enlightenment (though precisely how is controverted)[9]—one thinks of the Calvinist slogan *post tenebras lux*, emblazoned today on the International Monument to the Reformation in Geneva—and in the heyday of the Enlightenment's confidence in reason and education, J. P. Gabler stepped forth to formalize the fracture between what had become academic biblical studies and theology in the 1787 inaugural address for his chair at the University of Altdorf, titled (here in English) "On the Correct Distinction between Dogmatic and Biblical Theology and the Right Definition of Their Goals."[10] With Protestant lands having both their Protestant churches and their universities serving as arms of the state, biblical studies and theology became ever more academic even while ostensibly serving the churches—with the result that biblical studies, theology, and the churches often functioned to serve *Staatsinteresse* in a situation of near-total Erastianism,[11] under which members of the *Freikirchen* suffered much and institutionalized in 1648 under the principle of *cuius regio eius religio* when the Peace of Westphalia ended the Thirty Years War.

Gabler's goal was to have the Bible serve as the basis of all theological dogmatics. Biblical theology thus became an independent discipline but was not an end in itself. It was intended to mediate between biblical religion and dogmatic theology by enabling a description of biblical religion to function as the ground of prescriptive dogmatic theology. Gabler's program involved three distinctions. First, Gabler separates religion and theology, asserting that the Bible contains not theology as such but only religion not yet systematized, divine teaching handed down in documents. Second, Gabler separates biblical theology from dogmatic theology; biblical theology is the endeavor of providing an accurate description of the disparate religious data of the documents the Bible comprises in a

---

8. Luther, "Concerning Letter and Spirit," 80.

9. See Gregory, *Unintended Reformation*.

10. Gabler, "De justo discrimine theologiae biblicae et dogmaticae regundisque recte utriusque finibus," in *Kleinere Theologische Schriften*, 179–98.

11. See again Hahn and Wiker, *Politicizing the Bible*, and Hahn and Morrow, *Modern Biblical Criticism as a Tool of Statecraft 1700–1900*.

sort of exercise in cataloguing. Third, Gabler makes a distinction between "true" and "pure" biblical theology. "True" biblical theology was descriptive; the scholar here is to describe all the elements of religion as found in the Bible; it is thus "true" in a historical, factual sense. Fourth, the scholar (also functioning necessarily here as a philosopher, if only on the level of unreflective assumptions) eliminates contingent, particular concepts from what has been catalogued, leaving only the "pure," timeless truths of Scripture. Then, once those pure, supposedly timeless truths have been isolated, dogmatics can systematize them into a coherent theology.

Gabler's intention was to reestablish the Bible as the foundation and ground of all theology, but consequences have a way of becoming unintended: biblical theology became an independent discipline within biblical studies, itself separated from theology. The failure and thus fracture between biblical studies (whether descriptions of biblical religion or biblical theology more narrowly) and theology resulted because descriptive history was being performed on the biblical texts as dead artifacts, much like a forensic pathologist treats a corpse. No robust theological vision provided inspiration or exercised control. Indeed, Gabler's philosophical assumptions necessitated a broad, ugly ditch between the contingent facts of history and the (perhaps) necessary truths of theology. God was no longer author and referent of the entirety of Scripture but one who somehow might have spoken through parts of the Bible. The supposedly timeless parts just happened to accord with what educated Western Europeans happened to want to believe about faith and morals already (in Germanic lands, determined largely by Kant), rendering the Bible increasingly superfluous and thus irrelevant.

Protestantism, then, from Luther himself through the periods of Protestant orthodoxy and Protestant liberalism in the context of the Enlightenment in Protestant lands, flowed from Ockham's nominalism and voluntarism, with implications for biblical interpretation well before the Copernican revolution upended our view of the cosmos and the Enlightenment gave us mechanistic modernity, Deist at best, atheist at worst. For Catholicism, on the other hand, scriptural interpretation came to fruition, and today comes to fruition, in the eucharistic liturgy. We live in salvation history even today. The Old Testament points forward to the New Testament, which fulfills the Old, and the events of the New Testament are fulfilled throughout the ages in the Church and her sacred liturgy, in which we not just anticipate but experience heaven (as Jesus Christ comes to us with his body, blood, soul, and divinity, under the appearance of bread and wine). That is why Catholics have sometimes seemed to privilege the Eucharist over Scripture and preaching (though a right understanding sees Christ coming to us both at the altar and the ambo). That is also why the Mass looks back to the Old Testament as it looks forward to the eschaton, to heaven. Catholics have an all-male priesthood that wears vestments in churches that are supposed to look like temples while offering the sacrifice of the Eucharist, because the Old Testament presents an all-male priesthood wearing vestments while offering sacrifices in the tabernacle and later temples.

Protestant orthodoxy, however, focuses much more on content than ritual. The New Testament does fulfill the Old, but instead of seeing the New continued in the present in the Church's eucharistic liturgy, Protestantism sees the next step as a matter of extracting content from the Bible and presenting it in the sermon. And there are again philosophical and cosmological reasons for this. For in Ockham's proto-Protestant way of thinking, there was no stable metaphysical realm. Things existed as they were purely by God's will, which, in principle, could change at any moment, though God had graciously bound his *potentia absoluta* by his *potentia ordinata*; God chooses freely not to change himself or anything else, but nothing stops his *potential absoluta* from deciding upon a new *ordinata*. As such, the sacraments (or ordinances, as some Protestants came to prefer to call them) as signs could not point to or participate in any metaphysical reality they might signify; they had to point to what God had done in the past and thus merely remind contemporary Protestant Christians in a given place and time of what God has done for them; at best, they were understood as occasions where the Holy Spirit was specially present. This is why most Protestants have some sort of symbolic understanding of the Lord's Supper; lacking classical metaphysics, they distance the elements from the reality of the risen Christ. (Luther was an exception; for him it was enough to grant that "is" means "is" when Jesus says "this is my body" and "this cup is the new covenant in my blood," and he felt that we should not complicate the matter with philosophy.)

Indeed, whereas for Catholics, grace has been conceived of as a real thing, a substance that changes believers who participate in the sacraments with the proper dispositions, Protestants have conceived of grace in forensic (that is, legal) terms, merely as God's attitude towards the sinner. God's grace in this model does not metaphysically exist, so grace cannot really change us (as taking a medicine would change the chemistry of our bodies to encourage health—think here of St. Ignatius of Antioch's description of the Eucharist as "the medicine of immortality")[12]—for neither grace nor we are Real. Rather, we do not change—whatever we are, we remain sinners, but God regards us *as if* we were righteous. This is of course the classical orthodox Protestant doctrine of imputed justification (or righteousness; the two words are the same in Hebrew, Greek, Latin, and German). Neither sacraments nor grace really touch the Christian, though the ritual and the believed fact of grace might somehow motivate her, as might the Holy Spirit.

We thus see that sacraments and Scripture stand in parallel in theology. For Catholicism, which operates with the classical metaphysics of the invisible, stable realm behind the visible realm of flux, the words of Scripture and the matter of the sacraments (bread, wine, oil, water, etc.) are visible signs of invisible realities, which participate in and make present that which they signify. For Protestantism, which employs not the fourfold sense but the grammatico-historical method using rhetorical tools to get at the human meaning of the words of the Bible, Scripture proclaims truths that God wanted (and wants) proclaimed. And that Protestant turn towards the use of rhetorical tools to get at the human meaning of the words (willed and inspired by God nonetheless) would issue forth as historical criticism once the new cosmology (with its concomitant if nascent Ockhamite anti-metaphysics) worked itself out in human history. Ockham could not have foreseen the result, which, once the Enlightenment's deistic influence on theology removed God from any real ongoing providential role in creation, was to leave the Bible a relic of the past, useful only for moral encouragement.

Cosmology itself was upended not only by Ockham but later by the Copernican Revolution in science (of course, Tycho Brahe, William Kepler, and Galileo are also important here). In the later Middle Ages, Aristotelian cosmology prevailed, with earth at the center of the cosmos and the Holy Trinity outside creation but sustaining creation as (in the words of Dante) "the love that moves the sun, and the other stars,"[13] with a perfect if asymmetrical relational polarity between the Triune Creator outside the created cosmos and his ultimate creature made in his image, humanity, as his steward of the earth at the pinnacle of the created cosmos.

---

12. Ignatius, *To the Ephesians*, ch. 20.
13. Alighieri, *Divine Comedy: Paradise*, 33.

Early modern geocentrism shattered this vision, and the West has been searching for a coherent, dominant replacement ever since, now with physics seeking a GUT (Grand Unifying Theory) or TOE (Theory of Everything). Further, Descartes cut Aristotelian causality in half. St. Thomas and other medievals, following Aristotle, assumed that all natural things are "caused" by formal, material, efficient, and final causes, with the formal cause determining what a thing metaphysically is and the final cause in tandem with the formal determining its purpose—finality follows form. Descartes found no cause for the necessity of formal and final causes, believing material and efficient causes sufficient to explain existence and motion, which led to the modern materialist idea that there is nothing but atoms and the forces of physical laws. The loss of final and formal causes means, ultimately, there is no meaning. For theological voluntarists, God's dominant will made things what they were, but once the dominant powers in the West surrendered the Triune God, neither rocks nor human beings were actual real things, and everything came to be seen as a random constellation of atoms. Scripture thus has nothing metaphysical to refer to; the words of Scripture cannot refer to realities like ultimate, perennial truths but only to events in history, in the past, and where earlier generations came to believe God is unknowable, many contemporary scholars and historians think the past is unknowable, too.

Perhaps here lies the best way of understanding the difference between historic Catholic scriptural interpretation and modern historical criticism of the Bible. As regards the former, the letter of Scripture comprised meaningful signs, pointing above the metaphysical line to spiritual meanings and ultimately to God, whereas for the latter, the words refer only to the author's thoughts and thus the historical situation of the ancient author below any metaphysical line. And in postmodern interpretation, with its severe lack of confidence in historical epistemology, history can never finally be known, leaving the reader and contemporary communities supreme to do what they wish with the biblical materials, unmoored from God, reality, and history, leaving the reader firmly in charge. The Protestant principle of *sola Scriptura* degraded itself into *sola historia*, and *sola historia* degraded and collapsed in those circles that regarded objective knowledge of the past as an impossibility.

The Diagnosis: Mere Moralism

By the nineteenth century, then, the old cosmology had been displaced, as had classical voluntarist Protestant theology of the orthodox variety, in which the divine will (totally free, but never changing by God's own free choice) guaranteed the stability of the world we encounter and the truth of Scripture. But the dominant picture of God had shifted well away from that. God was either removed from having any real role in the cosmos (so deism) or identified with the cosmos in a pantheistic way (so Spinoza and his legacy in the nineteenth century).

Rather than jettison Jesus, however, Christian Europe and America sought to remake him in their image, more mascot than Master. Miracles, prophecy, and sacrifice were rejected, leaving Jesus to be nothing more than a moralist who happily anticipated Immanuel Kant's works on morals by 1752 years. So too with the rest of Scripture, which was read for its moral lessons, and where the lessons disagreed with Enlightenment morality, they were rejected. Another way of thinking about it is that the nineteenth century rejected allegory (except when describing what Paul, for instance, was trying to do in his obvious mangling of the Old Testament) and anagogy but kept a weak sense of the letter and some sort of moral sense.

So historical critics investigated the biblical writings supposedly for the sake of knowledge for its own sake but also to wrestle with the meaning of the Bible and Jesus for their own generations. But lacking a robust Christian theology and metaphysics, the Bible fell apart. It came to be seen as a random collection of contradictory texts, documentary artifacts left by long-dead Israelite, Jewish, and Christian communities, for there was no stable, metaphysical reality and no living God overseeing time in providence to provide for its unity.

The Prognosis: A Sane God in a Sane Reality in a Sane Scripture

In the twentieth century, serious churchmen and churchwomen found this to be a major problem for believing communities. Historical criticism (as practiced by those who regarded themselves as believing Christians) had promised to provide the ultimate facts about the biblical materials, especially the person of Jesus of Nazareth, apart from any dogmatic or philosophical traditions, so that Christian faith might have firm bedrock.

Here, *sola Scriptura* had become *sola historia*. But just as orthodox Protestant theologians attempting to root their work in Scripture alone could not agree on important points—one thinks here of Lutheran and Calvinist polemics against each other in the sixteenth and seventeenth centuries—neither could historical critics agree with each other after rescuing the Bible from the theologians.

The academic quest for the historical Jesus provides the most accessible and important example. Was the historical Jesus an apocalyptic prophet, as Johannes Weiss[14] and Albert Schweitzer[15] contended? If so, the risk was that he was useless for modern Christians. Or was Jesus a non-apocalyptic prophet or teacher of sorts, as Ernst Renan presented?[16] If so, his presentation seemed at odds with many of the textual Jesus's clear statements of the Bible (see Mark 9:1 for the *locus classicus*), and it seemed as if these critics were peering down the well of history and finding their own reflection there.[17] Perhaps Jesus was a preacher who proclaimed an incremental coming of the kingdom of God over a long time in history, as C. H. Dodd suggested.[18] In any event, historical criticism did not provide the assured results it promised, a promise now routinely and rightly mocked, and what it did provide seemed useless for the life of modern Christians and purposes of modern theologians.

And so, closer to our own day, scholars and theologians like Walter Wink, Brevard Childs, and Karl Barth engaged in what has been called a postcritical retrieval of theological ways of reading Scripture. They pointed out the problems with historical criticism and endeavored to provide new models that would take Scripture seriously for Christian faith and theology in the modern (and postmodern) age without engaging in fundamentalism or mere repristination.

---

14. Weiss, *Predigt Jesu*.
15. Schweitzer, *Quest of Historical Jesus*.
16. Renan, *Life of Jesus*.
17. The image is usually credited to Schweitzer, but it actually comes from George Tyrrell's work *Christianity at the Crossroads*: "The Christ that Harnack sees, looking back through nineteen centuries of Catholic darkness, is only the reflection of a Liberal Protestant face, seen at the bottom of a deep well" (44). Schweitzer expressed similar sentiments: "Thus each successive epoch of theology found its own thoughts in Jesus; that was, indeed, the only way in which it could make him live" (*Quest of Historical Jesus*, 6).
18. Dodd, *History and the Gospel*; Dodd, *Parables of the Kingdom*.

THE LITERAL AND SPIRITUAL SENSES OF SACRED SCRIPTURE

Wink regarded historical criticism as "bankrupt" in a literal way, asserting that it had not paid what it had promised to pay[19] (and Wink lost a position over the book in which the claim was made). Childs asserted a neo-Protestant model in which attention was paid to the process leading to the final canonical form of the text as "the arena in which each new generation of believers stood and sought to understand afresh the nature of the faith."[20] This allowed the use of historical-critical methods like form, source, and redaction criticism, while also privileging the scriptural canon and maintaining a necessary role for the community of faith, which was part of the process leading to the final form of the canon and which hears the word of God in its arena today. Barth paid less attention to the world behind the text of Scripture (and thus the tools of historical criticism designed to access it) and more to the text itself. His *Church Dogmatics* are full of truly masterful interpretations of Scripture driven by the best of academic exegesis within a robust dogmatic framework. All three men took the dynamic of the Spirit's role in illuminating believers and believing communities in the contemporary moment as a chief point of departure, paying little attention to any possible doctrine of inspiration or cosmology. For this reason, they are critiqued from opposite sides for heterodoxy or fideism (Bonhoeffer once referred to the logical end of Barth's project as "positivism of revelation").[21]

Narrative theology (developed chiefly in the divinity schools of Yale University and Duke University) is perhaps the most recent and robust attempt to unite Scripture and theology by taking recourse to the grand narrative of Scripture and the narratives within it, such as the exodus and the story (or stories, depending on how one relates the Gospels to one another) of Jesus. The story of Scripture and its component stories provide a structure within which theology thinks, and they provide a place within which believers and their communities act in the present day. Theology draws out the implications of the particulars of the stories for God and his relation to the world and the Church, and believers live within the grand story, acting as the nonviolent Jesus and earliest Church acted (narrative theology is almost always pacifist, thanks to the influence of Stanley Hauerwas).

---

19. Wink, *Bible in Human Transformation*, 1–12. The particular chapter is titled "The Bankruptcy of the Historical Critical Paradigm."

20. Childs, *New Testament as Canon*, 29.

21. Bonhoeffer, *Letters and Papers*, 92.

Critiques have, of course, been offered. There are many competing ways of construing the Christian story and acting upon it and many different ways of drawing its theological implications. It may be ahistorical, concerned only with the story and not history. Further, some have said it is a-theological: "Talk about 'text' stands in place of talk about 'God.'"[22] Further, the text refers to itself; in narrative theology, the symbols or signs of the text are irreducible to anything else (it sets itself against the apologetics of liberal theology, like those practiced by Tillich and Bultmann who sought to transform the scriptural signs, symbols, and claims into new forms, new signs, symbols, and claims accessible to "modern man"). As such, it does not make any first-order truth claims about God or the world; no metaphysics is involved. What counts is simply doing the story in one's own day as a believer and simply sketching an accurate picture of the story's implications if one is a theologian proper. Finally, its emphasis on ethics—acting in accord with the story is the point, after all—risks reducing Christian faith and practice to a system of ethics and reducing Jesus yet again to a moral teacher (whatever claims the story actually makes about his divine person and saving work). Postliberalism is thus liberal at its core. And yet narrative theology is certainly on to something: the unity of Scripture as Scripture is indeed found in its overarching narrative of creation, fall, redemption, and glory, whereas if one does not see that story presumed and presented by the biblical canon of Scripture, then the biblical materials can appear as a disparate, random collection of texts standing often in stark contradiction with each other.

Perhaps the way forward is the way back. In 1980, church historian and mainline Methodist David Steinmetz published a piece titled "The Superiority of Pre-Critical Exegesis." His thesis, delivered at the end of the article, was audacious:

> The defenders of the single meaning theory usually concede that the medieval approach to the Bible met the religious needs of the Christian community, but that it did so at the unacceptable price of doing violence to the biblical text. The fact that the historical-critical method after two hundred years is still struggling for more than a precarious foothold in that same religious community is generally blamed on the ignorance and conservatism of the Christian laity and the sloth or moral cowardice of its pastors. . . .

---

22. Lindbeck, "Postcritical Canonical Interpretation," 43, quoting Thiemann, "Response to George Lindbeck," 378.

> I should like to suggest an alternative hypothesis. The medieval theory of levels of meaning in the biblical text, with all its undoubted defects, flourished because it is true, while the modern theory of a single meaning, with all its demonstrable virtues, is false. Until the historical-critical method becomes critical of its own theoretical foundations and develops a hermeneutical theory adequate to the nature of the text which it is interpreting, it will remain restricted—as it deserves to be—to the guild and the academy, where the question of truth can endlessly be deferred.[23]

Steinmetz, being a church historian, could make such claims, whereas biblical scholars, like Wink, could not at that time—not so long ago—and still be taken seriously as biblical scholars.

But some Protestant biblical scholars today who are also serious believers are finding that the way forward is the way back. They do not engage in simple repristination of the past but draw on it for insight today and resources to critique the arid desert of historicism in biblical studies. They see that the decline of classical medieval metaphysics left the Reformers with nothing more than the literal sense of Scripture, and the loss of their traditional concept of the triune nature of a transcendent God left Enlightenment figures with nothing for the words of Scripture to refer to but the mental intentions of the ancient human authors. They see that the result in our own day has been fracture: the Bible has become separated from the Church, the Testaments from each other, their constituent parts (e.g., Torah, Prophets, Wisdom/Psalms, Gospels, Letters) from each other, Jesus from the Gospels and the Gospels from each other, and in our postmodern day even words separated from meaning.

Now, serious believing Catholics would assert that the struggle to bring the Bible and theology together, and thus to read the Bible theologically, is won by embracing the Catholic Church's historic way of reading Scripture according to the fourfold sense: the literal, allegorical (or typological), moral (or tropological), and anagogical (which concerns the soul's progress towards heaven). Serious Protestants and Evangelicals who have attempted to recover the theological interpretation of Scripture actually engage in the fourfold sense but usually unwittingly. Everyone has to deal with the letter of Scripture, including Protestants and Evangelicals. But Protestants and Evangelicals also engage in allegory when they consider the relationship between the Testaments. What they usually

---

23. Steinmetz, "Superiority of Pre-Critical Exegesis," 82.

call typology, St. Thomas calls *allegoria*, allegory.[24] They also engage in reading for the moral sense, tropology, any time they ask, "What would Jesus do?" And presumably they are reading Scripture with the intent of refining their love of the God with whom they will spend eternity in heaven—that is, anagogy (though, of course, Protestants and Evangelicals, on the one hand, and Catholics, on the other, differ on whether reading Scripture actually contributes towards one's ultimate salvation, thanks to their differing perspectives on justification).

Perhaps no Protestant figure exemplifies how attempts to interpret Scripture theologically for the good of Christian believers today involves subtle use of the fourfold sense more than Richard Hays, George Washington Ivey professor emeritus of New Testament at Duke University. Associated with Yale and Duke, Hays was trained not only in the ways of historical criticism as a biblical scholar but also in literature as an undergraduate and so has been able to bring literary approaches to bear on the Bible, which are often fruitful for theological interpretation because they take the form and claims of a biblical text seriously prior to the making of hypotheses of the intent of the author or editor behind the text.

Hays knows historical criticism and uses it, like any New Testament scholar trained in the modern academy; in the wake of the phenomenon of the Jesus Seminar in the 1990s, he had plenty to say about the historical Jesus. Of course his profound readings of Paul[25] (and lately the Gospels)[26] engage in allegory (typology), showing how Paul and the evangelists found Christ prefigured in the Old Testament and that Testament fulfilled in the New. Hays later wrote a famous book entitled *The Moral Vision of the New Testament*—hence the tropological or moral sense. And Hays is a man of profound Christian faith—a committed Methodist—who reads Scripture devotionally for the good of his soul—hence anagogy. And so once when asked, he conceded publicly and readily in a major session of an annual meeting of the Society of Biblical Literature that his body of work effectively employs the classical fourfold sense of Scripture.

If anyone, then, is reading and interpreting Scripture as a believing Christian, he cannot ultimately avoid using the fourfold sense, for in many ways it is simply a codification of how Christian believers and their communities of faith use the Bible as a practical matter when they

---

24. Aquinas, *Summa Theologica* I, q. 1, art. 10 (I answer that).
25. Hays, *Faith of Jesus Christ*; Hays, *Echoes of Scripture in Letters*.
26. Hays, *Echoes of Scripture in Gospels*.

attempt to apply it. If anyone is more than a pure historical critic, she finds herself interpreting Scripture in the fourfold way, often unwittingly.

Is Steinmetz thus correct? Is pre-critical exegesis superior? He is correct on the point that pre-critical interpretation did meet (and meets today!) the needs of the believing community, and historical criticism does not. Is he ultimately correct? That depends (as Steinmetz observes) on theoretical commitments, and one's position on those are dependent upon convictions (acknowledged or unacknowledged, articulated or unarticulated) on matters philosophical, theological, and ultimately cosmological.

Steinmetz's piece is pragmatic in that he is asking (and answering) what ways of interpreting Scripture are helpful and unhelpful for Christian believers and communities today; he is not asking whether either particular approach is *true*. Perhaps historical criticism is right in seeing the Bible as a contradictory, random accident of documentary collation through history. For our purposes, we are assuming that the Catholic faith is true and asking, "What interpretive approach to the Bible would be salutary for believing Catholics?" And yet although beyond the scope of this chapter, it is incumbent for Catholics not only to believe but to show, in a plausible way even under the conditions of human finitude, that the Catholic faith is true—whether it can today be shown plausible as far as religion can be defended and whether it fits with what we think we know of the cosmos today.

Certainly the fourfold sense is the salutary, fruitful approach to Sacred Scripture that Scripture itself contains (consider the examples from St. Paul above) and demands for the perception of its inherent unity and use by the contemporary Church (consider the manifest relationships between the Testaments and the moral and anagogical significance of Scripture). But if the fourfold sense is not to be just another approach among many in Church and academy, Catholics must articulate and defend its theoretical foundations, however much the matter and materials of the biblical canon of Scripture itself demand the fourfold sense, which means developing and articulating adequate, and true, philosophical, theological, and cosmological underpinnings.

The Prescription: A New and Doubtless Very Different Medievalism

Faithful Catholics ought to hold to the use of the fourfold sense in the interpretation of Sacred Scripture. Is that tenable? It is, if the Catholic conception of God is true, if God is the uncreated Creator who can signify even today not just by means of signs but also by means of things as further signs of spiritual things. But did not early modernity and the later Enlightenment put paid to this possibility of God, removing him ever further from the world and eventually eliminating him altogether?

Perhaps so, sociologically, in history, among those who came to dominate the West's institutions. And yet a Platonic or Aristotelian (and thus Augustinian or more Thomistic) approach remains possible today. For what matters is less the ultimate results or the particular views of these saints about the actual structure of the visible universe and invisible realm behind it, which have indeed been superseded both in physics and philosophy, and more their approach, their way of philosophizing, theologizing, and investigating. If we refrain from ruling certain possibilities out of court a priori thanks to the lingering legacy of the Enlightenment, we might find our way forward to a cosmological structure similar to the classical structure, with the uncreated, triune Creator superintending it all, which would provide a solid cosmological, philosophical basis for the fourfold sense in our own day beyond Steinmetz's mere pragmatics.

Just as the Copernican Revolution and later Newtonian physics displaced medieval physics—and eventually removed the triune God as traditionally understood, as an active, providential agent in human affairs—modern physics (called such even though it feels postmodern to nonspecialists) after Einstein and Heisenberg has made room for classical conceptions of God and tracks well with beliefs premoderns had about the cosmos.[27] For instance, St. Augustine famously argued in the *Confessions* that time and space—that is, the visible realm—were created by the uncreated Creator, himself necessary to explain reality (creation visible and invisible) as it really is.[28] For St. Augustine, space and time are effectively the same thing, which permits both divine will and human will to exist cooperatively in God's providence, as God sees all things at once in an eternal, everlasting moment. Einstein and the other fathers

---

27. See Barr, *Modern Physics and Ancient Faith*.

28. See the discussion in books XI and XII of the *Confessions*, especially XI.10 (12)–XI.12 (14).

and mothers of modern physics may not have thought their theories required the existence of the triune God, but certainly the idea of the continuum of space-time tracks very well with St. Augustine's reflections, as often observed.[29] Indeed, as Nobel laureate in physics Steven Weinberg states, "Book XI of Augustine's *Confessions* contains a famous discussion of the nature of time, and it seems to have become a tradition to quote from this chapter in writing about quantum cosmology."[30]

Or consider multiverse theory, which claims that instead of there being one simple universe of whatever character and origin (say, having a beginning as explained by the Big Bang Theory), there are infinite universes "out there" (to speak colloquially), or, all that exists, exists in multiple domains beyond our known universes. And so speculative physics considers the possibility of infinite universes necessitated by the infinity of space-time, the finite possibilities of the arrangement of particles therein, and the limits of light (which travels at a fixed speed)—meaning that outside the boundaries of light emitted from the Big Bang over thirteen billion years ago there is still "room" (as it were) in the continuum for other universes. It also considers "daughter universes," the most popular form of multiverse theory, necessitated by the theory of quantum mechanics in its affirmation of probabilities as opposed to deterministic certainties. (If I may, one way of summarizing Heisenberg's uncertainty principle is to say that electrons behave how they do because they *want* to.) That is, events are not determined by any immutable iron laws of physics but are matters of probability, and thus is implied the existence of other universes in which different results obtain from the same situation.

In theological perspective, it may be that multiverse theory is necessitated by the exclusion of the classical conception of God. For the odds of our perceived universe being just how it is are so infinitesimal, it would seem that an infinite number of other universes is required to balance out the rather peculiar particularity of our own. If you flip a quarter ten times and manage to get heads ten times in a row (odds are 1/1024, or 0.09765625%), you would assume that it has already or will come up tails ten other times (not necessarily in a row, though at some point that too will obtain) if the chance of a quarter coming up heads (or tails) is 50%. That is, you cannot beat the odds over time, as corporate gambling interests know. Our universe may be likened to a quarter coming up heads

---

29. See Russell, *History of Western Philosophy*, 373, and Carter, "St. Augustine on Time," 308, as well as Wilcoxen, "Augustine's Theology of Time," 668.

30. Weinberg, "Cosmological Constant Problem," 15n15.

millions of times in a row; somewhere (or somewhen!) else it must come up tails millions of times in a row to compensate. The providence of God as uncreated Creator, conversely, removes the need for multiverse theory, for it guarantees the unity of the cosmos as universe and means that our world can be exactly as it is by his will as a reflection of his nature.[31]

That order pointed the ancients to the divine and ancient Christians to the triune Divinity, Creator of heaven and earth. For them, beauty was rooted in order, and so in perceiving the order of the cosmos, they perceived beauty and the God who was beauty behind it. As St. Augustine wrote:

> Question the beauty of the earth, question the beauty of the sea, question the beauty of the air distending and diffusing itself, question the beauty of the sky, . . . question all these realities. All respond: "See, we are beautiful." Their beauty is a profession [*confessio*]. These beauties are subject to change. Who made them if not the Beautiful One [*Pulcher*] who is not subject to change?[32]

The ordered beauty of the universe has also impressed modern physicists. Edward Witten has said, "The laws of nature as they've been uncovered in the last few centuries, and especially . . . the last century, are very surprising. . . . They have a great beauty, which is a little hard to describe, maybe, if one hasn't experienced it."[33] Avraham Loeb, chair of Harvard's astronomy department, recently offered the following musings:

> I was secular to start with. I am not religious. I am struck by the order we find in the universe, by the regularity, by the existence of laws of nature. That is something I am always in awe of, how the laws of nature we find here on Earth seem to apply all the way out to the edge of the universe. That is quite remarkable. The universe could have been chaotic and very disorganized. But it obeys a set of laws much better than people obey a set of laws here.[34]

---

31. Some might protest that the perceived order of the cosmos in spite of such long odds implies God intervening to make it so. But the Christian view is not so brute. Nature simply displays order without God intervening to keep it in order, as if he were at an absent remove but needed to step in every so often to restore its order. Further, the above is neither an adversion to a *Deus ex machina* nor an argument for today's "intelligent design" theories, but simply to say with Einstein that God does not play dice.

32. Augustine, *Sermo* 241:2, PL 38, 1134, quoted in the *Catechism*, §32.

33. Quoted by Barr, "Orderliness of the Cosmos."

34. Chotiner, "Have Aliens Found Us?," quoted by Barr, "Orderliness of the

I am no physicist nor scientist (though I have taken courses in physics and various other sciences in the course of my broader education). The point of the above is negative: to suggest that we are no longer constrained by the straitjackets of modern philosophies and their implications for theology and thus scriptural interpretation. But it has become clear to me as I have researched the history of biblical interpretation that debates and disputes about how to properly interpret Scripture revolve at a deep level around philosophy, metaphysics, and cosmology. It is therefore both possible and necessary to articulate a cosmology adequate to Catholic faith and to contemporary, if fluid, understandings of physics if the fourfold sense is to flourish and be found once again at the heart of Catholic exegesis, interpretation, and proclamation. Doing so will aid in healing the fracture between Scripture and theology, for it would put both biblical exegesis and theology in the same universe, on the same sane foundation.

In fact, God is prior to any cosmology, and both are prior to scriptural interpretation. For Scripture is a divine gift meant to aid us in knowledge and love of God, world, neighbor, and self, and our use of Scripture depends on prior Christian convictions (even as Scripture must accord with them). Luther did not forget that, but other Reformers and later Protestantism often did. And since Scripture does not provide an explicit set of instructions (though one might attempt to model proper scriptural interpretation on inner-biblical exegesis), serious attempts to found all Christian belief and practice on Scripture were bound to fail, because Christian Scripture is itself a *product* of Christian belief and practice: the canon was determined by the community, and the contents of the canon were written first as a record (oblique or direct) by those the community regarded as luminaries. And as God is prior to all, the community God founded by salvation in time—first Israel, and then also the Church—is prior to the Scriptures that narrate, regulate, and nourish the relationship of God's people with our God.

What, then, does healthy scriptural interpretation look like? The *Catechism of the Catholic Church* provides the answer in sections 109–19.[35] It draws on *Dei Verbum* (indeed much of the section is simply indirect and direct quoting of *Dei Verbum*, §12), assumes the classical visible/invisible structure of the cosmos, and makes the normativity of the fourfold sense explicit. Drawing out what is implicit in the text of the

---

Cosmos."

35. See Huizenga, "Tradition of Christian Allegory."

Second Vatican Council's *Dei Verbum* section 12, the *Catechism* in sections 109–19 makes the fourfold sense explicit. Titled "The Holy Spirit, Interpreter of Scripture," these sections essentially insert the fourfold sense back into *Dei Verbum* section 12. The *Catechism* here first reads, "To interpret Scripture correctly, the reader must be attentive to what the human authors truly wanted to affirm and to what God wanted to reveal to us by their words."[36]

The first part of this thesis statement concerns the letter of Scripture with its reference to human authors. And so the letter is affirmed and is to be investigated using modern tools and awareness of ancient cultural conditions and ways of communicating in an appropriate manner adequate to scriptural interpretation.[37] Here, historical-critical tools have a place but as prolegomena to the letter, in service of understanding the letter—this is no absolute endorsement of the so-called historical method. The point is not to recreate a possible history behind the texts but to use what we know of history to understand the meaning of the signs of the lexematic surface of the text—that is, the words.

The second part of the thesis statement—"what God wanted to reveal to us by their words"—concerns then the threefold spiritual sense, namely allegory (Old Testament–New Testament relationships), tropology (the moral sense), and anagogy (the process of the soul's progress to heaven). That is, we know God's mind not merely through the letter interpreted using historical-critical tools but also by employing the remainder of the fourfold sense rooted in the letter. And so the *Catechism* quotes *Dei Verbum*: "Sacred Scripture must be read and interpreted in the light of the same Spirit by whom it was written."[38] This first involves attention to salvation history, which provides unity to Scripture on the level of the economy of salvation in history.[39] Then, second, Scripture is read according to the tradition of the Church.[40] Third, attention must be paid to the "analogy of faith," which is "the coherence of the truths of faith among themselves and within the whole plan of Revelation."[41] Here we are dealing with the unchanging metaphysical dogmatic truths of the faith in the invisible realm of the spirit, the signifieds to which the

---

36. *Catechism*, §109, alluding to Second Vatican Council, *Dei Verbum*, §12.1.
37. Second Vatican Council, *Dei Verbum*, §12.2.
38. *Catechism*, §111, quoting Second Vatican Council, *Dei Verbum*, §12.3.
39. *Catechism*, §112.
40. *Catechism*, §113.
41. *Catechism*, §114.

signified signs of the letter point, understood by the threefold spiritual sense. And right on cue, the *Catechism* delineates the four senses[42] and even provides the famous medieval couplet:

> The Letter speaks of deeds; Allegory to faith;
> The Moral how to act; Anagogy our destiny.
>
> Lettera gesta docet, quid credas allegoria,
> moralis quid agas, quo tendas anagogia.[43]

We also have to remember that the point of scriptural interpretation is not purely intellectual, as if the Bible simply delivered dogmatic and moral content we unlock with the key of method, whether classically Catholic or methodologically modern. Rather, scriptural interpretation is a matter of an existential encounter with the living God. The fourfold sense really means the Mass: in the story of salvation history (the letter), the Old Testament is fulfilled in the New Testament, with the Eucharist fulfilling all sacrifices (allegory), and that story is overflowing with moral import (tropology) we embody in our common life and individual lives, while the point of our scriptural engagement is the achievement of heaven by God's prior grace (anagogy).

Again, the *Catechism* teaches that the classic approach to Scripture is normative and binding for Catholics, closing this section by quoting again from *Dei Verbum*:

> It is the task of exegetes to work, according to these rules, toward a better understanding and explanation of the meaning of Sacred Scripture in order that their research may help the Church to form a firmer judgment. For, of course, all that has been said about the manner of interpreting Scripture is ultimately subject to the judgment of the Church which exercises the divinely conferred commission and ministry of watching over and interpreting the Word of God.[44]

The Holy Spirit does protect the Church. Although the Second Vatican Council did not explicitly teach the normativity of the fourfold sense, the later *Catechism*, authoritative for Catholics today and one of the greatest deliberate fruits of the Council, makes explicit what is implicit in the text of *Dei Verbum*. Far from crowning the historical-critical

---

42. *Catechism*, §§115–17.
43. *Catechism*, §118.
44. *Catechism*, §119, quoting Second Vatican Council, *Dei Verbum*, §12.3.

method as the Catholic approach to Scripture par excellence, as many have claimed,[45] the Second Vatican Council's *Dei Verbum* and the later *Catechism* maintain the interpretive tradition of the fourfold sense.

It is not too much, then, to speak of a new medievalism in speaking of salutary scriptural interpretation. Whether prior to the rise of modernity and its historical-critical method or after, Scripture and theology are rooted in God, and healing the fracture not only between the literal and spiritual senses of Scripture but also the concomitant fracture between theology and Sacred Scripture depends upon recovering both classical conceptions of God and the fourfold sense.

Bibliography

Alighieri, Dante. *The Divine Comedy: Paradise*. Translated by Mark Musa. New York: Penguin Classics, 1986.
Aquinas, Thomas. *Summa Theologica*. 2nd and rev. ed. Translated by the Fathers of the English Dominican Province. New York: Benzinger, 1981.
Augustine. *Teaching Christianity* [*De doctrina christiana*]. 2nd ed. Hyde Park, NY: New City, 2005.
Barr, Stephen. *Modern Physics and Ancient Faith*. Notre Dame, IN: University of Notre Dame Press, 2003.
———. "The Orderliness of the Cosmos Is Far Deeper Than the Ancients Ever Suspected." Church Life Journal, 1 Sept. 2020. https://churchlifejournal.nd.edu/articles/the-orderliness-of-the-cosmos-is-far-deeper-than-the-ancients-ever-suspected/.
Bonhoeffer, Dietrich. *Letters and Papers from Prison*. Translated by Eberhard Bethge. London: SCM, 1953.
Bultmann, Rudolf. "Is Exegesis without Presuppositions Possible?" In *New Testament and Mythology and Other Basic Writings*, edited and translated by Schubert M. Ogden, 145–53. London: SCM, 1985.
Carter, Jason W. "St. Augustine on Time, Time Numbers, and Enduring Objects." *Vivarium* 49 (2011) 301–23.
Catechism of the Catholic Church. 2nd ed. Washington, DC: United States Conference of Catholic Bishops, 1997.
Childs, Brevard S. *The New Testament as Canon*. Minneapolis: Fortress, 1985.
Chotiner, Isaac. "Have Aliens Found Us? A Harvard Astronomer on the Mysterious Interstellar Object 'Oumuamua.'" *New Yorker*, 16 Jan. 2019. https://www.newyorker.com/news/q-and-a/have-aliens-found-us-a-harvard-astronomer-on-the-mysterious-interstellar-object-oumuamua.
Dodd, C. H. *History and the Gospel*. New York: Scribner's Sons, 1938.
———. *The Parables of the Kingdom*. London: Nisbet, 1935.
Donahue, John R., SJ. "Scripture: A Roman Catholic Perspective." *Review & Expositor* 79 (1982) 231–44.
Gabler, J. P. *Kleinere Theologische Schriften*. Ulm, Germ.: n.p., 1831.

---

45. See, for instance, Donahue, "Scripture," 233–34.

Gregory, Brad. *The Unintended Reformation: How a Religious Revolution Secularized Society*. Cambridge, UK: Belknap, 2015.

Hahn, Scott, and Jeffrey L. Morrow. *Modern Biblical Criticism as a Tool of Statecraft 1700–1900*. Steubenville, OH: Emmaus Academic, 2020.

Hahn, Scott, and Benjamin Wiker. *Politicizing the Bible: The Roots of Historical Criticism and the Secularization of Scripture 1300–1700*. New York: Crossroad, 2013.

Hays, Richard. *Echoes of Scripture in the Gospels*. Waco: Baylor University Press, 2017.

———. *Echoes of Scripture in the Letters of Paul*. New Haven, CT: Yale University Press, 1993.

———. *The Faith of Jesus Christ: The Narrative Substructure of Galatians 3:1—4:11*. Grand Rapids: Eerdmans, 2002.

Huizenga, Leroy. "The Tradition of Christian Allegory Yesterday and Today." *Letter & Spirit* 8 (2013) 77–99.

Koppe, J. B. *Marcus non epitomator Matthaei*. Göttingen, Germ.: n.p., 1782.

Lindbeck, George. "Postcritical Canonical Interpretation: Three Modes of Retrieval." In *Theological Exegesis: Essays in Honor of Brevard S. Childs*, edited by Kathryn Greene-McCreight and Christopher Seitz, 26–51. Grand Rapids: Eerdmans, 1999.

Luther, Martin. "Concerning the Letter and the Spirit." In *Answer to the Hyperchristian, Hyperspiritual, and Hyperlearned Book by Goat Emser in Leipzig*; *Martin Luther's Basic Theological Writings*, edited by Timothy F. Lull, 76–92. Minneapolis: Augsburg Fortress, 2005.

McGrath, Alister. *The Intellectual Origins of the European Reformation*. 2nd ed. Oxford, UK: Blackwell, 2004.

Oberman, Heiko A. *Luther: Man between God and the Devil*. Translated by Eileen Walliser-Schwarzbart. New York: Image, 1992.

Renan, Ernst. *Life of Jesus*. Amherst, NY: Prometheus Books, 1991.

Russell, Bertrand. *History of Western Philosophy*. New York: Allen and Unwin, 1946.

Sandys-Wunsch, John, and Laurence Eldredge. "J. P. Gabler and the Distinction between Biblical and Dogmatic Theology: Translation, Commentary, and Discussion of His Originality." *Scottish Journal of Theology* 33 (1980) 133–44.

Schweitzer, Albert. *The Quest of the Historical Jesus*, edited by John Bowden. Minneapolis: Fortress, 2001.

Second Vatican Council. "Dogmatic Constitution on Divine Revelation [*Dei Verbum*]." Vatican, 18 Nov. 1965. https://www.vatican.va/archive/hist_councils/ii_vatican_council/documents/vat-ii_const_19651118_dei-verbum_en.html.

Steinmetz, David C. "The Superiority of Pre-Critical Exegesis." *Theology Today* 37 (1980) 27–38.

Thiemann, Ronald F. "Response to George Lindbeck." *Theology Today* 43 (1986) 377–82.

Tyrrell, George. *Christianity at the Crossroads*. London: Longmans, Green and Co., 1909.

Weinberg, Stephen. "The Cosmological Constant Problem." *Reviews of Modern Physics* 61 (1989) 1–23.

Weiss, Johannes. *Die Predigt Jesu von Reich Gottes*. Göttingen, Germ.: Vandenhoeck & Ruprecht, 1892.

Wilcoxen, Matthew A. "Augustine's Theology of Time: A Trinitarian Reassessment of Confessions 11." *Heythrop Journal* 57 (2016) 666–77.

Wink, Walter. *The Bible in Human Transformation*. Philadelphia: Fortress, 1973.

6

Theology, Preaching, and Apologetics

James Baxter, OP

There are Mass-going Catholics in the world who have only ever heard good preaching. Not much is known of these people. Where they live, where they go to Mass, we cannot say. The one certainty we have is this: they cannot have been Catholics for very long.

About any other practice, a comment like this might seem cynical and unkind. Made about preaching, it would meet with wide agreement from people who love and appreciate preaching and preachers. Recent popes have joined in the criticism. It is not simply that the occasional homily fails to fire but that poor preaching is the norm. What has gone wrong? Rhetorical matters such as delivery and homily length are important to preaching, but the core of preaching is always theology. Preaching cannot be good preaching unless it is theologically rich. This does not mean that a homily is awash with doctrinal terms. It means that the preacher shares with the congregation a vision of reality infused with God's revelation in the Scriptures and the theological reflection of the Church. That vision is one that he would not have unless he had the grace of ordination and years of theological training, prayer, and contemplation behind him. Why is this kind of preaching not the norm? That is the subject of the first part of this chapter, dealing with the fracture between theology and preaching.

The second part of the chapter turns to another fracture, this time between theology and apologetics, which is sufficiently dissimilar to

THEOLOGY, PREACHING, AND APOLOGETICS

preaching to require separate treatment. At the same time, apologetics has much in common with preaching, which permits them to be treated together in this chapter. They both aim at sharing the faith; they both demand rhetorical prudence; they are both necessarily theological.

Fractures in Theology and Preaching

Some caveats are necessary before identifying the fractures. Firstly, "preaching" in this chapter is confined to the liturgical homily, which is the preaching that most people in the Church encounter. It does not include preaching in the broader sense, such as retreat conferences or catechetical talks, which can be given by unordained speakers in variable settings, from schools to pubs.

Secondly, when critiquing preaching, we are in the realm of impressions. There has been little empirical research into Catholic preaching, and what little there is tends to focus on objective measurements such as sermon length and vocabulary.[1] To assess the state of contemporary preaching requires drawing on impressions from listening to multiple preachers over decades. We may also be guided by recent papal evaluations of preaching. Benedict XVI offered some pointed criticism: "Given the importance of the word of God, the quality of homilies needs to be improved."[2] Francis was at one with his predecessor, saying this of contemporary preaching: "We know that the faithful attach great importance to it, and that both they and their ordained ministers suffer because of homilies: the laity from having to listen to them and the clergy from having to preach them!"[3]

Both popes were concerned enough about preaching to offer constructive advice beyond their criticisms. Benedict requested the production of practical publications to assist preachers in cultivating the art of good preaching, such as a directory on the homily.[4] This request led to the *Homiletic Directory*, issued by the Congregation for Divine Worship in 2014. Francis devoted a remarkably lengthy section to preaching in his

---

1. See, for example, "Digital Pulpit" (2019). For a rare example of qualitative research, see Bellinger, "Are You Talking to Me?"
2. Benedict XVI, *Sacramentum Caritatis*, §46.
3. Francis, *Evangelii Gaudium*, §135.
4. Benedict XVI, *Verbum Domini*, §60.

first exhortation *Evangelii Gaudium*, including practical advice for homily preparation.[5]

The third caveat is the most important one. Even though one can speak of "fractures" between theology and preaching, the term is somewhat amiss. There can never truly be a fracture between preaching and theology, for while it is true that "some theology is preaching," it is equally true that "all preaching is theology." *Anything* that a preacher chooses to say or not to say in response to revelation is a theological statement. If a preacher on Trinity Sunday fails even to attempt to relate the doctrine of the Trinity to the Christian life, or ignores the doctrine entirely, the preacher is making a theological statement about the importance of the doctrine—that is has none. If a homily is indistinguishable from a newspaper editorial or a self-help column, the preacher is making an implicit theological statement about the difference that faith makes to our vision of reality—none at all.

With those caveats in mind, there are three critical fractures between theology and preaching. The first is in the content of the homily, between what is preached and what could be preached. At every Mass, the prayers and lectionary readings throw forth a vast number of theological themes. Many of these themes are patent immediately, even before the study and prayer that is part of homily preparation. If the preacher needs guidance, among scriptural commentaries alone there are thousands of patristic, medieval, and contemporary sources that indicate possible directions in which a preacher could take a homily. Put simply, there is a *lot* to say. Part of the difficult task of preaching consists in selecting and rejecting these possible directions. But when so much is already there to be drawn upon in our theological tradition, when a preacher says nothing much of substance in a homily, the lost opportunity is all the clearer.

The second fracture is located in the preacher himself, between the quality of preaching of which the preacher is capable and that of which he should be capable. It is about preaching as a craft. The preacher may have years of learning behind him, with lots of knowledge in his head and close at hand on bookshelves. He may have good habits of study and reading. But to formulate that knowledge into a homily is a different matter. Although there is necessarily a difference between preaching and public speaking, between being a preacher and an orator, one cannot overlook the basic rhetorical components of a homily, of matters such as

---

5. Francis, *Evangelii Gaudium*, §§135–59.

capturing and holding attention, speaking at a good volume, not going on for too long, and the like. A preacher might say wonderful things, but if half of his homily should have fallen to the cutting room floor and been left there, it will not be good preaching.

The third fracture is again found in the preacher, this time between the depth of preaching of which he is capable and what he actually delivers. A preacher in the Catholic Church has spent considerable time as a tertiary student. Across six to seven years, often many more, he attends lectures, does readings, writes essays, and takes exams on subjects ranging from metaphysics to ecclesiology, history to bioethics. He is familiar with different Christian spiritualities. More often than not, he has the broad cultural exposure that immersion in the Catholic faith brings. He is aware of the sort of different approaches one might take to scriptural passages and theological issues, and he knows where to go to refresh his knowledge. In some preachers, this formation is palpable in their preaching. In others, it flows out in their conversation, in spiritual direction, in the confessional, but not in their preaching. One is left with the sense that the preacher is capable of preaching with much greater theological depth, but there is an impediment. Something—an approach, an attitude, perhaps a fear—is holding the preacher back from sharing his theological formation in his preaching.

Causes of the Fractures

Content, quality, and depth. These fractures are variations on a single theme—that Catholic preaching is less theologically rich than it could be. A gap between the ideal and the reality of preaching will always exist to greater or lesser degrees, given the immensity of the wisdom contained in God's revelation and the struggle of our own human efforts to speak about it. It is no surprise that there have been criticisms of the quality of preaching from the patristic era to our own day. Yet healing the fractures, and making the reality closer to the ideal, should always be our aim. This healing requires us first to investigate the causes of the fractures.

The first cause, affecting the *content* of preaching, is the weight of expectation placed on the homily, such that it is required to carry a load that it was never intended to carry alone. The Sunday homily is often the only theological discourse to which a parishioner will be exposed all week. Some parishioners regularly study Scripture and Aquinas, but this is not the norm. Further, theological literacy has been in long-term decline. Those who received a Catholic school education in recent decades come to Mass with a level of theological knowledge lagging far behind their sophistication in mathematics, technology, and other sciences. The preacher cannot assume familiarity with the who's who and what's what of theology. He cannot throw off names like Augustine and Aquinas nor use terms like "transubstantiation," "eschatological," or even "incarnation," and assume that people will know who or what they are and why they matter.[6]

The fracture is therefore less evident, even absent, when the theological load is being borne elsewhere. Consider some different settings for a homily: Mass during a day retreat where there have been talks and time for reflection; daily Mass at a Catholic university or chaplaincy; Sunday Mass in a parish that has Bible studies, catechetical programmes, and communal devotions like eucharistic adoration and the Rosary. In these settings, the preaching is generally able to be pitched at a higher level, if the preacher is confident that there is a higher theological knowledge among his listeners. The listeners come to Mass already receptive to theological thinking and so can take whatever insights the preacher offers and connect them to the theological input they receive outside of Mass.

A second cause of the fracture in content is everything else to which the Western mind is exposed outside of Mass. A daily flow of noise and images presents the preacher with a lot of clutter into which he must speak. The challenge is not a new one. In 1952, the English Dominican Ferdinand Valentine commented on the effect of radio on Catholic congregations of his day. After first noting the ways in which radio had done some good, including helping to change preaching from "sermonizing" to a more intimate mode of address, he lamented the effect of the new media on mental clarity:

> The radio and the cognate influences of the cinema and television have spoon-fed the human mind. The faithful who listen to our sermons are impressionable rather than thoughtful, and find it increasingly difficult to collaborate with—to *think-with*—the

---

6. Michael Connors and Ann Garrido observe about the place of doctrinal terms: "Some of the erstwhile tension between doctrine and preaching flows from the compressed nature of doctrinal language: a language never intended to be used verbatim from the pulpit, at least not without Scripture, additional explanation, and other supportive forms of rhetoric, images, and illustrations" (Connors and Garrido, "Doctrine and Catechetical Preaching," 127).

preacher, preferring to sit back quite passively and absorb. We shall never succeed in teaching them unless we bear this in mind. Our people are mentally sick.[7]

This pungent assessment ironically may have lost some of its force. Valentine was writing as one who had watched the early effects of electronic media as they happened. Preachers and members of a congregation today have no experience of any other world. This can work in the preacher's favor, if the seriousness of the preacher's message and the ritual of the liturgy come as a welcome relief from noise and triviality. But it requires serious preparation to preach to congregations more generally distracted than any others before in history.

Is that serious preparation happening? Here we find a cause of the fracture in the *quality* of preaching. For men who will spend the rest of their lives most days of the week in front of an audience, students for the diaconate and priesthood receive precious little preparation even in public speaking, let alone in preaching. Formation in preaching is not standardized across the Church, so it is left to each seminary or religious order to train its preachers as it sees fit. Usually, preparation is limited to a course in homiletics across a semester or two, or sometimes several short courses that incorporate a brief practical component.[8] Often, it is left to the last two years or less prior to ordination, or even limited to the occasional short homily at Sunday vespers. Given all that we read in magisterial documents of the importance of preaching, there is nothing here of the intensity of preparation that we would expect. The message this sends to the student is that preaching is one task among many that he will do after ordination, so a bit of preparation is called for, and a bit of preparation suffices.

A second cause of this fracture consists of the simple fact that theological preaching is easy to do badly and hard to do well. Perhaps the preacher has never even witnessed excellent preaching, or if so, only rarely. Preaching is not like tennis or ballet where people know where to go to watch the best of the best in action. On the other hand, the preacher has almost certainly sat through negative examples of preaching as a member of a congregation. While that experience could spark off a worthy ambition towards good theological preaching, it could equally lead the

---

7. Valentine, *Art of Preaching*, 20.

8. For a survey of some different preaching programs in the US, see Bosso, "Best Preaching Practices."

preacher to avoid it entirely. He knows, too, that what is profound and powerful for the preacher may be hopelessly abstract for the congregation. If anything will dissuade a preacher from theological preaching, it is the criticism that his preaching is too theoretical, too removed from the real concerns of the people. This criticism can be doubly effective, because preachers are still widely assumed to be removed from everyday life in the first place. It is not unheard of for priests themselves to depreciate their understanding of "real life." All these criticisms and fears can create the illusion—an awful one for a preacher to fall prey to—that theology is not real life.

This illusion also leads to a fracture in the *depth* of preaching. In reaction to the fear of being too theoretical, the preacher can overcompensate. He shifts from an approach that starts with God and his revelation to an approach that starts with the people and their concerns (as the preacher perceives them) or the current events of the week. This "inductive turn" was popularized by the Disciples of Christ preacher Fred Craddock in his 1971 work *As One without Authority* and was taken up by other Christian churches in a trend often called the "New Homiletic."[9] In the Catholic Church, its extreme form was found in the dialogue homily, where the congregation were invited to share actively in the preaching. Its most everyday form is the homily that talks about the latest news, and as Pope Francis points out, "we have television programs for that."[10]

While certainly well-meant, the inductive turn had preaching totally backwards. It makes perfect rhetorical sense to consider the community in front of the preacher and the world in which we live. Moreover, it is common for magisterial documents to encourage preachers to relate their preaching to the concrete circumstances of the people in front of them.[11] The issue is where does the preacher start? Preaching, as part of the Liturgy of the Word, must always start with God and his revelation. Abstract ideas and terms will inevitably enter the preacher's head as he contemplates the readings, which simply reflects his academic training. Applying those to the concrete circumstances of life and finding the right

---

9. See ch. 3, "Inductive Movement in Preaching," in Craddock, *As One without Authority*. For an account of the influence of Craddock's work on the Catholic Church in the US, see Michael Monshau, "Preaching beyond Postmodernity," 188–91.

10. Francis, *Evangelii Gaudium*, §155.

11. See, for example, Benedict XVI, *Verbum Domini*, §59; Francis, *Evangelii Gaudium*, §§154–55; also Paul VI on evangelization generally, in *Evangelii Nuntiandi*, §§29, 63.

language to express them are further steps along in the process of preparing a homily. When the order is reversed, theology will only ever function as a veneer.

False Remedies

Before turning to suggestions for healing the fracture, some false remedies must be considered and dismissed. The first false remedy is to preach for longer. Although there are variations worldwide, the current trend is for a Sunday homily to go for between seven and ten minutes. Some preachers will push the homily to fifteen minutes or slightly beyond. If the average were extended to twenty minutes, would that not give the preacher more time to go into theological depth? In theory, yes, but this is likely to be true in practice only for a preacher who already preaches theologically with the time he has. There is no reason to think that quantity will improve quality.

The second false remedy is to return to sermon-cycles. This was the practice, common before the Second Vatican Council, where the preacher would preach on a catechetical topic, regardless of the readings of the Mass. Often this was in collaboration across a diocese. As a solution to the fracture, it has some immediate attractions: a preacher can simply work out the topics he thinks he should cover, consult the calendar, and off he goes. But there are many practical problems with the remedy, not least of which is that parishioners are not always at the same Mass or even the same church from week to week. Unless this new practice is taken on across a diocese, for the same preacher to work through cycles of topics with basically the same congregation is not as feasible today as it was in an earlier era. But the greatest problem with this remedy is theological. There may well be a catechetical element to the homily, but preaching is not catechesis. The theme of the homily should always arise from within the liturgy itself.[12] When the preacher reaches outside the liturgy to make the homily about something other than the Liturgy of the Word or the prayers of the Mass, such as the faithful's need to know about this or that subject, it ceases to be truly liturgical.[13]

---

12. For the liturgical status of the homily, see *Sacrosanctum Concilium*, §52, which states that the homily is to be "highly esteemed as part of the liturgy itself."

13. Benedict XVI was not opposed to thematic preaching per se. In *Verbum Domini* in §46 he wrote, "During the course of the liturgical year it is appropriate to offer the faithful, prudently and on the basis of the three-year lectionary, 'thematic'

The sermon-cycle remedy should have less attraction following the publication of the *Homiletic Directory*, which greatly assists preachers in drawing out theological themes from the lectionary readings. For every Sunday of the liturgical year, the directory offers specific paragraphs from *The Catechism of the Catholic Church*, to which the preacher may turn to give doctrinal support to the themes arising from the Scripture passages.[14]

Healing the Fractures

One method of healing the fractures may be immediately identified. If the fracture is partly because the homily is carrying too much of the load, then other means of theological formation can be provided to lessen the load. When a parish offers Bible studies, talks, discussion groups, and the like, it is committing itself to a culture where the members of the congregation are actively seeking understanding of their faith. They are becoming a congregation of theologians, of believers with a knowledgeable and thoughtful faith. If the preacher himself is involved in this formation, he also becomes familiar with the theological thought of his parishioners.

A second remedy, aimed at improving the quality of preaching, is to encourage a culture of preparation and feedback among future preachers. Greater preparation for future preachers can only benefit both preachers and congregations, so that the suffering spoken of by Pope Francis may be a rarer experience. There are many possible approaches to the formation of preachers, but since preaching is an action, preparation should emphasize practice rather than theory. The theology and history of preaching is important to study, as are the principles of classical rhetoric, but it is possible to have a solid grasp of the theory and to be hopeless in the delivery. Practice must dominate.

An approach used for Dominican students in Melbourne in recent years is heavily practical. It has no claim to be the best method, but it does have many virtues. Preaching practice takes place weekly, involving

---

homilies treating the great themes of the Christian faith, on the basis of what has been authoritatively proposed by the Magisterium in the four 'pillars' of the Catechism of the Catholic Church and the recent Compendium, namely: the profession of faith, the celebration of the Christian mystery, life in Christ and Christian prayer." The key phrase there is "on the basis of the three-year lectionary." Again, any thematic preaching must be liturgical.

14. Congregation for Divine Worship, *Homiletic Directory*, appendix 1.

students at all stages of priestly studies. Three or four students preach, one delivering a homily of seven to ten minutes based on the readings of the following Sunday, the others preaching weekday homilies of three to five minutes. The listeners—consisting of fellow students, formators, and members of the parish—are provided with forms on which to offer feedback, both graded and open-ended, on matters of content and delivery. Everyone then repairs to a room, where the feedback is delivered. The experience of receiving feedback is always helpful, sometimes humiliating, occasionally baffling. The preacher-in-training is often left wondering how people could have understood his main point to be so different from what, in his mind, it most definitely was. The homilies are often filmed for the preacher to watch later and to confirm feedback about verbal tics and poor eye contact. By the time the preacher delivers his first homily as a deacon, he already has five to six years of preaching practice behind him.

This method of formation reduces many of the risks that arise from limiting preaching preparation to courses in homiletics. It is not one academic course among many others. It is instead more of a habit, by which, through continually having preaching on his mind, the student learns to *be* a preacher, rather than someone who preaches. His theological studies and spiritual formation are integrated from the first into a developing spirituality. Another benefit is that many and various people provide feedback, none of whom necessarily has the dominant voice. This better mirrors the reality of preaching for a congregation at Mass, where the homily is for everyone present, bar none. If preachers are formed with regular feedback, they are more likely to be docile to any formal processes of feedback that may be introduced post-ordination. Preachers are already familiar with polite affirmations and hasty criticisms delivered on the steps after Mass, but methodical, root-and-branch feedback is lacking. If this is ever fruitfully introduced, it will be only when preachers themselves are convinced of the merits of formal feedback.

A third remedy is to restore the confidence of preachers in the value of theological preaching. One aspect of this remedy is to recall the relationship between the intellect and other aspects of God's action in the human person, including the action of the Holy Spirit and the role of the affections. Theological preaching aids the faithful in becoming more receptive to the gifts of the Holy Spirit, which work in concert with the intellect and affections. The better the faithful know and understand the teachings of the faith, the more they see reality from a divine perspective, with aid from the clarity and penetration that the gifts bring.[15] The more clearly, too, they can discern the gifts at work, purifying their intellects and ordering their affections. It is likewise crucial to see the importance of both the intellect and the affections in the spiritual life. After rightly identifying a place for "poetical, lyrical, and nondiscursive language" in preaching, Edward Foley writes that "today's reimagined homily is more about moving hearts than informing intellects."[16] There is a risk here of setting up a false dichotomy between the intellect and the affections. Foley does not do this (he does, after all, say "more . . . than," not "rather . . . than"), but there is no need to play them off against each other at all. The preacher does not have to choose between head and heart. If he wants his preaching to lead his congregation towards a greater love of God and neighbour, theological preaching is essential.

A second aspect of this remedy, addressing the reluctance to preach theologically, is for preachers and preachers-in-training to recall how much of the Church's theology is derived from preaching. Within the scriptural revelation, we have the preaching of the prophets, the apostles, and Christ's own preaching. The great works of the Church fathers and medievals are replete with homilies, both on scriptural texts and liturgical occasions. To take an example closer to our time, the homilies on Genesis delivered by Joseph Ratzinger in 1981 have been influential in contemporary discussions of creation and original sin.[17] There is no reason why the capacity for theological preaching should have been withdrawn from preachers of our own day, or why great contributions to the Church's theology should not come from homilies delivered in our time. To think otherwise amounts to theological nostalgia, where the glory years are always in the past. Perhaps it is merely pessimism. But preachers of today and the future can instead take pride in raising the standard and sharing in the revival of excellent preaching.

Fractures in Theology and Apologetics

Just as there are historical trends in preaching, the same is true for apologetics. Usually defined as the reasoned defence of the faith, apologetics

---

15. For more on this point, specifically on the gift of understanding, see Blankenhorn, "Aquinas on Spirit's Gift," 1130.

16. Foley, "Homily," 163–64.

17. See Ratzinger, *In the Beginning*.

was once a staple of theological and seminary formation, firmly entwined with theological thought. Owing to a series of fractures with academic theology, that has not been the case for many decades now.

The first fracture is in the institutional status and support of apologetics. Prior to the Second Vatican Council, apologetics formed part of the curriculum in theological studies and seminary preparation. There were chairs of apologetics at the major theological faculties, such as Tübingen, Fribourg, Le Saulchoir, the Gregorian, and the Angelicum. Today there are few faculties of Catholic theology in the world offering courses in apologetics. The Congregation for the Clergy's 2016 document on priestly formation does not mention any training in apologetics for students preparing for the priesthood.[18]

The effective expulsion of apologetics from seminaries and universities resulted in an almost total separation in the practitioners of apologetics and theology. While apologetics already had a strong lay involvement in the first half of the twentieth century (most famously with the Catholic Evidence Guild), the drive behind apologetics after the Council increasingly came from lay Catholics outside the academy. The most prominent apologists were often converts to Catholicism, usually from the United States, and their conversion stories formed part of their apologetics. Rather than publishing with academic publishing houses, they published for a popular readership. Their conference talks and answers to people's questions were initially disseminated by cassettes and CDs, and from the late 1990s, via websites and then online videos and podcasts.

Along with this difference in personnel, there was and remains a vast gap in the ecclesial attitudes of apologists and theologians. There is substantial uniformity among apologists on the more controverted questions of Church teaching. While many of the Church's most prominent theologians from the 1960s onwards have been critical of magisterial teaching, apologists in the main are not; rather, they are vocally supportive of papal and magisterial authority. They are defenders of Church teaching on bioethical questions and sexual ethics, rather than its critics.

These fractures were sufficiently entrenched in the latter part of last century that apologists and academic theologians could be viewed as inhabitants of almost entirely different cultures. One American theologian writing in the mid-1990s described the situation in cultural terms: "Though traditional Catholic apologetics languishes in the environment

---

18. Congregation for the Clergy, *Gift of the Priestly Vocation*.

of American academic theology, it has recently found a hospitable niche in the popular intellectual world of the conservative Catholic subculture."[19] In a similar vein is the introduction to Peter Kreeft and Ronald Tacelli's *Handbook of Catholic Apologetics*, where is predicted: "Liberal (or modernist or demythologist or revisionist) theologians will not like this book, especially its arguments for miracles, the reliability of Scripture, the reality of the Resurrection, the divinity of Christ and the reality of heaven and hell. We invite them to join the self-confessed unbelievers in trying to refute these arguments."[20] They then preemptively reject the description of the book as "conservative" or "right-wing." The choice of political terminology reveals how deeply entrenched the cultural divisions had become.

Causes of the Fractures

The causes of the fractures are largely historical, and although exacerbated by the post-Vatican II upheaval, some preceded the Council. An insight into preconciliar attitudes towards apologetics may be found in the notes of a discussion among seminary formators in 1958. The discussion opened with an address by Fr. Edward J. Hogan, where he posed many questions and observations about apologetics, including the following:

> Does apologetics "prove" the existence and authority of the supernatural Church, or does it merely demonstrate the reasonableness of faith already possessed? All too often the idea is conveyed that a complete and strictly scientific apologetical argument will necessarily lead to faith.[21]

This is not a tangential question to be asking about apologetics. It could not be more central. Though Hogan goes on to answer these questions, what follows is a digest of a lengthy discussion where formators raise further questions of this kind: What is apologetics? What is its purpose? What is it that apologetics seeks to "prove"? Should the apologetics manuals not be completely rewritten? Should the study of apologetics just be left to the individual seminarian?[22] It becomes clear in reading the

19. Huff, "New Apologists," 259. For a similar view, see Gaillardetz, "Do We Need a New(er) Apologetics?"
20. Kreeft and Tacelli, *Handbook of Catholic Apologetics*, 27.
21. Hogan, "Evaluation," 101.
22. Hogan, "Evaluation," 105–8.

summary of the discussion that, less than five years before the Second Vatican Council, although apologetics was certainly well established in seminary formation, those responsible for that formation were not at all clear about what it was actually doing there. We may assign this as the first cause of the fracture—a lack of clarity about the purpose and limitations of apologetics. If authority figures in any social structure are not sure what the purpose of a practice is, that practice will not have a long shelf life. And so it proved. Apologetics suffered the same fate as the rest of the manual tradition of pre-Vatican II seminary formation. The apologetics manuals were not rewritten at all. When the manuals were discarded from seminary shelves—physically discarded—in the postconciliar *aggiornamento*, the study of apologetics went with it.[23]

The second cause was the strongly critical and insular turn that Catholic theology took in the postconciliar era. High-profile theologians called into question long-established Catholic teachings, and the pattern of one theologian after another butting heads with the magisterium became a familiar one. An apologist who sought to defend the dogmas of papal infallibility and the assumption could find few supporting works by contemporary theologians. It is remarkable in postconciliar apologetics works how rarely the work of a contemporary theologian is invoked. For those Catholics who fully accepted the teaching of the Church and who wished to defend it against criticism, theologians were no longer looked upon as allies in the cause but as part of the problem.

Allied to this shift in theological attitudes was the professionalization of academic theology, which has seen theologians, as in so many of the humanities, pursue narrow specializations and unexplored research questions where the connection to concerns of non-theologians is, at best, distant. The responsive nature of apologetics protected it from drifting off into the rarefied air of the theology conference, away from the street and the pew. It remained fixed on responding to questions that people were actually asking. Unless theologians intentionally maintain involvement in the world of apologetics, the culture of academic theology will tend to draw them away from it. There are very few dual citizens who move between the two cultures.

A third cause of the fracture was that apologetics fell afoul of the ecumenical turn of the Second Vatican Council and the decades that

23. Avery Dulles comments that the mid-twentieth century was possibly the first time that apologetics acquired a bad name among Christians themselves (Dulles, "Rebirth of Apologetics," 19).

followed it, a turn that shaped theological study and, in particular, the Church's theological engagement with non-Catholics. While ecumenism received close treatment in many of the documents of the Council, the word "apologetics" was nowhere to be found.[24] The old language of apologetics had spoken of attack and defense, dogmas and heresies; the new language of ecumenism would be dialogue and unity. It was a change in tone and emphasis that flowed over into curricula, conference papers, and shelf-space in libraries.

A final reason for the fracture, which requires some extended attention, is the quasi-rationalistic approach to apologetics that prevailed prior to the Council. While post-Reformation apologetics was based on defending Catholic teachings against Protestant criticism, those debates were at least grounded in a shared faith in God's revelation of himself in Christ. Post-Enlightenment apologetics could not build on any such shared faith in supernatural revelation, so reason alone became the terrain for its disputes. Hogan explains this history and the effect on apologetics: "Deism and rationalism, with their denial of the supernatural in general and of revelation in particular, forced the defenders of the Catholic Church and of her doctrine to build their argument on truth as rationally known rather than on truth as divinely revealed."[25]

This is the approach taken in the classic text *Apologetics and Catholic Doctrine*, first published in 1918 and revised in 2001. The text has many strengths: clarity of expression, breadth of argument, confidence in the faith. It is clear on the distinction between reason and faith, that even if an unbeliever accepts the argument and conclusions of the text, that acceptance does not of itself amount to an act of faith.[26] Yet it still aims to demonstrate, using reason alone, many of the essential teachings of Christianity and the Catholic faith. Adopting a sequential method, it works through a series of proofs in first natural, then Christian, then Catholic apologetics, beginning from the proof of God's existence, and ending with the Catholic Church as the only one and true Church. This method is flagged in the introduction to the book: "Its aim is to prove from reason the divine authority of the Catholic Church. Advancing

---

24. Glenn Siniscalchi has nevertheless demonstrated that apologetics is not only compatible with the Vatican II documents but that the Council endorsed key elements of prominent genres of apologetics (Siniscalchi, "Conciliar Rhetoric").

25. Hogan, "Evaluation," 99.

26. Sheehan, *Apologetics and Catholic Doctrine*, 21.

through a series of connected truths, it concludes that the one and only guide of faith on earth is the Catholic Church, Holy and Infallible."[27]

The problem with this approach does not lie with the logical force of the argument, nor does it lie in the discrete topics considered in each chapter. Many of the chapters remain excellent as expositions and defenses of the teachings in question. The problem is the unreality of the approach. Who are these people who start out not believing in God's existence but, by the force of logic alone, are persuaded by one argument building on the next to belief in one true Church, awaiting only the grace to seek baptism? One might respond that it was not written for any such people at all, rather for apologists themselves. That is, in fact, what the text claims. Although the introduction does refer to "an unbeliever who is convinced by our argument,"[28] the text is written to give Catholics "a fuller vision of the reasonableness of our faith, of the enormous strength of its defenses, and of the weakness of the objections alleged against it."[29] That is a laudable aim at which the text succeeds. And it is nowhere stated in the text that an apologist is expected to sit an unbeliever down and go step by step through the proofs. So the method of sequential proofs from reason bears no resemblance to anyone's experience of coming to belief in God and his Church, neither of the apologists themselves nor of unbelievers. Even for the brainiest of intellectual converts, the process of coming to accept the teachings of the Church (including those truths about God accessible to reason alone) never occurs solely through the intellect but also through the affections.[30]

Texts like *Apologetics and Catholic Doctrine* are valuable as scientific study for people who already have the faith and who want to bolster their confidence in its conformity with reason. But apologetics is about much more than that narrow slice of intellectual formation. This is essential for understanding why apologetics fell out of favor. To return to the discussion among seminary formators, one of the topics of discussion was about the distinction between scientific and practical apologetics, and whether the distinction was being made clearly enough.[31] That is, it is one

27. Sheehan, *Apologetics and Catholic Doctrine*, 17.
28. Sheehan, *Apologetics and Catholic Doctrine*, 21.
29. Sheehan, *Apologetics and Catholic Doctrine*, 18.
30. The great apologist Ronald Knox also came to look unfavorably on an approach to apologetics that, with its "mathematical precision," seemed too glib and "machine-made" (Walsh, *Ronald Knox as Apologist*, 68).
31. Hogan, "Evaluation," 104–7.

thing—scientific apologetics—to learn the kind of intellectual objections that can be raised to the faith and the sort of responses that one might make. It is another thing—practical apologetics—to apply that scientific knowledge when people ask those questions. In failing to be clear about these distinctions, apologetics had morphed into a single entity. The rationalistic method was identified with the whole apologetic enterprise.

Could not the Church have genuinely renewed its approach to apologetics? Were ecumenism and apologetics really at odds? Would it not have been worthwhile for theologians to nail their colors a bit more firmly to the magisterial mast? Certainly. But once the Church has travelled away from a certain path, it takes only a few decades before half its earthly members have no personal familiarity with anything else. Healing the fractures will therefore require some serious departures from the status quo.

Healing the Fractures

A first path to healing is to see *unity* as the motive, theme, and goal of apologetics. There is more to apologetics than defending teachings of the faith. It is also about defending people from intellectual error and its effects, and so liberating the intellect to embrace truth. There is therefore a higher purpose to apologetics: to remove the intellectual impediments to a person's unity with God. Behind every objection to Catholic teaching is a person who, aware of it or not, desires closer unity with God. This is what should motivate people to practice and study apologetics. If unity is its guiding theme, apologetics can be saved from being an exercise in parrying with Bible verses and pointing out fallacies, so that it may be truly theological and truly pastoral.

The theme of unity can also give integration to the work of apologetics itself. Because it responds to questions posed by all manner of different people, apologetics can have a scattergun quality that lacks integration. An apologist may field and reply to multiple objections to Catholic teaching on the Eucharist without ever addressing why Christ gave us the Eucharist in the first place. After the Eucharist, the discussion moves on to the papacy, the atonement, and whatever the other objections may be. But what are these objections all ultimately about? Unity is the quality—so often prayed for throughout the liturgy—that runs as the connecting thread through every truth of the faith: unity with God and his creation; unity within ourselves; unity with each other. From teachings about the Trinity, the sacraments, prayer, and the moral life, unity explains these teachings and the effects they have in the lives of those who believe them and live by them.

Unity is also the goal of the Church in its ecumenical efforts. We find the second path to healing in the firm rejection of any inconsistency between apologetics and ecumenism. Apologetics at its worst can certainly take the form of the polemics that are so disastrous for Christian unity. But those most involved in apologetics are often the least polemical. The preponderance of converts among apologists means that apologists are often highly familiar with different expressions of Christianity and non-Christian faiths. Even more than familiar, they are respectful and grateful for what they have received from those faiths. While there are certainly instances of polemical apologetics, particularly online, this reflects more the personal weaknesses of the participants rather the apologetic undertaking itself.[32] Ecumenism can run its own risks of indifferentism and syncretism. Those risks do not detract from its worth.

Ecumenical dialogue entails learning from collaborators and seeking points of agreement, but it also requires the discussion of doctrinal differences with the aim of removing impediments to unity.[33] This is precisely where apologetics can play a complementary role to ecumenism. In willingly addressing doctrinal objections with reasoned explanations, apologetics helps to bring impediments to Christian unity into the light and give greater clarity to Catholic teaching. If apologetics remains out of favor, it is hard to see how the Church is doing all it can to seek Christian unity. John Paul II asked of believers: "How could they refuse to do everything possible, with God's help, to break down the walls of division and distrust, to overcome obstacles and prejudices which thwart the proclamation of the Gospel of salvation in the Cross of Jesus, the one Redeemer of man, of every individual?"[34] Apologetics has much to contribute to overcoming obstacles and prejudices, and breaking down division and distrust, particularly when engaged in by well-trained theologians.

---

32. An excellent guide to engaging in apologetics while avoiding polemics is Brumley, *How Not to Share Your Faith*.

33. John Paul II praised dialogue as "a natural instrument for comparing differing points of view and, above all, for examining those disagreements which hinder full communion between Christians" (John Paul II, *Ut Unum Sint*, §36).

34. John Paul II, *Ut Unum Sint*, §2.

The third path to healing is to recognize the substantial overlap between theology and apologetics. Although they are distinct disciplines, where one begins and the other ends is not always clear-cut. To demonstrate, take several questions that someone might pose: How can God be good and all-powerful when there is so much suffering in the world? How can the Church teach that Jesus is divine when he says that the Father is greater than he is? Why is eating and drinking the body and blood of Christ not cannibalism? Why do Catholics call priest "Father" when Jesus said to call no man your father on earth? These are familiar questions to anyone with experience in both apologetics and catechesis. But who is asking the questions? Would they be posed by a Catholic or a non-Catholic? Would answering those questions be a case of explaining the faith or defending it? We do not yet know. Each of those questions is capable of being asked as a theological question from a believer who wants a better grasp of the coherence of Church teaching. Each is also capable of being posed as an objection by a nonbeliever, or a non-Catholic Christian, who wishes to demonstrate that Catholic teaching is unreasonable. What makes the exchange apologetic is not so much its subject matter but the disposition of the person asking the question.

For someone who is a believer, and so whose intellect and will are united to God through the theological virtues, the problem behind the question lies in their intellectual grasp of the teaching about the goodness of God, the divinity of Christ, and so on. They do not doubt the truth of the teaching; they simply want to understand it better. For someone who poses those questions as objections in order to attack Catholic teaching, the problem lies both in the intellect and will. Not only do they not understand why the teaching is true, but they believe it to be false and so also lack any attraction towards the goodness of the teaching *as a truth*. The exchange in that case will be more apologetic in nature. What both exchanges have in common is this: if the question or objection is answered convincingly, an intellectual impediment to faith is removed—to deeper faith on the part of the Christian believer, to any faith at all on the part of the nonbeliever. To the extent that there is an overlap, it demonstrates that apologetics is not something wholly extraneous to theology. It most certainly has a place, if not *within* theology, then *with* theology.[35]

---

35. This distinction comes from James Beilby, who goes on to comment, "Apologetics comes as part of the theological enterprise because the Christian theologian claims that the theological core of the Gospel is neither expendable nor negotiable" (Beilby, *Thinking about Christian Apologetics*, 34).

A fourth path to healing follows from the third: to restore the study of apologetics to theological institutions. If this is to be done, it is essential to be clear about what apologetics is doing in the curriculum and what the limitations of the subject are. The main necessary distinction is between *scientific* apologetics—or "theological apologetics"—and *practical* apologetics. The priority for study should be theological apologetics, where the focus is on the objections simply as theological questions. Practical apologetics requires a different treatment, and although some classroom formation can certainly help, it is learnt more through experience than through teaching. It is about responding to a question posed by a particular person in a particular setting. Theologians and ministers of the Church will have more knowledge upon which to draw if they are familiar, through the study of theological apologetics, with the principal impediments that people have in accepting the Church's teaching.[36] A sole course can touch only very lightly on the subject, but it would nonetheless give students a more outward-facing turn to their theological formation, as well as place their theological assumptions under some worthwhile interrogation.

A fifth path to healing the fracture is to recall the service that apologetics has made to theology, then to draw the obvious conclusion that it may yet have more to offer. Just as preaching's contribution to theology is not a thing of the past, the same is true for apologetics and theology. Theologians will usually be aware that several great theological works of the Church have been explicitly apologetic. Among the works of the Church fathers, the apologetic nature of the work is often in the title: Tertullian's *Against Praxeus*, Origen's *Against Celsus*, Irenaeus's *Against Heresies*. If academic theology has moved on from apologetics, that decision comes at a cost to theology. Apologetics gives refinement and creativity to the thinking of the theologian. It provokes questions that the theologian would not have thought to ask and then draws on the best of the theological tradition to engage with those questions with respect and confidence. In their turn, Catholic theologians can aid the work of apologetics by making their work accessible to a more general public.[37] Postconciliar

---

36. Stuart Nicolson comments, "While there is some academic involvement in apologetics, this is clearly not sufficient to reflect the importance of the field today, particularly taking into account its status in Scripture, Tradition, and Church history, and, particularly of note, the Second Vatican Council" (Nicolson, "Field of Apologetics Today," 422).

37. On this point see also Gaillardetz, "Do We Need a New(er) Apologetics," 30.

apologetics is almost always highly readable and easy for a nonacademic reader to follow. The same can be said much less frequently of works in theology, which are invariably written with professional theologians and theology students in mind. The result is that many who become involved with apologetics are much less informed about contemporary theology than they could be, and their suspicion towards theologians remains.[38]

A Healthy Relationship

Despite some scattered signs of healing, for the most part, these fractures between theology, preaching, and apologetics remain in place. It is to the Church's loss. If the fractures were to be healed, what would we see? We would see first of all a Church that, in response to people's desire to know God, is demonstrably committed to excellence in preaching. Its preachers would be confident that not only do they understand real life but that with the wisdom of theology they can offer the congregation a higher perspective on everyday realities. That confidence would come from being skilled in the craft of preaching, having been well trained from the time they begin their formation. They would know the theory of both classical rhetoric and homiletics, but more importantly, their abilities would have been honed through practice and critique. Gradually a culture will have developed where students, preachers, formators, and laity are all committed to excellence in preaching, and those who do not preach to their capability will be helped to reach a level of excellence. The people of God deserve no less.

Responding to people's desire to know God also means taking their questions and intellectual difficulties seriously, not only from those people who belong to the Church but also from those who at present express no such desire to belong. The postconciliar hang-ups towards apologetics would have dissipated to the extent that it is welcomed back into institutional theology. Students would be able to study classic and

---

38. Thomas Joseph White's *The Light of Christ* has removed the long-time problem of which book to recommend to general readers seeking a modern and comprehensive introduction to the Catholic faith. It is highly readable, scholarly, and perhaps an enduring classic. Most importantly for those drawn to apologetics, it lacks any ambivalence towards Church teaching. Similar work would be welcome from scholars prepared to tackle some of the more difficult scriptural questions that arise in apologetics, using the best of the historical-critical method in concert with the magisterial teaching of the Church. An excellent example is Ramage, *Dark Passages*.

contemporary objections to Catholic doctrine and so be well prepared to share their theological knowledge with all manner of people. Those seeking answers to objections would be able to access resources from authors and speakers academically trained in theology, including from some of the best among professional theologians. As resources become more accessible, different apologetic initiatives may emerge spontaneously in parishes, chaplaincies, and elsewhere, as well as online. These would strengthen Catholics' own grasp of the faith and equip them to help others with their own impediments to the faith.

Finally, the classic definition of theology as "faith seeking understanding" will not be viewed solely as the faith of the individual theologian or preacher but as the faith of the whole Church, so that those who have received the call to study theology may share the fruits of their learning with confidence and generosity.[39]

Bibliography

Beilby, James. *Thinking about Christian Apologetics: What It Is and Why We Do It*. Downers Grove, IL: IVP Academic, 2011.

Bellinger, Karla. "Are You Talking to Me? A Study of Young Listeners' Connection with Catholic Sunday Preaching." PhD diss., Aquinas Institute of Theology, 2012.

Benedict XVI, Pope. *Sacramentum Caritatis*. Vatican City: Libreria Editrice Vaticana, 2007.

———. *Verbum Domini*. Vatican City: Libreria Editrice Vaticana, 2010.

Blankenhorn, Bernard. "Aquinas on the Spirit's Gift of Understanding and Dionysius's Mystical Theology." *Nova et Vetera* 14, no. 4 (2016) 1113–31.

Bosso, Stephen C. "Best Preaching Practices in Homiletic Programs in Roman Catholic Theologates in the United States." PhD diss., Aquinas Institute of Theology, 2018.

Brumley, Mark. *How Not to Share Your Faith: The Seven Deadly Sins of Apologetics and Evangelization*. El Cajon, CA: Catholic Answers, 2002.

Congregation for the Clergy. *The Gift of the Priestly Vocation: Ratio Fundamentalis Institutionis Sacerdotalis*. Vatican City: Libreria Editrice Vaticana, 2016.

Congregation for Divine Worship and the Discipline of the Sacraments. *Homiletic Directory*. Vatican City: Libreria Editrice Vaticana, 2014.

Connors, Michael E., and Ann M. Garrido. "Doctrinal and Catechetical Preaching." In *A Handbook for Catholic Preaching*, edited by Edward Foley, 124–33. Collegeville, MN: Liturgical, 2016.

Craddock, Fred B. *As One without Authority*. 4th ed., revised and with new sermons. St. Louis: Chalice, 2001.

DeBona, Guerric. "Preaching before Vatican II." In *A Handbook for Catholic Preaching*, edited by Edward Foley, 84–94. Collegeville, MN: Liturgical, 2016.

39. I would like to thank Sr. Mary Helen Hill, OP, and Fr. Matthew Boland, OP, for their comments on an earlier draft of this chapter.

"The Digital Pulpit: A Nationwide Analysis of Online Sermons." Pew Research Center, 16 Dec. 2019. https://www.pewforum.org/2019/12/16/the-digital-pulpit-a-nationwide-analysis-of-online-sermons/.

Dulles, Avery. "The Rebirth of Apologetics." *First Things* (May 2004) 18–23.

Foley, Edward. "The Homily." In *A Handbook for Catholic Preaching*, edited by Edward Foley, 156–65. Collegeville, MN: Liturgical, 2016.

Francis, Pope. *Evangelii Gaudium*. Vatican City: Libreria Editrice Vaticana, 2015.

Gaillardetz, Richard R. "Do We Need a New(er) Apologetics?" *America* (2 Feb. 2004) 26–33.

Hogan, Edward J. "Evaluation of the Traditional Seminary Course in Apologetics." *Proceedings of the Catholic Theological Society of America* 13 (1958) 97–108.

Huff, Peter A. "New Apologists in America's Conservative Catholic Subculture." *Horizons* 23, no. 2 (1996) 242–60.

John Paul II, Pope. *Ut Unum Sint*. Vatican City: Libreria Editrice Vaticana, 1995.

Kreeft, Peter J., and Ronald K. Tacelli. *Handbook of Catholic Apologetics: Reasoned Answers to Questions of Faith*. San Francisco: Ignatius, 2009.

Monshau, Michael. "The Influence of Pope Benedict XVI's Liturgical Initiatives on Preaching beyond Postmodernity." *Antiphon* 22, no. 2 (2018) 186–98.

Nicolson, Stuart. "The Field of Apologetics Today: Responding to the Calls of Scripture and the Second Vatican Council." *Heythrop Journal* 59, no. 3 (2018) 410–23.

Paul VI, Pope. *Evangelii Nuntiandi*. Vatican City: Libreria Editrice Vaticana, 1975.

Ramage, Matthew J. *Dark Passages of the Bible: Engaging Scripture with Benedict XVI and St. Thomas Aquinas*. Washington, DC: Catholic University of America Press, 2013.

Ratzinger, Joseph. *"In the Beginning . . .": A Catholic Understanding of the Story of Creation and the Fall*. Translated by Boniface Ramsey. Grand Rapids: Eerdmans, 1986.

Second Vatican Council. *Constitution on the Sacred Liturgy [Sacrosanctum Concilium]*. Vatican City: Libreria Editrice Vaticana, 1963.

Sheehan, Michael. *Apologetics and Catholic Doctrine*. Revised and edited by P. M. Joseph. London: Saint Austin, 2001.

Siniscalchi, Glenn B. "Conciliar Rhetoric: An Integrated Model of Catholic Defense." *Heythrop Journal* 53, no. 6 (2012) 943–60.

Valentine, Ferdinand. *The Art of Preaching: A Practical Guide*. London: Burns Oates & Washbourne, 1951.

Walsh, Milton. *Ronald Knox as Apologist: Wit, Laughter, and the Popish Creed*. San Francisco: Ignatius, 2007.

White, Thomas Joseph. *The Light of Christ: An Introduction to Catholicism*. Washington, DC: Catholic University of America Press, 2017.

7

Theology and Ethics

Paul Morrissey

We live in a fragmented age. The human person, created in the *imago Dei*, is an integrated being, called to flourish body and soul, neighbor to neighbor, and in relationship with God and creation. And yet, through sin, we disintegrate, seeking solace in ourselves, separate from God, creation, our neighbor, and society. Contemporary culture and technology have exacerbated this fragmentation, and the academy has not been exempted from this trend. As argued by Alasdair McIntyre, universities have become *multiversities*, where overarching wisdom—philosophy and theology—have been sidelined, resulting in hyper-specialization between and within disciplines.[1] This volume seeks to unite that which has become disparate in theology. The argument goes that individual theological disciplines, to their detriment, have cut themselves adrift from each other, as well as from traditional sources of unity such as Scripture, authority, doctrine, liturgy, and prayer. This is no less true in Christian ethics (moral theology) than it is in other theological specializations.

In an important essay, the late Avery Cardinal Dulles summarized well the argument for a reintegration of Catholic theology. He begins his reflection with something of a lament:

> Over the past fifty years we have all heard the repeated complaint, amounting sometimes to a lamentation, that theology has lost its unity. Like Humpty Dumpty it has suffered a great fall, and all the pope's theologians have not succeeded in putting

1. MacIntyre, *God, Philosophy, Universities*.

it together again. Theology is splintered into sub disciplines that insist on their own autonomy without regard for one another. Biblical studies go in one direction, historical scholarship goes in another, ethics in a third, and spirituality in a fourth. In addition to this fragmentation of disciplines, there is a growing breach between past and present. The classic statements of the faith are studied historically, in relation to the circumstances in which they arose. If their contemporary relevance is not denied, they are reinterpreted for today in ways that preserve little if anything of their original content. The Magisterium, which has traditionally been the guardian of theological orthodoxy, is simply ignored by some theologians and bitterly criticized by others. Dogmatic theology, which seeks to ground itself in official Catholic teaching, is shunned as being servile and unprogressive.... Each theologian is expected to be creative and is encouraged to say something novel and surprising. A theologian who reaffirms the tradition and fails to challenge the received doctrine is considered timid and retrograde.[2]

Dulles pleads for an integration of theology on several levels: between theological disciplines; between the past and the present; between philosophy (and other human sciences) and theology; between the wisdom that is gift and theological wisdom in the more academic sense; and between different theological systems. In Dulles's mind, wisdom is a lost concept today, having been replaced by technical knowledge, calculated reasoning, and artistic creativity—that is, wisdom as the ability "to understand the real connections between things and to be able to answer broad speculative and practical questions."[3] Dulles underlines several cultural reasons for the fragmentation of theology and theological wisdom:

Democratization, individualism, and the mobility of populations. The ever-accelerating progress of technology has brought different cultures and ideologies into close contact. The slow moving, culturally unified traditional society seems to be a thing of the past. In the current situation it is easy to fall into the historical and cultural relativism and abandon the quest for permanent and universal truth.[4]

Thus, theology's perennial value in the wider world, as well as its innate confidence in pursuing universal truth, has diminished. Theology is

2. Dulles, "Wisdom as the Source," 59.
3. Dulles, "Wisdom as the Source," 61.
4. Dulles, "Wisdom as the Source," 60.

fragmented because there is surer footing in a more specialized expertise—any universal knowledge or reality is unattainable.

Dulles argues that it will be through a retrieval of the sapiential dimension of theology that the fragmentation of theology will be overcome. This will be through a renewal of understanding that the principle of unity of theology comes from its formal object, God and his revelation of saving truth. It is true that theology necessarily comprises a study of human questions; however, primarily, it must remain the study of God. Dulles points out that in recent centuries, theology has become increasingly secular and, in some respects, a de facto type of religious studies whereby divine revelation is subjected to human standards. Therefore, if theology is to recover its unity, each discipline that comprises the whole must be refocused on the primary object of theology's goal, God. This is true whether one speaks of biblical studies, historical theology, patristic theology, dogmatics, or moral theology.[5]

This chapter will focus on the renewal of moral theology in the context of Vatican II. This renewal, called for by the magisterium, asks moral theologians to reintegrate their discipline more fully with Christian faith and revelation so that the moral and spiritual life of Christians may be suitably assisted. There is no better champion and exponent of this renewal than the Dominican moral theologian Servais-Théodore Pinckaers. It is his work that will form the focus of this chapter.

After a brief introduction to Pinckaers's life and work, the chapter will look at three key areas through his moral theology: first, the

---

5. "Moral theology, in recent years, has tended to degenerate into a merely ethical discipline heavily dependent on the methodologies of social and behavioural sciences. As Pope John Paul II insisted in *Veritatis splendor*, it needs to retain its character as theology by acknowledging 'that the origin and end of moral action are found in the One who "alone is good" and who, by giving himself to man in Christ, offers him the happiness of divine life' (*Veritatis splendor*, no. 29). Faithful to the supernatural sense of the faith moral theology must take account of the 'spiritual dimension of the human heart and its vocation to divine love' (no. 112). In so doing moral theology retains its authentic links with Scripture and tradition in its various expressions" (Dulles, "Wisdom as the Source," 69–70). In its 2011 document "Theology Today," the International Theological Commission (ITC) also sees sapiential theology as providing a unifying vision. Wisdom integrates and unifies the various sciences. "The human person is not satisfied by partial truths, but seeks to unify different pieces and areas of knowledge into an understanding of the final truth of all things and of human life itself" (§86.). Thus, while the individual disciplines of human knowledge (and those that exist within theology itself) are essential, wisdom "strives to give a unified view of the whole of reality. It is, in effect, a knowledge in accordance with the highest, most universal and also most explanatory causes" (§90).

importance of St. Thomas and retrieving his unifying vision of ethics and the moral life; second, how prior, during, and post-Vatican II, a renewal of moral theology was sought; and third, the renewal of moral theology as exemplified in the most important magisterial teaching post-Vatican II, John Paul II's *Veritatis Splendor*, which seeks to incorporate a unitive rather than fragmented approach to moral theology.

Significance of Servais Pinckaers

Servais-Théodore Pinckaers was born in Liege in 1925 and is considered one of the most important Catholic moral theologians of the latter half of the twentieth century.[6] His output includes the writing of 21 books, 254 articles, and 27 book reviews.[7] His influence has been most keenly felt in Thomistic circles. For example, the moral philosopher Alasdair MacIntyre, writing in the preface to the English edition of Pinckaers's brief introduction to moral theology, *Morality—The Catholic View*, calls Pinckaers an "extraordinary author," who has written an "extraordinary book."[8] MacIntyre goes on to say that Pinckaers's most significant scholarly work, *The Sources of Christian Ethics*, was "the single most striking exposition of the ethics of Christianity for a long time."[9] However, it must be noted that his influence is relatively muted in the English-speaking world. For example, in two histories of moral theology in the twentieth century, Pinckaers rates barely a mention. Paulinus Odozor in his study of Catholic moral theology since Vatican II devotes only two pages to Pinckaers's thought, and this only to highlight Pinckaers's critique of contemporary Catholic moral theology.[10] In James Keenan's *A History of Catholic Moral Theology in the Twentieth Century*, Pinckaers is mentioned only briefly on four pages.[11]

---

6. The biographical details presented here are taken from Sherwin, "Eulogie"; Berkman, "Introduction"; Cessario, "On the Place"; and Cessario, "Hommage."

7. Taken from the bibliography compiled by Berkman and Titus, *Pinckaers Reader*, 397–411.

8. MacIntyre, "Preface," vii.

9. MacIntyre, "Preface," vii.

10. Odozor, *Moral Theology*, 9–10.

11. The lack of reference to Pinckaers in these two works has a number of probable reasons, foremost of which is that relatively little of his work that has been translated into English. Also, moral theology has been at the forefront of much of the controversy in Catholic theology since Vatican II, and the principal players in this controversy

Within Thomistic thought, Pinckaers is seen as far more influential. For example, Thomas O'Meara in his overview of Dominican moral theology in the twentieth century spends considerable time considering the importance of Pinckaers.[12] O'Meara labels him a "Biblical Thomist," seeing in Pinckaers a return to a more authentic Thomistic moral theology where historical and biblical studies are at the forefront. O'Meara notes that Pinckaers rarely touches concrete moral issues or controversies due to his more speculative approach, in line with St. Thomas himself.[13]

The January 2009 issue of *The Thomist* dedicated a section to the life and work of Pinckaers. Romanus Cessario, OP, sought to place the significance of Pinckaers in light of the recent summary of twentieth-century Catholic theology by Fergus Kerr, OP.[14] Kerr chose ten theologians whom he felt were the most influential of the twentieth century. Cessario suggests that perhaps the name of Pinckaers should have been added. Cessario makes a strong case that Pinckaers assisted significantly in two of the most important documents of the pontificate of John Paul II, *The Catechism of the Catholic Church* and *Veritatis Splendor*. Certainly, the moral section of the *Catechism* bears significant resemblance to Pinckaers's *Sources of Christian Ethics*. Pinckaers also participated in the workshop that provided John Paul II with a draft that he would use for the 1993 encyclical *Veritatis Splendor*.[15] Cessario believes that "Fr. Pinckaers merits a place of greater significance in the history of twentieth-century Catholic theology than Fergus Kerr seems prepared to acknowledge."[16]

Other contemporary Thomist theologians also acknowledge the place of Servais Pinckaers in twentieth-century Catholic theology. Matthew Levering, for example, considers Pinckaers the greatest moral theologian of the twentieth century and says that his own approach to reading

---

(such as Charles Curran and Richard McCormick) appear frequently in these histories. Pinckaers tended to shy away from these controversies. Still, the neglect of Pinckaers in these works is surprising. Gallagher notes something similar in his review, "History of Catholic Moral Theology," 347–49. All that being said, it is interesting to note that in the first issue of the *Journal of Moral Theology*, dedicated to formative figures in contemporary American Catholic moral theology, there is an article on Pinckaers's contribution (see Titus, "Servais Pinckaers").

12. O'Meara, "Interpreting Thomas Aquinas."
13. O'Meara, "Interpreting Thomas Aquinas," 366.
14. Cessario, "On the Place," 1–27.
15. Cessario, "On the Place," 1–2.
16. Cessario, "On the Place," 5.

St. Thomas owes a profound debt to Pinckaers.[17] Michael Sherwin, OP, who has succeeded Servais Pinckaers in the chair of Moral Theology at the University of Fribourg, says of his predecessor that Pinckaers is his mentor, whose "writings have shaped my way of living the Dominican life. His insights into the two distinct conceptions of freedom (freedom of indifference vs. freedom for excellence) at work in theology and the two distinct perspectives on morality (morality of obligation vs. morality of virtue) that these freedoms generate are insights that remain with me."[18] For John Corbett, Servais Pinckaers was a leading light in moral theology, whose genius lay in his historical exposition of Aquinas. This *ressourcement* of the historical sources (Scripture, the fathers, and Aristotle) was married to a rigorous scientific systematic theology that was critically sympathetic to the Thomist commentatorial tradition.[19] We should note here, too, the recent symposium in the *Josephinum Journal of Theology* entitled "Servais Pinckaers and the Renewal of Thomistic Ethics."[20] Also, introducing a volume of *Journal of Moral Theology* dedicated to the work of Pinckaers, Matthew Levering and William Mattinson describe Pinckaers's approach to theology using four characteristics. These characteristics, they believe, can help drive the renewal of Catholic moral theology called for by Vatican II. First, as this chapter argues, moral theology cannot be isolated from other areas of theology, especially biblical studies, systematic theology, and spirituality. Second, it needs to be ecclesial, a theology done in the heart of the church, always close to her sacramental and spiritual life. Third, it is a theology characterized by a joyful engagement with the world. And fourth, it is a *ressourcement* Thomist moral theology, rooted in the theology and sources of the Angelic Doctor.[21]

---

17. "Interview with Dr. Matthew Levering."

18. Leget, "Courage of Imaginative Sympathy."

19. Corbett, "Function of Paraclesis," 89. One theologian from outside strictly Thomist circles, Tracey Rowland, also sees the significance of Pinckaers. In her essay "Natural Law," Rowland states that Pinckaers is the twentieth-century Thomist who arguably came closest to offering a moral theology "with an accent on theo-dramatics," her point being that Pinckaers reconstituted Thomistic ethics in the framework of St. Thomas's theological sources (especially Augustine). Rowland suggests that Pinckaers's work might stand as a bridge between Thomists and Balthasarians (Rowland, "Natural Law," 383, 395).

20. *Josephinum Journal of Theology* 17, no. 2 (2010).

21. Mattinson and Levering, "A Peek at Renewal," 2–3.

It is no surprise to note that Pinckaers viewed St. Thomas as his principle theological influence. He noted in a reflection in the later years of his life the following:

> The rational power of his thought and of his scholastic method taught me to listen to diverse opinions, to confront loyally with objections, to be rigorous in reflection and concise in expression, to discern what is essential among the details, to follow the logic of things behind the words, and to love reality and truth. This is the rational side of the formation one receives at the feet of St. Thomas, and it balances its theological and spiritual dimension.[22]

In reading St. Thomas, Pinckaers was deeply influenced by the historical method that was developed and used at La Sarte. This method was inherited from the University of Louvain. His principal teachers were Dominican fathers Louis Charlier[23] and Jerome Hamer in dogmatic theology and Fr. Bernard Olivier in moral theology. They were working out of an approach to theology in which Marie-Dominique Chenu, Henri de Lubac, Jacques Leclercq, and Jean Daniélou were key figures. The general thrust of the historical method was to study St. Thomas in the context of history. As Pinckaers himself reports, they would study a treatise first with relevant passages of Scripture and the fathers of the Church, followed by an analysis of the text of St. Thomas, though always placed in its historical context. "Thomas did not float in isolation," writes Pinckaers, "but was presented as rooted in a rich and specific soil, and his biblical, patristic, and medieval (as well as his philosophical roots) were clearly delineated."[24] It was in this milieu that Pinckaers could discern the limitation of the manualist/casuist method of moral theology that had become the norm in Catholic moral theology since the 1700s. Although based on St. Thomas, the casuist approach represents in essence a break from the theology of the common doctor. As Pinckaers writes:

> It is easy to compare these two perspectives in fundamental moral theology: the manuals exclude the treatises on happiness, the virtues, the gifts, the New Law, and grace; reducing the moral part of theology to four treatises: the treatise on human

---

22. Pinckaers, "My Sources," 913.

23. On Charlier and his influence in Thomistic *ressourcement*, see Mettepenningen, "Thomism and the Renewal."

24. Pinckaers, "My Sources," 914.

acts (considered as cases of conscience), the treatise on law (based on the natural law), a treatise on conscience (replacing the virtue of prudence), and the treatise on sin (constructed in view of the sacrament of penance and taking the place of the virtues); the perspective of the manuals reduces moral theology entirely to the domain of legal obligations, an impoverishment arising from the separation of moral theology from asceticism and mysticism, both of which were now viewed as annexed disciplines. The theology of St. Thomas and that of the manuals constitute two different moral systems, both of which have their own inner logic.[25]

Apart from St. Thomas, Pinckaers cites his great love for St. Augustine as an abiding influence on his work. This also helped him to see clearly the patristic influence at the heart of St. Thomas's writings. Pinckaers's thought was also nourished by monastic spirituality. He mentions by name Cassian, St. Bernard, and Leo the Great; Rhineland and Carmelite mysticism; and the classics of the Dominican tradition. Later in his life, the works of John Henry Newman, particularly, he says, the *Parochial and Plain Sermons*, would be important.[26] Pinckaers also notes the philosophical influences that helped him "acquire a mind that is open to all that is human."[27]

A Thomistic Renewal in Moral Theology

At one point in *The Sources of Christian Ethics*, Pinckaers asks the provocative question: is St. Thomas's moral teaching Christian? The question, although seemingly odd, is valid, because—for many—St. Thomas relies so much on Aristotle's ethics that the morality one finds in his works is more philosophy than theology. And it is true that when one turns to the second part of the *Summa*, Christ is rarely mentioned.[28] In answering this

---

25. Pinckaers, "My Sources," 913.
26. Pinckaers, "My Sources," 915.
27. Pinckaers, "My Sources," 915. Among others, he mentions particularly Plato, Aristotle, the Stoics, Descartes, Spinoza, Kant, Nietzsche, Sartre, Scheler, Bergson, and Maritain. He also notes that Kierkegaard's defence of faith and critique of Hegel was important for him.
28. Pinckaers, *Sources of Christian Ethics*, 168. Using a concordance for the *secundae secundum*, Pinckaers notes the following in terms of number of citations. Vis-à-vis non-scriptural sources, Augustine is cited 1,630 times, Aristotle 1,546 times. The Old Testament is cited 1,839 times and the New Testament 2,003 (Pinckaers, "Sources of

critique, Pinckaers recognizes two pitfalls when reading St. Thomas. The first is what he calls myopia: choosing to read only what one is interested in, and thus ignoring the entire theological vision of the *Summa* as well as its general structure. Countering this myopia, Pinckaers says that the *Summa* can be compared to a great medieval cathedral. Each part of the cathedral is separate, but it cannot be split off from the whole. So, while the moral section of the *Summa* seems devoid of the Trinity and Christ, this is because St. Thomas begins his masterpiece with God and the Trinity and completes it in part 3 with Christ.

> It is no cause for surprise to find the Blessed Sacrament is located in only one place in the cathedral: we know that radiates throughout the whole edifice. In the same way, the Summa, a well-planned work, treats of Christ, the Trinity, and the Eucharist in specific sections designed to stand out in eminence for those who know how to take an overall view of the theological construction in its entirety.[29]

The second pitfall that Pinckaers recognizes when interpreting St. Thomas is double vision. This is where we bring preconceived categories to a particular work. Thus, the modern reader brings the divisions of a modern theologian to the work of St. Thomas. For example, the modern theologian divides morality and dogma, philosophy and theology, morality and spirituality. So, whereas St. Thomas saw no divisions in theology, the modern theologian sees them everywhere in St. Thomas's work. For example, St. Thomas's treatment of happiness seems completely philosophical and not even concerned with morality as it is presently understood. Therefore, when the modern moral theologian goes to St. Thomas for inspiration, he skips past the treatment of happiness and the]s on virtue and simply looks at the section on human acts.

> Clearly these distinctions, usually lodged incognito in the reader's head, have so dissected St. Thomas's moral teaching that there is hardly anything left but human acts, a smattering of passion, and a small sampling of virtue. The place in the sun is turned over to natural law and sin. We also note that when the most explicitly Christian treatises have been removed from

---

the Ethics," 4). For a more developed overview of Pinckaers's approach to this question, see my essay "Is St. Thomas Aquinas's Moral Teaching Christian?"

29. Pinckaers, *Sources of Christian Ethics*, 170.

moral theory proper we have witnessed the decapitation of St. Thomas.[30]

Pinckaers cites the prologue of the *tertia pars* of the *Summa* as the key to how St. Thomas links morality to dogma, especially to Christology:

> Forasmuch as our Saviour the Lord Jesus Christ, in order to "save His people from their sins" (Mt 1:21), as the angel announced, showed unto us in His own Person the way of truth, whereby we may attain to the bliss of eternal life by rising again, it is necessary, in order to complete the work of theology, that after considering the last end of human life, and the virtues and vices, there should follow the consideration of the Saviour of all, and of the benefits bestowed by Him on the human race.[31]

There is a grave risk when consulting St Thomas's theological ethics to divorce it from his theology as a whole. Among other reasons, this risk stems from the scholastic methodology of the time, particularly its use of questions and sections, to concisely break down the different theological issues. However, this risk needs to be avoided. In fact, at the beginning of the *Summa Theologiae*, Thomas considers the unity of theology, asking: "Is Christian theology (*sacra doctrina*) a single science?"[32] The affirmative answer that Thomas gives is based on the oneness and simplicity of divine knowledge. The unity of theological wisdom is greater than philosophical wisdom, as the latter has natural divisions while theology "extends to everything."[33] Thus theology, for Thomas, "possessed a more intrinsic unity than philosophy, since the latter admits the innate duality of metaphysics and ethics?"[34] In theology, all things are treated under the aspect of God, "either because they are God Himself or because they refer to God as their beginning and end."[35] God is the subject of theological *scientia*; therefore, the end that the theologian pursues is not simply an accumulation of objective facts about God but the living God himself.[36] This means that although theological knowledge treats of different aspects

---

30. Pinckaers, *Sources of Christian Ethics*, 171.
31. See Pinckaers, "Body of Christ," 29.
32. Aquinas, *Summa Theologiae*, I, q. 1, a. 3. See my essay "Sapiential Dimension of Theology."
33. Aquinas, *Summa Theologiae*, I, q. 1, a. 3.
34. Pinckaers, *Sources of Christian Ethics*, xxi.
35. Aquinas, *Summa Theologiae*, I, q. 1, a. 7.
36. Torrell, "St. Thomas Aquinas," 5.

such as creation, salvation, Christ, and so forth, its overarching object remains God, who is the source of the intrinsic unity of theology.[37] Louis Bouyer sums up well this unitive dimension: "Theology, as St. Thomas quite expressly understood it, is an organic whole, not artificially and as it were externally unified by an independent philosophy, but proceeding from the inner unity of God's revelation and his whole saving design, a unity which in any case is essentially mysterious."[38]

Renewal of Catholic Moral Theology

Commencing his academic career just prior to the Council, Servais Pinckaers would dedicate his life to the call of the Council fathers to the renewal of moral theology. In the "Decree on Priestly Training [*Optatam Totius*]," the fathers write:

> Likewise let the other theological disciplines be renewed through a more living contact with the mystery of Christ and the history of salvation. Special care must be given to the perfecting of moral theology. Its scientific exposition, nourished more on the teaching of the Bible, should shed light on the loftiness of the calling of the faithful in Christ and the obligation that is theirs of bearing fruit in charity for the life of the world.[39]

However, this citation, specific to moral theology, needs to be read in light of the preceding paragraph, which focuses on a student's theological training in general. Here, the fathers begin by noting that the study of the Bible is the "soul of theology." This study is to be nourished by daily reading and meditation on the sacred texts. Dogmatic theology is to be arranged in light of biblical themes, and its historical study should begin with the Eastern and Western fathers. Only after this are students encouraged to penetrate the mysteries of salvation more deeply with speculative study under the guidance of St. Thomas. Finally, students

> should be taught to recognize these same mysteries as present and working in liturgical actions and in the entire life of the Church. They should learn to seek the solutions to human problems under the light of revelation, to apply the eternal truths of

---

37. Aquinas, *Summa Theologiae*, I, q. 1, a. 7.
38. Bouyer, *Invisible Father*, 255.
39. Second Vatican Council, *Optatam Totius*, §15.

revelation to the changeable conditions of human affairs and to communicate them in a way suited to men of our day.[40]

Here we find themes that are central to Pinckaers's theological vision: the importance of Scripture, the fathers, history, the speculative (contemplative) guidance of St. Thomas, and the liturgical life of the Church.[41]

Even in his writings prior to Vatican II, Pinckaers called for a renewal of moral theology. This renewal, he believed, had already begun. His first book, a collection of essays, has as its unifying theme this renewal. It is, he argues, a renewal that needs to take place in each generation. This ongoing renewal, according to Pinckaers, is necessary because of what moral theology is.

> Christian morality is, in brief, the terms of an action between God and men, the study of the conjunction of human action and divine action; the latter has the initiative, and the former is orientated towards union with God. Moral theology can be defined as the reasoned expression of the active quest of God by man. But, this quest, this search through action, starts anew with each man, begins over again at each generation, at each epoch, under a new form, to cope with the problems peculiar to each. God remains always a mystery to us, always new, always to be sought out. And, since he transcends all our categories, since no human language can completely enclose him within its concepts or its formulas, since no system of theology schematized at a determined period can ever transmit to the following generation an ethics which can fully satisfy, in a certain sense moral theology will always have to be renovated, will always have to be bought up to date.[42]

Pinckaers noted that moral theology was being renewed *ad extra* and *ad intra*. Externally, she was being challenged by the rise of secular sciences such as sociology and psychology. Furthermore, the personalist tendency in contemporary philosophy (phenomenology and existentialism) was also affecting moral theology. Internally, moral theology was being renewed by a return to biblical studies in theology, helping Christian ethicists better understand and appropriate Scripture to their task. The reintegration of dogma, especially Trinitarian and christological, was

---

40. Second Vatican Council, *Optatam Totius*, §15.

41. For Thomas, the words *speculative* and *contemplative* are interchangeable terms. Contemplative in this sense is theological rather than mystical contemplation. See Pinckaers, "Recherche de la signification."

42. Pinckaers, "Revival of Moral Theology," 56.

an especially important development for moral theology. The liturgical movement was also an important contributor, "generating the desire to pivot Christian living and morality on participation in the sacraments which unites us to Christ."[43] Other important factors were the retrieval of St. Thomas Aquinas as a theologian of genius who successfully integrated the thought of Aristotle to the service of Christian theology, the need to proclaim again the primacy of charity in any discussion of the Christian moral life, and the desirability of integrating moral theology in a deeper way in the life of the church—to move away from the individualistic morality of previous centuries to a more ecclesial vision of the Christian moral life and to fill the lacuna in the moral theology manuals of the supernatural life. Moral theology should not be focused solely on laws, obligations, and what is forbidden; rather, the Christian life is a call to perfection, to joy, and to happiness.[44]

Moreover, prior to Vatican II, Pinckaers understood that the most essential element in any renewal of theology was a return to faith as a primary source. Before any other source, whether biblical, patristic, or theological, the contemporary theologian needs to return to the source that inspired every Christian writing or theology, that is, "the Spirit of God promised to Christians."[45] Pinckaers highlights the illuminating nature of Christian faith as essential in the theological enterprise. Faith is the living source that illuminates ancient doctrines, sacred writings, and theological masterworks.

> For us Christians, the ultimate goal of our nature is God, the living and inexhaustible source, creator of every nature; our *cogito* is the *credo*, the act where God attains to us personally and illuminates us, he the Sun of the mind. This is not that credo, the act of faith, as all too often it is imagined, which is rather only the notion of faith, an abstraction and a skeleton outline, but that act achieved, constituted in its reality so rich that it transforms us for the length of our time, overwhelming and reinvigorating all our mental outlook. There is not involved here the faith which would go begging to reason for a glimmer of intelligibility, but

---

43. Pinckaers, "Revival of Moral Theology," 59.

44. Cf. Pinckaers, "Revival of Moral Theology," 59–60. It is worth noting that Pinckaers's thought remained remarkably consistent throughout his academic life. The themes he discusses prior to Vatican II are themes to which he returns four decades later.

45. Pinckaers, "Revival of Moral Theology," 62.

the act which irradiates in us mysteriously that divine light of which reason is only a reflected flash.[46]

In light of his thought prior to Vatican II, we can understand how Pinckaers viewed the Council with such optimism: a real chance for the renewal of theology in general and moral theology in particular—although, it must be said, Pinckaers expresses surprise that the conciliar documents have so little to say about moral theology. At one point, he gives an account of why Vatican II did not explicitly address the moral life. He notes that in 1961, a schema for the Council was composed on morality, *De re Morali*.[47] However, this schema was evidently situated

> in the long line of classical manuals of moral theology with their four fundamental tracts: law, conscience, human acts, and sins. A first chapter deals with the foundation of the moral order. It affirms the existence of an objective and absolute moral order. The basis of this moral order is God, who is the author, guardian, judge, and agent of retribution, and more precisely, the divine will, which is the source of moral obligation.[48]

Pinckaers observes that the schema only briefly acknowledges the role of the new law, and only then in so far as it discloses the obligatory nature of the moral life.[49]

De re Morali was met with two substantial critiques, one by Cardinal Döpfner and another by Marie-Joseph Le Guillou, OP. Pinckaers summarises the critique of Döpfner as one that sees in the schema a focus on the new law that conflates it with the natural and divine law—as something imposed from without.[50] This is a far cry from St. Thomas's own description of the new law: "That which is foremost in the Law of the New Testament and in which all its virtue resides, is the grace of the Holy Spirit given by faith in Christ; the New Law is therefore, above all, the grace of the Holy Spirit, which is given to Christ's faithful ones."[51] The intervention by Döpfner is important, according to Pinckaers, because it highlights the centrality of a faithful reading of St. Thomas on the

---

46. Pinckaers, "Revival of Moral Theology," 62.

47. Franz Hürth, SJ, was the principal redactor, assisted by Louis-Bertrand Gillon, OP, and Ermenegildo Lio, OFM.

48. Pinckaers, "Return of New Law," 372.

49. Pinckaers, "Return of New Law," 373.

50. Pinckaers, "Return of New Law," 373.

51. Aquinas, *Summa Theologiae*, I–II, q. 106, a. 1.

evangelical law—a very important source in any renewal of moral theology: "In this intervention we clearly see the beginnings of a line of renewal in the sense of a better biblical grounding for moral theology, and more particularly a revaluation of the New Law in fundamental moral theology, thus avoiding the tendency to reduce it to the treatment of Natural Law."[52]

The critique of the schema by Le Guillou is even more withering. "Dominated by an intellectual climate of conceptualist rationalism and written in a deficient style, which is not that of the great theological tradition, [the document] represents a lack of appreciation of true Christian values.... The more essential exhortations of the Gospel and of contemporary thought are radically disregarded."[53] The schema, according to Le Guillou, avoids speaking about the central mystery of Christ, the mystery through which all of the moral life can be presented—the natural law, the old law, the new law of the interior life. It is only through Christ that the human person and his glorious destiny can be fully realized. A presentation through this mystery would make moral theology more attractive.[54] Unfortunately, Pinckaers notes, these criticisms did not have the desired affects. Despite some further interventions, including one from Jean Daniélou, the schema was not judged to be ready to be presented to the Council fathers. The Council's attention was, by this stage, firmly set on the Church and her relationship with the world; the possibility of a document on the moral life had been sidelined. As Pinckaers notes: "Apparently the time was not yet ripe; minds had not yet been prepared for the carrying through of the desired renewal of moral theology. This explains the relative silence of Vatican II on moral theology."[55]

Although Vatican II explicitly mentions moral theology only once,[56] Pinckaers sees that the Council as a whole inspires a renewal in Catholic moral thinking in a more implicit way. This would give rise to a number of

52. Pinckaers, "Return of New Law," 374.

53. Pinckaers, "Return of New Law," 374. Pinckaers quotes Le Guillou: "The Schema is characterized by an almost total absence of the mystery of Christ and of the New Law given in the Spirit and constituted by love."

54. Pinckaers, "Return of New Law," 374.

55. Pinckaers, "Return of New Law," 376.

56. "Special care must be given to the perfecting of moral theology. Its scientific exposition, nourished more on the teaching of the Bible, should shed light on the loftiness of the calling of the faithful in Christ and the obligation that is theirs of bearing fruit in charity for the life of the world" (Second Vatican Council, *Optatam Totius*, §16).

magisterial documents of importance on moral theology. Pinckaers cites the example of *Gaudium et Spes* and its holistic teaching on the situation of the human person in the contemporary world: vocation, life in Christ, dignity of marriage and the family, work, politics, and so forth—all topics, notes Pinckaers, which had been neglected in preceding centuries but were once part of the Christian moral tradition.[57]

Of the postconciliar documents, Pinckaers takes special note of the document from the Congregation for Catholic Education, "The Theological Formation of Future Priests," written in 1976. In fact, one can see in this document many themes dear to the heart of Pinckaers. For example, the document decries the fragmentary nature of contemporary theology:

> Consequently, the teaching of theology has in many cases lost its unity and compactness, and presents an incomplete fragmentary aspect so that it is often said that theological knowledge has become "atomized." When order and completeness are lacking, the central truths of the faith are easily lost to sight. Therefore, it is not at all to be wondered at, if, in such a climate, various fashionable theologies, which are in great part one-sided, partial, and sometimes unfounded, gained ground.[58]

The document goes on to call for a synthesis, where theology and doctrine are one, and the different levels of theological studies—for example, systematic, scriptural, moral, etc.—are brought together.[59] In terms of moral theology in particular, the document calls for a renewal as referenced at Vatican II. This renewal should be inspired by the gospel and avoid the legalistic tendencies of previous centuries. Moral theology should never be divorced from dogmatic theology. The model for this should be St. Thomas Aquinas, who,

> like other great masters, never separated moral from dogmatic theology, but, instead, inserted it in a unified scheme

---

57. Pinckaers, *Sources of Christian Ethics*, 302–3. A representative quote would be: "Therefore, the council focuses its attention on the world of men, the whole human family along with the sum of those realities in the midst of which it lives; that world which is the theater of man's history, and the heir of his energies, his tragedies and his triumphs; that world which the Christian sees as created and sustained by its Maker's love, fallen indeed into the bondage of sin, yet emancipated now by Christ, Who was crucified and rose again to break the strangle hold of personified evil, so that the world might be fashioned anew according to God's design and reach its fulfilment" (Second Vatican Council, *Gaudium et Spes*, §2).

58. Congregation for Catholic Education, "Theological Formation," 183.

59. Congregation for Catholic Education, "Theological Formation," 184.

of systematic theology, as a part that concerns the process by which man, created in the likeness of God and redeemed by the grace of Christ, tends towards his full realization, according to the demands of his divine calling, in the context of the economy of salvation historically realized in the church.[60]

Also, not to be neglected is the spiritual dimension of the moral life.[61]

The Importance of the Encyclical *Veritatis Splendor*

The most important—and specific—magisterial document after Vatican II on moral theology is John Paul II's encyclical letter *Veritatis Splendor*.[62] This encyclical encapsulates for many what was envisioned by the Council fathers when they spoke about a renewal of moral theology.[63] In the encyclical, one finds a return to Scripture, especially the Gospels, as a primary source for moral reflection, a source that is not just a proof text.[64] One also finds a reunification between moral theology and Christology,

---

60. Congregation for Catholic Education, "Theological Formation," 187.

61. Pinckaers, *Sources of Christian Ethics*, 303. "In my opinion," writes Pinckaers, "this document ['Theological Formation of Future Priests'] is very fine. In line with the biblical, patristic, and spiritual renewal of recent decades, it indicates the most positive and enriching orientations that should guide the current renewal of moral theology. It is in accord with the main inferences we have drawn from our historical research: teachings on recourse to scriptural sources together with philosophical openness within the context of the faith, as evidenced by the fathers of the church; systematic reflection, unified and capable of integrating the offerings of philosophy within theology as the great scholastics did; attention to the sciences and adaption to modern problems as illustrated by the best Renaissance theologians—but here, perhaps, with a more critical, penetrating eye in the name of the Gospel and the faith" (Pinckaers, *Sources of Christian Ethics*, 303).

62. This letter was predicted in John Paul II's apostolic letter *Spiritus Domini*, issued to commemorate the second century of the death of St. Alphonsus Liguouri. He stated that he wished to write "an encyclical with the aim of treating more fully and more deeply the issues regarding the very foundations of moral theology."

63. This is certainly the view of theologians collected in the work, issued to commemorate the fifth anniversary of the encyclical, edited by Di Noia and Cessario, *Veritatis Splendor*.

64. Thus, ch. 1 of the encyclical is a prolonged meditation on ch. 19 of the Gospel of Matthew and the dialogue between Jesus and the rich young man. John Paul II uses this text to situate moral theology in the context of the human person's quest for fulfillment (beatitude) and the answer to this question being found only in Christ. On this point, see the essay by Di Noia, "*Veritatis splendour*: Moral Life as Transfigured Life" in Di Noia and Cessario, *Veritatis Splendor*, 1–10.

as well as an eschewing of the casuistry of previous centuries.[65] There is a reconnection between moral theology and beatitude.[66] It is for these reasons, Servais Pinckaers sees this encyclical as so important for the renewal of moral theology, calling it an "encyclical for the future." One finds in the encyclical a "discreet revolution in the concept of Christian morality, down to its very foundations." Why? Because "it carries us far beyond the so-called progressive positions which it critiques, and invites us to revise many ideas which have been accepted unquestioningly or are too narrow."[67] It is evident that within *Veritatis Splendor*, we see many of the themes that Pinckaers deems to be crucial in the practice of moral theology after Vatican II.

Pinckaers outlines six guidelines for the renewal of moral theology that he finds within the first chapter of *Veritatis Splendor*, the reflection on the Gospel text from Matthew.[68] The first guideline is the relationship

---

65. See, for example, "The light of God's face shines in all its beauty on the countenance of Jesus Christ, 'the image of the invisible God' (*Col* 1:15), the 'reflection of God's glory' (*Heb* 1:3), 'full of grace and truth' (*Jn* 1:14). Christ is 'the way, and the truth, and the life' (*Jn* 14:6). Consequently the decisive answer to every one of man's questions, his religious and moral questions in particular, is given by Jesus Christ, or rather is Jesus Christ himself, as the Second Vatican Council recalls: 'In fact, *it is only in the mystery of the Word incarnate that light is shed on the mystery of man*. For Adam, the first man, was a figure of the future man, namely, of Christ the Lord. It is Christ, the last Adam, who fully discloses man to himself and unfolds his noble calling by revealing the mystery of the Father and the Father's love'" (John Paul II, *Veritatis Splendor*, §2).

66. "*The Beatitudes* are not specifically concerned with certain particular rules of behaviour. Rather, they speak of basic attitudes and dispositions in life and therefore they *do not coincide exactly with the commandments*. On the other hand, *there is no separation or opposition* between the Beatitudes and the commandments: both refer to the good, to eternal life. The Sermon on the Mount begins with the proclamation of the Beatitudes, but also refers to the commandments (cf. *Mt* 5:20–48). At the same time, the Sermon on the Mount demonstrates the openness of the commandments and their orientation towards the horizon of the perfection proper to the Beatitudes. These latter are above all *promises*, from which there also indirectly flow *normative indications* for the moral life. In their originality and profundity they are a sort of *self-portrait of Christ*, and for this very reason are *invitations to discipleship and to communion of life with Christ*" (John Paul II, *Veritatis Splendor*, §16.)

67. Pinckaers, "Encyclical for the Future," 12.

68. The importance of this first chapter for Pinckaers is evident in the following: "I maintain that the first chapter of *Veritatis splendor* is every bit as important as the second, because it traces the broad lines of a renewal of Catholic moral theology through a return to its chief source—the Gospel—which means bridging the gap which has been created between morality and spirituality" (Pinckaers, "Encyclical for the Future," 13).

between moral theology and Scripture. This includes the centrality of the Gospels and the person of Christ for the moral life. As John Paul II writes: "Following Christ is thus the essential and primordial foundation of Christian morality."[69]

The second guideline identified by Pinckaers is that the essential question for the moral life is posed by the rich young man, "Teacher, what good must I do to inherit eternal life?" This is the question that arises in the heart of every human person—the question of happiness, of fulfillment. This is a return to pre-casuist days, to St. Thomas and the fathers who see morality not so much in terms of law, rules, and obligations but as related to happiness and beatitude.

The third guideline, says Pinckaers, is a reinterpretation of the Decalogue with love as the starting point. The Ten Commandments need to be seen first as a gift from God in the context of the covenant rather than simply a list of obligations. Love is the end to which the Decalogue points. John Paul II quotes St. Augustine: "Does love bring about the keeping of the Commandments, or does the keeping of the Commandments bring about love? But who can doubt that love comes first? For the one who does not love has no reason for keeping the Commandments."[70]

The fourth guideline involves the reintegration of the Sermon on the Mount and the new law in moral theology. This is a particularly important aspect of the renewal in moral theology, according to Pinckaers.

> The introduction of the New Law into fundamental moral theology is an innovation which I believe is prophetic. It is still far from being generally accepted. Yet it is an absolute condition for the evangelical renewal of moral theology and an essential contribution to the undertaking of "re-evangelization" promoted by John Paul II. In this regard *Veritatis splendor* is ahead of current ideas in the field of moral theology, which are still determined by casuistic categories.[71]

The fifth guideline identified by Pinckaers is a reintegration of the link between observance of the commandments and the search for perfection. This means a reintegration of the moral life and spiritual perfection. For a long time, there had been an implicit understanding in the Catholic tradition that there were two levels of morality: one for the laity who were simply obliged to obey the commandments and another for

---

69. John Paul II, *Veritatis Splendor*, §19.
70. John Paul II, *Veritatis Splendor*, §22.
71. Pinckaers, "Encyclical for the Future," 27.

religious who were called to the spiritual perfection exemplified in the Sermon on the Mount. As Pinckaers notes, John Paul II sees the inherent unity between the two questions and the two responses of the young man and Jesus. The first involves the commandments in order to inherit eternal life; the second involves the search for perfection reached through radically following Christ. Following the commandments sets us free so as to reach perfection in charity by following and imitating Christ.[72]

The sixth and final guideline is the need for grace. The new law, as expressed in the Sermon on the Mount, is not achievable through human effort. By definition, the new law is given by the Holy Spirit, written on our hearts. "The law was given so that we might ask for grace; grace was given so that we might fulfil the law."[73] Therefore, moral theology needs to account for grace: "According to *Veritatis splendor*, we can no longer teach moral theology without referring to grace, giving it a major role and showing how it intervenes in the life of every Christian."[74]

Conclusion

Servais Pinckaers is a model for a contemporary reintegration of moral theology with theology as a whole. The inherent unity of theology, as espoused by Aquinas (and all significant authorities in theology), was a key part of Pinckaers's project. At the beginning of his major work, *The Sources of Christian Ethics*, Pinckaers attempts to define Christian ethics, which, he admits, is no easy task. He favors a broad, integrated definition: "Christian ethics is the branch of theology that studies human acts so as to direct them to a loving vision of God seen as our true, complete happiness and our final end. This vision is attained by means of grace, the virtues, and the gifts, in the light of revelation and reason."[75] Unlike terms such as discipline, field, or specialization, "branch of theology" highlights this integrated vision. A branch is connected and stems from the same root ("revelation and reason") as all theology. In elaborating on his definition, Pinckaers notes how in recent centuries, Christian ethics has been cut adrift from dogma, exegesis, and spirituality. Although this is important and necessary for pedagogical purposes, theology is no longer a single science; rather, it is "in actual fact a tangle of disconnected

---

72. See John Paul II, *Veritatis Splendor*, §17.
73. St. Augustine, as quoted by John Paul II, *Veritatis Splendor*, §23.
74. Pinckaers, "Encyclical for the Future," 37.
75. Pinckaers, *Sources of Christian Ethics*, 8.

parts."[76] "One of the principle tasks of theology today," writes Pinckaers "is to restore its own unity."[77] The lines of communication between the different branches of theology need to be reopened for the mutual benefit of all. After all, writes Pinckaers, "Did not St. Thomas claim that theology, with all its branches, possessed a more intrinsic unity than philosophy, since the latter admits the innate duality of metaphysics and ethics?"[78] Following St. Thomas and the vast majority of theologians of the tradition, a theologian should not be shut off from the rest of theology and be willing to venture to other parts of the tree. Some giants—Balthasar and Ratzinger—of twentieth-century theology make this same point in the preface to their work on Christian ethics:

> Yet it must be said that the great fundamental questions of theology never fit neatly into the specialists' categories; they always need to be discussed in open forum. What would become of dogmatics without the interventions and observations of scriptural exegetes? And how could exegesis pursue its path without philosophical and theological reflection on its governing principles? So we hope that, precisely because we come to the fundamental issues of moral theology from other disciplines, we may have a contribution to make to a question which, after all, affects the whole of both theology and faith.[79]

---

76. Pinckaers, *Sources of Christian Ethics*, 9.

77. Pinckaers, *Sources of Christian Ethics*, 9.

78. Pinckaers, *Sources of Christian Ethics*, 9. Before explaining the connection between the image of God and Christian ethics, Pinckaers states: "I approach the theme as a moralist, it is true, but one whose concern is to re-establish close bonds between Scripture, dogmatic theology, and the Christian experience, each of which expresses itself in its own way, converging in our theme" (Pinckaers, "Ethics and Image of God," 131).

79. Ratzinger et al., *Principles of Christian Morality*, 8.

Bibliography

Aquinas, Thomas. *Summa Theologiae*. Translated by the English Dominican Fathers. New York: Christian Classics, 1981.

Berkman, John. "Introduction." In *The Pinckaers Reader: Renewing Thomistic Moral Theology*, edited by John Berkman and Craig Steven Titus, xi–xiii. Washington, DC: Catholic University of America Press, 2005.

Berkman, John, and Craig Steven Titus, eds. *The Pinckaers Reader: Renewing Thomistic Moral Theology*. Washington, DC: Catholic University of America, 2005.

Bonino, Serge-Thomas, OP. *Pour lire le document "La théologie aujourd'hui: perspectives, principes et critères."* Paris: Cerf, 2012.

Bouyer, Louis. *The Invisible Father: Approaches to the Mystery of Divinity*. Translated by Hugh Gilbert, OSB. Petersham, MA: St Bede's, 1999.

Cessario, Romanus, OP. "Hommage au Père Servais-Theodore Pinckaers, OP: The Significance of his Work." *Nova et Vetera*, English Edition 5, no. 1 (2007) 1–16.

———. "On the Place of Servais Pinckaers (+7 April 2008) in the Renewal of Catholic Theology." *The Thomist* 73, no. 1 (2009) 1–27.

Congregation for Catholic Education. "The Theological Formation of Future Priests." *Origins* 6, no. 12 (1976) 180–91.

Corbett, John, OP. "The Function of Paraclesis." *Thomist* 73, no. 91 (2009) 89–107.

Di Noia, J. Augustine, OP, and Romanus Cessario, OP, eds. *Veritatis Splendor and the Renewal of Moral Theology: Studies by Ten Outstanding Scholars*. Princeton, NJ: Sceptre, 1999.

Dulles, Avery, SJ. "Wisdom as the Source of Unity for Theology." In *Wisdom and Holiness, Science and Scholarship: Essays in Honor of Matthew L. Lamb*, edited by Michael Dauphinais and Matthew Levering, 59–72. Naples, FL: Sapientia, 2007.

Gallagher, D. B. "A History of Catholic Moral Theology in the Twentieth Century: From Confessing Sins to Liberating Consciences—By James F. Keenan." *Reviews in Religion & Theology* 18, no. 2 (2011) 347–49.

International Theological Commission. "Theology Today: Perspectives, Principles and Criteria." Vatican, 29 Nov. 2011. https://www.vatican.va/roman_curia/congregations/cfaith/cti_documents/rc_cti_doc_20111129_teologia-oggi_en.html.

"Interview with Dr. Matthew Levering." 1 Mar. 2008. http://www.thomisme.org/index.php?option=com_content&view=article&id=22. Site discontinued.

John Paul II, Pope. *Veritatis Splendor*. Vatican, 6 Aug. 1993. https://www.vatican.va/content/john-paul-ii/en/encyclicals/documents/hf_jp-ii_enc_06081993_veritatis-splendor.html.

———. *Spiritus Domini*. *L'Osservatore Romano*, Weekly Edition in English, 17 Aug. 1987.

Keenan, James, F., SJ. *A History of Catholic Moral Theology in the Twentieth Century*. London: Continuum, 2010.

Leget, Carlo. "The Courage of Imaginative Sympathy—An Interview with Michael Sherwin OP." Thomas Instituut te Utrecht, 11 Sept. 2002. http://www.thomasinstituut.org/nws.php?nws_id=48.

MacIntyre, Alasdair. *God, Philosophy, Universities: A Selective History of the Catholic Philosophical Tradition*. London: Rowman & Littlefield, 2009.

———. "Preface." In Servais Pinckaers, OP. *Morality: The Catholic View*. South Bend, IN: St Augustine's, 2000.

Mattinson, William C., III, and Matthew Levering. "A Peek at Renewal in Contemporary Moral Theology: The Pinckaers Symposium." *Journal of Moral Theology* 8, no. 2 (2019) 2–3.

Mettepenningen, Jürgen. "Thomism and the Renewal of Theology: Chenu, Charlier, and Their Ressourcement." *Horizons* 39, no. 1 (2012) 50–68.

Morrissey, Paul. "Is St. Thomas Aquinas's Moral Teaching Christian? The Answer of Servais Pinckaers, OP." *Solidarity: The Journal of Catholic Social Thought and Secular Ethics* 5, no. 1 (2015). https://researchonline.nd.edu.au/solidarity/vol5/iss1/3/.

———. "The Sapiential Dimension of Theology According to St. Thomas Aquinas." *New Blackfriars* 93, no. 1045 (2012) 309–23.

———. "Servais-Théodore Pinckaers, O.P., and the Renewal of Sapiential Thomistic Theology." *Nova et Vetera*, English ed., 12, no. 1 (2014) 172–91.

O'Meara, Thomas, OP. "Interpreting Thomas Aquinas: Aspects of the Dominican School of Moral Theology in the Twentieth Century." In *The Ethics of Aquinas*, edited by Stephen J. Pope, 355–73. Washington, DC: Georgetown University Press, 2002.

Odozor, Paulinus Ikechukwu, CSSP. *Moral Theology in an Age of Renewal: A Study of the Catholic Tradition since Vatican II*. Notre Dame, IN: University of Notre Dame Press, 2003.

Pepler, Conrad. "The Basis of the Mysticism of St. Thomas." *Aquinas Paper* 21. London: Blackfriars, 1953.

Pinckaers, Servais-Théodore, OP. "The Body of Christ—The Eucharistic and Ecclesial Context of Aquinas's Ethics." In *The Pinckaers Reader: Renewing Thomistic Moral Theology*, edited by John Berkman and Craig Steven Titus, translated by Craig Steven Titus, 26–45. Washington, DC: Catholic University of America Press, 2005.

———. "An Encyclical for the Future: *Veritatis Splendor*." In *Veritatis Splendor and the Renewal of Moral Theology: Studies by Ten Outstanding Scholars*, edited by J. Augustine Di Noia, OP, and Romanus Cessario, OP, 11–72. Translated by Sr. Mary Thomas Noble, OP. Princeton, NJ: Sceptre, 1999.

———. "Ethics and the Image of God." In *The Pinckaers Reader: Renewing Thomistic Moral Theology*, edited by John Berkman and Craig Steven Titus, 130–43. Translated by Sr. Mary Thomas Noble, OP. Washington, DC: Catholic University of America Press, 2005.

———. "My Sources." *Communio: International Catholic Review*, English ed. 26, no. 4 (1999) 913–15.

———. "Recherche de la signification véritable du terme speculative." *Nouvelle revue théologique* 81, no. 7 (1959) 673–85.

———. "The Return of the New Law to Moral Theology." In *The Pinckaers Reader: Renewing Thomistic Moral Theology*, edited by John Berkman & Craig Steven Titus, 369–84. Translated by Hugh Connolly. Washington, DC: Catholic University of America Press, 2005.

———. "The Revival of Moral Theology." Translated by F. A. McGowan. *Cross Currents* 7, no. 1 (1967) 56–67.

———. *The Sources of Christian Ethics*. Translated by. Sr. Mary Thomas Noble, OP. Washington, DC: Catholic University of America Press, 1995.

———. "The Sources of the Ethics of St. Thomas Aquinas." In *The Ethics of Aquinas*, edited by Stephen J. Pope, 17–29. Washington, DC: Georgetown University Press, 2002.

Ratzinger, Joseph, et al. *Principles of Christian Morality*. San Francisco: Ignatius, 1986.

Rowland, Tracey. "Natural Law: From Neo-Thomism to Nuptial Mysticism." *Communio* 35, no. 3 (2008) 374–96.

Second Vatican Council. "Pastoral Constitution on the Church in the Modern World [*Gaudium et Spes*]." Vatican, 7 Dec. 1965. https://www.vatican.va/archive/hist_councils/ii_vatican_council/documents/vat-ii_cons_19651207_gaudium-et-spes_en.html.

———. "Decree on Priestly Training" [*Optatam Totius*]. Vatican, 28 Oct. 1965. http://www.vatican.va/archive/hist_councils/ii_vatican_council/documents/vat-ii_decree_19651028_optatam-totius_en.html.

Sherwin, Michael, OP. "Eulogie pour le P. Servais Pinckaers O.P." *Nova et Vetera* 84, no. 2 (2009) 133–36.

Titus, Craig Steven. "Servais Pinckaers and the Renewal of Catholic Moral Theology." *Journal of Moral Theology* 1, no. 1 (2012) 43–68.

Torrell, Jean-Pierre, OP. "St. Thomas Aquinas: Theologian and Mystic." *Nova et Vetera* 4, no. 1 (2006) 1–16.

8

Theology and Social Theory

Matthew John Paul Tan

THIS IS AN ESSAY about borders. It will look at the location of disciplinary borders, as well as the terms and means by which these borders can be traversed and even breached. More specifically still, it will look at theology's place in these border crossings.

This chapter will move within the terrain opened up by John Milbank's work, which shares a common title with this chapter. However, the latter does not seek to revisit the debates that the former generated, since they have been dealt with far more comprehensively elsewhere. This chapter's concerns are far more limited, for it seeks to identify the points in the terrain where the borders of theology and social theory appear to intersect with each other, and it will explore the possible responses when these intersections arise. I intend to navigate a path between the uncritical capitulation to social theory or condemnation of it, by analyzing both the promises and pitfalls of these intersections.

It will be argued that, as a discipline, theology cannot avoid these intersections with social theory. As a discipline dedicated to the outlining the contours of revelation vis-à-vis creation, theology contains a built-in imperative to breach the seemingly impervious borders of a "pure secularity." I will start by outlining the background for this imperative and highlight how it is not a recent trend but the latest phase of a long-standing tradition going back at least to the Middle Ages. The chapter will tackle the need to reckon with social theory with reference to Thomas

Aquinas in the medieval period and the Second Vatican Council's pastoral constitution *Gaudium et Spes* in the modern.

Having identified the grounds for this border crossing, I will lay out some preliminary contact points along these borders. I will first identify the apparent signs of external and internal strain on the supposed self-contained immunity to transcendence in social theory. Externally, in the name of multi-disciplinarity, social theory is gradually giving way to an openness to incorporate a transcendent horizon within the analyses of social phenomena. Internally, we are seeing a self-reflexivity within social theory that recognizes its own epistemological and metaphysical limitations, which has created an opening through which the transcendent can be smuggled in through an otherwise immanent analysis. The chapter will provide one example of self-reflexivity in the work of critical realism. After establishing the possibility for the border crossings between theology and social theory, I will then identify some of the openings whereby this crossing is possible.

Fundamentally, it will be argued that theology is both a transcendent and immanent mode of analysis and critique of the real, a study of and within places.[1] As a human response to revelation, theology works within a place as much as social theory does. Before concluding, the final task of this chapter will be to locate the precise places that both social theory and theology occupy, by indicating how one provides the place for the other in the common task of coming to terms with reality.

Background

Aquinas

If one listens only to the *commenterati*, one can be forgiven for thinking that the question on the relationship between theology and social theory emerged only in the wake of the Second Vatican Council. What is implied in this commentary is the presumption that giving any credence to a relationship between theology and social theory undermines the explanatory purity of the theological discipline, which exceeds that of every other discipline. According to this line of argumentation, social theory is a pollutant that dulls the explanatory power of theology.

---

1. Snell, *Acedia and Its Discontents*, 81.

The impression expressed above can be reinforced by a cursory reading of Aquinas, when Aquinas looked into this matter in the first question of the *Prima Pares* of his *Summa Theologica*. This question is dedicated to the scope of divine revelation. Article 5 explicitly deals with the comparison between the study of revelation and the study of other disciplines, asking if the study of theology is superior to the other sciences. Aquinas ranks the disciplines in accordance to certitude and treats the conclusions of divine revelation as more certain than divine revelation's natural counterparts, hemmed in as they are by the human tendency to get things wrong.[2]

A reader might believe that Aquinas is dismissing the need for these human disciplines, until he or she pays closer attention to one of his replies to an objection. The second objection of article 5 states that sacred doctrine depends on the secular—Aquinas uses the term "philosophical"—disciplines to make its claims. In response, Aquinas says that divine revelation

> does not depend upon other sciences as upon the higher, but makes use of them as of the lesser, and as handmaidens: even so the master sciences make use of the sciences that supply their materials, as political or military science. That it thus uses them is not due to its own defect or insufficiency, but to the defect of our intelligence, which is more easily led by what is known through natural reason (from which proceed the other sciences) to that which is above reason, such as are the teachings of this science.[3]

Aquinas makes a very subtle point here. In and of itself, divine revelation can make its own claims independently of the other sciences. However, this unfiltered discourse would escape the apprehension of a limited human intellect. Put another way, our intellects are not capable of receiving theology qua theology. This gives rise to the need for divine revelation to bridge the gap in apprehension by emptying itself into the methods and vocabularies of the philosophical sciences. Thus, Aquinas affirms that theology is indeed superior to the other disciplines on account of the greater certitude of its claims. Be that as it may, our limited intellect presents theology with a problem of *communicating* its claims to the faithful. Graham Ward puts the problem raised by Aquinas in this

---

2. Aquinas, *Summa Theologica*, I/I, 1:5.
3. Aquinas, *Summa Theologica*, I/I, 1:5.

way: in and of itself, theology has no proper *social* discourse.⁴ Ward's reading opens up an interesting nuance, which becomes clearer when we consider that the ends of divine revelation are redemption, salvation, and divinization. This good news, however, needs to be comprehensible and communicable. Theology is therefore wedded to the human attempt to understand and communicate what salvation means for the human person, in the context of the places it inhabits. This means that as a discipline, theology must speak *into* the cultures of those whom God seeks to save. Be that as it may, theology per se lacks the means to inhabit these cultures. This creates a gap in understanding between theology on the one hand and the cultures in which the gospel is disseminated on the other.

For Thomas, what bridges this divide is theology having to parallel the Lord's *kenosis* to take human form; theology must undergo a *kenosis* of its own, so that divine categories can indwell human ones to accommodate the limits of the intellect. The fact that our intellect can receive theology's claims is because theology's claims are woven into the secular sciences. Because these sciences are the fruits *of* the human intellect, they ease the reception of theology's claims *by* the human intellect. This is why Aquinas acknowledges in his response to the second objection that theology has the capacity to recruit these seemingly lower sciences to communicate the truths of the higher; the more finite disciplines can aid in the communication of more infinite truths. In Ward's reading of this article, it is not only possible but *necessary* for theology to speak via the voice of the other disciplines in order for theology to be a properly discursive voice. Theology is thus "a discourse that requires other discourses for its very possibility." For theology to operate therefore, it must be in the business of "the transgression of boundaries."⁵

Vatican II

A more contemporary counterpoint to Aquinas on the matter of transgressing boundaries can be found in the Second Vatican Council. While Aquinas presents the authority of a single thinker, we have here a statement of an ecumenical council pertaining to this matter. Like Thomas, we have in the Council an affirmation of the capacity for cooperation

---

4. Ward, *Christ and Culture*, 19.
5. Ward, *Theology*, ix.

between the disciplines, and crucial here is section 36 of the "Pastoral Constitution of the Church in the Modern World [*Gaudium et Spes*]."

Unlike in Aquinas's time, the drafting of *Gaudium et Spes* was responding to a different set of presumptions, which sought to sanitize reason by sequestering it from bodies of knowledge tainted by the sacred. To this attitude, the Council gave a twofold response. First, it acknowledged the fear "that a closer bond between human activity and religion will work against the independence of men, of societies, or of the sciences."[6] At the same time, however, the Council expressed a concern that the overreliance on the secular sciences would undermine humanity's recognition of its dependence on the Creator—in the mind of the Church, this was a mentality that fueled the political systems that generated two world wars not too long before and were fueling a cold war at the time of the Council. In order to address these macro-political concerns, it was crucial that the epistemological question on the relationship between the sacred and the secular was addressed. This meant that the Council had to find a path between two extremes: a methodological monism on the one hand (where theology overrides the sciences) and a methodological atheism on the other (where the sciences exclude theology). In this, section 36 of *Gaudium et Spes* becomes crucial.

On the one hand, *Gaudium et Spes* reaffirms the constant dependence of creation on its Creator. Creaturely existence itself hung off the hook of God's goodness and "without the Creator ... the creature would disappear."[7] At the same time, however, creatures were not *so* dependent on God as to become mere automatons of their Creator. Creatures still had a legitimate sphere of temporal autonomy, what section 36 calls the "autonomy of earthly affairs." While the document as a whole covers a number of areas in which this autonomy is enjoyed, the area of interest in section 36 concerns how human knowledge is acquired through the natural sciences. In the course of investigating various objects of study within the world, the secular sciences will inevitably have within them "their own stability, truth, goodness, proper laws and order." Rather than being ignored or overwritten, the Council fathers decreed that these constitutive elements "must be gradually deciphered, put to use, and regulated by men." Where the autonomy of the secular becomes further sharpened is when the article covers the need not only to decipher the inner laws of

---

6. Second Vatican Council, *Gaudium et Spes*, §36.
7. Second Vatican Council, *Gaudium et Spes*, §36.

the world of things but to do so using the "appropriate methods of the individual sciences and the arts."[8] We see here a conciliar recognition of a twofold autonomy worked into secular affairs, in terms of their inner order and in terms of the methods and disciplines by which to discern that order. In recognizing this autonomy of the secular from the sacred, the Council fathers were nevertheless confident that this distinction would not simply unhook the former from the latter. Instead, section 36 states that such a "methodological investigation within every branch of learning . . . carried out in a genuinely scientific manner" would actually contribute to harmonizing the world to the will of its Creator.

Social Theory as Theological Method: The Imperative

Divine Love

There is an intriguing passage in the third chapter of Paul's Letter to the Ephesians, in which Paul expresses the hope that "with all the saints you will have the strength to grasp the breadth and the length, the height and the depth; so that knowing the love of Christ, you may be filled with the utter fullness of God" (Eph 3:18).

At one level, the passage spells out the fulcrum of the Christian faith, which is human reception of divine love. This kind of understanding, however, does not leave the person who comes to know this love to fold into his or her own interiority, whether by reducing love to a feeling or confining it to an intellectual concept. Rather, as D. L. Schindler reminds us, the love of God is a principle that orders the whole world. "Love is the basic act and order of things," and by this he means that "God creates and sustains being out of love; and being itself, all of being . . . is most truly conceived as at root a logos or logic of love."[9]

If what Schindler says is true, then the encounter with divine love puts the one so loved in touch with the Word of God, which is at once incarnate in Jesus Christ and imprinted into everything in the universe, the beating heart of the cosmos. Divine love flings our horizons outwards into the texture—the breadth, length, height, and depth—of the world of things. We should not be surprised to find Paul's exhortation to the Ephesians running against the grain of the tendency towards interiorizing

---

8. Second Vatican Council, *Gaudium et Spes*, §36.
9. Schindler, *Ordering Love*, 1.

the faith. To know God's love is to know the universe God made, which means that one should not withdraw from the world. Instead, to be loved by God is to be thrust into the universe that God loved into being. Put conversely, exploring the breadth, length, height, and depth of the universe does not turn one *away* from God. It is the very means by which one *enters* into the mystery of God.

Theology is thus a strange discipline that must straddle two realms, the divine and the human. As a discipline, theology records a human response to the divine. At the same time, it speaks *in the name of* God, the God who in turn relates to creation. What is more, this divine revelation is articulated most intensely in God becoming flesh to us, as the prologue of John makes clear. My submission here is that this kind of revelation is not nakedly divine but clothed in the anthropological and, consequently, the cultural and the social. This has important consequences for the discipline of theology. To borrow from Graham Ward, any action (including the act of theologizing) done in the name of the Lord is "undertaken 'in the name of' that which transcends the social, but it is conducted, examined and made sense of only in and with respect to the social."[10]

For Ward, the main implication for theology is that when theology speaks in the name of God, its claims and its object must be "gauged, recognised, shared and comprehended in negotiation with all the other social activities (and the public truths they assert and contest) that inform it."[11]

Human Person

Ward alerts us to the importance of contextual awareness in our knowledge, and this is important when read in light of Paul's instruction to the Ephesians. This instruction is to be read not only as an extrinsic divine order but also as an anthropological reality, experienced by an embodied person. Acknowledging our embodied personhood has implications for our knowledge, especially for our knowing faithfully. Embodiment links our knowledge to our contexts, because to be embodied is not to be static. To have a body, Ward says, is to be constantly "in transit" and to be "located in a space of flows."[12] To know in this fashion means to be embod-

---

10. Ward, *Cultural Transformation*, 15.
11. Schindler, *Ordering Love*, 15.
12. Ward, *Christ and Culture*, 64.

ied is to *be moved* as much as it is to move, and to be continually drawn out of self as a fundamental condition of being. Emmanuel Mounier's personalism bears this out when he says that to have a body "takes me constantly out of myself into the problems of the world and the struggles of mankind. By the solicitation of the senses it pushes me out into space, by growing old it acquaints me with duration, and by its death, it confronts me with eternity."[13]

Mounier's link between body and eternity highlights another crucial link between personhood and Paul's injunction: embodiment is not secular, and neither is the embodied knowing of the breadth, length, height, and depth. This goes beyond mere begrudging acknowledgment to the existence of an infinite soul—even if it is locked up in a prison of flesh. Rather, for Mounier, the body is the very means by which the soul comes to know infinity. Even the body's most basic engagements with the textures within the world—such as touch—can become the very site for knowing the eternal at work in the world. For touch, Ward says, realizes this infinity by doing two things. First, touch "bridges the different flows within which each body is situated and lives." It draws the person out of its stasis and solipsism and places it at the threshold of another, be that other animate or inanimate. Touch is the basis of communion with that other. Moreover, Ward reminds us that the incarnation—that union between the divine and human natures in the person of Jesus—makes "touch trigger a divine operation" in the world.[14] Because of the incarnation, the body's touch, which crosses the border between solipsism and communion to engage the texture of the world, also puts us in an encounter with that which transcends the world, enfolding us into the divine love that orders this world.

In short, embodied existence constantly opens up the field of inquiry to consider not only the material arena with all its motions and change. It also connects the knower to the arena that transcends all motion and change. Therefore, inquiring into the person's experience of that material arena via social theory does not turn our attention away from the divine. Indeed, to lean into social inquiry is a step in investigating the material operations of grace.

---

13. Mounier, *Personalism*, 11.
14. Ward, *Christ and Culture*, 65.

Social Theory as Theological Method: The Contours

Communicating Reality

We must now shift our focus to the need for theology's cooperation with social theory as a means to transmit revelation. To do this, we must first outline the purpose of any science or theory, which is to give an account of reality.[15] This simplicity of the word "reality" belies the multiple dimensions that constitute it, since no single science has the monopoly on its capacity to apprehend all dimensions of reality. This includes theology qua theology.

As Aquinas makes clear, it is true that theology, as queen of the sciences, sheds light on all dimensions of reality. This claim, however, has one very important qualifier: it does not reveal the material dimensions of reality. Theology might shed insight on the origins of the animal kingdom, for instance, but it does not have the tools necessary to shed any insight on the migratory paths of humpback whales or the psychology of urban millennials. Furthermore, Aquinas puts forward another important qualifier on the scope of theology's claims in his *Summa contra Gentiles*. Whilst asserting the superiority of the theological science in terms of certainty, Aquinas nonetheless qualifies it with the proviso that this certainty must rest on the foundation of the knowledge being true, both at a natural as well as a supernatural level. This is why he says that "no opinion or belief is sent to man from God contrary to natural knowledge."[16] As a discipline that provides input on the social dimensions of natural knowledge, social theory has a vital role to play in developing theology's socio-discursive voice. Conversely, the theological science can provide an account of the divinity that gave rise to that social discourse.

However, doing the cross-border work is not as straightforward as putting a theological gloss on an insight from social theory. It also does not involve simply reiterating the same theological formulas with certain items of terminology replaced by elements of a sociological glossary. To form a theological discourse that reckons with social reality, we must reckon with these disciplinary borders and with the terms of the policing of these borders.

---

15. Snell, *Acedia and Its Discontents*, 81–82.
16. Aquinas, *Summa contra Gentiles*, I, 7:4.

Opening the Epistemic Field

In the preceding sections, we looked at how the encounter with divine mystery requires us to delve into the mystery as present in creation. This is an enterprise of the theological discipline yet also implicates the insights from other disciplines, in accordance with the dimension of reality being investigated. This kind of inquiry requires theology to transgress disciplinary borders, but how feasible is a sacred transgression of what has become a highly secularized border? More specifically, are there openings in walls of the social disciplines through which theology may enter?

I suggest a shift in the line of questioning. Having acknowledged the limits of the theological discipline above, is social theory so self-sufficient in giving a proper account of social reality? Here, the critique following the tradition of Nietzsche is especially insightful. Following Nietzsche's critique of the intellectual self-sufficiency of modernity, the heart of this post-Nietzschean critique is the observation that social inquiry is not so much intellectually self-sufficient as arbitrarily self-enclosed. These attempts at artificial theoretical closure end up arbitrarily excluding from consideration any theoretical remainders.[17] As Roy Bhaskar's work in scientific method suggests, these remainders exist because social inquiry establishes scientific credibility by breaking down the whole into various isolated parts for analytical purposes. Following that, however, Bhaskar observes that the outcomes from that partial analysis were then expected to become standardized and apply to the whole.[18] Under such a methodology, seamless standardizability (defined in terms of mathematical measurability) becomes the criterion for rationality and credibility. Anything that escapes this kind of standardizability, such as experience, the esoteric, and even the social with all its complexity and contradiction—never mind the transcendent—is regarded as analytically irrelevant or even suspect.[19] At work in this drive to equate rational credibility with mathematical standardizability, McLennan puts plainly, is a bias that "screens out or actively delegitimates types of evidential reasoning . . . that may well be perfectly valid from a more encompassing perspective."[20] There is now the question: what might this more encompassing perspective on social

---

17. Johnson, *Theology, Political Theory*, 85.
18. Bhaskar, *Realist Theory of Science*, 75.
19. Herman, "Beyond Postmodernism," 78–80. See also Lapid, "Culture's Ship," 9.
20. McLennan, "Postsecular Cities," 30.

inquiry look like? Here we should return to the perspective articulated in *Lumen Gentium*, that there are those who "in shadows and images seek the unknown God."[21] At first glance, this reads like an extrinsic imposition of the divine standpoint on the secular—here you are seeking God, and here we are to give God to you. However, I suggest that we see echoes of this line from within certain streams of secular social theory.

Recall Bhaskar's observation that the drive for empirical credibility created remainders that are still empirically relevant but nonetheless ignored. What Bhaskar creates is a possibility of an openness within immanent analysis to what transcends the immanent—more specifically, an openness to the theological in social analysis. This is not an extrinsic imposition, exerted by the theological discipline from the outside by secular social theory. McLennan puts it another way: rather than being anti-secularist, an openness to a post-secular critique and to the transcendent can come from an *intra-secular* impulse. For McLennan, it is little more than social theory interrogating itself regarding its own assumptions—especially its assumptions of a radically self-enclosed material sphere—with the same skepticism as when it is applied to claims concerning matters that transcend the material.[22] We can put this more constructively: the self-reflexivity encouraged by McLennan widens the zone of epistemological possibility. Within this expanded epistemological space, social theory has the possibility to consider that, at the very least, "the causal mechanisms characteristic of one order of being might turn out to be dependent upon, and interactive with, higher-level generative mechanisms of an altogether different sort."[23] Acknowledging that there are generative orders beyond that which is currently under analysis should open social theory to treating with the ignored remainders mentioned above, especially the remainders comprising discourses that transcend the social and material.

At the heart of this epistemological widening is the broadening of the sites of the rational. If it is possible to do this widening within secular inquiry, we then need to identify the avenues of inquiry opened up by social theory's engagement with the remainder. To do this, we must locate the contact points between the immanent claims of social theory on the one hand and the transcendent claims of theology on the other. Three

---

21. Second Vatican Council, *Lumen Gentium*, §16.
22. McLennan, "Postsecular Cities," 27.
23. McLennan, "Postsecular Cities," 30.

will be suggested in this chapter, namely, the metaphysical, the narratival, and the theological.

Metaphysics

McLennan's insights mentioned above are helpful in guiding us through the limits of modern *epistemic* presumptions. McLennan also alerts us to another presumed fault line, one that justified the overlooking of the remainder in the name of objectivity. In the name of giving objectivity to secular discourse, this remainder was deemed unworthy for scientific analysis due to what might be described as "subjective freight." This freight emerged from the metaphysical, moral, or narrative claims that were in turn baked into the claims coming from the humanities, especially literature, philosophy, and theology. Because the claims of those disciplines could not align with scientific standards of objectivity, they could be legitimately excised from secular theory to create a clinical space free from any subjective contagion. The claims coming out of this clinical space of objective analysis were thereby afforded superiority over any other claim.

Because of the epistemic superiority touted by this clinical space, the fields of study excluded from this clinical space adopted the strategy of reentering that clinical space by ceding to the terms of entry. In other words, they sought to prove their credentials by proving their objectivity according to the terms set by the gatekeepers. This was done either by narrowing their claims to what can be subjected to scientific quantification, making these claims internally consistent in accordance with formal logic,[24] or making them verifiable in accordance within a squarely immanent, that is to say materialist, frame.[25] The effect this has on the discipline of theology is that references to phenomena outside of a materialist frame either were sequestered as "irrational" or "superstitious" or became internalized in forms of natural theology. We see a secularizing of theology or attempts to make the study of the supernatural credible by treating it as a purely natural category. Another subtler sanitizing operation that took place came in the form of shedding any "subjective freight" by weeding out any normative content, on the grounds that such claims emitted from personal opinion rather than objective statements of fact.

24. Pickstock, *After Writing*, 58.
25. Tyson, *Seven Brief Lessons*, 13.

Put another way, theological claims became credible only insofar as they subjected themselves to what Pickstock calls a "geometric spatial rule" over any qualitative claim of the good.[26]

This drive for epistemological credibility was underpinned by a more profound backstage philosophical drama, which is a drama of metaphysical proportions. Put another way, the drive to establish epistemological credibility belied an overt denial of legitimacy to the claims of metaphysics. In this respect, critical realism has provided helpful spadework. As an intellectual movement, it has argued that all secular sciences—physical and social—may have provided a wealth of empirical data that could enter the clinical space we have discussed above. However, it has also uncovered how, in the drive to provide metrically verifiable data as the only reliable basis for any public knowledge claim, there was also an upending of the ground of reality. According to Bhaskar, in order to create this clinical space and the rubrics of entry into that space, epistemology, rather than ontology, had to be regarded as the surer foundation for reality. In the drive to attain scientific credibility by playing by the rules of the secular sciences, "statements about being can be reduced to or analyzed in terms of statements about knowledge."[27] When this happens, metaphysics per se becomes sequestered from the arena of verifiable knowledge claims. Ironically, the sequestering of metaphysics from public inquiry was in itself a revolution in metaphysical affairs. Thus, social theory's creation of a space free from the "subjective freight" of metaphysics was not the elimination of opinion in the name of gaining a foothold on objective reality. Rather, it was the smuggling of an account of reality, a metaphysics, into that very space.[28] Paul Tyson puts it another way, saying that disenchantment, this removal of the subjective freight of the nonempirical accounts of reality, is not so much an eviction as a relocation. In Tyson's words, "Enchantment has not vanished from our ordinary experience of reality. What has really happened is that our understanding of *where* enchantment *is* has moved ... out of the categories of knowledge and factual reality, and completely into the categories of imagination and subjectivity."[29]

---

26. Pickstock, *After Writing*, 59.

27. Bhaskar, "Philosophy and Scientific Realism," 27.

28. Bhaskar, "Philosophy and Scientific Realism," 29. See also Milbank, *Theology and Social Theory*, 106.

29. Tyson, *Seven Brief Lessons*, 31.

However, disenchantment was itself the replacement of one metaphysical framework for another, under the guise of procedural efficiency. There are two facets to this metaphysical restructure. One dimension of this is what Jeff Bishop has described as an obsession with efficient causation, which concerns one immanent thing generating motion in another. Though Bishop's observations are confined to the medical sciences, his more general observation is that this obsession with proximate immanent causes led to questions of less proximate, first, and final order causes being willfully unexplored.[30] For Bishop, this was not so much an innocent procedural convenience as it was a revolution in metaphysical affairs, a posture that presumed a flattened metaphysical universe. The other dimension of this metaphysical restructure comes into sharper relief when one considers the diagnosis of Eric Voegelin. While space does not permit a full exploration of his thought, a constant reminder within Voegelin's writings can be summarized in his *From Enlightenment to Revolution*, in which he identifies a drive towards "substituting for transcendental reality an intrawordly evocation which is supposed to fulfill the functions of transcendental reality."[31] Voegelin adds another dimension to the metaphysical drama at which Bishop only hints. There is not merely a rejection of primary or final causes in the name of epistemological credibility. What is taking place is a smuggling in of primary and final causality to the realm of efficient causes or, in Voegelin's terms, collapsing supernatural significance into the structure of the immanent. Furthermore, Voegelin's work is significant precisely because he directs this analysis squarely at social theory. This is especially apparent in his *New Science of Politics*, in which he takes aim at the positivism in the study of politics, which "subordinate[d] the search for truth to methodology."[32] Rather than a study of reality, Voegelin argues that positivism created a *logophobia* in political study, in which "metaphysical questions . . . should not be asked" and in which "realms of being which are not accessible . . . by the model methods were irrelevant, and in the extreme . . . did not exist."[33]

---

30. Bishop, *Anticipatory Corpse*, 65–66.
31. Voegelin, *From Enlightenment to Revolution*, 95–96.
32. Federici, *Eric Voegelin*, 49–50.
33. Voegelin, *New Science of Politics*, 4.

Narrative

In the rush to sanitize the disciplines in the name of public credibility, two things were overlooked. First, in the name of being credible to everyone, the scope of credibility for any claim became drastically narrowed, as these claims became subjected to the terms set by a single discipline, namely the physical sciences. Secondly, when clinical space demanded that everything be shorn of preloaded presumptions, it had actually retained presumptions of its own. Such presumptions determined not just the extraction of data but also the meaningfulness of that data. The drive to subject all data to a "geometric spatial rule" set aside the task of explaining why the data was meaningful.[34]

On its surface, meaning was denied legitimacy, because meaningfulness relied on myth and narrative to provide the crucial undergirding to that data. Ironically, the attempts to disenchant knowledge did not purge myth from facts. As Tyson argues, what took place under the banner of a demythologizing objectivity was actually the introduction of another "life-world defining myth, ordering our understanding and experience of reality."[35] The reference to "myth" is important here, because the subjective freight smuggled into this clinical space is the freight of normative claims packaged in a narrative, one that was presumed yet unarticulated by the champions of the "geometric spatial rule."

On this score, James K. A. Smith's twist on Jean Francois Lyotard's claim of "incredulity towards metanarratives" becomes particularly insightful. Rather than signifying a collapse of belief in narratives, Smith argues that what Lyotard is referring to is incredulity towards any knowledge claim that claims legitimacy on the basis of being freestanding and shedding any narrative presumptions. Put more constructively, Smith has argued that such freestanding knowledge claims—that is, claims purporting to provide universal truth that transcends any narrative freight—"mask their own particularity," denying "their narrative ground even as they proceed on it as a basis."[36]

---

34. Lapid, "Culture's Ship," 9.
35. Tyson, *Seven Brief Lessons on*, 31.
36. Smith, *Who's Afraid of Postmodernism*, 69.

Theology

The project of creating an objective clinical space was not just an act of metaphysical or narrative smuggling. The project was also over-coded by a new theological charter. As Milbank argued, the metaphysical freight brought into any physical or social scientific inquiry rides on the waves of debates that are fundamentally theological in nature. This is because both metaphysics and theology form not two fundamentally distinct discourses but two elements of a single discourse.[37] This gives rise to what Milbank calls a "critical non-avoidability of the theological."[38]

What is fascinating here is that this is not a point raised by theologians but by social theorists of the political left and in the tradition of Nietzsche. In Milbank's words, these "assert the inevitably religious or mythic-ritual shape" of any regime of thought that equates atheism with objectivity. Thus, they seek to establish credibility by excising any subjective freight concerning the transcendent[39] and focus instead on the sheer presence of the immanent and concrete.

However, what gets ignored here is the need for a constant presence in order for an immanent fact to establish itself. Immanence, in order to maintain that constant presence, would require a "privileged transcendent factor,"[40] which, as Milbank's phrase suggests, requires a point of reference that transcends the immanent, as well as an account that can explain how that transcendent point of reference relates to the immanent. The moment we arrive at this point of the inquiry, we arrive at the need to furnish an account that is, strictly speaking, theological.[41] As a discipline that requires a stable immanence for analytical purposes, social theory is not exempt from this need for the transcendent, even as it strives to gain entry into the clinical space of objective analysis. Social theory does not simply give an account of "the facts," but also dragoons us into this clinical space governed by the authority of the physical sciences so that we might accept these as "the facts." In effect, Milbank argues, "theology encounters in sociology not only a theology, and indeed a church in

---

37. Milbank, *Theology and Social Theory*, xxix.
38. Milbank, *Theology and Social Theory*, 2.
39. Milbank, *Theology and Social Theory*, 2.
40. Milbank, *Theology and Social Theory*, 2.
41. Ward, *Cities of God*, 2.

disguise, but a theology and a church dedicated to promoting a certain secular consensus."[42]

On the pretensions of this secular consensus, Nietzscheans have provided crucial genealogical spadework to expose the unarticulated cultural and mythological underpinnings of the seemingly pristine scientific claims of sociology. For Milbank, these underpinnings are not simply "naturalistic, evolutionary stories about the whole of human history" but are also "religious and mythic-ritual" in nature.[43] In other words, built into the structure of social inquiry is a "practical non-avoidability of worship,"[44] a theological substructure smuggled into the clinical space. From the left, Terry Eagleton's *Reason, Faith, and Revolution* has stated more plainly than most that championing rationality by creating this clinical space did not simply make the nonrational disappear. More specifically, the creation of a secular space of deliberation did not prove the irrationality of theology or remove it from consideration altogether. All it did, Eagleton suggests, was present an objectivity that was really a set of "secular myths" which were "degutted versions of sacred ones."[45] For Eagleton, as for Milbank, "all reasoning is conducted within the ambit of some sort of faith, attraction, inclination, orientation, predisposition, or prior commitment."[46] This includes scientific reasoning, which "trades on articles of faith like any other form of knowledge."[47] What this means is that, just as faith precedes reason, theological claims precede any knowledge claim, including those that do not relate explicitly to God.

As indicated earlier, the heart of these knowledge claims is the relationship between the divine and the temporal, and how God makes sense *in relation* to the world. If social theory is a consideration of temporal causal relationships that ultimately have an indispensable transcendent factor, then we must inevitably grapple with the question of how that transcendent causal factor interacts with these temporal causes. The moment we get to this point of the inquiry, we arrive at the threshold of theology. For Graham Ward, theology's heart is not about the identity of God per se but the identity of the causal relationship between God and

---

42. Milbank, *Theology and Social Theory*, 4.
43. Milbank, *Theology and Social Theory*, 36.
44. Milbank, *Theology and Social Theory*, 3.
45. McLennan, "Postsecular Cities," 35.
46. Eagleton, *Reason, Faith*, 120.
47. Eagleton, *Reason, Faith*, 131.

the world.[48] Understanding this is important, because giving an account of the shape of this relationship will ultimately become a narrative and metaphysics bound up in a theological account of providence. As Milbank observes, this unveils the hidden substrate of any reason that seeks to prove its objectivity via its secularity. "Secular reason," Milbank argues, "produces a discourse about providence, which, unlike medieval theology, violates the distinction between primary and secondary causes, and invokes a final cause—'God' or 'nature'—to plug some supposed gap in immanent understanding."[49] In other words, theology is not a makeshift filler in social theory but its necessary completion.

Placing Theology and Social Theory

If the "subjective freight" of narrative, metaphysics, or theology has not—and cannot—be excised from social theory, our next question concerns the place and purpose of theology vis-à-vis social inquiry. We therefore face three more queries. First, if there is a place for theology to "position, qualify, and criticise"[50] the claims of social inquiry, where is that place situated? Secondly, how would a theology so situated further social inquiry? Thirdly, can social inquiry provide a feedback loop for theological inquiry?

The Place of Theology

We said earlier that theology and social theory serve a common purpose in providing accounts of different facets of reality. We also said that each discipline does not come as a neutral given but with a set of preloaded assumptions. As such, the same question can yield a different nuance to an answer, depending on the subdiscipline that has been recruited into the inquiry.[51] This should give us a hint as to the first kind of placement: theology has a role in placing social theory by identifying the presumptions that are baked into social theory. In doing so, theology can fruitfully cooperate with the project of critical realism, help social theory step out

---

48. Ward, *Cities of God*, 13.
49. Milbank, *Theology and Social Theory*, 4.
50. Milbank, *Theology and Social Theory*, 1.
51. Ward, *Theology*, xii.

of its confinement in the allegedly presumption-free clinical space, and help it face up to its need to reckon with its own subjective freight.

Where theology's assistance is at its most potent is when it helps articulate the transcendent dimension of diverse human experiences. This is a concrete extension of Peter Berger's sociological observation that in diverse human experiences, there are the possibilities of something beyond these experiences.[52] Theology can assist in empirical observation by giving shape to these possibilities, articulating a mode of relation with the temporal world and the experiences that take place within it. Once that which transcends temporal experience is identified, the inquiry can fork into a number of possibilities.

The first possible avenue of inquiry was identified by Peter Berger who, in the name of searching for meaning, argued that this transcendence provides a *nomos* to cohere the array of different human experiences.[53] This can come in the form of unearthing and decoding a meta-discourse that gives meaning to the experience of human triumph and tragedy, the wonders of the cosmos and the tedium of the mundane.[54] I say "unearthing" because the meta-discourse may be baked into the structures of social theory and left unarticulated; I say "decoding" because, where articulated, the meta-discourse may be theological in substance but secular in its expression. The second possibility is that, having articulated that which coheres temporal experience, theology can transform the contours of theoretical accounts pertaining to that experience, with a view to better align social theory's account of experience with reality. In this instance, theology can call out and interrogate the partial nature of the inquiry and the clinical space in which that inquiry is conducted. For instance, theology can push the boundaries of providing a merely descriptive account of reality and add its voice in attempts to provide a normative edge to the inquiry. To borrow from Eagleton, theology can be counted among those that speak to the "primitive conviction that *this is not how it is supposed to be*,"[55] by supplementing the vocabulary which can be used to interrogate the status of the present moment as reality, when these voices have been tranquilized by the clinical space. Put another way, theology can speak

---

52. Berger, *Rumor of Angels*, 32–46.
53. Berger, *Sacred Canopy*, 27.
54. Polkinghorne, "Fields and Theology," 795.
55. Eagleton, *Reason, Faith*, 123; italics added.

on behalf of the normative remainder excluded from the inquiry.[56] The third possibility is that the meta-discourse would have a more qualified impact, with theology identifying the blind spot but having no transformative effect in the content of social theory per se. David Brown suggests the possibility that though theology might have instigated the opening up of social theory's range of possible insights, the insights themselves could have been acquired by social theory, given greater attunement to that experience. In other words, those insights could have been acquired independently of the theological discipline's intervention.[57] Whichever the outcome, theology can assist social theory in opening up a zone of what Ward calls "radical exteriority" opened up by divine revelation.

The Place of Social Theory

It must be noted, however, that theology's placing social theory does not mean that theology is itself unplaced. Although theology's meaning is at its most comprehensive from a transcendent standpoint, Ward makes clear that this standpoint is not available to anyone but God. When theology speaks, it speaks not only in relation to the God who is transcendent but also in relation to the world and those within it who are not. Therefore, though theology may come with a divine reference point, it still speaks from a place that is "embedded within historical and cultural situations."[58] In recognizing God's voice speaking to the world, we must also recognize "the ecclesiological and anthropological basis for that speaking and recognise the limits and horizons of both those bases."[59] To deny this embedded status would leave divine revelation as a historical and cultural event "necessarily compromised."[60]

Thus, just as theology provides its corrective to social theory's accounts of reality, social theory also applies its own placing effects on theology. In light of Ward's observation about theology's relation to both

---

56. This applies to both modern and certain postmodern modes of social inquiry. According to Louis Herman, both suffer from the same penchant for the partial over the holistic but in different ways. While the former does so out of a narrow view of objectivity, the latter does so out of a reactive denial of objective accounts altogether. See Herman, "Beyond Postmodernism," 81.

57. Brown, *Continental Philosophy*, 11.

58. Ward, *Cultural Transformation*, 14.

59. Ward, *Cultural Transformation*, 14.

60. Ward, *Cultural Transformation*, 15.

God *and* humanity mentioned above, social theory provides a cartography of the territory within which theology is meant to traverse and that theology must speak to and negotiate with. For theology itself to come up with this cartography would be to dabble in illusion since, as Aquinas indicated earlier, theology has not the means to provide an account to this temporal dimension of reality. Put more constructively, social theory places theology insofar as the former provides the raw material of reality with which the latter can interface.

A proper theological voice, therefore, is one integrated with the horizons that frame the temporal outer limits of that voice. These horizons do not stifle the theological voice. Rather, as *Gaudium et Spes* made clear, they *incarnate* that voice and provide the very means for it to mature the faith of those living within those horizons.[61] Ultimately, these horizons frame the conditions for the human reception of divine revelation. To build on the Thomist maxim that "grace builds on nature," grace does not impose itself onto nature, destroying the latter so that the former can be expressed in its proper glory. Rather, it is through the integrity of nature as nature that grace begins its articulation, though it will eventually surpass it. In being so received by those horizons, the stage is also set for the transformation of those very horizons.

What the above indicates is the need to be mindful of theology's limitations whilst also remaining confident of its capacities. Like any discipline, theology's insights emerge from a series of abstractions and distillations, a "reduction of the heterogeneity and complexity of the material and its contexts."[62] Claims are made only when these reductions are also made, and these claims might be accounts of reality, but they are not reality as such. This is why Ward argues that every claim comes with "blind spots," and every subdiscipline is enabled only with a series of built-in limitations. Whilst revelation as such is an infallible source of knowledge, it must be distinguished from the human intellectual response to revelation—theology—which is anything but infallible. McLennan takes this to mean that our intellectual articulations must inevitably "always be couched fallibly," in the sense of being open to the possibility that the human response and its articulation might be mistaken.[63] We must put a slight qualification here, for the critical realist perspective does not take

---

61. Second Vatican Council, *Gaudium et Spes*, §62.
62. Ward, *Theology*, xii.
63. McLennan, "Postsecular Cities," 31.

into account the possibility of participation, where otherwise fallible articulations can participate in the infallibility of revelation. The possibility of participation modifies McLennan's caution, because theology's similitude to the infallibility of divine revelation is a partial one, awaiting a final consummation. The impact that this has on the claims of theology is that they are not so much mistaken, as McLennan would have it, but provisional. The claims of theology do not so much lack veracity as they lack finality, which will come only at the *eschaton*. On this side of the eschaton, it is thus necessary to have a self-reflexivity, borne from an awareness of the boundaries of each discipline.

Conclusion

There is much ground that this short work did not cover. It did not, for instance, locate the contours of reality that social theory can lay out, nor did it itemize the contact points in social reality whereby theology can complete the analysis. This chapter had a much more modest aim of showing the point from which these analyses can begin: from a mutual recognition of the partiality of both theology and social theory in apprehending a portion of reality. Recognizing the partial nature of each discipline's inquiry should lead us to discern the borders between the disciplines. To apprehend every dimension of reality, therefore, necessitates a method of cross-border activity.

The chapter sought to open this space by highlighting two themes. The first is that social theory has not captured the full picture of social reality simply because the theory has tried to be "objective." Objectivity confined in a supposedly presumption-free analytical space is a method of analysis that has not admitted to the smuggling in of its own presumptions—especially the philosophical, mythological, and theological—concerning reality beyond the immanent. The second observation, however, is that theology does not provide a whole picture either simply because it is "the queen of the sciences." Its claims might be more certain in relation to its object of study, but the purview of those claims does not extend to shedding light on immanent reality in and of itself. Understanding the whole of social reality, therefore, requires the insights of *both* theology *and* social theory, and this in turn requires that each discipline be properly positioned by the other.

This need for placing theology and social theory should instill both humility and confidence in theologians. On the one hand, theology should recognize the lack of its own apprehension of the contours of social reality. This should bring theology to a point of encounter with the disciplines that lay out the dimensions of social reality. On the other hand, theology ought to recognize its own capacities in unveiling social theory's own pretensions to knowing the full scope of reality, in particular its transcendent dimensions. The extent to which theology lacks this confidence, or the extent to which theology cedes full analytical competence over its own claims to purely social analytical methods, is the extent to which theology ensures its own obsolescence. The extent to which theology properly exercises this combination of confidence and humility in the service of apprehending reality is the extent to which it can facilitate the Church to be a site of encounter of both sacred and secular, as well as the locus for a real dissemination and reception of the gospel in every time and place.

Bibliography

Berger, Peter L. *A Rumor of Angels: Modern Society and the Rediscovery of the Supernatural*. New York: Open Road, 2011.

———. *The Sacred Canopy: Elements of a Sociological Theory of Religion*. New York: Open Road, 2011.

Bhaskar, Roy. "Philosophy and Scientific Realism." In *Critical Realism: Essential Readings*, edited by Margaret Archer et al., 16–47. London: Routledge, 1998.

———. *A Realist Theory of Science*. London: Routledge, 2008.

Bishop, Jeffrey P. *The Anticipatory Corpse: Medicine, Power, and the Care of the Dying*. Notre Dame Studies in Medical Ethics and Bioethics. Notre Dame, IN: University of Notre Dame Press, 2011.

Brown, David. *Continental Philosophy and Modern Theology: An Engagement*. Eugene, OR: Wipf and Stock, 1987.

Eagleton, Terry. *Reason, Faith, and Revolution: Reflections on the God Debate*. New Haven, CT: Yale University Press, 2009.

Federici, Michael P. *Eric Voegelin: The Restoration of Order*. Wilmington, DE: ISI, 2002.

Herman, Louis G. "Beyond Postmodernism: Restoring the Primal Quest for Meaning to Political Inquiry." *Human Studies* 20 (1997) 75–94.

Johnson, Kristen Deede. *Theology, Political Theory, and Pluralism: Beyond Tolerance and Difference*. Cambridge, UK: Cambridge University Press, 2007.

Lapid, Yosef. "Culture's Ship: Returns and Departures in International Relations Theory." In *The Return of Culture and Identity in IR Theory*, edited by Yosef Lapid and Friedrich Kratochwil, 3–20. New York: Lynne Rienner, 1996.

McLennan, Gregor. "Postsecular Cities and Radical Critique: A Philosophical Sea Change?" In *Postsecular Cities: Space, Theory and Practice*, 15–32. Continuum Resources in Religion and Political Culture. London: Continuum, 2011.

Milbank, John. *Theology and Social Theory: Beyond Secular Reason*. 2nd ed. Oxford, UK: Blackwell, 2006.

Mounier, Emmanuel. *Personalism*. South Bend, IN: University of Notre Dame Press, 2010.

Pickstock, Catherine. *After Writing: On the Liturgical Consummation of Philosophy*. Oxford, UK: Blackwell, 1997.

Polkinghorne, John. "Fields and Theology: A Response to Wolfgang Pannenberg." *Zygon* 36, no. 4 (2001) 795–97.

Schindler, David L. *Ordering Love: Liberal Societies and the Memory of God*. Grand Rapids: Eerdmans, 2013.

Second Vatican Council. "Dogmatic Constitution on the Church [*Lumen Gentium*]." Vatican, 21 Nov. 1964. http://www.vatican.va/archive/hist_councils/ii_vatican_council/documents/vat-ii_const_19641121_lumen-gentium_en.html.

———. "Pastoral Constitution on the Church in the Modern World [*Gaudium et Spes*]." Vatican, 7 Dec. 1965. http://www.vatican.va/archive/hist_councils/ii_vatican_council/documents/vat-ii_cons_19651207_gaudium-et-spes_en.html.

Smith, James K. A. *Who's Afraid of Postmodernism? Taking Derrida, Lyotard and Foucault to Church*. Grand Rapids: Baker Academic, 2006.

Snell, R. J. *Acedia and Its Discontents: Metaphysical Boredom in an Empire of Desire*. Kettering, OH: Angelico, 2015.

Tyson, Paul. *Seven Brief Lessons on Magic*. Eugene, OR: Cascade, 2019.

Voegelin, Eric. *From Enlightenment to Revolution*. Edited by John H. Hallowell. Durham, NC: Duke University Press, 1975.

———. *The New Science of Politics*. Chicago: University of Chicago Press, 1952.

Ward, Graham. *Christ and Culture*. Oxford, UK: Blackwell, 2005.

———. *Cities of God*. London: Routledge, 2000.

———. *Cultural Transformation and Religious Practice*. Cambridge, UK: Cambridge University Press, 2005.

———. *Theology and Contemporary Critical Theory*. New York: St. Martin's, 2000.

9

Dogmatic and Pastoral Theology

Tracey Rowland

In an essay titled "Why I Am a Catholic," the English historian Christopher Dawson wrote that at a certain moment in his life he "realised that the Incarnation, the Sacraments, the external order of the Church and the internal working of sanctifying grace were all parts of the one organic unity, a living tree, whose roots are in the Divine Nature whose fruit is the perfection of the saints."[1] This is an excellent description of someone perceiving the whole without the fracture. The fact that Dawson had such a radically life-changing moment of perception, raises the question of why this understanding is not immediately obvious to anyone living in an ostensibly Christian culture. Why should Dawson's experience be remarkable?

The Fracture

The fact that the vision of the whole, the organic unity, is not immediately obvious, is due to a number of fractures in the theological tradition that have widened over the centuries. A lopsided emphasis on particular elements of the tradition have given rise to spiritual pathologies that occlude the vision of the whole. As with many problems in the life of the Church, a quintet of "villains" may be summoned before the tribunal of an authentic Christian culture and indicted on charges of undermining

---

1. Dawson, "Why I Am a Catholic," 112–13.

the unity. They are: William of Ockham, Francisco Suárez, Martin Luther, Immanuel Kant, and Georg Wilhelm Friedrich Hegel. While the fracture between dogmatic and pastoral theology cannot be attributed to these five alone, it is nonetheless the case that the fracture bears the deeply stamped hallmarks of the intellectual influence of each of these players.

Ockham is responsible for the first fissure in what Dawson called "the organic unity." Ockham separated the morality of the divine commandments, the commandments that he accepted were necessary for eternal salvation, from a form of morality based on human reason without any reference to the divine law.[2] In other words, Ockham drew a sharp distinction between "right reason" and moral precepts found in the Scriptures, without establishing a necessary link between the two.

Following Ockham, the next major impetus for the fissure was the theory of revelation associated with Francisco Suárez. Suárez's view of revelation occluded the historical dimension of revelation with its accent on Trinitarian relationships and the relationship between the Persons of the Holy Trinity and human persons. It fostered the idea of Christianity as an intellectual system of propositions rather than as a network of sacred relationships whose meaning is illumined by reference to doctrinal principles. Gerard O'Shea explains the problem:

> For St. Thomas, the symbolic apprehension of divine truth conveyed by Revelation implied at the very least a desire for intimacy with God as a means of entering into the perception of this truth. But by the sixteenth century language was largely cut off from its participatory role, and was reduced to simply pointing at objects . . . [Suárez] no longer sees faith primarily as a supernatural habit (virtue) by which human beings participate in the very life of God. For him, faith is concerned with the knowability and believability of an object. In using these categories, he has accepted a rupture between intelligibility (the way in which an object is known) and assent (whether what is presented to the intelligence is to be believed).[3]

Consistent with O'Shea's reading, in his essay on "The False Legacy of Suárez," John Montag argues that the difference between the classical Thomistic understanding of revelation and the baroque Thomism of Suárez is due to the loss in the late Middle Ages of the metaphysical

---

2. Clark, "William of Ockham."
3. O'Shea, "Historical Discontinuity," 290.

framework of participation and with it the connection between the sign and the thing signified.[4]

The relationship between doctrine and the personalist dimensions of the faith and their consequences for pastoral theology was addressed by Martin X. Moleski in his *Personal Catholicism* by using an analogy drawn from the world of information technology. Moleski writes:

> The rigidity and formalization of theology plays exactly the same role in carrying the message of God's love to his people as does a communications protocol in delivering messages over the tangled web of the internet. Unless there are strict rules of interpretation about how to transmit and receive, there will be no communication from one computer to another. All of the elements of the message will fall into disarray and be lost in the noise and confusion of the environment. From time to time, when the message is deteriorating, someone has to trace the circuits and determine why the transmission is being corrupted. When someone is downloading a new piece of software from the internet, for example, they do not want the intermediary computers to add or subtract a single byte from the original. Personal or random reinterpretations of what is sent would destroy the functionality of the program and prevent it from performing as it was designed to perform.[5]

In other words, dogmatic theology and the network of doctrinal principles that comprise it are analogous to the communications protocols. They are absolutely necessary to ensure that the deposit of the faith is not corrupted. If corruption or "deterioration" appears to be taking place, then someone, such as those scholars who work for the Congregation of the Doctrine of the Faith or, in extreme cases, popes and whole councils of the Church, needs to trace the circuits and correct the corruption. Nonetheless, as Moleski goes on to note, "the person seeking the new software generally does not want to receive the communications protocol itself. They want the software, not a set of rules and regulations that describe how the software may be sent and received. If the rules did not exist, the transmissions could not take place, but the rules are no substitute for the files transmitted by the rules."[6] The "files," in this analogy, are

---

4. Montag, "Revelation."
5. Moleski, *Personal Catholicism*, 188.
6. Moleski, *Personal Catholicism*, 188.

the personal relationship with the Holy Trinity. As Moleski expresses the idea:

> The dogmatic propositions in the treasury of the Church are precious because they preserve the definitive revelation given once for all time by the incarnate Word. But the dogma that can be put into words is not the real dogma. Many Catholic theologians, especially in the manualist tradition of the nineteenth and early twentieth century, give the impression that knowing all of the facts about Jesus is all that is required. I know many facts about the President of the United States, more perhaps than I do about many of my friends, but I do not know him personally. For many Catholics, the transition from knowing about Jesus to knowing Jesus personally seems to be inhibited rather than served by the richness of the articulate [dogmatic] tradition.[7]

The problem is not therefore that it is wrong for Catholics to have a knowledge of dogmatic theology or that dogmatic theology is, in itself, problematic but that dogmatic theology is not the meaning and purpose of Christian life. It is a means, not an end. The meaning and purpose of Christian life is participation in the life of the Holy Trinity. For this to occur, dogmatic theology needs to be partnered with other dimensions of theology, including theological anthropology, moral theology, and what today is called pastoral theology.

The tendency of the Suárezian account of revelation to foster a notion of Christianity as intellectual assent to a pocketbook of doctrines runs parallel to another pathological account of Christianity as the obedience of the will to a moral code. This is what Hans Urs von Balthasar and Joseph Ratzinger call Christianity as "moralism." The logic of the process of fracture and dissolution begun by Ockham revealed itself in the trajectories taken by the theologians of the Reformation, especially the trajectory of viewing God as some "being" beyond reason and morality, that is, beyond the true and the good. Foremost among the Reformers was Martin Luther, who played his part in increasing the fracture by constructing moral theology as an autonomous discipline separate from dogmatic theology and by treating ethics as a doctrine of duties rather than as a doctrine of virtues.[8] Luther was, in other words, the forerunner to Kant. Kant's project was to defend Christian ethics by reference to "reason alone" once Luther had decoupled moral theology from dogmatic

---

7. Moleski, *Personal Catholicism*, 186.
8. Melina, *Sharing in Christ's Virtues*, 93.

theology. This becomes the source of liberal social theory, the source of the current project to build a community and a state without any reference to God. While Suárezian presentations of revelation gave rise to a lopsidedly intellectual Christianity or Christianity as a mere intellectual framework, Immanuel Kant's project to defend Christian moral teachings without any reference to Christian doctrine at all fostered the notion that Christianity is a mere moral code that can just as well be defended by eighteenth-century "pure reason" as by recourse to sacred texts.

In *Sharing in Christ's Virtues*, Livio Melina argues that the quintessentially liberal idea of using prudence, or practical reason, rather than revelation, as a foundation for social ethics is an idea of Lutheran provenance.[9] He further observes that once "disjointed from its connection with salvation and from a rootedness in faith," morality has only two roads open to it.[10] These are social utilitarianism and philanthropic altruism. The political liberalism of John Rawls is an example of the first. It expressly excludes recourse to theological or even more generally metaphysical principles in its jurisprudential framework. The ostensibly philanthropic projects of contemporary billionaire celebrities is an example of the second. Typically, here, "philanthropy" takes the form of marketing social engineering policies or providing money to political causes in the name of social progress. As Melina explains:

> The separation of morality from dogmatics and spirituality, which was to become "classical" for modern moral theology, is of relatively recent origin. It prevailed and remained undiscussed with post-Tridentine manualistic theology. This development has its roots in a legalistic understanding of moral obligation, viewed as a fact that is justified by itself, which begins with the will of a legislator. Morality thus becomes a doctrine of precepts that are imposed on conscience under the pain of sin. It is detached from its anthropological roots (the ontology of a new creature in Christ) and from the concrete supernatural end of the beatific vision. Separated from dogmatics, it assumes an ever-more voluntaristic character: it becomes a "human" morality organized as a code of precepts of the natural or ecclesiastical law, to be realized by human effort alone. Separated from spirituality and centered on single acts, it is preoccupied only with the minimum for not falling into sin, leaving to ascetics

---

9. Melina, *Sharing in Christ's Virtues*, 94.
10. Melina, *Sharing in Christ's Virtues*, 95.

and mysticism the way of perfection—something viewed as optional and only for the few elect.[11]

This fracture therefore led to the absurd situation where Christians were encouraged to think with reference to "reason alone" in some contexts, while the "faith alone" maxim prevailed in others. The Christian soul became bifurcated. Its faculties (the intellect, will, memory, and imagination) could no longer operate as a harmonious synergy. The more that morality was separated from dogmatic theology and the idea of sanctification and participation in the life and love of the Holy Trinity, the closer it became to social utilitarianism and philanthropic altruism—projects that require neither grace nor faith, nor anything like personal holiness.

Pastoral Theology

The adjective "pastoral" refers to the care of the Christian faithful or "sheep." Christ is the Good Shepherd who cares for his sheep and goes after those who are lost or in danger. Pastoral theology is therefore concerned with the conditions of the sheep, their problems, their challenges, their dangers and predators. It has a constant range of concerns, but its content differs according to the situation in which it finds the sheep. In other words, the pastoral needs of the sheep will vary from one "paddock" or diocese to another. In some, the pastureland will be lush and wolves nowhere on the horizon; in others, the pastureland may be stricken by drought and predators of all kinds abound. Good "animal husbandry" requires a knowledge of what it is that the sheep need in order to flourish, what dangers they encounter, and what deprivations they face. An understanding of the unity of the faith, of the symphonic operation of the faculties of the soul, of the work of the theological virtues and the sacramental graces, is foundational for such husbandry. Without an understanding of the unity of the faith, of Christianity as a mode of being within the life of the Holy Trinity, and the sanctification that accompanies this life, the so-called "pastoral theologian" will not know where to begin. This foundational theological anthropology requires a preliminary knowledge of dogmatic theology in the same manner as a human body requires a skeletal structure to support its organs. Without the structure provided

---

11. Melina, *Sharing in Christ's Virtues*, 177.

by doctrine, pastoral theology veers in the direction of mere social work and offers, at best, a kind of "Band-Aid" theology.

Moreover, a person who has been baptized but not catechized and who is the recipient of a form of "Band-Aid" pastoral care that lacks the organic vision is likely to find it hard to distinguish Christianity from philanthropy. Once moralism becomes the default position, it easily morphs into social utilitarianism and philanthropic altruism, leaving the Trinity with nothing to do. This is precisely what the sociologist Julie Pagis argues happened in the spiritual formation of many Catholics of the generation of 1968. She was interested in how students from ostensibly Christian homes found themselves attracted to Marxism when they arrived at university in the late 1960s. One of the key concepts used in Pagis's research was the distinction between "mass religiosity," understood as the need for ritual and institutionally dispensed supernatural aid (what in theological parlance is called sacramentality), and what Pagis calls the "religiosity of the virtuous," which is about ethics. Those whose Christian education and experience fell into the type of the "religiosity of the virtuous" were the more readily politicized. The "religiosity of the virtuous" was a kind of moralism, and their moralism morphed into political activism when presented by Marxists with an array of alleged social injustices.[12]

In contrast, what Pagis describes as a religion that takes the form of "institutionally dispensed supernatural aid" requires a doctrinal support structure. As Melina argues:

> The dynamics of the "vocation to holiness" permit the rooting of Christian morality in dogmatics, by exalting the primacy of the grace of Christ and the work of the Holy Spirit; it opens up the horizon for an itinerary of perfection to the glory of God the Father, thus intimately linking the ethical dimension to spirituality. At the same time, by overcoming the limitations of legalistic conceptions, it allows for a discussion of the human struggle for happiness in the specific perspective of the moral journey, which is that of the maturation of the human subject's communion with God and the brethren.[13]

The importance of rooting Christian morality in dogmatics and the importance of the work of the Holy Trinity within the economy of salvation history are two theological themes amplified in the Apostolic

---

12. Pagis, "Politicisation of Religious Commitments."
13. Melina, *Sharing in Christ's Virtues*, 177.

Exhortation *Evangelii Gaudium* of 2013, the first exhortation of the Francis pontificate. In section 39, Francis writes:

> Just as the organic unity existing among the virtues means that no one of them can be excluded from the Christian ideal, so no truth may be denied. The integrity of the Gospel message must not be deformed. What is more, each truth is better understood when related to the harmonious totality of the Christian message; in this context all of the truths are important and illumine one another. When preaching is faithful to the Gospel, the centrality of certain truths is evident and it becomes clear that Christian morality is not a form of stoicism, or self-denial, or merely a practical philosophy or a catalogue of sins and faults.[14]

In section 164, Francis adds that "in catechesis too, we have rediscovered the fundamental role of the first announcement or kerygma, which needs to be the centre of all evangelizing activity and all efforts at Church renewal. The kerygma is Trinitarian."[15]

Kerygma is a Greek word used in the New Testament for "proclamation." It is related to the Greek verb κηρύσσω/*kēryssō*, literally meaning "to cry or proclaim as a herald" and is being used in the sense of "to proclaim, announce, preach." Proclamation is thus a primary concern of pastoral theology, and the proclamation needs to be Trinitarian. Immanuel Kant may have believed that it matters not whether there are "ten persons in the deity or three," but this is not Christian teaching. In order to have any understanding of Christianity, one must at least understand the role that each Person of the Trinity plays in the economy of salvation. Presenting this knowledge as a kind of Christianity 101 lesson was the work of the early Church councils culminating in the Nicene Creed. The Creed is, in content, a treasury of doctrines.

The Contribution of John Paul II and Benedict XVI to Healing the Fracture

The separation of dogmatic theology from moral theology and the effects of this severance on pastoral theology was one of the crises the pontificate of John Paul II sought to address. In the early years of his pontificate, John Paul II devoted his Wednesday audiences to the delivery of a

---

14. Francis, *Evangelii Gaudium*, §39.
15. Francis, *Evangelii Gaudium*, §164.

catechesis on human love in which he situated sexual ethics within the framework of a couple's participation in the life and love of the Holy Trinity. He also devoted his early encyclicals to explaining the human person's relationship to each of the Persons of the Trinity. *Redemptor Hominis* (1979) begins with an exposition of the relationship between Christ and the human person. *Dives in Misericordia* (1980) then addresses the relationship between God the Father and the human person, and finally *Dominum et Vivificantem* (1986) reflects upon the role of the Holy Spirit in the economy of salvation. Taken as a suite, these encyclicals provide an outline of a Trinitarian anthropology.

Added to this was the Christocentric moral theology of the encyclical *Veritatis Splendor* of 1993. This encyclical defended moral absolutes and set them on a firm christological foundation. When combined with the Catechesis on Human Love,[16] this body of scholarship brought dogmatic theology, moral theology, and pastoral theology back together. As John Paul wrote in *Dives in Misericordia*:

> Through the gift of grace, which comes from the Holy Spirit, man enters a "new life," is brought into the supernatural reality of the divine life itself and becomes a "dwelling-place of the Holy Spirit," a living temple of God. For through the Holy Spirit, the Father and the Son come to him and take up their abode in him. In the communion of grace with the Trinity, man's "living area" is broadened and raised up to the supernatural level of divine life.[17]

Proclaiming this truth and explaining its foundations and assisting the faithful to embrace this unified vision of the meaning of human life and to embody it in their social practices is central to the work of pastoral theology.

Benedict XVI added to this Trinitarian theological anthropology his own suite of encyclicals, providing an account of the work of the theological virtues. *Deus Caritas Est* (2005) explains the importance of the theological virtue of love, *Spe Salvi* (2007) addresses the theological virtue of hope, and *Lumen Fidei* (2013), drafted by Benedict but settled and promulgated under the name of Francis, completes the trilogy with an exposition of the importance of the theological virtue of faith.

---

16. John Paul II, *Man and Woman*.
17. John Paul II, *Dives in Misericordia*, §58.3.

In *Deus Caritas Est*, Benedict argues that God's way of loving becomes the measure of human love. As he expresses the principle in section 17:

> The love-story between God and man consists in the very fact that this communion of will increases in a communion of thought and sentiment, and thus our will and God's will increasingly coincide: God's will is no longer for me an alien will, something imposed on me from without by the commandments, but it is now my own will, based on the realization that God is in fact more deeply present to me than I am to myself.[18]

The concept of an alien will imposed from without is, of course, a reference to Kant's criticisms of a theologically inspired moral framework. Pope Benedict's point is that Catholic moral theology does not give rise to what Kant perceived as a conflict between law and desire if the person is united through the sacraments with the Holy Trinity. As Cardinal Marc Ouellet has argued, Christian ethics is radically theological! The "practice of the Christian virtues does not obey a self-sufficient moral ideal but proceeds from a 'spiritual transformation of judgment' (Eph. 4:23) that allows a 'discerning of what is pleasing to God' (5:10)."[19]

In *Deus Caritas Est* and in his social encyclical *Caritas in Veritate* (2009), Benedict XVI also emphasizes that there is something problematic about the fracture between the Church's teachings in the area of personal morality and the Church's teachings about the obligations Christians owe to other people, including those within their family circles and beyond. Pastoral theology needs to address both of these branches of Christian morality, not one or the other.

Logos Precedes Ethos

All social practices embody some logic, some meaning intrinsic to the practice itself and not imposed on the practice by someone's mental decision to give the practice meaning *y* rather than meaning *z*. The typical theological expression of this principle is that *logos* precedes *ethos*. This principle was a central theme in the theology of Romano Guardini. In various works, including the final chapter of his *The Spirit of the Liturgy*, Guardini argued that ethos is now taking precedence. Many moderns and

---

18. Benedict XVI, *Deus Caritas Est*, §17.
19. Ouellet, *Divine Likeness*, 140.

especially postmoderns try to impose meaning on their actions *ex post facto* by a will that declares itself to be autonomous of God, of nature, and even of fate. For example, the "fate" of having been born male or female is now regarded by proponents of gender ideology as something that can be overcome by a mere mental decision. One can simply "identify" as a person of the opposite gender from that of one's biological sex. Rejected is the notion, common to Hebraic, Greco-Roman, and Christian modes of thought, from the author of the book of Genesis to Aristotle and Virgil and onto the Church fathers, of there being such a thing as a human ecology, or natural way of being human.

Ontology is now generally regarded by postmodern scholars, including postmodern theologians, as an oppressive concept, limiting human freedom. Ratzinger regards the philosophy of Hegel as a watershed moment in this movement of opposition to ontology and to nature and natural law. He observes that, for Hegel, being itself is now regarded as time, and the *logos* becomes itself in history.[20] Accordingly, "truth becomes a function of time; the true is not that which simply *is* true, for truth is not simply that which *is*, it is true for a time because it is part of the becoming of truth, which *is* by becoming."[21] From this, Ratzinger concludes:

> This means that, of their very nature, the contours between true and untrue are less sharply defined: it means above all that man's basic attitude to yesterday's truth consists precisely in abandoning it, in assimilating it into today's truth; assimilation becomes the form of preservation. What was constitutive yesterday is constitutive today only as that which has been assimilated. In the realm of Marxist thought, on the other hand, this ideology of reconciliation (as it might be called) is converted into an ideology of revolution; assimilation becomes transformation. The concept of the continuity of being in the changeableness of time is now understood as an ideological superstructure conditioned by the interests of those who are favoured by things as they are. ... The notion of truth comes to be regarded as an expression of the vested interests of a particular historical moment; it gives place to the notion of progress: the "true" is whatever serves progress, that is, whatever serves the logic of history.[22]

---

20. Ratzinger, *Principles of Catholic Theology*, 16. For a more extensive treatment of this subject, see the author's article, Rowland, "Ratzinger on Timelessness."

21. Ratzinger, *Principles of Catholic Theology*, 16.

22. Ratzinger, *Principles of Catholic Theology*, 16–17.

Having offered this account of the logic driving Hegelian historicism, Ratzinger makes the observation that discussions about theological content remain mere "isolated and losing skirmishes" if no consideration is given to these questions: Is there, in the course of historical time, a recognizable identity of man with himself? Is there a human "nature"? Is there a truth that remains true in every historical time because it *is* true?[23]

Ratzinger, of course, answers in the affirmative. He believes in human nature, and he believes in truth that transcends history. This might be described as a classically Christian position. However, the spirit of Hegel has infused significant schools of contemporary theology, some of them claiming the Catholic appellation. Thomas Guarino has summarized the significance of this in the following paragraph:

> If one accepts postmodernity more fully, thereby abandoning some form of foundationalist ontology, one's entire understanding of revelation, especially the role of Christian doctrine, is deeply affected. Either the truth of the gospel must simply be asserted, breaking its link with a rationally elaborated infrastructure. Or, by opening a fissure between ontology and theology, one develops a quite different understanding of what the deposit of faith is, how it develops, and the type of continuity and identity proper to it. Particularly affected is the type of truth mediated by it.[24]

Ratzinger would no doubt strongly concur with Guarino's observation. He has described the issue of the correct understanding of the relationship between ontology and history as the most severe crisis faced by Catholic theology in twentieth century.[25] Moreover, using an expression borrowed from the psychoanalyst Albert Görres, Ratzinger has described the mentality that wants to give priority to *ethos* over *logos* as the "Hinduization" of the faith.

The Hegelian influence on Catholic theology is strongest in versions of liberation theology where there is an express preference for the "priority of praxis" and where, at its most extreme, dogmatic theology in the form of the creeds is dismissed as unacceptable "logocentrism."

---

23. Ratzinger, *Principles of Catholic Theology*, 17.
24. Guarino, "Postmodernity," 660–61.
25. Ratzinger, *Principles of Catholic Theology*, 160.

The Unity of Truth, History, and the Kerygma

In a collection of essays titled "Dogma and Method: Toward Interdisciplinarity in Dogmatic Theology," Robert Wozniak echoes Ratzinger and argues that revealed truth, history, and the proclamation of the word (kerygma) need to be kept together. He writes:

> These formulae [doctrines], for their part, do not replace history, but reveal it in what is most important to it. For Ratzinger, therefore, there is an important relationship between history, metaphysics, kerygma, and dogma. The word of faith (kerygma) always refers to a specific history. Together with faith, it seeks to be understood and effectively communicated. To this end, they enter into a creative dialogue with metaphysics. Ratzinger is, in such a perspective, one of the clearest exponents of synthetic theology, maintaining the need for dialogue with culture. Christianity is inscribed in such a vision in the great odyssey of the human spirit, which seeks the supreme truth. An important moment here is the emphasis placed on dogma, which preserves the historical experience of the Church. It is not, therefore, a form of speculative metaphysics, an expression of the Hellenization of Christianity, but a living transmission of faith based on experience. The dogma uses metaphysical concepts to the extent that they help to concretely express, preserve, and transfer this historical experience of the Church based on the deposit of Revelation. Any negative dialectic between history, preaching, metaphysics, and dogma becomes unacceptable. The dogma is, in fact, a shortened formula in which all these elements are synthesized: the historical experience is expressed by means of precise concepts which ultimately serve the kerygma.[26]

Wozniak concluded that "among such issues as historical thinking, the dynamics of the proclamation of the evangelical message (kerygma), metaphysics looking for the most adequate understanding of existence, and finally, theology with its dogmas—all these constitute a kind of differentiated whole."[27]

Wozniak's list of elements that constitute the kind of differentiated whole Christopher Dawson found so compelling can also be found in Josef Andreas Jungmann SJ's 1936 publication *Die Frohbotschaft und unsere Glaubensverkündigung* (*The Good News and Our Proclamation of*

---

26. Wozniak, *Dogma and Method*, 24.
27. Wozniak, *Dogma and Method*, 25.

the Faith). Jungmann emphasized the importance of not simply teaching dogma and "rejoicing in its systematization" but of linking the "logical unity of the system to the teleological unity of the good news which, as a conceptual unity, guarantees insight into the objects of the divine plan for salvation in that all mysteries merge to a 'mysterium of the divine will' (Ephesians 1:9)."[28] For this to occur, Jungmann observed that there must also be an engagement with Scripture, the theology of the Church fathers, and with the liturgy, and thus, as a supplement to strictly dogmatic theology, one must offer a "kerygmatic theology," the "central theme of which is the economy of salvation" and the language of which favors that of the "conceptual images" of the apostolic and ancient ecclesial proclamation.[29]

In other words, dogmatic theology needs to be presented in the context of other elements of the kerygma and the links between each of the elements made obvious to the faithful; otherwise, the organic unity of the Christian life that has appealed so strongly to numerous converts like Dawson lies hidden from vision.

Reading the Signs of the Times

In addition to the proclamation of the kerygma as a "differentiated whole," or "organic unity," pastoral theology needs to address the issue of the dangers to the faith in different parts of the world. It needs, in other words, to warn the sheep about the various threats to their flourishing. This is sometimes called "discerning the signs of the times." This expression is one of those phrases that was popularized at the Second Vatican Council and can mean different things to different people. For some, it has come to mean being sensitive to social trends so as to correlate the faith to these trends. This project was highly popular among pastoral theologians in the 1960s and '70s and went by the label "correlationism." Their aim was to correlate the faith to the culture of modernity. The theologian whose name was most strongly associated with this project was Edward Schillibeeckx. Today second-generation Schillibeexkxians, located in Belgium and Holland, speak of "re-contextualizing the faith to the culture of postmodernity." Either way, it is something other than the faith that positions the faith. For this reason, correlationism and its postmodern

---

28. Jungmann, *Frohbotschaft und unsere Glaubensverkündigung*, 59.

29. Jungmann, *Frohbotschaft und unsere Glaubensverkündigung*, 59. Quoted by Gottlieb Söhngen in *Symbol und Wirklichkeit*, 53.

twin, recontextualization, are not popular with Catholic theologians who believe that the kerygma needs to be unapologetically Trinitarian. As Bishop Robert Barron has summarized the issue: the question is whether Christ positions culture or whether some culture, be it modern, postmodern, or something else, positions Christ. Both St. John Paul II and Ratzinger/Benedict were firmly of the view that pastoral strategies need to be thoroughly Trinitarian and Christocentric, and Ratzinger argued that the references to the signs of the times in the Synoptic Gospels are thoroughly eschatological (not sociological) and are therefore making a point about the significance of the incarnation and hence Christology and Trinitarian theology. Ratzinger was critical of a sociological reading of these scriptural passages and the pastoral project of correlationism. The Church, he declared, is not a haberdashery shop that updates its windows with each new fashion season.[30] Even more emphatically, his *Communio* colleague, Hans Urs von Balthasar, states:

> The Church, they say, to appear credible, must be in tune with the times. If taken seriously, that would mean that Christ was in tune with the times when he carried out his mission and died on the Cross, a scandal to the Jews and folly to the Gentiles. Of course, the scandal took place in tune with the times—at the favourable times of the Father, in the fullness of time, just when Israel was ripe, like fruit ready to burst, and the Gentiles were ready to receive it on their own soil. Modern is something Christ never was, and God willing, never will be.[31]

To criticize a sociological reading of the "signs of the times" passages in Scripture is not to say, however, that one should ignore social trends, to place one's head in the sand like an ostrich and simply dismiss social practices or social fashions that are not derivative of the Christian proclamation as of no concern to the Christian. Rather, one must, in the words of Graham Ward, "unmask the cultural idols, providing genealogical accounts of the assumptions, politics, and hidden metaphysics of the specific secular varieties of knowledge—with respect to the constructive, therapeutic project of disseminating the Gospel."[32] In other words, one must make an intellectual and moral assessment of the compatibility of fashionable social practices and their *zeitgeist* with the kerygma. One

---

30. Ratzinger, *Co-Workers of the Truth*, 314.
31. Balthasar, *Wer ist ein Christ*, 30.
32. Ward, "Radical Orthodoxy," 104.

finds this kind of analysis in the publications of Wojtyła/John Paul II and Ratzinger/Benedict and many other theologians associated with the International Catholic Review named *Communio*. A concrete example is found in the fact that the very first lines of John Paul II's first encyclical, *Redemptor Hominis*, were directed against the first lines of Karl Marx's *Communist Manifesto*, while the first footnote in the first encyclical of the pontificate of Benedict XVI was directed against Nietzsche's indictment of Christianity as a crime against life itself, presented most forcefully in Nietzsche's *Beyond Good and Evil: On the Genealogy of Morality*. Unmasking "hidden metaphysical assumptions" is not an easy academic exercise; it requires a high level of learning and scholarship, and thus forms part of the "brief" or "mission" of the pastoral theologian.

Conclusion

Returning to the pastoral ovine metaphor, one might argue that pastoral theologians need to alert the sheep to the presence of "bad pasture" or "bad social practices inconsistent with the kerygma," and they also need to identify wolves in sheep's clothing, that is, purveyors of ideas and social practices hostile to the faith. It is impossible for the pastoral theologian to perform this service without a sound background in dogmatic theology. Conversely, dogmatic theologians need to follow the advice of Moleski, Jungmann, Wozniak, and others and present Catholic dogma within the context of the whole kerygma, so that its pastoral relevance is obvious to the faithful and a panoramic vision of the organic unity of the faith is unveiled. Above all, the fracture between dogmatic theology and moral theology needs to be healed, so that the faithful understand that moral precepts are not random decrees handed down from a God who is beyond goodness and truth but are, rather, our guidelines for sharing in Christ's virtues and participating in the life and love of the Holy Trinity.

Bibliography

Balthasar, Hans Urs von. *Wer ist ein Christ*? Freiburg, Germ.: Johannes Verlag Einsiedeln, 1965.

Benedict XVI, Pope. *Caritas in Veritate*. Rome: Editrice Vaticane, 2009.

———. *Deus Caritas Est*. Rome: Editrice Vaticane, 2005.

———. *Spe Salvi*. Rome: Editrice Vaticane, 2007.

Clark, David W. "William of Ockham on Right Reason." *Speculum* 48 (1973) 13–36.

Dawson, Christopher. "Why I Am a Catholic." *Chesterton Review* 9, no. 2 (1983) 110–13.
Francis, Pope. *Evangelii Gaudium*. Rome: Editrice Vaticane, 2013.
———. *Lumen Fidei*. Rome: Editrice Vaticane, 2013.
Guarino, Thomas. "Postmodernity and Five Fundamental Theological Issues." *Theological Studies* 57, no. 4 (1996) 654–90.
John Paul II, Pope. *Dives in Misericordia*. Rome: Editrice Vaticane, 1980.
———. *Dominum et Vivificantem*. Rome: Editrice Vaticane, 1986.
———. *Man and Woman He Created Them: A Theology of the Body*. Translated by Michael Waldstein. Boston: Pauline, 2006.
———. *Redemptor Hominis*. Rome: Editrice Vaticane, 1979.
———. *Veritatis Splendor*. Rome: Editrice Vaticane, 1993.
Jungmann, Josef Andreas. *Die Frohbotschaft und unsere Glaubensverkündigung*. Regensburg, Germ.: Pustet, 1936.
Melina, Livio. *Sharing in Christ's Virtues: For a Renewal of Moral Theology in the Light of Veritatis Splendor*. Washington, DC: Catholic University of America Press, 2001.
Moleski, Martin X. *Personal Catholicism: The Theological Epistemologies of John Henry Newman and Michael Polanyi*. Washington, DC: Catholic University of America Press, 2000.
Montag, John. "Revelation: The False Legacy of Suárez." In *Radical Orthodoxy: A New Theology*, edited by John Milbank et al., 38–64. London: Routledge, 2002.
O'Shea, Gerard. "Historical Discontinuity in Contemporary Views on Revelation." PhD diss., John Paul II Institute for Marriage and Family, Melbourne, 2007.
Ouellet, Marc. *Divine Likeness: Towards a Trinitarian Anthropology of the Family*. Grand Rapids: Eerdmans, 2006.
Pagis, Julie. "The Politicization of Religious Commitments: Reassuring the Determinants of Participation in May '68." *Revue Française de Science Politique* 60, no. 1 (2010) 61–89.
Ratzinger, Joseph. *Co-Workers of the Truth: Meditations for Every Day of the Year*. San Francisco: Ignatius, 1992.
———. *Principles of Catholic Theology: Building Stones for a Fundamental Theology*. San Francisco: Ignatius, 1987.
Rowland, Tracey. "Ratzinger on the Timelessness of the Truth." *Communio International Catholic Review* (Summer 2017) 242–65.
Söhngen, Gottlieb. *Symbol und Wirklichkeit im Kultmysterium*. Bonn: Hanstein, 1937.
Ward, Graham. "Radical Orthodoxy and/as Cultural Politics." In *Radical Orthodoxy: A Catholic Enquiry*, edited by Laurence Paul Hemming, 97–111. Aldershot, UK: Ashgate, 2000.
Wozniak, Robert J. *Dogma and Method: Toward Interdisciplinarity in Dogmatic Theology*. Rome: Santa Croce, 2021.

10

Theology and the Koinonial *Christian Life*

Kevin Wagner

> ἢ ψυχῆς ἐπιστασίαν δέξασθαι, ἢ θεολογίᾳ προσβαλεῖν, οὐκ
> ἀσφαλὲς εἶναι γινώσκω.
>
> *I think it is dangerous either to accept the responsibility for other souls or to take up theology.*
>
> —ST. GREGORY OF NAZIANZUS, *ORATION* 20.1

St. Gregory Nazianzen, the fourth-century Cappadocian father, is considered such a master of theology that he is known simply as Gregory the Theologian. Despite his mastery—or perhaps because of it—Gregory feigns reticence to theologize on account of his belief that the theologian ought to be one who "first presents himself to God as a living sacrifice, or rather, becomes a living holy temple of the living God."[1] In fact, what Gregory demands before one can theologize is purity forged through an encounter with God himself.[2] For both Hebrews and Christians, purity is attained through ritual—ritual that is performed by and within the community and, once performed, has communal implications. The task of the theologian is deeply embedded in the life of the community (NT: *koinōnia*). Divorced from it, the theologian is unfit to perform her or his

---

1. Gregory, *Oration* 20.4, 109.
2. Gregory, *Oration* 20.4, 109.

task. The claim of this chapter is that separated from the community, the work of the theologian suffers. Here, we will seek to demonstrate some of the dangers of separating theology from its proper ecclesial foundation and theologians from their natural home, the Christian community. We hope, however, that this will be counterbalanced by an optimistic account of ways to bridge these divisions, some of which have grown more markedly in the post-Vatican II era.

We will begin our discussion by establishing what we mean by our key terms: theology, *koinonia*, and the *koinonial* Christian life. Following this, we will offer a brief reflection on why the fracture between theology and the *koinonial* Christian life has grown more concerning in the years following the Second Vatican Council. Here, we will focus particularly on the fact that many theologates in the West are now often secular in nature and corporatized, and that they are often comprised primarily of lay theologians, rather than secular priests and religious brothers and sisters. In our third and final section, we will directly address the problem of theology done outside of communal life, paying particular attention to the drawbacks this has for both individual theologians and the *ecclesia*. In the process we will proffer some thoughts on how the theologian and the theologate might work to heal the fracture for the benefit of the individual theologian, the theologate, and the wider *ecclesia*.

Before launching into our argument proper, it behoves me to give some personal context for this discussion, a disclaimer, as it were. This is necessary as I am not writing as a disinterested bystander but rather as an advocate for theology being done by those who are tapped into the *ecclesia*, a unified body comprised of diverse members. I am a member of the international *Communauté de l'Emmanuel* (Emmanuel Community). Beginning in 1972 in Paris, and formally founded in 1976, the Emmanuel Community is a fruit of the Catholic Charismatic Renewal. While the Community is still predominantly a lay organization (11,500 lay members), there are also around 275 priests, 100 seminarians, and 225 women and men consecrated celibates. There are also ten priests of the Community who have been consecrated bishops.

Since the earliest years, the Community has worked to ensure the successful integration of members in these various states of life in order to better support the flourishing of individual members and to be better able to work as a united ecclesial body for the mission. Underpinning the efforts of the Community to bring together members in these different states of life has been the ecclesiology of the Second Vatican Council. In the preamble to the latest version of the Community's statutes, we read:

> The Ecclesiology of Communion, and in particular the communion between baptismal priesthood and ministerial priesthood lived in the complementarity of states of life, is at the heart of the spiritual, fraternal and missionary life of Emmanuel Community members.[3]

The Community thus affirms that "the presence of all the states of life in the Community is an essential part of the Community vocation."[4] Furthermore, in its statutes, the Community explicitly acknowledges the interrelated nature of the common and ministerial priesthoods, quoting *Lumen Gentium* directly:

> Though they differ from one another in essence and not only in degree, the common priesthood of the faithful and the ministerial or hierarchical priesthood are nonetheless interrelated: each of them in its own special way is a participation in the one priesthood of Christ.[5]

What we see then, is that the Emmanuel Community seeks to bring together persons in various states of life, recognizing the essential difference and complementarity of the various states. In seeking a unity that embraces, rather than rejects, diversity, the Community members are better placed to answer the call of the Council fathers to "bear witness to Christ and give an answer to those who seek an account of that hope of eternal life which is in them."[6]

---

3. Emmanuel Community, "Statutes," §90.

4. Indeed, "it is essential both in evangelisation and in the sanctification of each person. Experience has shown how productive working together is in mission. The faithfulness of each person to his or her own calling contributes to the sanctification of all" (Emmanuel Community, *Guide to Community Life*, 20).

5. Translation as used in Emmanuel Community, "Statutes," §90n3.

6. Second Vatican Council, *Lumen Gentium*, §10.

Definitions—Theology, *Koinonia*, and the *Koinonial* Christian Life

Theology

Gavin D'Costa, in his 2012 article "On Being a Catholic Theologian," makes the claim that "all theology is ecclesial theology, that is, it originates from a churched context."[7] Here we will argue that Catholic theology deserves the name only really when the theologian is embedded within a living Christian community. So, what is theology, and what is its relationship to the Christian community? D'Costa defines Roman Catholic theology as "basically prayerful, intellectually rigorous, communally tested and accountable reflection upon the three sources of authority that feed theology: Scripture, tradition, and magisterium."[8] Essentially an expansion on the Anselmian definition of theology (*fides quaerens intellectum*), D'Costa sets out useful criteria for assessing how "theological" particular works of theology actually are. Of particular utility for our purpose are D'Costa's descriptors: prayerfulness, intellectual rigor, communal testing, and accountability. A claim we will make here is that it is too often the case—even amongst excellent theologians—that theological reflection does not meet these four D'Costian criteria.[9] There are, no doubt, innumerable reasons for this, but here we will examine how a failure to theologize in a strong ecclesial setting tends to lead to theological reflection that does not meet these criteria.

Koinonia and the *Koinonial* Christian Life

The nuances of the noun *koinonia* have been widely addressed in post-Vatican II literature. Benoît-Dominique de La Soujeole, OP, crafts a definition of the term as it is used in the New Testament. In his view,

> *koinōnia* expresses three aspects of the same reality and not three different realities: the fact of sharing along with the correlative fact of taking part (receiving what is proposed) make up a reciprocal relationship that thereby engenders the communal

---

7. D'Costa, "On Being a Catholic Theologian," 3.
8. D'Costa, "On Being a Catholic Theologian," 4.
9. While failure to meet these criteria does not automatically invalidate the theology done, the omission of one or more of these criteria does leave the work open to critique.

reality. We find ourselves here at the heart of the doctrine of the Mystical Body.[10]

Koinonia, in this scriptural sense, is thus a mutual donation and reception of gifts and persons that make manifest the Body of Christ.

The Dominican goes on to offer helpful analyses of *koinonia* (and its Latin equivalent *communio*) as used in patristic theology and Vatican II documents. He concludes with the following proposal:

> The ecclesiological notion of *koinonia-communio* expresses the divine community inasmuch as man participates in it according to a Christic economy that conforms individuals to Christ. This *koinonia-communio* is perfect in the Church in heaven. It is still characterized by pilgrimage, progress, and a fight against evil in the Church here below. Yet these different states do not form different churches, for these are different states of participating in the same reality—the one community-as-divine-beatitude— and always through the same mediation of Christ's humanity.[11]

De La Soujeole thus aids us in clarifying the meaning of the phrase "the *koinonial* Christian life." Such a life is one that is embedded in the *ecclesia militans* with a view to the *ecclesia triumphans*—in sum, a pilgrim's life.

The Fracture

The principal claim of this chapter is that theology is best done as a pilgrim amongst pilgrims and that when it is not, there is substantial risk of this theological work failing to meet the D'Costian criteria set out above. It is the view of the editors of this book (and myself) that there are significant numbers of Catholic theologians who do not live fully the *koinonial* Christian life and that this is to the detriment of both the theologians themselves and the wider *ecclesia*. So why has this situation developed, and what can be done to improve it? There are, no doubt, plenty of reasons for this. Here we will focus particularly on the changing nature of Catholic theologates and the implications this development presents for those who staff them.

When once theological faculties were established, overseen, and funded by bishops for the purpose of priestly and religious formation, now the links between faculties and bishops are often far weaker. One

---

10. La Soujeole, *Introduction to the Mystery*, 455.
11. La Soujeole, *Introduction to the Mystery*, 464.

significant reason for this is the fact that theologates are often now corporatized and subject to the demands of secular regulators.[12] Sometimes this is because these faculties are embedded within secular institutes (such was the case of the University of Bristol when D'Costa wrote his article in 2012).[13] Other times, this is due to a desire for the institute to offer degrees recognized by secular regulators (which is the case for Vianney College in Wagga Wagga, Australia, which seeks to satisfy the requirements of both Charles Sturt University in Wagga Wagga and the Urbaniana University in Rome).[14]

A major result of this shift to a secular and corporate market for theology has been a shift in the staffing of the theologate. In many countries, faculties of theology are no longer the domain of only the cleric and religious. Certainly, the increase in lay theologians being employed in theological faculties has brought with it some benefits. For instance, the mingling of academics in different vocational states brings with it a certain richness, making *koinonia* manifest in a new way. This development has also freed up clerics and religious for other activities. On the other hand, this movement from clerical and religious theologians to lay practitioners has brought about significant challenges, both for institutions and for individual theologians. Most markedly, being a theologian has become one way among many by which one may earn a living. Consequently, it may no longer be presumed that the theologian understands his or her work as a vocation, for he or she may instead treat it merely as a job. Furthermore, given that corporate workplaces are competitive by nature, the theologian can fall easily into an individualistic mindset in order to protect her or his job. This can often have serious consequences for the quality of the theology "produced."[15] Before moving on to consider the consequences of individualism in the theologate, it is useful to clarify what is meant by the vocational nature of the theological occupation in order to highlight the ecclesial nature of the role.

---

12. Hand in hand with this corporatization of theology faculties is the shift in view of tertiary education from being useful in and of itself to being yet another commodity to purchase. See Hanchin's wonderful, but grim, account of other consequences of the commodification of the higher education sector, "From Below Upwards."

13. D'Costa, "On Being a Catholic Theologian," 13.

14. "Seminary and Vocations."

15. We use this word intentionally to reflect the corporate nature of theologates.

The Vocation of the Theologian

The French philosopher and spiritual writer Antonin-Gilbert Sertillanges, OP, is possibly best known in the English-speaking world for his book *The Intellectual Life*. Written in 1921, this text seeks to inspire and direct those who wish to live a life less ordinary, an intellectual life. Sertillanges begins his work arguing that the intellectual life—regardless of one's chosen field of study—is a vocation. The Dominican is not referring here merely to anyone who seeks to engage the intellect. Rather, he uses the term "vocation" to refer to

> those who intend to make intellectual work their life, whether they are free to give themselves up to study, or whether, though engaged in some calling, they hold happily in reserve, as a supplement of their activity and as a reward, the development and deepening of their mind.[16]

Why, might we ask, is this decision to pursue the life of the intellect a vocation? It is thus, Sertillanges declares, as "it is written in our instincts, in our powers, in a sort of inner impulse of which reason must judge."[17] He continues, using an analogy, to link vocation to nature; he states, "Our dispositions are like the chemical properties which determine, for every body, the combinations into which that body can enter."[18] One's vocation, however, is not simply a gifted product of nature. Rather, it is a call from God and a call from, what Sertillanges describes beautifully, our "first nature."[19] The intellectual life, then, is a gift and a call that engages the will.

Almost seventy years after Sertillanges wrote his *Intellectual Life*, the Congregation for the Doctrine of the Faith published its instruction, *Donum Veritatis*. Here the Congregation described theology as an exercise in truth-seeking that is rooted in the *ecclesia*; that is, it is a mission of the Church that is at the service of truth.[20] The practitioner of theology is therefore engaged in the mission of the Church and is tasked with helping her pastors to preach, teach, and explain the truth of the gospel in new times and contexts. Given that theology is a mission, and missions

---

16. Sertillanges, *Intellectual Life*, 3.
17. Sertillanges, *Intellectual Life*, 4.
18. Sertillanges, *Intellectual Life*, 4.
19. Sertillanges, *Intellectual Life*, 4.
20. Congregation for the Doctrine of the Faith, *Donum Veritatis*, §§6, 8, 11.

are bestowed rather than grasped, it follows that the theological life is a vocation.

If this is so, what shape ought this vocation take? Mary Ann Donovan, in her examination of the vocation of the theologian, posits that "taken in its entirety, no. 12 of *Lumen gentium* can serve as an outline of the vocation of the theologian."[21] She explains:

> With the whole people of God, the theologian is called to adhere to the faith, to penetrate it more deeply through right judgment, and to apply it more fully in daily life. Specifically as theologian, she or he is to perform these tasks by the exercise of the scholarly discipline of teaching, with the research and writing that solid teaching demands. As a member of the people of God gifted with a charism for teaching, then, the theologian is called to exercise that gift for the renewal and building up of the Church, and can expect his or her gift to be tested by those who hold office in the Church.[22]

On the one hand then, the theologian has certain obligations and expectations imposed on her or him by virtue of the missionary nature of the vocation. On the other hand, the Church as a body is responsible for the nurturing and growth of the theologian who is called to serve the Church. One needs only to consider the figure of Paul, the *Didache*, or the tumultuous life of Origen of Alexandria to see that the Church has long recommended supporting the work of evangelists, prophets, preachers, and teachers.[23] This support is not, however, limited to the financial and practical but extends also to the provision of a milieu in which the intellectual life is encouraged and stimulated, and where spiritual aid and direction is forthcoming.

This is affirmed by Joseph Cardinal Ratzinger, in his introductory statement on the occasion of the promulgation of *Donum Veritatis*. Here he declared two things essential for the Catholic theologian:

> First, the methodological rigor which is part and parcel of the business of scholarship; in this regard, the document [*Donum Veritatis*] refers to philosophy, the historical disciplines and

---

21. Donovan, "Vocation of the Theologian," 9.
22. Donovan, "Vocation of the Theologian," 9.
23. Examples of such support include for Paul, Phil 4:15–20; from the *Didache* 13.1–7; and in Holmes, *Apostolic Fathers*, 365; while regarding Origen, we note the financial assistance given by Julia Mammaea, the mother of the Roman emperor Alexander Severus (McGuckin, *SCM Press A-Z*, 11).

the human sciences as privileged partners of the theologian. But [the theologian] also has need of inner participation in the organic structure of the Church; he [or she] needs that faith which is prayer, contemplation and life. Only in this symphony does theology come into being.[24]

The first of these essential components ought to be provided for by the life of the theological academy, though as we shall soon see, the corporatization and commodification of tertiary education can hinder this. Engagement in prayer and contemplation and participation in the life of the Church are, however, perhaps harder to guarantee, as these activities presume freely chosen faith and the will to submit to the Divine Other who reveals himself through and in the Church. Given the invitational nature of faith, the Church cannot ensure provision of spiritual nourishment to those who reject the invitation to participate in the life of the *ecclesia*.

Consequences of Individualism and Solutions

So, what are the consequences of theology done by individuals who fail to invest themselves in the give-and-take of the *koinonial* Christian life? There are, one suspects, plenty of possible consequences, but here we will focus on five, the first three of which are drawn directly from our reflection on D'Costa's definition of theology:[25]

1. Theology may not benefit from prayer;
2. Theology may not be intellectually rigorous or communally tested and theologians not held accountable for their work;
3. Theology may not be founded on the three sources of Catholic theology;
4. Theology may lead to division rather than to unity; and
5. Theology may lack grounding in reality.

---

24. Ratzinger, "On the 'Instruction,'" 105. Ratzinger defends the necessity of applying both faith and reason to questions of theology, declaring that "theology presupposes faith" and that "both faith and rational reflection are integral to theology." Indeed, "the absence of either principle would bring about theology's demise" (Ratzinger, "Spiritual Basis," 55, 57).

25. We do not claim this list is exhaustive. Furthermore, we do not adopt a fatalistic view that individualism must, by necessity, lead to these consequences.

For each of these consequences, we will first set out the problem and then show how the *koinonial* Christian life can serve to prevent these consequences.

1. Theology May Not Benefit from Prayer

Evagrius of Pontus famously stated, "If you are a theologian, you will pray truly; and if you pray truly, you will be a theologian."[26] Indeed, divorcing theology from prayer and the spiritual life risks emptying theology of its Divine Object, reducing it to a science of a foreign or distant god. It is necessary then that the theologian has an active life of prayer. However, while prayer is first and foremost the act of an individual person, it is also a practice that is nurtured and promoted by communal life. Acts 2:42 shows that involvement in the prayer life of the early Church was one of the four characteristics of Christian living, alongside listening to the teaching of the apostles, fellowship (*koinonia*), and participation in the breaking of the bread. Communal and personal (not individual) prayer were, we may presume, normative experiences for the first Christians.

The vibrant Christian community can provide numerous supports for helping the theologian to have a fruitful prayer life. In the first instance, the Eucharist is the source and summit of the Christian life, so therefore its regular celebration is a powerful means by which one can come to knowledge of God. Next, nonliturgical communal prayer is a typical feature of *koinonial* Christian life. In the Emmanuel Community, for instance, a daily time of praise, preferably in a communal setting, is mandatory for all members. This is not an imposition but, rather, an invitation to turn one's gaze outward to the Source of all blessings. Parish life should also provide opportunities for nonliturgical community prayer. Another way communal living can help the theologian to remain faithful to prayer is through the prayerful support of community members. As fellow members of the Body, community members are able to offer prayer and supplication for each other (Eph 6:18). Finally, communal living should involve encouraging one another to keep the commitments one makes when becoming Christian; this includes the commitment to pray. To take another personal example, members of the Emmanuel Community commit to a long time of prayer each day. Each member is encouraged to discuss his or her efforts to keep to this commitment with

---

26. Evagrius, *Chapters on Prayer*, §60.

one trusted member (a companion). This private forum provides a safe space for encouraging and challenging fellow members in living faithfully the commitments of community life, including the commitment to prayer.

All this is well and good, one might say, but how can the benefits of this way of life be replicated in the theologate? This is a good question, as the theologian does not sign up to join an ecclesial community.[27] Furthermore, the realities of the academic life are such that it is very difficult to incorporate prayer—liturgical or otherwise—into one's day. On a related note, we could argue that there has been an increase in technological-based communication in our theology faculties and a paralleled decrease in real personal interaction that is detrimental to the spiritual lives of theologians.

A key reason for this is the rapid development of communication technologies. New technologies have made it possible for people to be connected to the world twenty-four hours a day. There would be few active theologians who pass a day without being distracted, for good or ill, by students, colleagues, or administrators through email, student management systems, telephone and video conferencing, and other forms of communication. In themselves, these technologies are useful and can be used to build communion, to show charity, to teach, and to help build the earthly and heavenly kingdoms. They can, however, make it difficult for one to focus on the truly essential. Furthermore, this electronic noise can make silence—both exterior and interior—an impossibility.

Silence, Cardinal Robert Sarah declares, "has come into disrepute."[28] He continues, asserting that "this is the symptom of a serious, worrisome illness [for the] real questions of life are posed in silence."[29] Such a claim ought to give even the most secular thinker pause to think. For the theologian, the one who is called to make God the object of her or his work, the cardinal has an even stronger message:

---

27. D'Costa makes precisely this point, though he declares that prayer is necessary for the theologian: "The theologian is part of a community of prayer, involved and shaped by its liturgies and practices—which includes 'personal' prayer (not 'individual' prayer, for such a category is a modern invention). I choose this feature as this is not a prerequisite to do theology in the university, but I would argue that it is a necessary condition for an ecclesial theologian" (D'Costa, "On Being a Catholic Theologian," 9).

28. Sarah and Diat, *Power of Silence*, 27.

29. Sarah and Diat, *Power of Silence*, 27.

Silence is the only means by which to enter into this great mystery of God. I am certain that silence is a divine liberation that unifies man and places him at the center of himself, in the depths of God's mysteries. In silence, man is absorbed by the divine and the world's movements no longer have any hold on his soul. In silence, we set out from God and we arrive at God.[30]

Silence is thus essential for intimate communion with God (*theosis*, divinization), in whose image and likeness we are made. Certainly, this communion is a prerequisite for salvation, but it is also necessary—to speak colloquially—in order that heart knowledge can inform head knowledge; that is, intimacy with God transforms and informs the intellect such that it is purified and perfected. In a nutshell, theological acumen needs to be partnered with spiritual growth, which demands that the theologian discover, or rediscover, the power of silence.

So, to return to the essence of our question, how can our theology faculties transform to become truly prayerful Christian communities? First, our faculties must become liturgical communities—in particular, eucharistic communities. Second, prayer must become a regular feature of faculty life. Here, one must guard against prayer being "tacked on" to faculty events; rather, prayer should develop organically to respond to the needs and desires of faculty members. A feature of this prayer could be formal and informal moments of prayer for one another.[31] Third, space should be found in the faculty calendar for regular moments of silence. These moments could include, for example, annual retreats, monthly "desert days," or weekly holy hours. On a related note, some businesses and schools implement a policy of not sending or replying to emails outside of business hours. This could be a useful means for reducing electronic "noise."

---

30. Sarah and Diat, *Power of Silence*, 48. Later, the cardinal declares poignantly and powerfully, "I realize that theologians study this mystery [of God's very self] and translate into human words the results of their research. But these words will be tolerable only if the study of them is rooted in silence and leads to silence. Otherwise they will become vain chattering. Theology must rediscover a contemplative language" (Sarah and Diat, *Power of Silence*, 127–28).

31. While it would be wonderful for faculties to develop a culture of accountability to help members to remain faithful to prayer, it is difficult to imagine widespread uptake of this idea!

2. Theology May Not Be Intellectually Rigorous or Communally Tested and Theologians Not Held Accountable for Their Work

In medieval universities, the *disputatio* was a fundamental feature of the pedagogy.[32] Livesey notes that

> disputations were central to the university scholar's formation: part of the bachelor's training involved attendance at his master's disputations, and in time he was obliged to "respond" in a private mock dispute with his master or other students.[33]

These disputations were held to demonstrate "competence and creativity [and] the ability to 'think on one's feet.'"[34] While there were, no doubt, instances when the power of the master was abused in the context of these disputations, there is much to recommend the practice for ensuring academic rigor.[35]

A healthy culture of organized and civil disputation or debate in the university theological faculty is a powerful remedy for poor theology. Such a culture can develop, however, only in the right type of environment. In commercial workplaces, like modern university faculties, there are significant barriers to establishing a sympathetic environment for debate. Where competition for funds, promotions, and prestige take precedence over sharing in the success of one's colleagues, it is difficult to foster an environment in which debating builds bridges and bolsters rigor.

Ratzinger raises the related matter of dialogue in his 1983 article "The Essence of the Academy and Its Freedom." Here, Ratzinger begins by noticing that the academy is primarily a "place of dialogue."[36] He then sets out the elements of the dialogue in the order in which they present themselves: speech, listening, encounter, comprehension, and, finally, reciprocal understanding.[37] What Ratzinger seems to be describing as

---

32. Conti notes Aristotle's articulation of the characteristics of dialectical encounters in his *Topics* (Conti, "Using Debate," 357). See also Livesey, "Medieval University," 233.

33. Livesey, "Medieval University," 233.

34. Livesey, "Medieval University," 233.

35. Indeed, Conti argues that the practice of the disputation, adapted to the modern form of the debate, should be promoted as a valid pedagogical tool in Italian universities today (Conti, "Using Debate," 355–66).

36. Ratzinger, "Essence of the Academy," 32.

37. Ratzinger, "Essence of the Academy," 32–33.

the fruit of true dialogue is an exchange of persons, for "after the act of listening," he states, "I am another man, my own being is enriched and deepened because it is united with the being of the other and, through it, with the being of the world."[38] This dialogue, however, is contingent on each of the persons taking heed of "the interior master, the truth." Failure to do so, Ratzinger poignantly declares, would lead to dialogue being "nothing more than a discussion among the deaf."[39] While Ratzinger does not at this point identify truth with God, he does later assert that "to think through the essence of truth is to arrive at the notion of God."[40]

Our discussion on debate and Ratzinger's reflection on dialogue could seem overly optimistic; sometimes civility and basic cooperation are lacking, so how likely is it that a theologate could grow to allow for constructive debate and the exchange of persons that results from effective dialogue? Whilst acknowledging the danger of overoptimism, it is still legitimate to posit that the transformation of the theologate into a legitimate Christian community is worth striving for as an antidote to individualism and competition. The theologate must celebrate the success of the other, recognizing that the accomplishments of one member add to the glory of the whole body. Charity, mercy, and humility—which ought to be features of all Christian organizations—act as brakes on selfish ambition and hubris. Furthermore, if the faculty is genuinely Christian, it will not settle for debate on ideological or emotive grounds but, rather, will appeal to reason and shared faith in order to mutually seek truth.[41] In sum, faculties in which members experience genuine fellowship (*koinonia*) are most conducive to constructive theological debate and are thus better placed to "produce" theology that meets the D'Costian criterion of rigor, communal testing, and accountability.

---

38. Ratzinger, "Essence of the Academy," 33.
39. Ratzinger, "Essence of the Academy," 34.
40. Ratzinger, "Essence of the Academy," 40.
41. We use the term "ideology" in a pejorative sense, meaning a system of ideas or beliefs, particularly relating to social, economic, or politics, that are not in accord with Catholic teaching. It is recognized that the term may be understood otherwise, particularly by scholars in the field of critical social theory. See Crossley, "Ideology," in *Key Concepts*, 148–56.

3. Theology May Not Be Founded on the Three Sources of Catholic Theology

Other writers in this volume address the relationship between theology and each of the foundations of Catholic theology: Scripture, tradition, and magisterial teaching. Here we will focus simply on the relationship between the three and will offer some reflections on how the *koinonial* Christian life, and the liturgy in particular, can assist the theologian to theologize on this triune basis.

To begin, we can turn our attention to the statement of *Dei Verbum*, section 10, on the unity of the Scripture and tradition—the "one sacred deposit of the word of God"—and the magisterium, which is entrusted with interpreting, teaching, and handing on what it has received from this sacred deposit.[42]

> It is clear . . . that sacred tradition, Sacred Scripture and the teaching authority of the Church, in accord with God's most wise design, are so linked and joined together that one cannot stand without the others, and that all together and each in its own way under the action of the one Holy Spirit contribute effectively to the salvation of souls.[43]

These three foundations are therefore like the three legs of a tripod upon which rests the light of Christ drawing all men and women to himself (cf. Ps 119:105).[44] This salvific dimension to theologizing on the basis of these three foundations highlights a key link between the foundations and communal life; theology done rightly has the power to build up the Body of Christ.

In his 1979 article "Was Ist Theologie?," Ratzinger emphasizes the connection between scriptural exegesis and the living Christian community:

---

42. Second Vatican Council, *Dei Verbum*, §10.
43. Second Vatican Council, *Dei Verbum*, §10.
44. It would take us too far afield to engage with the question of the weight one ought to put on the use of each of the three sources of Catholic theology. It is not unreasonable to declare that Catholic theologians fit broadly into camps marked out by collective stances on the weight one ought to put on each of the three sources of authority—Scripture, tradition, and magisterium. Much ink has been spilt by individuals in each camp seeking to justify their position; we will not add to that debate here. Rowland deals with the relationships between Scripture and tradition, and the magisterium and theologians in her monograph *Catholic Theology*, 36–38, 40–41.

> The reality that is the Church transcends any literary formulation of it. Of course, what she believes and lives can be, and is, contained in books. But it is not totally assimilated by these books. On the contrary, the books fulfill their function as books only when they point to the community in which the word is to be found. The living community cannot be replaced or surpassed by historical exegesis; it is inherently superior to any book. By its very nature, the word of faith presupposes the community that lives it, that is bound to it and that adheres to it in its very power to bind mankind.[45]

Here Ratzinger shows that the Scriptures, magisterial documents, and the great works of theology must be subordinated to the reality of the *ecclesia*, for the simple fact that books and the words they contain have a symbolic function and do not constitute reality itself. Additionally, Ratzinger underscores the importance of baptism into this community as the key interpretive rule in relation to revelation (the sacred deposit of the word) and literature.

The sacrament of baptism initiates one into the *ecclesia*, builds it up, and is an activity of it.[46] Ratzinger emphasizes that baptism and its related catechesis—the content of which is "Christ, the Son of God, who was anointed by the Holy Spirit, and the consequently trinitarian character of faith"[47]—provide the "common knowledge [which is] itself the measure of every interpretation."[48] This ecclesial sacrament supplies, therefore, the knowledge needed to properly pay attention to the analogy of faith, and thus, to correctly interpret the word.[49] With this in mind, we can see that drawing on the graces of baptism provides one with the common knowledge that allows one to properly interpret the word. The *koinonial* Christian life, which is simply the living out of one's baptismal call, is thus essential for theologizing.

One aspect of this life, the liturgy, deserves mention here. The communal celebration of the liturgy "is the ontological condition for what is

---

45. Ratzinger, "What Is Theology," 329–30.

46. "The passive side of becoming a Christian calls for the *acting Church*, in which the unity of believers as a single subject manifests itself in its bodily and historical dimensions" (Ratzinger, "Spiritual Basis," 52; italics added).

47. Ratzinger, "What Is Theology," 330.

48. Ratzinger, "What Is Theology," 330.

49. *Catechism*, §114.

itself a genuine theology," what David Fagerberg calls "*theologia prima*."[50] Fagerberg states this more descriptively in his account of the fictitious Mrs. Murphy:

> Theology's more relevant practitioner is Mrs. Murphy who has been capacitated by the mystery of God in the liturgy to see the world in the light of Mount Tabor. She may not be able to say something about the other theologians, but she can do something more important: she can say something theological about everything else in the world.[51]

Without wanting to sound utilitarian, if Mrs. Murphy can theologize on the basis of the graces given to her through baptism and her participation in the liturgy, then it behooves the academic theologian to avail himself or herself of these same opportunities.

4. Theology May Lead to Division Rather than to Unity

The International Theological Commission's 2011 document "Theology Today: Perspectives, Principles and Criteria" stresses that the "sheer fulness and richness" of revelation "is too great to be grasped by any one theology."[52] That multiple theologies exist is not a problem—and is, in fact, a beautiful expression of the catholicity of the Church—so long as theology remains "united in its service of the one truth of God."[53] Indeed, "the plurality of theologies should not imply fragmentation or discord, but rather the exploration in myriad ways of God's one saving truth."[54] Another way of expressing how a plurality of theologies is possible is supplied by Ratzinger in the assertion that "unity rests in faith, while theology is the domain of plurality. To that extent, the very act of fixing the common reference point—faith—makes plurality in theology possible."[55]

The diversity of Protestant churches is a poignant reminder that plurality in the realm of theology is not a good in itself; there can be, of course, theologies that claim to be founded on faith that fracture the unity of this faith. So how can we ensure that the faith on which our

---

50. Fagerberg, *Theologia Prima*, 41.
51. Fagerberg, "*Theologia Prima*: Liturgical Mystery," 62.
52. International Theological Commission, "Theology Today," §5.
53. International Theological Commission, "Theology Today," §5.
54. International Theological Commission, "Theology Today," §5.
55. Ratzinger, "Pluralism as a Problem," 93.

theologies are based is sure and that these theologies take their place in the symphony—not cacophony—of Catholic theology?

In the first instance, attention must be paid to an accurate discernment of the *sensus fidei*, which is helpfully defined by the ITC:[56]

> On the one hand, the *sensus fidei* refers to the personal capacity of the believer, within the communion of the Church, to discern the truth of faith. On the other hand, the *sensus fidei* refers to a communal and ecclesial reality: the instinct of faith of the Church herself, by which she recognises her Lord and proclaims his word.[57]

This distinction between the personal and the communal and ecclesial realities of the *sensus fidei* serves to remind us that the individual theologian, whose task it is to interpret the *sensus fidelium*, must take heed of the instinct of the *ecclesia* when developing his or her theology.[58] This is only possible for the theologian who actively and intentionally takes her or his place amongst the flock under the one Shepherd, for to attempt to theologize outside the sheepfold would be to engage in a study of religion, not theology.[59]

A second way to ensure that one is contributing symphonically to the body of Catholic theology is to develop an adequate understanding of the role of the magisterium as an instrument for discerning the truth claims of faith. Ratzinger is again helpful on this matter as he points out that "the priority of faith, which lends the Magisterium authority and a final right of decision, does not obliterate the independence of theological research but guarantees it a solid basis."[60] On this view, those who claim

---

56. For discussion on the distinction between the *sensus fidei* (the personal dimension) and the *sensus fidelium* (the ecclesial or communal dimension), see International Theological Commission, *Sensus Fidei*, §3.

57. International Theological Commission, *Sensus Fidei*, §3.

58. International Theological Commission, *Sensus Fidei*, §81. See also International Theological Commission, "Theology Today," §35.

59. *Donum Veritatis* affirms the necessity of prayer for the theologian in order that he or she may better understand the *sensus fidelium*: "Since the object of theology is the Truth which is the living God and His plan for salvation revealed in Jesus Christ, the theologian is called to deepen his own life of faith and continuously unite his scientific research with prayer. In this way, he will become more open to the 'supernatural sense of faith' upon which he depends, and it will appear to him as a sure rule for guiding his reflections and helping him assess the correctness of his conclusions" (Congregation for the Doctrine of the Faith, *Donum Veritatis*, §8).

60. Ratzinger, "On the 'Instruction,'" 106.

the priority of faith over the dictates of the magisterium seem to overlook the fact that "those who exercise the magisterium, namely the pope and the bishops, are themselves, first of all, baptised members of the people of God, who participate by that very fact in the *sensus fidelium*."[61] It follows that those who argue for the prioritization of the *sensus fidelium* over the authority of the magisterium must apply some unconvincing mental gymnastics, as this line of argument must simultaneously affirm the authority of the faithful who are charged with playing "an active role in the development of Christian belief" and place limits on who constitutes this body of the faithful.[62]

Catechumens coming to seek baptism are asked what they are seeking from God's Church. One valid response to this question is "faith." Both Mrs. Murphy and the academic theologian can draw on this gift of baptism in their efforts to expound the mysteries of the Christian faith. Both can, however, fail to pay heed to the *sensus fidelium* and to the magisterium that gives theology its certainty.[63] In both instances, active engagement in the *koinonial* Christian life is an aid to shoring up one's defense against the tendency to theologize in ways that can be divisive. Acts 2:42 details life in the post-Pentecostal Christian community. Following baptism on that first Christian Pentecost, the followers of the Way committed to the celebration of the Eucharist, prayer, fellowship (*koinonia*), and devotion to the teaching of the apostles. These four aspects of early Christian life are integral to Christian life still today. Trust in the teaching office of the apostles and their successors is hard to imagine for those theologians who are not fully integrated into the Christian community. Collectively, prayer, the sacramental life, and fellowship empower the Christian to grow in faith, hope, and charity. This growth then serves to help one place trust in the Church, Christ's Body, and in his vicars, those bishops who are in communion with Peter. In sum, we can say that the Christian life, lived fully and in communion with brothers and sisters in

---

61. International Theological Commission, *Sensus Fidei*, §76. The ITC reinforces this further in §77, saying of the magisterium that "the faith which it serves is the faith of the Church, which lives in all of the faithful, so it is always within the communion life of the Church that the magisterium exercises its essential ministry of oversight."

62. International Theological Commission, *Sensus Fidei*, §72.

63. Ratzinger states plainly that "there can be no office of teaching theology if there is no ecclesiastical magisterium, for in its absence theology would enjoy no greater certainty than any of the liberal arts, that is, the certainty of hypothesis, which no one can stake his life on" (Ratzinger, "Spiritual Basis," 46).

Christ, is a sure bulwark against divisive and insipid theology, and some guarantee of theology that builds unity and leads others to salvation.

5. Theology May Lack Grounding in Reality

In February 2006, the late British educationalist Sir Ken Robinson gave a TED Talk on the theme "Do Schools Kill Creativity?" This presentation has clearly struck a chord with the public, as by the end of 2020, the talk had been viewed more than sixty-eight million times. A former professor of education at the University of Warwick, Robinson speaks with both affection and a certain realism on the topic of the stereotypical academic.[64] He states,

> There's something curious about professors. In my experience—not all of them, but typically—they live in their heads. They live up there and slightly to one side. They're disembodied, you know, in a kind of literal way. They look upon their body as a form of transport for their heads.[65]

Robinson's observation, while clearly intended as a caricature, points to an ever-present danger faced by anyone who is engaged in the intellectual life, the proclivity to individualism and subsequent retreat from reality to the intellect. The theologian is just as susceptible to this hazard as any academic.

Without wanting to labor the point, a theologian ought to be protected somewhat if she or he is fully integrated into the *ecclesia*, a state of being which would include taking one's part in assuming the Church's "three-fold responsibility . . . of proclaiming the word of God (*kerygma-martyria*), celebrating the sacraments (*leitourgia*), and exercising the ministry of charity (*diakonia*)."[66] Signs of successful integration into the *ecclesia* would be found both in the choice of topics of study taken up and in the absence of ideological influences in the work produced.[67] In

---

64. One cannot reasonably doubt Robinson's affection for academics. His principal concern is that the academic and the academic life "should not be held up as the standard for other forms of human achievement" (Robinson, *Out of Our Minds*, 66).

65. Robinson, "Do Schools Kill Creativity," 9:44.

66. Benedict XVI, *Deus Caritas Est*, §25. For members of the Emmanuel Community, this threefold responsibility is expressed in terms of the particular charisms of the Community: adoration, compassion, and evangelization (Emmanuel Community, "Statutes," 89–90).

67. Again we use the term "ideology" in its pejorative sense.

the first case, the projects a theologian chooses to undertake should be informed by the needs of the Church. For example, the theologian should act prophetically to discern the signs of the times, looking at contemporary culture and the Church to determine what would be most helpful for leading the flock to know, love, and be saved by Christ. In the second case, the theology produced should be "scientific reflection on the divine revelation which the Church accepts by faith as universal saving truth."[68] This precludes theologizing that allows ideology to taint reason or the substitution of divine revelation with secular "truth" claims.

In its conclusion, "Theology Today: Perspectives, Principles and Criteria" provides a useful summary of the relationship between theology and the *koinonial* Christian life:

> it may be said that Catholic theology studies the Mystery of God revealed in Christ, and articulates the experience of faith that those in the communion of the Church, participating in the life of God, have, by the grace of the Holy Spirit, who leads the Church into the truth (Jn 16:13).[69]

In this chapter we have examined what happens when a theologian fails to be well integrated into an ecclesial community—that is, when he or she does not have a *koinonial* Christian life. More positively, we have noted the benefits that come from participating fully in the give-and-take of the ecclesial life. We have shown, for instance, that baptism, prayer, liturgy, and fellowship afford the theologian "access" to the supernatural gift of faith, the sense to interpret it, and the spiritual help to trust in the guidance of the magisterium. Furthermore, we have shown that debate and dialogue, which are fruits of a culture of charity and demand an exchange of persons, help to ensure intellectual rigor, accountability, and the testing of one's theological work. Much work needs to be done to convert our theologates into places of communion, prayer, silence, collaboration, and fidelity to the word. Care must be taken, however, for the conversion of institutions must not be driven by ideologies. Rather, change starts with personal decisions and growth in moral virtue, and it is on that front that efforts to heal the fracture between theology and the *koinonial* Christian life must begin.

---

68. International Theological Commission, "Theology Today," §5.
69. International Theological Commission, "Theology Today," §100.

Bibliography

Benedict XVI, Pope. "On Christian Love [*Deus Caritas Est*]." Vatican, 25 Dec. 2005. http://www.vatican.va/content/benedict-xvi/en/encyclicals/documents/hf_ben-xvi_enc_20051225_deus-caritas-est.html.

Catechism of the Catholic Church. 2nd ed. Strathfield, Aus.: St Paul's, 2009.

Congregation for the Doctrine of the Faith. "Instruction on the Ecclesial Vocation of the Theologian [*Donum Veritatis*]." Vatican, 24 May 1990. http://www.vatican.va/roman_curia/congregations/cfaith/documents/rc_con_cfaith_doc_19900524_theologian-vocation_en.html.

Conti, Manuele. "Using Debate in University Lectures." *Form@re* 19 (1 Jan. 2019) 355–66.

Crossley, Nick. *Key Concepts in Critical Social Theory*. London: Sage, 2005.

D'Costa, Gavin. "On Being a Catholic Theologian." *Theology* 115, no. 1 (Jan. 2012) 3–13.

Donovan, Mary Ann. "The Vocation of the Theologian." *Theological Studies* 65 (2004) 3–22.

Emmanuel Community. *Guide to Community Life of the Emmanuel Community and of the Fraternity of Jesus*. 3rd ed. Paris: Éditions de l'Emmanuel, 2012.

———. "Statutes of the Association of the Faithful and of the Clerical Association." Emmanuel, 15 Aug. 2017. https://emmanuel.info/wp-content/uploads/2018/05/Statuts-2017_anglais.pdf.

Evagrius of Pontus. *Evagrius of Pontus: The Greek Ascetic Corpus*. Edited and translated by Robert E. Sinkewicz. New York: Oxford University Press, 2003.

Fagerberg, David. "*Theologia Prima*: The Liturgical Mystery and the Mystery of God." *Letter & Spirit* 2 (2006) 55–67.

———. *Theologia Prima: What Is Liturgical Theology?* 2nd ed. Mundelein, IL: Hillenbrand, 2004.

Gregory of Nazianzus. *Select Orations*. Translated by Martha Vinson. Washington, DC: Catholic University of America Press, 2004.

Hanchin, Timothy. "'From Below Upwards': Worship and Wonder in Catholic Higher Education." *Logos: A Journal of Catholic Thought & Culture* 20, no. 3 (2017) 75–94.

Holmes, Michael W., ed. *The Apostolic Fathers*. 3rd ed. Translated by Michael W. Holmes. Grand Rapids: Baker Academic, 2007.

International Theological Commission. *In the Life of the Church* [*Sensus Fidei*]. Vatican, 2014. http://www.vatican.va/roman_curia/congregations/cfaith/cti_documents/rc_cti_20140610_sensus-fidei_en.html.

———. "Theology Today: Perspectives, Principles and Criteria." Vatican, 29 Nov. 2011. http://www.vatican.va/roman_curia/congregations/cfaith/cti_documents/rc_cti_doc_20111129_teologia-oggi_en.html.

La Soujeole, Benoit-Dominique. *Introduction to the Mystery of the Church*. Translated by Michael J. Miller. Washington, DC: Catholic University of America Press, 2014.

Livesey, Steven J. "The Medieval University." In *A Companion to the History of Science*, edited by Bernard Lightman, 228–44. Hoboken, NJ: Wiley & Sons, 2016.

McGuckin, John A., ed. *The SCM Press A-Z of Origen*. Louisville: SCM, 2006.

Ratzinger, Joseph. "The Essence of the Academy and Its Freedom." In *The Nature and Mission of Theology*, translated by Adrian Walker, 31–41. San Francisco: Ignatius, 1995.

———. "On the 'Instruction Concerning the Ecclesial Vocation of the Theologian.'" In *The Nature and Mission of Theology*, 101–20. Translated by Adrian Walker. San Francisco: Ignatius, 1995.

———. "Pluralism as a Problem for Church and Theology." In *The Nature and Mission of Theology*, 73–98. Translated by Adrian Walker. San Francisco: Ignatius, 1995.

———. "The Spiritual Basis and Ecclesial Identity of Theology." In *The Nature and Mission of Theology*, 45–72. Translated by Adrian Walker. San Francisco: Ignatius, 1995.

———. "What Is Theology?" In *Principles of Catholic Theology: Building Stones for a Fundamental Theology*, translated by Sr. Mary Frances McCarthy, SND, 315–31. San Francisco: Ignatius, 1987.

Robinson, Ken. "Do Schools Kill Creativity?" TED, Feb. 2006. https://www.ted.com/talks/sir_ken_robinson_do_schools_kill_creativity/transcript#t-774658.

———. *Out of Our Minds: Learning to Be Creative*. Hoboken, NJ: John Wiley & Sons, 2011.

Rowland, Tracey. *Catholic Theology*. London: Bloomsbury T&T Clark, 2017.

Sarah, Robert C., and Nicolas Diat. *The Power of Silence: Against the Dictatorship of Noise*. Translated by Michael J. Miller. San Francisco: Ignatius, 2017.

Second Vatican Council. "Dogmatic Constitution on Divine Revelation [*Dei Verbum*]." Vatican, 18 Nov. 1965. http://www.vatican.va/archive/hist_councils/ii_vatican_council/documents/vat-ii_const_19651118_dei-verbum_en.html.

———. "Dogmatic Constitution on the Church [*Lumen Gentium*]." Vatican, 21 Nov. 1964. http://www.vatican.va/archive/hist_councils/ii_vatican_council/documents/vat-ii_const_19641121_lumen-gentium_en.html.

"Seminary and Vocations." Catholic Diocese of Wagga Wagga. https://wagga.catholic.org.au/seminary-catholic-vocations/.

Sertillanges, A. G. *The Intellectual Life: Its Spirit, Conditions, Methods*. Translated by Mary Ryan. Washington, DC: Catholic University of America Press, 1998.

11

Theologians and Non-Theologians

JOHN R. CIHAK

FEW OF THOSE IN the pews on Sunday could name a contemporary theologian, and even fewer would have read anything from that theologian. Rarely, if ever, is a theologian prominent in any meaningful way in the other sciences, the public square, or in the lives of ordinary people. One notable exception perhaps is Bishop Robert Barron, who is having meaningful conversations with a wide variety of non-theologians, such as Jordan Peterson and Dave Rubin, as well as engaging the lives of many ordinary believers. But most theologians do not seem relevant to non-theologians. Theologians study, write, and teach, and only occasionally is this voice heard in the public discourse or even invited to contribute to the conversation. This is not good. The organic unity of theologians and non-theologians has been fractured. Why is this the case, and what can be done about it? This chapter will outline the causes for this rift, describe what a renewed unity would look like, and offer some proposals for a way forward toward healing this fracture.

The first task is to define the three fundamental terms of our inquiry: theology, theologian, and non-theologian. G. K. Chesterton famously stated, "Theology is simply that part of religion that requires brains." Theology is thinking about what is believed. In its classical Anselmian definition, theology is faith seeking understanding. More precisely, theology is rational reflection on what is revealed by the Triune God in Jesus of Nazareth and believed by faith. Faith unlocks access to divine revelation. Divine revelation is the "data" received in faith, which then is reflected upon rationally. This rational reflection is systematic, organized, and methodical, qualifying theology as a science. Theology is unique among sciences, because faith is essential for this way of knowing. Without faith, rational reflection on the Christian claim is more properly called "religious studies," since it is the study of a revealed religion from a philosophical, historical, sociological, or psychological perspective. The two fundamental exercises comprising theology are the *auditus fidei* (positive theology) and the *intellectus fidei* (speculative theology).[1] The *auditus fidei* listens to the sources of theology arising from Sacred Scripture and Sacred Tradition, mining these sources, thereby producing the material for speculative theology.[2] The *intellectus fidei* derives further conclusions and discovers new connections between what is already known. Because theology involves rational reflection, it appropriates and transforms categories of philosophy.

The theologian is a believer who takes intellectual responsibility for the faith. He or she articulates the intelligibility of divine revelation in a scientific way. Thus, three qualities are required of the theologian: 1) faith, 2) intellectual acumen, and 3) ecclesial communion.[3] Faith, if it is a living faith, implies communion with the Church. In other words, the theologian is a living member of the mystical Body of Christ who possesses the intellectual competence to examine and to expound the intelligibility of divine revelation, that it is something understandable and reasonable, and therefore human and believable. In Catholic theology, the theologian is a fully integrated member of the Church and has a *mandatum* from the local bishop to teach Catholic theology. Throughout the centuries, theologians have been primarily bishops (patristic age), monks (early Middle Ages), and mendicants (high Middle Ages). Until recent decades, theology was primarily the domain of the clergy, but now many lay people are theologians. Today, theology is generally understood as an academic endeavor and so is done mostly in universities and seminaries. However, I have argued elsewhere, following St. Bonaventure, that

---

1. See Latourelle, *Theology*, 62–86.

2. The classic list of sources, delineated by the Dominican Melchior Cano (1509–1560) are seven proper places: Sacred Scripture, Sacred (apostolic) Tradition, the universal Church, the councils, the papal magisterium, the fathers of the Church, theologians and canonists, and three sources borrowed by theology: natural reason manifested in science, philosophers and jurists, history and human tradition.

3. See Congregation for the Doctrine of the Faith, *Donum Veritatis*.

theology is far more than merely an intellectual exercise.[4] The material for theological inquiry is not inert data but a living relationship with the God who reveals himself historically. Given the subject matter of the science—the living God revealed in Jesus of Nazareth—and the prerequisite of faith to access that subject matter, the exercise of theology by its very nature engages and transforms the one thinking, engaging the will, emotions, and moral action. Hans Urs von Balthasar writes, "From the standpoint of revelation, there is simply no real truth which does not have to be incarnated in an act or in some action ... and 'walking in the truth' is the way the believer possesses the truth."[5] In a broad sense, because it is proper for human nature to think, any believer who seeks to understand the faith can be understood as a "theologian." For the purposes of our inquiry, I will use the term to mean an academic theologian.

Who is the non-theologian? This category is more fluid and can encompass a wide and diverse range of people. In general, the non-theologian is anyone who is not academically trained in theology. The non-theologian could be an academic specialized in another field like philosophy, history, mathematics, psychology, or neurochemistry. The non-theologian could also be a bishop or priest who does not have more than basic seminary training. The non-theologian could also be a lay believer in the pews on Sunday and, finally, could be a non-believer who is academically trained or not. For the purposes of this essay, I will focus attention on the non-theologians who are believers, as I believe healing this rift will help facilitate the connection with non-theologians who do not yet believe. Because of the various causes of the fracture between theologians and non-theologians, the material of this chapter inevitably will overlap with other chapters that treat theology's relationship with philosophy, liturgy, and spirituality.

Giving a Diagnosis

The causes of this rift between theologians and non-theologians arise in both groups from fundamental problems in philosophical and cultural currents in Western civilization since the Enlightenment. We begin with the causes from non-theologians. A first cause is the widespread religious

---

4. See Cihak, "Forging a Reason"; see also LaNave, *Through Holiness to Wisdom*; LaNave, "Why Holiness is Necessary"; and Rowland, "How Does Spirituality Supply."

5. Balthasar, "Theology and Sanctity," 181–82.

indifference and consequent religious ignorance of non-theologians, even highly educated ones. This indifference and ignorance has come about through the rise of atheism,[6] which gained ground as certain philosophical currents from the Enlightenment worked toward their inevitable conclusions and following the tragedy and horror of world wars and totalitarianism, the moral quagmire of the sexual revolution in the 1960s, the destruction of family life, the clergy sex-abuse crisis, and the materialism from economic prosperity. To these we can also add the lightening-quick rise of the digital age, which fosters technological over philosophical knowing, and the "liquid culture" and hyper-busy pace of most people's lives, which leave them fragmented and spiritually anemic. All of these currents have fostered ideas and lifestyles that imply that God either does not exist or is not meaningfully active in the world and in one's daily life. Thus, no historical revelation of said God seems possible, any reflection on that historical revelation would not be considered rational, authority is not trustworthy, and there is simply no time to cultivate a spiritual life. The big questions of existence, especially those of God, simply are not considered in the daily life of many people. This indifference is not so much an articulated intellectual position as something simply lived. Recent data indicate that the "Nones," those who claim no religious affiliation, have now surpassed Catholics as the largest "religious" group in the United States.[7] Even practicing Catholics are not immune from these currents of indifference, especially intellectual indifference toward the faith.

An inevitable consequence of indifference is ignorance. If God and the things of God are not relevant to people's daily life, then one tends not to bother to seek out and to know them. Vast swaths of lay faithful, even those who are in the pews every Sunday, cannot recognize or articulate basic truths of the faith.[8] It is difficult, if not impossible, to engage

---

6. See the authoritative text on the subject: Buckley, *At the Origins*.

7. See Burge, "How Many 'Nones.'" Nones now account for 23.1 percent of the U.S. population, a 266 percent increase since 1980, which now surpasses the largest group (Catholics), which stands at 23 percent. A 2017 Pew Research survey reported only 22 percent of Nones listed "not believing in God" as the most important reason for their lack of religious affiliation.

8. Take, for example, the basic truth of the real, substantial presence of Jesus in the Blessed Sacrament. A Pew Research poll in 2010 reported that a majority of those *practicing* the faith do not believe in this truth and cannot articulate it. Another Pew Research poll recently found that large numbers of Americans are uninformed about the teachings and practices of their own faith as well as the other major faith traditions

theologians if the non-theologian does not know the basic truths that the theologian studies and expounds upon. This ignorance is not entirely the non-theologians' fault. For most non-theologians, their primary encounter with theology or any intellectual articulation of the faith would be in Sunday preaching or in some sort of catechesis in the parish. After the Second Vatican Council, seminarians for decades were often formed in the mistaken notion that doctrine and conceptual content were not appropriate for preaching.[9] Moreover, catechetical formation was often deficient in developing faith to keep pace with a child's growing intellectual development into adolescence and adulthood.

A second cause is that non-theologians tend not to consider faith as something to think about, which points to an underlying presupposition that faith and reason are somehow in conflict and even incompatible. This cause perhaps can be seen most clearly in the perceived conflict between faith and the empirical sciences.[10] The underlying perception is that faith is not a way of knowing or something "scientific." If faith and reason are not understood as compatible and even complementary and symphonic, then faith becomes understood more and more as irrational and something relegated to the realm of emotion. Faith as simply a feeling is what I frequently encounter in pastoral life, even among those who practice their faith. Although most believers today have never heard of Friedrich Schleiermacher (1768–1834), his idea that faith is mere religious sentiment seems to have the upper hand. If the non-theologian considers faith as sentiment, then he or she is not likely to seek out the intelligibility of what is believed.

I would suggest that beneath this emotional understanding of faith is an implicit, cultural appropriation of a type of philosophical skepticism that nothing can be known for certain. Whether it is Immanuel Kant's unknowable *noumenon* or the full-blown philosophical deconstructionism of Jacques Derrida and Michel Foucault, non-theologians often do not think that there is certainty in knowing, period. Most non-theologians have never read the works of these philosophers or even heard of their

---

("U.S. Religious Knowledge Survey").

9. See Ratzinger, *Dogma and Preaching*.

10. A Pew Research poll in 2015 reported that 59 percent of American adults say in general that science often is in conflict with religion, while 38 percent consider science and religion to be mostly compatible. This perception of conflict increased 4 percent from 2009 to 2015. See Pew Research Center, "Perception of Conflict," and Barron, "Does Religion."

names, yet their ideas are operative in mainstream culture. John Paul II observes in *Fides et Ratio* that reason in the postmodern age has lost faith in itself.[11] This philosophical skepticism is then extended to what faith proposes as true and certain. Philosophy's abandonment of the quest for meaning, beyond nihilism or psychology, gives momentum to the religious indifference and religious ignorance of the non-theologian.

A third cause of the rift between theologians and non-theologians from the non-theologian side lies in the undermining of trust in authority. The act of faith, whereby the will moves the intellect to give assent to God who reveals, means that loving trust of authority is essential to the act. Nearly all human knowing, even knowing through reason, comes from interpersonal relationship and trusting an authority.[12] A longstanding cultural situation of divorce; broken family life; child abuse; and the ongoing cultural denigration of fatherhood, motherhood, and other authority harms people's ability to trust and love, and specifically the ability to trust truth that comes from authority. Moreover, the deficient example of those in authority, whether they be fathers, mothers, civil leaders, or clergy, has fueled that distrust. It is difficult to overstate the impact divorce and abuse have on a child's ability to trust in relationships and thus on the whole question of truth and certainty, even into adulthood.

A fourth cause comes from the aftermath of the sexual revolution in the 1960s and its ensuing explosion of sexual impurity and the denigration of the virtue of chastity. The statistics on pornography addiction, especially among males, are particularly distressing. Jesus himself says, "Blessed are the pure of heart, for they shall see God" (Matt 5:8 RSV). Unchastity causes a blindness in the soul toward God and, if unrepented, leads to *odium Dei* (hatred of God), according to Aquinas.[13]

---

11. John Paul II writes, "The role of philosophy itself has changed in modern culture. From universal wisdom and learning, it has been gradually reduced to one of the many fields of human knowing.... Some philosophers have abandoned the search for truth in itself and made their sole aim the attainment of a subjective certainty or a pragmatic sense of utility. This in turn has obscured the true dignity of reason, which is no longer equipped to know the truth and to seek the absolute" (John Paul II, *Fides et Ratio*, §47).

12. "There are in the life of a human being many more truths which are simply believed than truths which are acquired by way of personal verification.... This means that the human being—the one who seeks the truth—is also *the one who lives by belief*" (John Paul II, *Fides et Ratio*, §31).

13. See Aquinas, *Summa Theologica*, II–II, q. 153, a. 5, corpus.

If the non-theologian tends to be characterized by religious indifference and ignorance, by an understanding of faith as mere emotion and not something reasonable, and by distrust of authority, the theologian, who has also been affected by these long philosophical and cultural currents, has contributed to the rift as well. A first cause for the rift from the theologian side is that theologians themselves have also been affected by the problems mentioned above, especially in the postconciliar period. Theology has lost its, more or less, univocal voice, because theologians have been divided about the fundamental nature of their science in object and method. The repeated clarifications by the Church's magisterium in the postconciliar period on the nature of theology and the ecclesial vocation of the theologian indicate this division. Personal, living faith has not always been understood as essential to the theological enterprise, despite the fact that only by a living faith does the theologian have access to divine revelation *qua* divine revelation. Faith is the *sine qua non* for rational reflection on divine revelation. Theologians suffer from a lack of faith and a lack of the spiritual life that vivifies and develops faith. As a result, theology itself has become despiritualized.[14]

A second cause lies in the above-mentioned suspicion of authority that manifests in theology in the rejection of ecclesiastical authority. The Church's teaching magisterium is seen not as a help but as an obstacle and even a threat to freedom of inquiry. Two notable historical moments in this regard were the Land O' Lakes Conference in 1967 and Pope St. Paul VI's publication of *Humane Vitae* in 1968. The explicit rejection of legitimate authority, manifested in the praise given to the resolutions of the Land O' Lakes Conference and the public repudiation of *Humane Vitae* on the part of many theologians, obscured the intrinsic connection of the theologian to the living community of faith, the Church, and her magisterium. Living communion with the Church has not always been understood as essential to theology. Theologians do not always see themselves as living members of the believing community of the Church, as being called to a vocation in service of the believing community, and as being given a mandate from the Church to pursue their craft.

A third cause lies in the impact the above philosophical currents have had on theology, resulting in an overly pluralistic approach to how theology proceeds as a science. Non-theologians find this excessive pluralism confusing and easier to dismiss, making the theological voice

---

14. Hans Urs von Balthasar traces this progressive despiritualization of theology in "Theology and Sanctity."

difficult to be heard. Fundamentally, it is a question of method. Not every philosophical approach is compatible in providing a rational exposition of divine revelation.[15] The dissatisfaction with the problems and limitations in conceptual Thomism in the first half of the twentieth century and its jettisoning in favor of transcendental Thomism, Hegelianism, Marxism, and even deconstructionism have created other, and perhaps worse, problems. Some of these methods infect the science of theology with philosophical skepticism, rationalism, fideism, and relativism. Pope Benedict XVI characterizes the difficulty with the terms "hermeneutic of continuity" versus "hermeneutic of discontinuity and rupture."[16] Theology today lacks a unified, coherent methodological and metaphysical point of reference. Theology must be in conversation with prevailing philosophical currents, but not all of these currents are adequate for theology's own way of proceeding as a science. The question of method has no easy solution, because theology attempts to articulate an understanding of infinite, divine realities within finite (and fallen) human rationality. It always involves the two fundamental philosophical conundrums discovered by Plato and Aristotle in relating the finite and the infinite, the one and the many, as well as the analogy of being. Theology must always wrestle with the difficulty of expressing the infinite God in human concepts and language that adequately correspond to the object studied.

A fourth cause lies in the hyper-specialization happening within theology itself. Theology has developed into many complex disciplines that necessarily involve hyper-specialization. The two-thousand-year theological tradition is too much for a single theologian to master, and so he or she is forced into a small area of expertise. When not unified methodologically, these specializations easily become fragmented from each other. Even the various disciplines of theology have difficulty dialoguing with each other.

A fifth cause for the rift with non-theologians on the part of theologians is the format and communication of most theology, which fail to connect with non-theologians. For centuries, theology has been expressed through the essay or monograph format. This is a format that today is read by very few. Theologians are still catching up to the new formats of communication provided by the rapid advance of digital technology. These new communication platforms bring with them their own

---

15. See John Paul II, *Fides et Ratio*, §50.
16. Benedict XVI, "Address."

difficulties in fostering the deeper, thought-provoking examination, the time and intellectual effort required to assimilate and consider a theologian's work. Furthermore, the platform where most non-theologians encounter theology would be in preaching. How many homilies or sermons has the reader heard that actually taught something theological or are remembered a month later? Behind this cause has been the all-too-frequent anti-intellectualism within seminary theological formation in the 1970s and 80s, which has persisted in some places down to the present day.

Giving a Prognosis

If this fracture between theologians and non-theologians were healed, what would it look like? Both the non-theologian and theologian would overcome the skepticism and indifference of the current age and rediscover the sapiential dimension of knowledge, a rediscovery of knowing as wisdom, awakening them to think philosophically about life in general and the things of faith. This sapiential approach means a reengagement with the perennially big questions about God, the world, human existence, love, suffering, sexuality, and death, instilling in non-theologians what Robert Sokolowski calls "the philosophical habit."[17] It would mean a renewed vision that faith seeks understanding and that faith has something profound to say about the meaning of the world and of human life to Nones as well as to believers. Furthermore, family life would be renewed so that children can grow up in loving, intact families and habitually encounter authority as loving, nurturing, and disciplining, which fosters trust in relationships and the knowledge transmitted through interpersonal trust. Non-theologians would also be connected to theologians through adequate preaching and formation through institutions and apostolates.

Theologians would have a renewed sense of their vocation to examine and expound divine revelation through a renewed identity as believers in living communion with the Church, allowing themselves to be transformed spiritually and morally by the living God they study. Theologians would rediscover the sapiential dimension of their science. While continuing in the details of the various theological disciplines and the myriad investigations into theology's sources, theologians would

17. Sokolowski, "Acquiring the Philosophical Habit," 319.

dialogue intelligently with non-theologians on the big questions. Theologians would also promote a common metaphysical point of reference for their science that would help present a more unified scientific voice to the non-theologian. There would be a mature, trusting approach toward ecclesiastical authority and robust dialogue between the various theological disciplines. Finally, theologians would integrate new forms of communication and of encounter to engage non-theologians.

Offering a Prescription

To heal this fracture between theologians and non-theologians, the following proposals are suggested. In order to address the religious indifference and ignorance of the non-theologian, an awakening is needed in the postmodern soul to a sapiential approach to knowledge and life, which would help to overcome the underlying skepticism, relativism, excessive empirical and technological emphasis on knowledge, and seeing faith as mere sentiment. Hans Urs von Balthasar's great theological contribution lies in his argument that beauty—ultimately, the beauty of divine love that is encountered personally—is a powerful way, perhaps the only way, of awakening the postmodern soul to the questions of truth and goodness. Where do most non-theologians encounter theological beauty in an interpersonal way? A privileged place of encountering theological beauty is in the holiness of life of believers; a Christian witness that is authentic and offered in friendship gives non-theologians an encounter of a living embodiment of theological truths. A second privileged place is the Sacred Liturgy. The Eucharist is the "source and summit of the Christian life,"[18] and a massive amount of theology is expressed symbolically to the senses and personally through the Sacred Liturgy. The spiritual and theological awakening of the non-theologian can be greatly helped through beautiful churches, a faithful and beautiful celebration of the Sacred Liturgy, well-sung sacred music, beautiful sacred vestments and vessels, and so forth. A third privileged place of theological beauty is in the works of charity. When the non-theologian witnesses and participates in the corporal or spiritual works of mercy, he or she comes into personal contact with theological beauty.[19]

---

18. Second Vatican Council, *Lumen Gentium*, §11; see *Catechism*, §1324.

19. One apostolate that is having an impact in this area among young adults and those who are homeless is Christ in the City, founded by Dr. Jonathan Reyes and

From the personal encounter with theological beauty, the non-theologian can enter into a renewed engagement with the big questions and form the philosophical habit. Sokolowski describes the philosophical habit as thinking critically about the things of faith through the ability to make comparisons and draw distinctions in order to relate them. He writes, "Philosophy . . . articulates the human and worldly things that serve as the basis and the contrast for theological definitions. Philosophy can bring out the integrity of those things that are important for a theological understanding."[20] The philosophical habit works to clarify, compare, contrast, distinguish, and define, and therefore brings about someone "who appreciates the nuances, contours, definitions, and shapes of important human things and can articulate them clearly."[21] He continues, "We must recover the philosophical exercise of reason precisely in response to the triumph of technological reasoning."[22] Fostering the philosophical habit will help overcome the perceived division between faith and reason and rescue reason from the reductionism of technological reason. Theologians can help in this regard by addressing the perceived conflict between faith and reason, showing that faith and reason have their proper function and mutually enrich each other in the quest for truth and meaning. Following the lines of *Fides et Ratio*, theologians can draw out the interpersonal dimension of knowing in both faith and reason. Both reason and faith come to knowing things for certain through interpersonal trust. We must trust in order to know. Thus, the trust involved in faith can be understood as something reasonable. The theologian can also challenge Schleiermacher's understanding of faith as mere religious sentiment, showing that faith is something to think about, that when the non-theologian seeks understanding about faith, he or she is, in fact, theologizing. An indispensable way to reengage the big questions and foster the philosophical habit is through interpersonal encounters between theologians and non-theologian, such as interviews, conversations, and debate in a spirit of friendship and authenticity. Bishop Barron's interview with Jordan Peterson in 2019 is an excellent example of such an encounter.[23]

---

operating in several cities in the United States (https://christinthecity.org).

20. Sokolowski, "Acquiring the Philosophical Habit," 320.
21. Sokolowski, "Acquiring the Philosophical Habit," 322.
22. Sokolowski, "Acquiring the Philosophical Habit," 324.
23. Peterson, "Bishop Barron."

A further way to bring about this greater closeness between theologians and non-theologians on the big questions and the philosophical habit is to reexamine the identity and curriculum of Catholic universities. Up until the time of the Second Vatican Council, Catholic universities commonly required all their undergraduates to receive a minor in philosophy and theology regardless of their major area of study. This practice fostered the philosophical habit, worked against the overly empirical and technological understanding of knowledge, and helped ensure that educated non-theologians would be at least somewhat versed in philosophy and theology. My mother relates that when she was studying pre-medicine at a Catholic university in the 1960s, she was required to take courses in philosophy, and in one course the professor took them through a detailed study of Aristotle's *Metaphysics*. Most Catholic universities today have reduced this practice to one or two basic courses. Catholic high schools and parish K-8 schools should make basic philosophy part of their curriculum and implement catechetical curricula that stirs the minds of students with theological content developmentally consonant with their age.[24]

The challenge for theologians is to engage the big questions while having to work in a narrow field of expertise. One way to meet this challenge is to increase the interaction of the various theological disciplines, to relate one's specific area of study to the greater whole of the theological enterprise. Theologians in the English-speaking world might consider the value of the specific discipline of fundamental theology. In the English-speaking world, the two disciplines of fundamental and dogmatic theology are usually merged into the single discipline of systematic theology, while many European faculties maintain the distinction. Fundamental theology's distinct object is critical reflection in faith on the nature, transmission, and credibility of divine revelation with the aim of providing the other theological disciplines a common framework and presenting the reason for belief to the other. As such, fundamental theology has an apologetical and evangelistic focus *ad extra* toward non-theologians to fulfill the apostle's injunction to "always be prepared to make a defense to any one who calls you to account for the hope that is in you, yet do it with

---

24. Sophia Institute Press's *Spirit of Truth* K-8 curriculum, for which the author served as one of the theological consultants, is a good example of a catechetical curriculum that is theologically well-informed.

gentleness and reverence" (1 Pet 3:15 RSV).[25] This theological discipline is specifically equipped to engage non-theologians.

I would suggest increasing interdisciplinary interaction between theologians and academic non-theologians. One example of this kind of interaction is the work of the Society of Sacred Liturgy and its *Antiphon* journal, which purposefully seeks membership from many academic fields on the Sacred Liturgy: theology, philosophy, architecture, music, and so forth. An increasingly important area of dialogue and collaboration between theologians and non-theologians is mental health. In the United States, nearly one in five people experiences mental illness each year.[26] The emerging studies on millennials and Gen Zers are showing a dramatic increase of anxiety and depression in these segments of the population. The *Harvard Business Review* reported in 2019 that 50 percent of millennials and 75 percent of Gen Zers left a job partly for mental health reasons, compared to 20 percent of the general population.[27] Several reasons are proposed for this dramatic increase of mental health problems, ranging from overprotective parents to the loss of economic upward mobility to the way social media has negatively altered interpersonal relationships. Theology has much to offer these problems. With the psychological sciences discovering in recent years, through their own research, that faith and religion play a very positive role in mental health, these sciences have been shedding their historically hostile bias toward faith and religion. This discovery opens up a promising area of collaboration. One example of such collaboration was my own co-authoring of a popularly written book on depression with a psychiatrist, which brought together philosophy, theology, psychological therapy, and pharmacology in a coherent whole.[28]

One area of theology that is connecting very well and producing much fruit among non-theologians, especially among the young, is John Paul II's theology of the body. The meaning of human sexuality is in the forefront in the lives of nearly everyone, and purity of heart is essential to "see God." In my years of priestly ministry, I have encountered many

---

25. John Paul II writes, "With its specific character as a discipline charged with giving an account of faith, the concern of fundamental theology will be to justify and expound the relationship between faith and philosophical thought" (John Paul II, *Fides et Ratio*, §67).

26. "Mental Health."

27. Greenwood et al., "Research," paras. 6–7.

28. Kheriaty and Cihak, *Catholic Guide to Depression*.

young people who, disillusioned with the brokenness and misery produced by living the Western culture's view of human sexuality, have come back to the practice of the faith by discovering theology of the body. Several competent theologians have taken up the task to digest and render in an understandable way the often complex and verbose thought of the late pope. Catechists and educators have developed effective curricula to implement theology of the body into K-12 education.[29]

Another area of building the relationship between theologians and non-theologians, especially believing ones, is the Bible. Sacred Scripture is not only "the soul of sacred theology"[30] but also the most familiar theological text to non-theologians. A renewed appropriation of Holy Scripture in all theological disciplines offers a unified point of reference in theology, fostering a less fragmented, hyper-specialized approach. For decades, the historical-critical dominance of biblical interpretation, important as it is for establishing the literal sense, has left non-theologians without much intellectual engagement with the Bible. Theology needs to continue a deeper engagement with Sacred Scripture in the *sensus plenior* described by Vatican I in *Dei Filius* and by Vatican II in *Dei Verbum* and further developed by Pope Benedict XVI's *Verbum Domini*.[31] The theologian needs to breathe the fullness of the written word, in letter and in spirit, and let it become part of his or her own theological vocabulary. Some positive contributions in this regard are the *Catholic Commentary on Sacred Scripture*, the *Brazos Theological Commentary on the Bible*, and the initiatives and publications of the St. Paul Center for Biblical Theology.[32] These sorts of resources are helpful to connect theologians and non-theologians.

The Church in recent years has made greater efforts to renew preaching among the clergy, and that ongoing renewal should continue,

---

29. For example, Ruah Woods (https://www.ruahwoods.org).

30. Second Vatican Council, *Dei Verbum*, §24.

31. Benedict XVI, *Verbum Domini*, §35: "In a word, 'where exegesis is not theology, Scripture cannot be the soul of theology, and conversely, where theology is not essentially the interpretation of the Church's Scripture, such a theology no longer has a foundation.'" He continues, "Care must be taken to ensure that the study of sacred Scripture is truly the soul of theology inasmuch as it is acknowledged as the word of God addressed to today's world, to the Church and to each of us personally" (§47).

32. *Catholic Commentary on Sacred Scripture* (https://www.catholiccommentary-onsacredscripture.com); *Brazos Theological Commentary on the Bible* (http://baker-publishinggroup.com/series/brazos-theological-commentary-on-the-bible); St. Paul Center for Biblical Theology (https://stpaulcenter.com).

since preaching is the privileged platform where the non-theologian engages theological truths. Jeremy Driscoll, OSB, offers helpful ways to integrate theology into preaching that flows from, and is centered on, the eucharistic mystery celebrated in the Sacred Liturgy.[33] The promulgation of the *Catechism of the Catholic Church* and recent resources such as the Congregation for Divine Worship's *Homiletic Directory* and the USCCB's "Preaching the Mystery of Faith: The Sunday Homily" are positive efforts to integrate Sacred Scripture, doctrine, and theological insight into preaching.[34] The formation of good preaching should be a priority in seminaries, so that theological realities are communicated clearly, thoughtfully, passionately, and relevantly. To achieve this end, seminary formation programs may have to confront an anti-intellectualism among seminarians and faculty, which would oppose theological clarity with "being pastoral."

Part of healing the rift between theologians and non-theologians is the theologian's understanding of his or her own identity and of the science itself. This renewed identity moves away from the maverick, dissenting voice toward a believer who thinks rigorously and scientifically with the mind and heart of the Church in a hermeneutic of continuity.[35] The latter understanding produces insight, creativity, and true doctrinal development. Dissent ultimately harms the relationship with non-theologians because it obscures the credibility of what is being proposed for belief. The theologian seeing him or herself tasked with the gift and responsibility of a vocation to the mystical Body of Christ to fulfill the Lord's great commission (Matt 28:19) will overcome an immature approach toward the magisterium and will offer a more united voice to the non-theologian. This renewed identity is supported by a renewed understanding of the science of theology itself. If theologians take seriously the object of their science as the living, personal God of revelation, then the practice of this science requires not just intelligence but the engagement of the entire person, humanly and spiritually, cultivating virtue, prayer, and a robust *sensus ecclesiae*. When theologians were almost exclusively taken from the clergy, the human, spiritual, and pastoral dimensions of formation were included with the intellectual formation needed for

---

33. See Driscoll, "Fathers and Eucharistic Preaching." See also Driscoll's video lecture, "New Perspectives on Preaching."

34. See Congregation for Divine Worship, *Homiletic Directory*, and Committee on Clergy, Consecrated Life, and Vocations, "Preaching the Mystery of Faith."

35. See Ratzinger, *Nature and Mission*.

theology. Since many theologians today are from the lay state, their formation as theologians needs to go beyond academic development to include human and spiritual development and greater engagement with pastoral life. Theology is more than intellectual understanding; it is ultimately expressive of discipleship; a following; a personal, living relationship with the object by which the theologian's understanding and life are continually undergoing purification, illumination, and union with the object. Theology is not some esoteric science but a necessary part of the Christian proclamation.

From a renewed identity of themselves and their mission, theologians will be in a position to overcome the problem of the excessive pluralism of method that impedes theologians from being heard by non-theologians. The debate about theological method goes well beyond the scope of this essay, but the issue is raised because it is important in healing the fracture with non-theologians. Some philosophical methods, such as Marxism or Freudianism, are inadequate for exploring the intelligibility of the faith. Excluding such methods within theology, however, does not preclude theologians from engaging in meaningful dialogue with those systems of thought; it simply means that using such methods will result in deficient expositions of what is known by faith. The difficulties in Catholic theology during the twentieth century, especially the modernist crisis and then the postconciliar period, demonstrate the need for caution in appropriating philosophies from the Enlightenment, as they often suffer from a deficient metaphysics.

The theological tradition of the Church has been heavily influenced by two major philosophical currents, either more Platonist or more Aristotelian, more Augustinian or more Thomistic. John Paul II writes in *Fides et Ratio* that the Church "has no philosophy of her own nor does she canonize any one particular philosophy in preference to others," while recognizing "the enduring originality of the thought of Saint Thomas Aquinas," and that the Church has consistently proposed him "as a master of thought and a model of the right way to do theology."[36] The philosophical and theological synthesis forged by St. Thomas Aquinas, with its subsequent development, has yet to be matched or surpassed and has proven itself a reliable, time-tested, coherent metaphysical system. Of course, it does not come in a neat package, as the theological debate over conceptual and transcendental Thomism during the twentieth century

---

36. John Paul II, *Fides et Ratio*, §§49, 43. See also Leo XIII, *Aeterni Patris*.

shows.[37] There is a provisionality of any philosophical system, as it develops over time with further thought, and no system can claim to embrace the totality of truth. However, the metaphysics of St. Thomas can serve as a unifying foundation and point of reference for constructing theological reflection, giving theology at least a unified metaphysical voice.

At the same time, it is essential to keep the two major philosophical lines in conversation with each other. I find encouraging the recent scholarship on St. Thomas that has given greater voice to him as a biblical commentator, a deeper hearing of his Augustinian influences, and an overcoming the sometimes overdrawn differences with St. Bonaventure.[38] On this last point, it is noteworthy that a scholar of St. Bonaventure, Gregory LaNave, serves as managing editor of *The Thomist*, and proposes vibrant, robust conversation between St. Thomas and St. Bonaventure, asking Bonaventurian questions of Thomas and Thomistic questions of Bonaventure. To propose Thomistic metaphysics as a unifying basis in theological method is not to propose a monolithic or ossified understanding of St. Thomas, but true to his own method, one that is dynamic and dialogical toward other thinkers and systems. A unified metaphysical outlook would help give theologians a more unified voice toward non-theologians. The Church expects that the metaphysical point of reference for philosophical studies be Thomistic. Unfortunately, that expectation is not realized in all seminaries. Furthermore, the metaphysical training of lay theologians is often left up to themselves, and whether they can be formed in Thomistic metaphysics depends upon the university they attend.

Parishes are also a vital part of the solution because the parish is often the only place most non-theologians encounter theology. Consistently thoughtful, passionate, theologically informed preaching that connects with people's lives will help a great deal. The preacher must expound on the word of God and the mysteries of the faith in a way that is intellectually stimulating, something worth knowing, and something that has great (eternal) relevance to one's life. This kind of preaching sustained over time will help non-theologians think about the faith. The importance of the Sacred Liturgy cannot be overlooked. We need faith-filled, beautiful celebrations of the Sacred Liturgy, allowing the full force of Catholic worship to have an impact on the non-theologian, not

---

37. See McDermott, "Methodological Shifts" and "Collapse of Manualist Tradition."

38. See Dauphinais et al., *Aquinas the Augustinian*, and Weinandy, *Aquinas on Scripture*.

only in intellect, will, and emotions but also the senses. The parish should also cultivate personal connection and develop a life of prayer (Ignatian meditation, *lectio divina*, eucharistic adoration, Liturgy of the Hours), retreats and missions, ongoing intellectual formation in catechesis (even the more informal groups such as Theology on Tap and Dead Theologian Society), involvement in the works of mercy, and strengthening family life. Intermediate structures between the academy and ordinary life, such as the Augustine Institute, Word on Fire, and Catechetical Institute at Franciscan University, have been making a significant contribution in bridging the gap between theologians and non-theologians.[39] As living members of the mystical Body of Christ, theologians can avoid the ivory-tower existence of the academy and re-root themselves in the believing community by increasing their presence in pastoral life for fruitful encounter with non-theologians. Like the patristic age where theologians were bishops and thus directly involved in the pastoral care of non-theologians, the theologian's direct engagement with pastoral life will be a source of fruitfulness in doing theology and make it more relevant to non-theologians.

Finally, it is worthwhile for theologians to reexamine the means by which they communicate, which for centuries has been almost exclusively the essay or monograph format, and take inspiration from other formats from the past, for example, the more pithy scholastic disputed question, which had the added advantage of the practice of "steel-manning" an opponent's argument rather than falling into straw-man characterizations. While a direct reappropriation of that mode is probably not the answer, theologians can take inspiration from that way of doing theology to forge new modes of communication. The explosion of digital social media brings opportunity as well as challenge. The social media platforms would be challenging as they tend to be dominated by the reductionism of soundbites and slogans. Theological truths and the philosophical habit that require time and attention are needed to absorb and discuss theological realities and foster the philosophical habit. On the other hand, podcasts and video interviews seem ideal platforms for communication, as they are less restricted by the time limits of television and radio.

---

39. Augustine Institute (https://www.augustineinstitute.org), Word on Fire (https://www.wordonfire.org), and the Catechetical Institute at Franciscan University (https://franciscanathome.com/about).

Conclusion

Just as the rift between theologians and non-theologians took years to form, the proposals outlined in this chapter may take years, as they involve cultural and institutional changes, the renewal of the mission and identity of theology and the theologian, and the formation of both theologian and non-theologian. These proposals—and perhaps more will emerge from discussion of this chapter—are possible to realize, and I have indicated the various ways in which these proposals are already being implemented. It is encouraging to discover that many within Catholic theology are already working on healing this rift. The healing of the fracture between theologians and non-theologians will bring great life and energy into theology and help theology accomplish its important contribution to the Great Commission.

Bibliography

Aquinas, Thomas. *Summa Theologica*. Translated by the Fathers of the English Dominican Province. New York: Benzinger Bros., 1947. https://www.ccel.org/a/aquinas/summa/home.html.

Balthasar, Hans Urs von. "Theology and Sanctity." In *Explorations in Theology 1: The Word Made Flesh*, 181–210. Translated by A. V. Littledale with A. Dru. San Francisco: Ignatius, 1989.

Barron, Robert. "Does Religion Really Have a 'Smart-People Problem'?" Word on Fire, 6 Jan. 2015. https://www.wordonfire.org/resources/article/does-religion-really-have-a-smart-people-problem/4610/.

Benedict XVI, Pope. "Address of His Holiness Benedict XVI to the Roman Curia Offering Them His Christmas Greetings." Vatican, 22 Dec. 2005. https://www.vatican.va/content/benedict-xvi/en/speeches/2005/december/documents/hf_ben_xvi_spe_20051222_roman-curia.html.

———. "On the Word of God in the Life and Mission of the Church [*Verbum Domini*]." Vatican, 30 Sept. 2010. http://www.vatican.va/content/benedict-xvi/en/apost_exhortations/documents/hf_ben-xvi_exh_20100930_verbum-domini.html.

Buckley, Michael J. *At the Origins of Modern Atheism*. Rev. ed. New Haven, CT: Yale University Press, 2009.

Burge, Ryan P. "How Many 'Nones' Are There? Explaining the Discrepancies in Survey Estimates." *Review of Religious Research* 62 (2020) 177–90. http://ryanburge.net/wp-content/uploads/2020/02/Burge-2020-Review_of_Religious_Research.pdf.

Catechism of the Catholic Church. Vatican City: Libreria Editrice, 1994.

Cihak, John R. "Forging a Reason Suitable for Theology According to St. Bonaventure." In *Entering the Mind of Christ: The True Nature of Theology*, edited by James Keating, 143–72. Omaha: Institute for Priestly Formation, 2013.

Committee on Clergy, Consecrated Life, and Vocations. "Preaching the Mystery of Faith: The Sunday Homily." United States Conference of Catholic Bishops,

Jan. 2013. https://www.usccb.org/beliefs-and-teachings/vocations/priesthood/priestly-life-and-ministry/upload/usccb-preaching-document.pdf.

Congregation for Divine Worship. *Homiletic Directory*. Vatican City: Libreria Editrice, 2015.

Congregation for the Doctrine of the Faith. *Donum Veritatis: Instruction on the Ecclesial Vocation of the Theologian*. Vatican City: Libreria Editrice, 1990.

Dauphinais, Michael, et al., eds. *Aquinas the Augustinian*. Washington, DC: Catholic University of America Press, 2007.

Driscoll, Jeremy. "The Fathers and Eucharistic Preaching." *Antiphon* 5, no. 3 (2000) 29–38.

———. "New Perspectives on Preaching *Verbum Domini*." Notre Dame Preaching Conference, "We Preach a Christ Crucified," 26 June 2012. http://www.youtube.com/watch?v=sc5RDWyltiI.

Greenwood, Kelly, et al. "Research: People Want Their Employers to Talk about Mental Health." Harvard Business Review, 7 Oct. 2019, updated 22 Nov. 2019. https://hbr.org/2019/10/research-people-want-their-employers-to-talk-about-mental-health.

John Paul II, Pope. *Fides et Ratio: On the Relationship between Faith and Reason*. Vatican City: Libreria Editrice, 1998.

Kheriaty, Aaron, and John R. Cihak. *The Catholic Guide to Depression*. Manchester, NH: Sophia Institute, 2012.

LaNave, Gregory. *Through Holiness to Wisdom: The Nature of Theology According to St. Bonaventure*. Rome: Istituto Storico dei Cappuccini, 2005.

———. "Why Holiness Is Necessary for Theology: Some Thomistic Distinctions." *Thomist* 74, no. 3 (2010) 437–59.

Latourelle, René. *Theology: Science of Salvation*. Translated by M. Dominic. Staten Island, NY: Alba House, 1969.

Leo XIII, Pope. "On the Restoration of Christian Philosophy [*Aeterni Patris*]." Vatican, 4 Aug. 1879. http://www.vatican.va/content/leo-xiii/en/encyclicals/documents/hf_l-xiii_enc_04081879_aeterni-patris.html.

McDermott, John M. "The Collapse of the Manualist Tradition." *Faith* 46, no, 1 (2014) 14–19.

———. "Methodological Shifts in Twentieth C. Thomism." *Seminarium* 31 (1991) 245–66.

"Mental Health by the Numbers." National Alliance on Mental Illness, last updated Mar. 2021. https://www.nami.org/mhstats#:~:text=Prevalence%20of%20Mental%20Illness.%20Approximately%201%20in%205,or%20limits%20one%20or%20more%20major%20life%20activities.2.

Peterson, Jordan B. "Bishop Barron on the Jordan B. Peterson Podcast." Word on Fire, Mar. 2019, Apr. 2021. https://www.wordonfire.org/peterson/?_ga=2.157491706.1501478384.1612899815-1976010359.1612899815.

Pew Research Center. "Perception of Conflict between Science and Religion." Pew Research Center, 22 Oct. 2015. https://www.pewresearch.org/science/2015/10/22/perception-of-conflict-between-science-and-religion/.

Ratzinger, Joseph. *Dogma and Preaching: Applying Christian Doctrine to Daily Life*. Edited by Michael J. Miller, translated by Michael J. Miller and Matthew J. O'Connell. San Francisco: Ignatius, 2011.

———. *The Nature and Mission of Theology: Approaches to Understanding Its Role in the Light of Present Controversy*. Translated by Adrian Walker. San Francisco: Ignatius, 1995.

Rowland, Tracey. "How Does Spirituality Supply Theological Study with the Correct Method?" In *Entering the Mind of Christ: The True Nature of Theology*, edited by James Keating, 23–46. Omaha: Institute for Priestly Formation, 2013.

Second Vatican Council. "Dogmatic Constitution on Divine Revelation [*Dei Verbum*]." Vatican, 18 Nov. 1965. https://www.vatican.va/archive/hist_councils/ii_vatican_council/documents/vat-ii_const_19651118_dei-verbum_en.html.

———. "Dogmatic Constitution on the Church [*Lumen Gentium*]." Vatican, 21 Nov. 1964. http://www.vatican.va/archive/hist_councils/ii_vatican_council/documents/vat-ii_const_19641121_lumen-gentium_en.html.

Sokolowski, Robert. "Acquiring the Philosophical Habit." *Theology Today* 44 (1987) 319–28.

"U.S. Religious Knowledge Survey." Pew Research Center, 28 Sept. 2010. https://www.pewforum.org/2010/09/28/u-s-religious-knowledge-survey/.

Weinandy, Thomas, ed. *Aquinas on Scripture: An Introduction to His Biblical Commentaries*. London: Bloomsbury/T&T Clark, 2005.

12

The Generation Gap between Gen X and Millennial/ Post-Millennial Catholics

Helenka Mannering

In her 2003 book, Colleen Carroll referred to the young people embracing Christian orthodoxy as the "New Faithful."[1] She wrote of a trend that she had noticed across the USA, where young adults were seeking a deeper, more authentic living of their Christian faith and wholeheartedly embracing aspects (such as a demanding sexual morality) that many of their elders had rejected. Carroll noted that, although "the New Faithful do not constitute the majority of their generation . . . they do seem to constitute the majority of young adults actively involved in the Church."[2] In this chapter, the term "New Faithful" will be used to refer to practicing Catholics of the millennial/post-millennial generations (Gens Y/Z), that is, those born roughly between 1981 and 2002. The attitudes of these Catholics to their faith will be compared to that of the previous generation (Gen X, 1961–1981). It will be suggested that the fracture that exists between these two groups can be traced back to different reactions to seismic cultural shifts that have occurred in the past fifty years.[3]

---

1. Carroll, *New Faithful*.
2. Carroll, "New Faithful," 26.
3. While the discussion presented here will be based on my own observations, as well as those of others, it is important to note that I am not writing as a detached observer: I am a millennial with post-millennial siblings; my parents are both Gen X.

Similarities between Gen X and Gens Y/Z

Although this chapter will be focusing on the rift between the two generations, it is important to note firstly that many of the cultural changes experienced by Gen Xers and by Gens Y/Zers are the same, although Gens Y/Zers are experiencing these changes with greater intensity. For example, both generations have experienced the damaging effects of the sexual revolution on families and society. The oldest of the Gen X generation were seven years old in 1968; both this generation and the following ones have experienced higher rates of divorce, marital infidelity, de facto relationships, and irregular family structures. In fact, Gen X were the first generation to experience this widespread collapse of the family unit as it had previously existed. In the book *Gen X Religion*, Donald E. Miller and Apri Misha Miller write, "GenXers became the experimental project of a society testing the effects of changes in family structure and dynamics. As a result, many Xers experienced loneliness in their childhood and entered adulthood confused by the meaning of love and relationships."[4] These changes were underpinned by the permeation of feminist thought throughout society, which challenged traditional approaches to marriage, family, bearing and raising children, and women's roles in the home and society.[5] Carrie Gress reports that, as a result of the deep infusion of these philosophies into culture, as well as various other economic and social pressures, mothers now spend 50 percent less time with their children than five decades ago.[6]

Another cultural change that has been experienced both by Gen Xers and Gens Y/Zers has been the constant rapid advance in technology. Today, it is the widely available content on the internet that is shaping the thought patterns, desires, and ideals of the generation; for Gen Xers, television played the same role.[7] In fact, as Miller and Miller write regarding the Gen X generation, "The television set became the moral mentor of this generation, with role models being drawn from a cast of sitcom

---

4. Miller and Miller, "Understanding Generation X," 4.

5. For example, as Carrie Gress writes, "In the '60s, Betty Friedan argued that mothers were over-nurturing their children and that heading to work would prevent us from mothering them. Germain Greer said that childbearing 'was never intended to be as time-consuming and self-conscious a process as it is. One of the deepest evils in our society is tyrannical nurturance'" (Gress, *Anti-Mary Exposed*, 21).

6. Gress, *Anti-Mary Exposed*, 21.

7. Miller and Miller, "Understanding Generation X," 4.

characters, rock stars, athletes, and moviemakers."[8] Some have argued that the omnipresence of television (and, by extension, the internet) has been the main contributor to the rapidly changing values in contemporary society, particularly in the sexual sphere, and to the widespread awareness of, and increasing tolerance of, diverse lifestyles. Further, according to Miller and Miller, this increased tolerance correlates to declining rates of religious practice in families, increasing parental ambivalence to religion, and the phenomenon of parents wanting children to choose religion for themselves.[9]

These cultural experiences of the Gen Xers and the millennials/post-millennials have led to several similar approaches to the Catholic faith. Those who come to the faith or persevere in the faith increasingly do so due to personal conviction rather than familial or social pressure. This trend of seeking authenticity,[10] structure, solidity, and permanence, and finding them within the Church, began with Gen Xers but has intensified with millennials and post-millennials.[11] Both generations have been disappointed with various authority figures in many ways,[12] and often their search for faith is a turning towards a love that is unconditional and, increasingly so for millennials and post-millennials, a truth that does not equivocate. Both these groups place a high importance on community, albeit in different ways: for example, Gen Xers seek to incorporate a sense

---

8. Miller and Miller, "Understanding Generation X," 4.

9. Miller and Miller, "Understanding Generation X," 4.

10. Carroll, "New Faithful," 23. See also Charles Taylor's analysis of "the age of authenticity" in Taylor, *A Secular Age*. Carroll states, "Over and over again, I heard a variation of this refrain: 'I want to live my faith all the way, or not at all.' These young Christians are adamant that their faith will consume their entire lives and inform every decision they make. They hate compartmentalization, and they don't want to just go to Church on Sunday and forget that they are Christians on Monday. They want a faith that animates every aspect of their lives" (Carroll, "New Faithful," 23).

11. Miller and Miller write, "Xers are a generation of young adults who have been bruised by their parents and disappointed by their society. When they turn to organized religion, it is often to get a little structure in their lives, as well as find a source of authority" (Miller and Miller, "Understanding Generation X," 10).

12. Carroll writes, "This is a generation whose authority figures rejected tradition, whose culture lived by the slogan, 'if it feels good, do it.' This is the generation of no-fault divorce and the fully implemented sexual revolution. And yet, a growing number of these young Americans are attracted to the most disciplined ways of practicing their faith and living their lives" (Carroll, "New Faithful," 23). Another way that both generations have been disappointed by authority figures is by the child sex abuse that was perpetrated by some clergy over the past few decades.

of (horizontal) community into liturgy,[13] while Gens Y/Z want to experience the (vertical) communion with God through the transcendental beauty of the liturgy while still heavily relying on the faith-based communities that form around churches for their social life.

Furthermore, both groups tend to reject an Enlightenment epistemology, although the way they do so is different. The Gen X approach to religion seems to be underpinned by a wholesale rejection of the modernist reification of reason and a return to other forms of knowing, such as mystery, intuition, the senses, and emotions.[14] Miller and Miller write, "Xers are a deeply spiritual generation, seeking meaning and purpose while simultaneously avoiding what they perceive to be inauthentic attempts to mediate the sacred. Indeed, a new worldview is emerging, and it stands in stark contrast to the text-based, linear, rationalist empiricism of the Enlightenment."[15] For Gen Xers, the importance of religious experience and personal conversion trumps the focus of previous generations of doctrinal adherence regardless of one's feelings. Charles Taylor summarizes this approach to religion, stating, "For many people today, to set aside their own path in order to conform to some external authority just doesn't seem comprehensible as a form of spiritual life."[16] This celebration of diverse sources of knowing and the downplaying of the importance of reason has had far reaching practical consequences in the Gen X practice of religion: philosophically, it has led to the rejection of

13. Miller and Miller write, "If traditional religions are going to have any meaning, it will be in the quality of their communal practice and experience of the faith, not because of pronouncements by external authorities" (Miller and Miller, "Understanding Generation X," 8).

14. "Rationalist apologetics are rejected in favour of experiential knowing. Abstract doctrines, propositional creeds, and dogmatic affirmations are viewed with suspicion. Instead, experience replaces reason, feeling is more important than form, and the heart triumphs over the head" (Miller and Miller, "Understanding Generation X," 8). Also, "subjective knowing is valued above propositional truth" (Miller and Miller, "Understanding Generation X," 9). Charles Taylor explains the general trend of the Romantic period as follows: "Now it appears to many that desiccated reason cannot reach the ultimate truths in any form. What is needed is a subtler language which can make manifest the higher or the divine. But this language requires for its force that it resonate with the writer or reader. Getting assent to some external formula is not the main thing, but being able to generate the moving insight into higher reality is what is important. Deeply felt personal insight now becomes our most precious spiritual resource" (Taylor, *Secular Age*, 489). Taylor claims that present expressivism comes from this Romantic outlook permeating the culture.

15. Miller and Miller, "Understanding Generation X," 3.

16. Taylor, *Secular Age*, 489.

metanarratives and deconstruction of absolute truth claims;[17] morally, it has inclined some Gen Xers to elevate tolerance[18] and being mellow[19] above other virtues; and socially, it has contributed to the embracing of pluralism. The philosophical trend of seeking to overthrow modernist rationalism and metanarratives combined with the cultural effects of the sexual revolution has led Gen Xers to approach religion "not asking what must I do to be saved, but what must I do to be loved."[20]

Differences between Gen X and Gens Y/Z

While the New Faithful, like Gen Xers, reject the dichotomy between mind and body,[21] nevertheless they have returned to recognizing the importance of reason, as well as the body, as a source of knowing. For Gens Y/Zers, therefore, a commitment to truth trumps pluralism and tolerance, and there has been a return to asking "What must I do to be saved?" and a willingness to suffer for this truth.[22] Rather than being embarrassed at the accusation of ontotheology, Gens Y/Zers operate according to an implicit theo-ontology:[23] recognizing that God is the source of truth and

---

17. "Many analysts of Generation X see parallels between postmodernism in its many manifestations and the spiritual commitments of young adults. One of the hallmarks of postmodern philosophy is rejection of metanarratives that relate a unified story of reality. For GenXers, reality is simply not that neat and simple. The possibility of universal principles is rejected, abandoned because they too often reflect someone's narrow self-interest. Xers tend to believe that values and metaphysical affirmations are conditioned by people in positions of power, with a desire to control others. Hence, the task of the critical thinker is to deconstruct all claims to supposed absolute truth" (Miller and Miller, "Understanding Generation X," 8).

18. Miller and Miller, "Understanding Generation X," 7.

19. Miller and Miller, "Understanding Generation X," 7.

20. Miller and Miller, "Understanding Generation X," 10.

21. Miller and Miller, "Understanding Generation X," 11.

22. Carroll states, "Their elders in the faith frequently accuse the New Faithful of being naïve and overly simplistic. Certainly, the young are prone to be idealistic and even judgmental of their elders. But to dismiss these believers as caught up in good feelings and lofty ideals would be to dismiss the very profound conversions they have experienced, the very serious study these young adults have engaged in to understand their faith, and the heavy crosses they have carried to remain true to it" (Carroll, "New Faithful," 25).

23. Here this term is being used as the opposite alternative to Heidegger's accusation of ontotheology, where ontotheology is understood to signify that knowledge and understanding of God is sought according to metaphysical concepts and the study of

we can share in this by his grace.[24] While Gens Y/Zers continue to seek authentic engagement with their faith, they tend to recognize that there is much more to Catholicism than they can subjectively experience. Speaking to his Dominican confreres of the Eastern Province (USA) about the new vocations to the Dominicans, Archbishop Di Noia states:

> The young men who are being drawn to the Dominican Order today—from God-knows-what kinds of personal and social experiences—know that the post-modern culture of authenticity leads to moral chaos, personally and socially, and they want no part of it. They see—probably by a pure grace of the Holy Spirit, for their family backgrounds and catechetical training surely cannot explain it!—that human authenticity is possible only by living in conformity to Christ.[25]

Furthermore, to many Gens Y/Zers, the liturgical styles of Gen Xers still seem deeply influenced by Cartesian dualism and rationalism. For example, the liturgical style where every act of the priest is verbally explained during the mass suggests that knowledge is best transmitted by words and leaves little to mystagogy and imagination. Gens Y/Zers often prefer a liturgy that does not rely so heavily on rational explanations—they know they can find answers to their questions online—but that has an underlying logic that can be perceived by attunement to beauty, by cultivating an interior silence that corresponds to external silence during particularly solemn moments of the liturgy (for example, the Canon of the Mass), and that contains a repetitive structure that speaks not only to our minds but also to our bodies. James K. A. Smith writes of this postmodern approach to liturgy:

> It is only Cartesian "thinking things" that can do without liturgy; for we embodied creatures, whether ancient or postmodern, the rhythms of ritual and liturgy are gracious practices that enable discipleship and formation. Thus postmodern worship stages a recovery of the aesthetic aspects of the Christian tradition as a

---

being.

24. "These young adults see Christianity not as logical but as super-logical—beyond the human intellect because it is imbued with mystery. This post-modern generation craves mystery—that's why so many of them are attracted to a sacramental faith found in Catholic, Orthodox, and Anglican churches—and they do not need their entire faith to fit into a modern, logical box" (Carroll, "New Faithful," 25).

25. Di Noia, "New Vocations."

crucial means for redirecting our imagination in community—a means for reordering our love.[26]

Gen X can be looked at in hindsight, perhaps, as a period of in-between: the negative effects of an exclusive focus on reason as a source of knowing were recognized, but the pendulum swung too far in the opposite direction; the sexual revolution had occurred, but Church teaching had not yet been explained for many of the faithful, nor had the negative effects of the sexual revolution been realized;[27] Vatican II had concluded, but there was a lack of clarity in the implementation of it, including a lack of clarity regarding the liturgical reforms. Perhaps Gens Y/Z, then, are the beneficiaries of a new clarity that has started to arise from the confusion of this in-between period. Today, the New Faithful are aware of and on board with the Church's teaching on sexual morality[28] (for example, accepting the teachings of Paul VI's *Humanae Vitae* [1968] and being educated in the deeper vision of true love presented by John Paul II in his theology of the body [1979–1984] as *Man and Woman He Created Them*). In fact, for some, this is what draws them to Catholicism over secular versions of the good life. They have experienced the damage that has resulted from sexual liberation and seek, as Carroll writes, "a road map for living lives of meaning and purpose, and for enjoying life-long romances instead of casual 'hook-ups' or purely transactional relationships."[29] Likewise, the period of liturgical experimentation has drawn to a close, and Gens Y/Z are the beneficiaries of drawing from the storehouse things both new and old (cf. Matt 13:52).

Differences in Theological Approaches

Unfortunately, the Gen X theology that arose out of this in-between period is a source of confusion for Gens Y/Zers, and a prevalent attitude seems to be one of mistrust towards much theology written after 1961. Many Gens Y/Zers associate the academic theology of the Gen X

26. Smith, *Who's Afraid of Postmodernism*, 140.

27. For this generation, Miller writes, there was "great confusion about the meaning of love and sex and how the two interact" (Miller and Miller, "Understanding Generation X," 7).

28. "These young adults are not naïve, and when they embrace Christian sexual ethics, they are well acquainted with the alternative celebrated in the culture. That's precisely why they are attracted to chastity" (Carroll, "New Faithful," 24).

29. Carroll, "New Faithful," 23.

generation with theological rebellion, particularly against the Church's teaching on sexual morality.[30] Millennial and post-millennial Catholics seeking to grow in a deeper knowledge of their faith or beginning to delve deeper into theology are faced with a minefield of differing theological opinions. These Catholics are aware of the need for good guides who will assist them through the literature, as well as form their critical discernment, so that they can perceive theological schools and philosophical or ideological commitments.[31] One theologian of the Gen X generation, Massimo Faggioli, has claimed that this has led many Catholics to write off theology as a "discipline corrupted by 'liberal opinion'"[32] and, as a result, for many Catholic leaders to turn their focus away from recognizing the importance of academic theology and towards fighting the "culture wars" instead.[33] Although insightful, this assessment is rather simplistic. It would be more accurate to claim that Gens Y/Z are deeply interested in theology but at the same time are aware that they lack the knowledge to sift the wheat from the chaff, and so turn to sources that they perceive do this for them, often on social media and blogs.[34] Furthermore, the impetus behind learning theology is different: Gens Y/Z desire clarity[35] and understanding of their identity as Christians, rather than being concerned with academic freedom and creativity.[36] Perhaps this is due to the

---

30. "What happened in the years between the Land O' Lakes Statement (1967) and the implementation of *Ex Corde Ecclesiae* emancipated the Catholic Church from academic theology. There was a breakdown between bishops and theologians throughout the late 1970s and early 1980s having to do with the theology of sexuality" (Faggioli, "Future of Academic Theology," 7).

31. One such resource is Rowland, *Catholic Theology*.

32. Faggioli, "Future of Academic Theology," 8.

33. Faggioli, "Future of Academic Theology," 8.

34. It could be claimed that social media has become a new kind of "manual" or textbook of theology for this generation, containing theology condensed and simplified for the average consumer but also often lacking the subtlety and balance found in original sources.

35. Archbishop Di Noia states of the young men seeking to become Dominicans today: "These young men are attracted by the clarity—if not always by the sophistication and subtlety—of the Dominican theological tradition, and by the Order's recognition of the harmfulness of doctrinal error and its apostolic commitment to doctrinal preaching and theological education" (Di Noia, "New Vocations").

36. Michael Hollerich writes that those who are just beginning their scholarly careers or considering higher degrees in theology lack the previous generation's "experience of growing up Catholic, [and] do not share our set of concerns about academic freedom and integrity. They are far more likely to be anxious about identity

fact that many budding Catholic theologians have grown up without the old Catholic subculture and are thus firstly seeking "character formation—both for themselves and for their students—so that they can live as Christians in a postmodern society."[37]

However, Faggioli's dismissal of the importance of fighting the "culture wars" points to another significant fracture between Gen X and Gens Y/Z. Generations Y/Zers are maturing in a world that is increasingly hostile to religion and are therefore aware that no compromise is possible when it comes to the truths of the faith. Hence, fortitude seems to have taken on a primacy among the virtues, over the tolerance and mellowness extolled by Gen X. Whereas, as Taylor wrote, the prosperity experienced by Gen Xers masked the need for God,[38] the seeming lightheartedness of the previous generation has been replaced by a seriousness and awareness of the darkness and dangers of an atheistic existence. What contributed to the utopian vision of the previous generation has now been exposed as deeply flawed: for example, the material prosperity of consumerism has been shown to be undergirded by exploitative labor in poorer countries.[39] In his address quoted earlier, Di Noia notes this change among the young men seeking to become Dominicans today. He states:

> My sense is that these 20- and 30-somethings have been radicalized by their experience before entering the Order in a way that we were not. I am not certain how they would articulate their experience for themselves. It is as if they had gone to the edge of an abyss and pulled back from it. Whereas we tended to experience modernity (and then post-modernity) as a kind of adventure that never or rarely touched the core of our faith, these 20- to 30-somethings have experienced the moral relativism and eclectic religiosity of the ambient culture—and possibly of their own personal experience—and recognised it as

---

questions—what it means to be 'Catholic' at all rather than something else" (Hollerich, as quoted in Faggioli, "Future of Academic Theology," 9).

37. Austin, "Review of *New Wine*," 281.

38. "The new prosperity came along with better communications, and this opened horizons; but then the new pursuit of happiness drew people so strongly that they began to desert the older ritual life which was built around the community and its common efforts to survive in the physical and spiritual world. This ritual life then itself begins to shrink, in part disappear, and there is less and less to hold those who might want to stay within it" (Taylor, *Secular Age*, 490).

39. Perhaps the most influential text, which began a revolution in the way we approach consumerism, is Klein, *No Logo*.

a chaotic but radical alternative to Christianity with which no compromise is possible.[40]

With the collapse of Christendom, the virtues and values of the Church can no longer be taken for granted as underpinning our society. We are coming to glimpse what a world that is no longer informed by Christianity looks like. The New Faithful do not experience secularity as something exciting and alluring; they experience it as a menacing force seeking to eradicate the presence of God, a force that must be struggled against and overcome within our own hearts, homes, and communities.[41] Rather than turning away from older traditions and rituals, therefore, Gens Y/Zers are returning to them, as well as to other ancient practices, such as regular prayer, penance, and fasting.[42] Hence, we can observe "a trend toward a robust, demanding practice of Christianity that belies the drift toward moral and theological relativism that has characterised the mainline Christian Church for many years."[43]

In this way, the mission and urgency experienced by many of the New Faithful is of rebuilding: creating communities where God is at the center, where virtues flourish, and where traditional values such as faith and family are incorporated into the fabric of daily life. This may be why books such as Rod Dreher's *The Benedict Option* and Stanley Hauerwas's *A Community of Character* have been popular with Gens Y/Z. The New Faithful are aware that they are living through Alasdair MacIntyre's "Disquieting Suggestion"[44] and that the eclectic religiosity that has arisen out of contemporary cultural instability is inadequate.[45] Their experience of a post-Christian civilization is like that of the hobbits Frodo, Sam, Merry,

---

40. Di Noia, "New Vocations."

41. "It may be hard for us to comprehend, but these young people do not share the cultural optimism that many of us learned to take for granted in the post-conciliar period, even if with deepening unease and disillusionment as the years of the late twentieth century wore on" (Di Noia, "New Vocations").

42. Miller and Miller, "Understanding Generation X," 11.

43. Carroll, "New Faithful," 22.

44. MacIntyre offers the analogy of a catastrophe that destroys all scientific knowledge but leaves random fragments unembedded within the structure of a scientific culture for future generations and suggests that this is what has happened to ethical discourse (and, we might say, Christianity) today (MacIntyre, *After Virtue*, 1–5).

45. "It is not only the practical moral relativism of our time that the 20- to 30-somethings reject. They are also acutely sensitive to the eclectic religiosity, with its doctrinal and theological relativism, that they perceive as a dominant feature of popular culture" (Di Noia, "New Vocations").

and Pippin returning to the Shire and seeing all that they loved and held dear has been destroyed and is in urgent need of fighting for and restoring.[46] As in the Shire, so in postmodern society, the technocratic Saruman has encroached on all aspects of life, and the New Faithful believe that it is up to them to rebuild and recreate, so that the sacramental beauty of creation can be perceived once again.[47] To do so, the New Faithful seek to create real local communities whose celebrations are marked by the Catholic calendar: a reaction to the timelessness and disembodied notion of persons advanced by modernity.[48]

Yet not all the New Faithful are heroes like Frodo and Sam. Some seek to recreate an imaginary past for which they are nostalgic rather than truly revivifying Christian tradition.[49] Others, in finding truth within Christianity, act uncharitably towards those who do not hold to this truth, or even to those who pursue Christian spirituality in diverse forms (for example, those inclined to more charismatic worship versus those inclined towards the traditional Latin liturgy). The fracture between Gen

---

46. "Many of the houses that they had known were missing. Some seemed to have been burned down. The pleasant row of old hobbit-holes in the bank on the north side of the Pool were deserted, and their little gardens that used to run down bright to the water's edge were rank with weeds. Worse, there was a whole line of the ugly new houses all along Pool Side, where the Hobbiton Road ran close to the bank. An avenue of trees had stood there. They were all gone. And looking with dismay up the road towards Bag End they saw a tall chimney of brick in the distance. It was pouring out black smoke into the evening air" (Tolkien, *Return of the King*, 1314).

47. An excellent book outlining a program for an education that awakens the sacramental imagination is Caldecott, *Beauty for Truth's Sake*.

48. "If modernity fosters an ahistorical penchant for timelessness and a disembodied notion of persons as merely thinking things, it also fosters a disconnection from space and locality. David Matzko McCarthy relates this to the increasing hegemony of the (modern, capitalist) market for which, Marx famously noted, all that is solid melts into air: 'Our modern growth economy,' he observes, 'requires that our attachments to people and things be superficial. We must be on the move in order to follow the market'"(Smith, *Who's Afraid of Postmodernism*, 141; internal quote from McCarthy, *Good Life*, 42).

49. Graham Ward writes of the difference between tradition and nostalgia as follows: tradition "is not just a transmission of ideas or a transmission of a Christ-consciousness but the outworking of a kingdom, the labouring through material practices of a hope that reaches into and forges a future. Nostalgia, on the other hand, has no future. The backward glance is petrifying. It petrifies by fetishizing. The nostalgic gaze sacralises concepts, forms, and states from the past and reproduces them in a present that simulates and commodifies their pastness" (Ward, "Between Virtue and Virtuality," 55). Furthermore, a nostalgic approach by the New Faithful fetishizes an imaginary past, as they never experienced that for which they are nostalgic.

X and Gens Y/Z cannot be healed when youthful ideals blind against charity. What is needed is for both sides to seek humility and be united in fidelity to the magisterium, in a true love of Christ and the Church. Generations Y/Zers need to learn that fidelity to the magisterium and to the Church's tradition is not incompatible with intellectual curiosity and creativity, and that "tradition is more than just the dead accumulation of custom; it is a living organism that overcomes time and death by a process of continual regeneration and gradual creative development."[50] In order to do so, they need Gen X role models and guides who teach this and embody these teachings in the way they live their lives. Both Gen Xers and Gens Y/Zers can also become more united through growing in a deeper understanding of Church and contemporary culture: rather than responding to issues of the past or seeking to recreate an imaginary past, both generations can grow by thinking theologically about problems facing Catholics in the world now.[51] Further, a deeper understanding of how the Church relates to culture would be beneficial to all: neither assimilation nor avoidance are healthy attachment styles.[52] Finally, the fracture can perhaps best be healed by a commitment to growth in virtue from both sides: if the tolerance and mellowness extolled by Gen Xers grows to be the cardinal virtue of prudence and combines with the other cardinal virtues, and if the fortitude extolled by Gens Y/Zers is balanced by prudence, temperance, and justice, then both sides increase their chances for fruitful collaboration. More essentially, all should seek deeper faith, hope, and love. The Holy Spirit can do all things, even heal generational divides.

---

50. Caldecott, *Beauty for Truth's Sake*, 101.

51. Moral theology today, according to David Cloutier, needs to "engage in cultural criticism; it must identify what in our culture disorders our desires. It also needs to address how we might grow in wisdom as we seek to order our desires" (Austin, "Review of *New Wine*," 283).

52. Joseph Ratzinger speaks, for example, of the doubling of cultures enabled by Christianity. A Christian lives in the world, and therefore understands and operates within its culture (hence resisting an avoidant mentality), while at the same time living a distinctly unique Christian culture (hence resisting assimilation) (Ratzinger, *Christ, Faith*).

Bibliography

Austin, Victor Lee. "Review of *New Wine, New Wineskins: A Next Generation Reflects on Key Issues in Catholic Moral Theology*, edited by William C. Mattison III." *Journal of the Society of Christian Ethics* 27, no. 1 (2007) 281–332.

Caldecott, Stratford. *Beauty for Truth's Sake: On the Re-Enchantment of Education*. Grand Rapids: Brazos, 2017.

Carroll, Colleen. "The New Faithful: Colleen Carroll in Conversation with Scott Cowdell." *St Mark's Review* 193 (2003) 22–26.

———. *The New Faithful: Why Young Adults Are Embracing Christian Orthodoxy*. Chicago: Loyola, 2003.

Di Noia, J. Augustine, OP. "New Vocations in the Province of St Joseph: Ecclesial, Historical and Cultural Perspectives." Dominican Friars Province of St Joseph, 2010. https://opeast.org/vocations/new-vocations-province-st-joseph/.

Dreher, Rod. *The Benedict Option: A Strategy for Christians in a Post-Christian Nation*. New York: Sentinel, 2017.

Faggioli, Massimo. "The Future of Academic Theology: An Exchange." *Commonweal* 145, no. 90 (2018) 7–11.

Gress, Carrie. *The Anti-Mary Exposed: Rescuing the Culture from Toxic Femininity*. Charlotte: Tan, 2019.

Hauerwas, Stanley. *A Community of Character: Toward a Constructive Christian Social Ethic*. Notre Dame, IN: University of Notre Dame Press, 1981.

John Paul II, Pope. *Man and Woman He Created Them: A Theology of the Body*. Translated by Michael Waldstein. Boston: Pauline, 2006.

Klein, Naomi. *No Logo: No Space, No Choice, No Jobs*. London: Flamingo, 2001.

MacIntyre, Alasdair. *After Virtue*. London: Bloomsbury Academic, 2011.

McCarthy, David Matzko. *The Good Life: Genuine Christianity for the Middle Class*. Grand Rapids: Brazos, 2004.

Miller, Donald E., and Arpi Misha Miller. "Understanding Generation X: Values, Politics, and Religious Commitments." In *Gen X Religion*, edited by Richard W. Flory and Donald E. Miller, 1–12. London: Routledge, 2000.

Paul VI, Pope. *Humanae Vitae*. Roma: Libreria Editrice Vaticana, 1968.

Ratzinger, Joseph. *Christ, Faith and the Challenge of Cultures: Meeting with the Doctrinal Commissions in Asia*. Roma: Libreria Editrice Vaticana, 1993.

Rowland, Tracey. *Catholic Theology*. London: Bloomsbury, 2017.

Smith, James K. A. *Who's Afraid of Postmodernism? Taking Derrida, Lyotard, and Foucault to Church*. Grand Rapids: Baker Academic, 2006.

Taylor, Charles. *A Secular Age*. Cambridge, MA: Harvard University Press, 2018.

Tolkien, J. R. R. *The Return of the King*. Vol. 3 of *The Lord of the Rings*. London: Harper Collins, 2008.

Ward, Graham. "Between Virtue and Virtuality." *Theology Today* 59, no. 1 (2002) 55–70.

13

Theologians and the Magisterium

Nigel Zimmermann

How very good and pleasant it is
when kindred live together in unity!
—PS 133:1

It is said that St. John Henry Newman (1801–1890), upon leaving the Church of England for communion with the Holy See, would occasionally be seen weeping at St. Paul's Cathedral while the choir voices soothed London's evening anxieties with the notes of Anglican Evensong.¹ Having become a Roman Catholic, Newman could not in good conscience attend a service of non-Catholic worship again, a qualm few of us have held since the Second Vatican Council, and he could only linger in the nave or upon the church steps to listen intently to that most beloved Anglican chant. A similar scene is described when Newman visited the Anglican parish in which he served as a young curate, that of Littlemore.² In the largely Irish migrant communities of English Catholicism, Newman staked his claim and found his home, despite the barrenness of its intellectual culture, one bereft of a general appreciation of the higher arts and attention to beauty in liturgy, for which he had grown so fond. He had made a journey of conscience, being received into the Church and, despite his

---

1. Morse-Boycott, *Lead, Kindly Light*, 7.
2. Ward, *Life*, 1:205–7.

high intellect and academic achievement, patiently sat through catechesis classes with young Catholic students who must have been bewildered at this ex-Anglican clergyman's presence in the schoolroom. The journey of conscience undertaken by Newman was a story of sacrifice and heartache but ultimately one of sweetness and joy. While Newman wept at what he lost, more deeply he rejoiced at what he had discovered and did everything he could to maintain the highest degree of unity-in-truth with his first love, that of Christ in Christ's own Church. The sight of this scholar-saint standing outside in the English winter, letting the sounds of beautiful worship touch his soul without bruising his conscience, is a memory to which I will return.

I want to consider how different Newman looks to the contemporary theologian who, although seemingly in communion with the Roman Catholic Church, might use conscience as a basis upon which to publicly disagree with the doctrine and morals of that same Church. Sometimes this is witnessed in the positioning of scholars such as Fr. Hans Küng, Sr. Elizabeth Johnson CSJ, or Fr. Charles Curran, who have entered into long-standing debates that have resulted in institutional instability or some other kind of public conflict with their Church; or in the example of a shrill reaction to Pope Francis's position against capital punishment in *Fratelli Tutti*.[3] At times, such conflicts center on a particular individual, usually a theologian with some form of university position, and at times, a number of voices will be raised on the same issue. It should also be admitted that in the university lecture hall, undergraduate theology students are not slow to recognize the particular prejudices and biases of their teachers, and the lecturer's disposition towards ecclesiastical authority is always noticed and absorbed in some fashion.

Newman gave up his position and public standing, his livelihood and scholarly respectability, his personal religious aesthetic, and many friends for the sake of conscience. He left friends and holy places of the heart, for the sake of following his head and his heart together. Some theologians have seemingly gained all these things precisely by defying the pope in a public fashion, not weeping for what they have lost but for a Church they would like to create. Such theologians might think me rude for saying this, but with Newman as a guide, it can be seen that the magisterium is an organic part of the Body of the Church, and a respectful and charitable disposition towards it is not simply good manners but

---

3. See Ratzinger, "Letter"; Committee on Doctrine, "Response to Observations"; Francis, *Fratelli Tutti*, §263.

an inherent requirement, if any Catholic theologian is to show fidelity and good faith.

In the Catholic Church, the term "magisterial" refers to those particular offices that carry a permanence and divine authority. They are, as it were, fixed points in the life of the Church, although holders of those offices will change, and the shape and style of those office holders will influence the way magisterial authority is exercised. The word refers to the authority to decide and to govern, and shares its roots with the English word "magistrate," denoting an office of judgment. The notions of authority and teaching offices in the Church have been under great pressure in modernity, and the need for renewal has taken hold since before the Second Vatican Council (1962–1965), calling for reconsideration of how theologians should relate to those in ecclesiastical authority.[4] I wish to avoid the lazy notion that there is some kind of natural antipathy between bishops and theologians, or that we are talking about a dichotomy of positions, as if there is the "side" of the theologians and the bishop's "side," caught in an unedifying cyclical conflict. Robert Coffy wrote a helpful essay on how bishops and theologians might build a habit of mutual awareness and collaboration but mistakenly says in his introduction, "In this delicate question, I will try to place myself on the theologians'

---

4. Anytime the Holy See intervenes in the work of a theologian, controversy arises. Questions of academic freedom enter into play, as well as of the appropriate scope for scholarly discussion about disputed questions that are as ecclesial as they are academic. Various examples might be drawn upon from the twentieth century preceding and following the Second Vatican Council, and excesses can be identified both on the side of the Holy See and on the part of individual theologians. This chapter is not a study of specific examples; however, a sound reflection on what we have learned and how we might move forward is found in *The Church: Learning and Teaching* by Ladislas Orsy, SJ, covering the topics of magisterium, assent, dissent, and academic freedom. Because the term "magisterium" has developed over the centuries, room must be allowed for a broad approach to teaching authority beyond strict juridical limits. For example, Avery Dulles, SJ, argues for a "dual magisterium" by the hierarchy and the theologians, exercising a corrective and a formative dimension of the one authority (see especially Dulles's articles "Criteria of Catholic Theology" and "The Two Magisteria"). On the other hand, Orsy joins with Francis Sullivan to argue that whatever distinctions are needed, in the end, there is only one magisterium, because the teaching of the Church is constant and derived from the one revelation of Christ Jesus (see Sullivan's *Magisterium*). Moreover, in ordinary usage, the faithful think of the magisterium as the teaching authority of the hierarchy, including pope and bishops, and altering this would be a monumental task.

side."[5] Partly this politicization of the relationship has emerged from the disunity and aggravation of dissenting voices after the Council.

One of the most powerful and cogent arguments was made by Yves Congar, OP, who reflected on the history of the term and concluded that "the period since the Council has been marked by argument, the breaking up of what had represented Catholic unity up to and including Pius XII."[6] Congar notes that the dogmatic environment has changed; in other words, many members of the Church, like their nonreligious peers, respect other modes of authority and ideas with as much dogmatic commitment as any Catholic ever respected the magisterium. The theologian works within this fractured environment and is called to connect the faith as transmitted and defined with the condition of contemporary human life, "but it cannot be a simple commentary on pontifical teachings."[7] Over fifty years on from the Council, what Congar said seems perfunctory and unsurprising. Primarily, when discussing the magisterium, we are considering the ordinary magisterium, being the office of the bishops in their teaching of the apostolic faith in its constancy, and the pontifical magisterium, in which the successor of St. Peter, the bishop of Rome, makes an authoritative statement or defines a matter of doctrine or morals. There is of course also the conciliar magisterium, referring to the teaching of an ecumenical council, such as the most recent, that of the Second Vatican Council.

In *Lumen Gentium*, the Council stated matter-of-factly that the teaching office of the Church continues to be the authoritative voice for every Christian believer, particularly on matters of faith and morals. The Council fathers affirmed that of those teachings, "about the institution, the perpetuity, the meaning and reason for the sacred primacy of the Roman Pontiff and of his infallible magisterium, this Sacred Council again proposes to be firmly believed by all the faithful."[8] Of course, the Church did not begin in 1965, and there is a long history in which the theologian finds his or her place. For example, *Lumen Gentium* makes its own the claim of the First Vatican Council and of preceding theologians, that the office of the episcopate is filled by those appointed successors to the apostles, and that Peter's successor, the bishop of Rome, has a legitimate

---

5. Coffy, "Magisterium and Theology," 206.
6. Congar, "Brief History of Forms," 327.
7. Congar, "Brief History of Forms," 328.
8. Second Vatican Council, *Lumen Gentium*, §18.

and authoritative role both with and above his brother bishops, and theologians have a critical and living relationship to these voices of authority.[9] The immediate decades following the Council were a time of upheaval and change, some of which have borne great spiritual fruit and some of which have remained barren and desolate in terms of faith. It is hard not to detect a naïvety in the idea of universal progress in modernity, "as man's social consciousness grows and his need to tap communal wisdom is more felt," as Daniel Maguire puts it.[10] There was in the Council a hopefulness for fresh approaches centered on the Holy Spirit, not constrained by this or that intellectual construct, and leading to a newness for the mission of the Church.[11] For example, John Thornhill writes positively of a new emphasis upon the theology of communion, situating papal authority within that ecclesiology instead of merely one of juridical power, as he identifies that of the First Vatican Council (1869–1870). Thornhill sways between hopes for change and the unchanging dimensions of the papacy quickly, revealing some of the fleeting feelings of theologians after the Council, reaching out creatively at the same time as retreating back to a settled position, all the time unsure of the broader cultural context in which they found themselves.

Ultimately, Thornhill argues that infallible statements by the pope should be made only in a time of crisis and upheaval, when ecclesial unity is under serious threat, and that the papal definitions of the assumption and the immaculate conception were rather luxuries we could not afford.[12] What he is striving for is a genuine realization of the shared mission of all believers, including theologians, who must remain in full communion with their own bishop and with the pope. For this purpose, he takes up a term commonly utilized by Dietrich Bonhoeffer in the activity of German Lutherans trying to be faithful to their evangelical calling during World War II, that of the "confessing Church," that communion of disciples who self-consciously professes, teaches, lives, and shares the faith of the apostles in the face of opposition and persecution. Thornhill writes: "The confessing Church must undertake this responsibility

---

9. Second Vatican Council, *Lumen Gentium*, §§8, 15, 18, 20, 22, 23–25, 28.

10. Maguire, *Moral Absolutes and Magisterium*, 38.

11. A legacy of the Council has been a theological struggle over "spirit" and "letter" and of the exegesis needed for authentic conciliar teaching. Francis Sullivan's book *Creative Fidelity* wrestles with the authority and weight of those documents and seeks to contrast the Council with the teaching authority of John Paul II.

12. Thornhill, *Sign and Promise*, 171.

through its *witness*, a witness of proclamation and quality of life, so that, through the Word, Christ is remembered in our age for what he really is, and challenges our contemporaries with what his message has to offer them."[13]

Each of us, individually and through our vocation or office, is called to give *witness*. The episcopate and, with it, the papacy are called to give witness, and both share this mission with every believer. Hence, we have contemporary language of co-responsibility and of co-leadership. Thornhill relates the giving of witness directly to the quality of our eucharistic faith and worship, and views our Catholic faith as a baptismal call to identify with the "struggles, sufferings and hopes of the people of our times."[14] Succinctly, we are called to worship and to serve fruitfully. If fractures take place, such as evidenced in the widespread rejection of *Humanae Vitae*, the onus of responsibility is upon both theologians and those in ecclesiastical offices to uphold the faith of the Church and to share it joyfully, not to fan the flames of dispute.[15]

Long before the fights of the 1960s about artificial contraception, John Henry Newman provided an intelligent and faithful example of how to respond to conflict. Newman, along with others, felt strongly that the doctrine of papal infallibility, if properly belonging to the tradition and worthy of definitive claim, ought to be proclaimed by an ecumenical council rather than the pope himself and, as a public figure in the English Church, was a quotable and controversial voice. In the lead up to the first Vatican Council (1869–1870), Newman had been largely focused on his book *An Essay in Aid of a Grammar of Assent*. In the course of developing that remarkable essay, those of an ultramontane disposition were influencing the pope and the Council, and Newman came to be associated with the anti-ultramontane party. Although he avoided Church politics, he offered his penmanship as a scholar to correct error and proclaim truth, and so, for example, he worked with William Monsell to

---

13. Thornhill, *Sign and Promise*, 175–76.

14. Thornhill, *Sign and Promise*, 176.

15. Gaillardetz's edited collection, *When the Magisterium Intervenes*, is an important critical reflection on how magisterial interventions have, might, and should operate, although it has a very American focus with its emphasis upon what can be gleaned from the situation of Sr. Elizabeth A. Johnson, CSJ. See especially a number of substantial contributions by Johnson included in that book and evidence of her interactions with North American bishops: Johnson, "To Speak Rightly"; Johnson, "To Speak Rightly: Appendix"; Committee on Doctrine, "Response to Observations"; Johnson, "Statement"; Gaillardetz, "Reflections."

translate and print copies of an address by Ignaz von Döllinger arguing strongly against the definition of papal infallibility.[16] Part of Newman's great fear was not simply about the reputation and understanding of the pope whom he deeply respected and to whom he offered sincere fidelity, but about the consequences of a definition that appeared to be overtly juridical rather than spiritual. For Newman, the Church was fundamentally a spiritual reality, but it was also one that, through the breath of the Holy Spirit, exercised the power of reason in a deeply personal way.[17] Reason, for Newman, developed fruitfully in the human person and was not the bare and plain canvas upon which were etched facts and merciless truths. That is why Mary is the archetype not just of the Church but of the development of doctrine and of the "realizing process" of the Church. The two elements Our Lady espoused were (a) to have a heart open to the divine message and its reality and (b) to be rooted in good principles.[18] As Bernard Trocholepczy puts it:

> It is from these elements, that the process of life, under the guidance of the Holy Spirit, becomes fruitful. While, on the contrary, a Church which only pursues principles and reduces life to formulae (one could almost say in a neology: a Church which reduces orthopraxis to orthodoxis) is correct but not fruitful. Newman would put it: "Barren knowledge is a wretched thing, when it ought to bear fruit."[19]

One can see here how strongly Newman felt about the need for knowledge to bear fruit, and more so in the Church than any other endeavor. His was not a dry scholasticism but of a knowledge seeking after wisdom without being shy of affection and childlike attentiveness. This all becomes crucial to the present discussion when one considers that

16. Campion, *John Henry Newman*, 99.

17. One must remember that Newman's ecclesiology is forged in the intellectual and personal path towards holiness, by which the Church is a teacher and a mother. For Newman, the Church's ancient claim of fidelity in Christ provides sometimes the only bulwark against the shameful excesses of each new generation. Newman took up St. Paul's maxim (cf. Titus 3:10–11) that the heretic accuses himself long before he is accused by any religious authority and that the constancy of Catholic orthodoxy as it permeates the *ecclesia communio* is itself a judgment on what is true and what is false. In most cases, the magisterium does not need to condemn the heretic at all, because the truth contrasts so beautifully with what is false. See especially Newman, *Essay on Development*, 254–59.

18. Newman, "Sermon XV," in *Fifteen Sermons*, 293–324.

19. Trocholepczy, "Newman's Concept of *Realizing*," 145.

the definition of papal infallibility came to be proclaimed in a manner contrary to Newman's preferred approach. It is in his next steps we witness the very model of the ecclesial theologian, of an intellect given fundamentally to humility and to the rigors of communion. Fundamentally, Newman failed in his argument, at least insofar as ecclesiastical politics played out. But he triumphed in his Christian discipleship, because he gave a personal assent to the newly defined doctrine without animosity or discontent. Newman, known for long periods of time in which depressive episodes or great highs and lows would overcome his days, did not despair of his beloved Church or of the papacy. In fact, his defense of the role of papal infallibility became one that, while not itself new in his work and considerations, was a great example of how he understood the authority of the Church to be expressed in the tumult of temporality. Avery Dulles describes it as Newman's pondering of the "dialectical interplay between ecclesiastical authority and private judgment."[20]

Newman wished to calm and reassure those in the Church worried by the new definition, remain in close dialogue and communion with those he had refuted, and, above all, honor the Holy Spirit as the principle of unity in the *ecclesia*. This was a theologian who gave formal assent to what the Church taught, while maintaining the critical analysis and the work of questioning that the theologian is called to conduct. Newman achieved both: fidelity and scholarly critique. In his regard, he is a model for our time, in which fractures divide and division becomes an ecclesiological disposition in and of itself. It is worth quoting Newman in full on this point:

> Every exercise of Infallibility is brought out into act by an intense and varied operation of the Reason, both as its ally and as its opponent, and provokes again, when it has done its work, a re-action of Reason against it; and, as in the civil polity the State exists and endures by means of the rivalry and collision, the encroachments and defeats of its constituent parts, so in like manner Catholic Christendom is no simple exhibition of religious absolutism, but presents a continuous picture of Authority and Private Judgment alternately advancing and retreating as the ebb and flow of the tide.[21]

---

20. Dulles, *Newman*, 100.
21. Newman, *Apologia pro Vita Sua*, 252.

To take the analogy a little further, it would seem that if a theologian wishes to advance and retreat faithfully, then purposefully entering into a kind of rivalry and collision with the magisterium is an unseemly conflict and to be avoided. Moreover, a fidelity that endures with and in communion with the papacy, even if it requires personal development and a submission of one's work to the authority of the Church, will be, in the long run, fruitful in the way that Newman contended faithful reason is called to be.[22]

When reading magisterial documents since the Second Vatican Council *after* reflecting on Newman's contribution to the Church, one is struck by Newman's impact on how we understand doctrinal orthodoxy. In *Veritatis Splendor* (1993), St John Paul II speaks of fruitfulness multiple times, connecting the search for truth with the flourishing of life in the Spirit. The responsibility of safeguarding what has been received remains paramount, but not as a locked treasure box to be barricaded and sealed. The Spirit desires the truth, in its fullness, to be shared generously. Even those aspects of the moral law that to contemporary ears sound negative and constrictive are orientated towards growth and communal happiness:

> In this way, moral norms, and primarily the negative ones, those prohibiting evil, manifest their *meaning and force, both personal and social.* By protecting the inviolable personal dignity of every human being they help to preserve the human social fabric and its proper and fruitful development.[23]

When those teaching the faith are working together, oriented towards the good, even with inevitable tensions and questions to be confronted intelligently, the truth is made more manifest as something offered for the sake of all people. In this way, the heart of the theologian, when oriented properly towards that which is true, is also oriented in an ethical way towards good outcomes for all whom Christ offers his love in plenitude. Again, on the fiftieth anniversary of the International

---

22. Inevitably, calls for renewal and a hope for the freshness of the Holy Spirit to breathe through the life of the Church have to deal with questions of dissent and disagreement, between theologians (itself a fracture) and also between dissenting theologians and the magisterium. These issues are evident in Gailliardetz, who on one hand calls for the effective assistance of the Holy Spirit (*Witnesses to the*, 184), and on the other places an accent on the "tentative and experimental" aspects of theologians (*Teaching with Authority*, 246).

23. John Paul II, *Veritatis Splendor*, §97.

Theological Commission, Pope Francis reflected on the attraction for people of a "beautiful theology."[24] Quite remarkably, after half a century of some theologians using their platform to shape a negativity towards the papacy and a bristling sense of hostility towards objective truth, the pope calls theologians to distinguish between the "in-house" debates of theology and what must be shared fruitfully with the people. He recognized that as scholars, theologians must wrestle with ambiguity and argue among themselves, but when it comes to God's people, he gives a clear instruction:

> And I would like to reaffirm, finally, something that I have said to you: the theologian must go ahead, must study what goes beyond; he must also face things that are not clear and risk in discussion. Among theologians, though. But he must give to the People of God the solid substance of faith, not feed the People of God with disputed questions. May the dimension of relativism, let's say, which will always be in discussion, remain between theologians—it is your vocation—but never take this to the people, because then the people lose their way and lose their faith. To the people, always the solid substance that feeds faith.[25]

The notion of providing the "solid substance that feeds faith" is derived from a disposition of love and care for the growth of God's people. In other words, it derives from the heart and is directed towards the heart, because it is focused on what is most needed. Theologians who place themselves in opposition to the Church's teaching place themselves outside of communion and depart from their vocation. It is not prophetic to disabuse one's work of Catholic orthodoxy, but, instead, such actions invoke a kind of hubris that lends itself to disunity and poorly formed students.

The Second Vatican Council offered much promise for Catholic Christians to gather in unity around a common purpose, facing modernity with boldness, charity, and conviction, but the following decades

---

24. Francis, "Address."

25. Francis, "Address." It is important to note here that the Holy Father refers to "*la dimensione di relativismo*" immediately following reference to what we would normally think of as disputed questions. It is most likely that Francis means "relativism" in its normal usage or simply as another way of describing the atmosphere of debate about unresolved theological questions. The rest of the pope's speech would indicate this interpretation.

resulted in something of a mixed legacy.[26] There are examples of great holiness and heroic Christian witness, and, on the other hand, great fractures that have not been healed. As the Council itself was coming to an end, theologians of various schools expressed hope for the future of theological science among Catholics, as well as some predictions of the conflicts to come. What might be called "liberal" and "conservative" theologies looked very different in the late 1960s to what operates under those labels over half a century later. Edward Schillebeeckx was particularly optimistic about the immediate postconciliar church but could see glimmers of a coming battle. Having reflected on what he saw as pioneering efforts by the Council on reconciling peoples in a time of great social conflict and of refreshing the Church's witness in a new technological age, he was concerned about conservative and liberal or progressive tribes at war:

> Another difficulty in the post-conciliar period is undoubtedly the possibility of an integralistic reaction, which is, in fact, already springing up in several countries, especially in connection with the so-called Schema 13. Whether this reaction will, in fact, take on violent proportions, depends, in my view, on two factors: for convenience we can call them "progressives" and "conservatives." On the progressives, in the measure that their legitimate renewed reflection on the faith may neglect the value of obedience as a form of loyal self-surrender. The faith is, after all, a liberating bond, not a liberation from all bonds, however difficult it may be here and now to establish in precise detail where the bond lies. On the conservatives, in the measure that they, legitimately concerned for the soundness and the authenticity of this bond, identify the treasury of the faith with traditional representations which they cannot give up, with the result that they constantly make their fellow believers suspect. The unavoidable outcome of a clash between these two extremes is integralism. This is why an examination of conscience—their own, not the others'—is called for from both.[27]

---

26. Gaillardetz has done some notable work on the theology of the magisterium, and attention should be drawn to his study of Scripture in relation to magisterial authority. See his book *By What Authority?* The present chapter does not focus on biblical texts, but in Newman and the conciliar documents, Scripture is of absolute centrality.

27. Schillebeeckx, *Vatican II*, 87.

Schillebeeckx wrote these words a year before *Humanae Vitae*, and, in many respects, he spent much time after that siding with one camp against the other.

In any such examination of conscience, a key question will be the role of Christ in one's notion of the Christian mission. That is to say, if one views the person and work of Christ as the creative motivation behind the whole Christian enterprise, then one will have a notion of one's mission as sharing in and giving life through the power of the Spirit. This is the work of evangelization, and a division can sometimes be observed between Church members who are active participants in that project and those wish to interrupt the story of growth and learning. George Pell, an Australian cardinal who had studied in Rome during the time of the Council, observed a tendency in the church to balk increasingly against the task of evangelization and describes it as a bleak enterprise that is more contraceptive than life-giving:

> In contraceptive Christianity, God is underplayed, sacrifice is not mentioned, repentance and forgiveness are not required and everyone has the right to happiness in heaven or perhaps to a convenient annihilation. Even Jesus can become like Harry Potter's foe Voldemort: "He who must not be named." This is nowhere good enough. The one true God and his Son deserve much better. Certainly the Second Vatican Council neither recommended nor silently condoned such a write-down, such a retreat from the call to repent and believe.[28]

These words describe the situation in both a theological and a sociological way. In terms of the theologians, their own particular retreat from the gospel call to repentance and belief is therefore part of a broader problem, one that they both cultivate and from which they spring. The problem that Pell identifies is well established and has been witnessed since the closing of the Council. Two examples reveal something of the extent of the problem, that of the publication of *Humanae Vitae* (25 July 1968) and of *Laudato Si'* (24 May 2015).

With *Humanae Vitae*, we see Paul VI reaffirm the Church's consistent teaching since the beginning, that artificial contraception or the intentional interruption of the sexual act between a husband and a wife for the purposes of stopping the conception of human life, was immoral.[29]

---

28. Pell, "Yesterday's Council," 16.
29. Paul VI, *Humanae Vitae*, §14.

Contextually, the Church was saying no to use of the pill, a product of new technology, built upon its yes to human life. In section 6 of *Humanae Vitae*, the pope acknowledges the work of experts who made a study of the pill in light of Christian moral teaching but says that, ultimately, the bishop of Rome had to make a personal enquiry into the matter. What follows is a dialogical format in which Paul VI replies to "grave questions" thrown up by the pill, and he explains the authoritative position he came to after honoring the natural law, the limits to human freedom, the glory of married life, and an appeal to other voices of authority, including scientists and God. Priests receive a particular call to be the voice of the merciful Redeemer to married couples in their care and to echo in their teaching what is made clear by the magisterium: "So speak with full confidence, beloved sons, convinced that while the Holy Spirit of God is present to the magisterium proclaiming sound doctrine, He also illumines from within the hearts of the faithful and invites their assent."[30]

Note that assent is not demanded but invited, and the burden is placed on pastors to speak confidently about this doctrine, trusting God is already present as a light that shines within the hearts of the faithful. In fact, it is not primarily the pope or bishops who invite assent but Christ. While no previous generation of Christians would have been surprised by the pope's teaching about artificial contraception, the mood of the times in 1968 was more "Revolution" than "Let It Be," and a theological revolt against the pope rippled through European and American institutions with long-term repercussions.[31] The decades after the closing of the Second Vatican Council have been described by Gerard Mannion as a time "when disagreement and division over magisterium were at a peak level of divisiveness across the Church."[32] While there are numerous cultural and historical reasons to which we can point, the exemplar of this "peak level of divisiveness" is the reaction to *Humanae Vitae*, which became symbolic of the Church's resistance to the totalizing forces for change overtaking Western institutions.[33] This explains why, in the early years of

30. Paul VI, *Humanae Vitae*, §28.

31. "Revolution" and "Let It Be" are songs by the British pop rock band The Beatles whose music and cultural associations are often viewed as epitomizing the cultural shifts of values in the 1960s. For a very useful Catholic perspective on the revolutions of that era, see Gourlay and Matthys, *Nineteen Sixty-Eight*.

32. Mannion, "Magisterium as Social Imaginary," 115.

33. Again, see the work of Charles Curran, including a reflection on his ongoing controversial position (Curran, "*Humanae Vitae*").

his pontificate, John Paul II gave significant pastoral attention to the place of the body in Christian anthropology. What became his "theology of the body" was an attempt to develop and explain the biblical foundations of the Church's vision of married love and to cultivate what is inherently good, what is life-giving, at the heart of the family.[34] John Paul II gave talks on this topic over a five-year period, mainly during his Wednesday public audiences, emphasizing the call to communion for every human person.

With *Laudato Si'*, Pope Francis gave depth to the Catholic commitment to nurturing and protecting creation as a gift of God and to the Church's solidarity with all efforts to avoid nature's destruction, including that of the human ecosystem itself. Contextually, the Church was saying yes to the balanced protection and care of all life, not just human life, and no to the inevitability of human-made climate change. *Laudato Si'* was not an endorsement of every theory in support of catastrophic climate change, but it did describe climate change as one of the "principal challenges facing humanity in our day."[35] What Francis achieved with *Laudato Si'* is impressive: an encyclical with all the gravity of the authority of the Holy See on a topic that was generating great social anxiety, political division, and constant media attention, but without the public rejection afforded to *Humanae Vitae*. And that is the fundamental difference between *Humanae Vitate* and *Laudato Si'*: the first generated widespread secular rejection and theological dissent in colleges and seminaries around the world, and the second generated broad approval from the secular media and positive acclaim within the Church's schools and universities.[36] See, for example, the headline of *The Guardian*: "Pope Francis Calls for a Cultural Revolution."[37] There were certainly politically conservative critics of *Laudato Si'*, but surveys of secular reactions have largely shown a tendency to speak glowingly of Francis for his position on climate change.[38] Others, more prone to criticizing the Church for inaction or cultivating discord between issues of justice and issues of truth,

---

34. For the full English translation, see John Paul II, *Man and Woman He Created Them*.

35. Francis, *Laudato Si'*, §25.

36. The public response has been significantly chartered in ways unimaginable in 1968. See, for example, McCallum, "Perspective."

37. "Editorial."

38. See Walter, "Secular Societies"; Dorff, "Comparative Analysis."

write of *Laudato Si*: "It's courageous, it's prophetic, it's challenging, it's holistic, it's wonderful."[39]

As a papal encyclical, *Laudato Si'* has authoritative weight and relevance equal to *Humanae Vitae*, and yet the broad social and ecclesiastical responses have been wildly different. A simple explanation might be that the central premise about climate change in *Laudato Si'* is shared by liberal and secular media, and hence the notion of the Catholic pope endorsing such a position was to be applauded. *Humanae Vitae* appeared at a moment in which the liberal and secular media were largely committed to a causal connection between artificial contraception and women's liberation, and hence the Church's leader teaching Catholics to reflect deeply on their own tradition and to reject the technological manipulation of otherwise healthy fertility was, on ideological grounds, to be rejected. In either case, it is hard to imagine that many secular readers sat down without their political bias and actually read either encyclical. The simple logic of *Humanae Vitae*, for example, or the much longer and great depth in *Laudato Si'* would have been counterintuitive, and so we find ourselves in the strange situation of the general public being encouraged to react positively to Pope Francis on the topic of climate change and, at the same time, to maintain a steady rage against the Church's intransigent position against what is usually called "birth control." This is relevant to the question of fractures between theologians and the magisterium because, as it happens, many theologians adopted a positive view of *Laudato Si'* in equal measure to their secular counterparts, entrenching the strange position that a number would embrace the climate-change narrative as the Church understands it while rejecting the contraception narrative as the Church understands that topic; and others have taken the polar opposite position.[40]

---

39. Magliano, "'Laudato Si" Is Inspiration"; for a long list of resources for schools and children, see "*Laudato Si'* in Schools." Goodchild has made a study of the encyclical in light of a broader social and economic crisis (Goodchild, "Creation, Sin and Debt").

40. What is described here as the superficial secular reaction is complicated by the reality that a close reading of *Laudato Si'* would in fact highlight the Church's countercultural position on a range of other matters to which the liberal intelligentsia and mainstream media of both conservative and liberal hues might strongly react, including an opposition to rampant materialism and the Church's commitment to protection of all human life, including the unborn, the elderly and dying, immigrants, and refugees.

In its sixth major publication, the International Theological Commission (ITC) focuses on "The Ecclesiastical Magisterium and Theology." There, the ITC, a body established by Paul VI after the Council, outlines twelve theses exploring the *relationship* between the magisterium (being both the extraordinary and the ordinary magisterium) and the work of theology. Despite the decades of fracture and distress between these two foci of the Church from 1968 onwards, the ITC attends to the relational aspects of both with eyes wide open, not shying away from the divisions that had become politicized and even tribalized. Its opening thesis is also historically informed, acknowledging what Gerard Mannion has pointed out so strongly, that the manner in which magisterium and other parts of the Church are manifest has varied over time and according to circumstance.[41] The ITC outlines the foundational bonds shared by the hierarchy and theologians, being the word of God, *sensus fidei*, the documents of the tradition, pastoral and missionary concern for the world. Each of these four elements bind those who either fulfil a role in the teaching office of the Church or who carry out the theological task of study and teaching, and those bonds are of a supernatural character because of the grace of baptism and the call to a common mission. While maintaining the integrity and uniqueness of each person involved in these tasks, such persons are, communally, living a life of witness through the Holy Spirit who speaks and motivates the Church through those four elements.

Out of this understanding come the various functions and qualitative differences between persons fulfilling these distinct and necessary roles in the Body of Christ. For example, in thesis 8, it is clear the magisterium operates within certain limitations and is not unbound in its authoritative scope, and conversely something similar can be said of theologians who do not have free reign in their research and teaching. The ITC maintains that theologians have a critical component in their work, not as an afterthought but as a necessary aspect of their right function in the Church's mission, but the ITC does qualify that this should be exercised "positively rather than destructively."[42] It is the common mission of all members of the Church, regardless of office, that determines the nature of this specific relationship, one that involves both freedom and critical thought, and thus is prone to natural tensions. Because of

---

41. International Theological Commission, "Ecclesiastical Magisterium and Theology," thesis 1. See also Mannion, "Magisterium as Social Imaginary," 114–15.

42. International Theological Commission, "Ecclesiastical Magisterium and Theology," thesis 8.

this, the ITC affirms that the relationship is one of a rich dialogue, assuming as it does that the truth is knowable and that there are limits to how that truth may be understood and diffused under the instruction of the Holy Spirit. In its final thesis, the ITC offers some advice for the magisterium when dealing with controversial theologians accused of heresy, endorsing a path of conversation and dialogical critique before entering into any kinds of "sanctions." Here it is crucial to understand the relational character of the magisterium–theologian dynamic, that the persons involved in either area do their work with a purpose given shape and content through the mission of the Church. There is, in none of the ITC's language, space to consider autonomous units of thought or authority disconnected from one another or from the common people of God, the lay faithful, who experience the fruits of that dialogue in various tangible and intangible ways.

Those arguing against magisterial authority in its definitional forms at the point of the Second Vatican Council, such as Daniel Maguire, tend to focus on the magisterium in terms of its prescriptive limits, seeking to deconstruct or erode those distinctions so that the voice of the faithful, or laity, may be seen as an authoritative voice, in and of itself. Those arguments are largely discredited by the biblical commitment to authoritative offices in the Church as well as Catholic tradition. However, a further point is made in *Lumen Gentium* that is often overlooked, which is not about the limits of magisterial teaching but about its *relationship* with and to others in the life of the Church:

> This religious submission of mind and will must be shown in a special way to the authentic magisterium of the Roman Pontiff, even when he is not speaking ex cathedra; that is, it must be shown in such a way that his supreme magisterium is acknowledged with reverence, the judgments made by him are sincerely adhered to, according to his manifest mind and will. His mind and will in the matter may be known either from the character of the documents, from his frequent repetition of the same doctrine, or from his manner of speaking.[43]

Whereas "submission of mind and will" sounds authoritarian to liberal democratic ears, the above words add to the notion of submission the dimension of personal and social manifestation. That is to say, it is not a bare expectation of internal and intellectual *submission* to the teaching

---

43. Second Vatican Council, *Lumen Gentium*, §25.

of the church but of its *manifestation* or its being "shown," such that the supreme magisterium (specifically, the bishop of Rome) is acknowledged in a spirit of reverence and sincerity. *Lumen Gentium* even goes so far as to say that the pope's "manner of speaking" carries the gravity of authoritative speech, which is a step further than previous ecumenical councils had ever gone.[44] The notion that it is not merely the magisterium that must be respected and its teaching to be given assent, but also the way that assent is manifested, tells us something about the means by which teaching authority in the Church is received and made clear in the lives of the faithful. That is to say, the dynamic between magisterium and individual believer has a relational quality and not one of mere bureaucratic order or obedience.

It is this relational quality that brings us back to St. John Henry Newman and the means by which fractures will be healed. Newman's motto was *Cor ad Cor Loquitur*: heart speaks to heart. The heart—the core of one's being—speaks and is heard in the core of the other. For Newman, the Body of Christ is that manifestation of the kind of relationality the ITC envisages between the magisterium and the theologians: "Christ binds us in the double tabernacle, of a house of flesh and a house of brethren, and He sanctifies both, not pulls them down. Our first life is in ourselves; our second in our friends."[45]

For Newman, the bodily integrity in which we move and have our being is the means by which the heart reaches out to another. The heart is that core of the self in which echo the sentiments of our hope and our longing, both those that are alight with the truth and those darkened by despair or sin. The heart that reverberates with the beat of Christ's own heart is that which is outward-directed, seeking others instead of an unhealthy reclusiveness within the self. This is a general truth and is a gift given to each human person for the sake of his or her sanctification, but it has a special relevance for the theologian, whose first life is also within a body of flesh and the distractions of the mind, and who is called to bind him- or herself freely to the truth of Christ in his Church. That bond is not of the scholar but of the Christian disciple, contained as it is within the life of every baptized believer and strengthened and nourished by the Holy Spirit through the Church over time. The theologian is accompanied by a great number of witnesses, spiritual and corporeal, and in an acutely personal sense, that body of thought and encouragement includes

---

44. Second Vatican Council, *Lumen Gentium*, §25.
45. Newman, *Parochial and Plain Sermons*, 5:279–80.

the magisterium. In this sense, the magisterium has a relationship with theologians peculiar to that particular bond in the life of the Church, one of mutual sharing in the tasks of learning wisdom and of teaching the faithful. Locally, these tasks are performed in the dust and debris of the local church, which is always messy with the stuff of human experience, all the while cultivating communion with the universal Church.

Theologians work in communion with their ordinary and ought to take an interest in the priorities, the teaching, the tone of the local apostle. Sometimes, that will be a natural and conflict-free dynamic, and at other times, it will be a burden. More broadly, the ordinary teaching of the bishops in the context of which one does the work of theology is of direct relevance to the shape of one's considerations and specialization, and it is a matter of conscience to ensure that one's writings are not in discord with the episcopal conference or foster disunity with the members of that conference without good and sound reason.[46] Lastly and, perhaps paradoxically, *firstly* is the relationship of each theologian with the living magisterium as exercised through the office of Peter. Hans Urs von Balthasar argues that the Petrine office meets a certain anthropological need in the heart of each human person in Christ's Church. That is to say, the supernatural character of each man and woman, which we often try to hide or ignore, is one to which Peter and his successors call from afar, reminding us of our origin and destiny. Balthasar writes: "The function of the Church's leadership, particularly that of the papacy, is unceasingly to focus attention on this transcendence and even to represent it."[47] It is no accident of history that the common name of the Catholic faithful for Peter's successor is the pope—*papa*—and that the familial echo resonant in this language speaks not to an arbitrary divine lawgiver but reflects the light of a loving father. When Peter speaks, he reaches out to the faithful with a father's concern, whether or not his tone and language are always entirely appropriate. The attention he gives to transcendence is a calling out of ourselves, to include the concerns of our local context as well as to be raised above and beyond them, pondering things greater and deeper than our most immediate of concerns.

According to Newman, the heart is that honest and vulnerable convergence within the person, by which the phantoms of what we project

---

46. By "writings," what is intended here is any kind of public teaching and utterance, including personal messages on social media, which have become an intense form of public announcement and political self-posturing.

47. Balthasar, *Office of Peter*, 8.

to be the truth are expelled, and we reveal the truth of the individual human person. Newman wished to expel his own phantoms, those visages of identity for which he had become known through gossip, slander, and news reports, and thoughtfully show his true self in communication with others. He wished for each in the Church to relate to the voices of authority primarily through the truthfulness of the heart in the same way, constantly displeased at fakery and episodes of dishonesty. He said, "I wish to be known as a living man, and not a scarecrow which is dressed up in my clothes. False ideas may be refuted indeed by arguments, but by true ideas alone they are expelled."[48] It was in that tone that Newman came to write his great personal defense, the *Apologia pro Vita Sua*. Newman's emphasis on the heart and on the role of truthfulness goes to the nature of the fracture between theologians and the magisterium and the means by which those fractures, appearing at times like a great gulf, must be overcome. They are not the stuff of mere personal differences nor of something as trite as a political conflict, as if magisterial authority were just about the exercise of power. The fractures between the pope and bishops, on the one hand, and the theologian, on the other, always bear the character of an ecclesial wound, which means it is about persons in communion between whom there exists an unnecessary divide. This is the case regardless of the medium by which the theologian is operating, be it a peer-reviewed journal article, a monograph, a public lecture, or an opinion piece. Perhaps the fractures run most deep in the classroom, the context in which the academic theologian teaches and forms students not just of intellectual knowledge and understanding but of disposition. For example, the rolling of the eyes and the disposition of the lecturer when introducing a papal encyclical on a topic of morality tell every student in the room with what respect that text should be treated.[49] Those of us who studied in theological colleges in the '80s and the '90s, and even in the first decade of the twenty-first century, are all too familiar with how many lecturers hold a personal prejudice against the authoritative voice of the magisterium. When we teach, we also convey meaning and value to the texts through which we guide our students.

---

48. Trevor, *Newman's Journey*, 208.

49. Following St. Thomas Aquinas, Fr. James V. Schall links the disorders of the spiritual life with the intellectual life in a number of essays, illustrating how the manner of teaching also conveys a spiritual reality. See for example his chapter "On Spiritual and Intellectual Life" in *Another Sort of Learning*.

Conclusion

Catholic theologians are called to apply the faculties of the mind and the heart to theological questions in communion with the magisterium. Expressing a living communion with the magisterium is not the only measure of faithfulness, but nor is it a dispensable one. The teaching authority of the Church is an aspect of its organic whole, a living witness to the gospel no less crucial than the witness of the martyrs or the testimony of Holy Scripture.

A clear project emerges since the Council, and one articulated boldly by Pope Francis and referred to above, that theologians owe a debt of service to God's people and not just a loyalty to institutions, peers, or personal career. As the Holy Father said, "To the people, always the solid substance that feeds faith."[50] Theologians who purposefully feed the flock with something other than nourishment and sustenance offer a disservice to the faithful who hunger for truth and goodness. The same can be said for bishops. Those who bristle against the teaching of the Church since the Second Vatican Council are an aberration in the longer story of Christian discipleship, and it is hard to imagine the Church of future generations looking back at the postconciliar era with anything but dismay in that respect. Having said that, being in the company of heretics and schismatics is not a problem new to the scholars of 1968 and thereafter, and we would be naïve to suggest there is any lasting approach that could permanently exclude the possibility of dissent. We have to continually drink from those deep wells dug and replenished by prayerful theologians whose knees are sore from kneeling and whose voices blend with that of the living magisterium. Such voices are less like a beautiful choir than they are part of a noisy family home. Occasional correction of bishops and popes can be welcome in such a context, for the fundamentals of dogma lay out the foundations upon which the relationship between magisterial authority and theological science rests, just as the authority of a mother and father lays the foundation for which children can, in their turn, learn to question some parental decisions with respect and love. The loyal questioning by theologians can then be made upon a foundation of faithfulness. Those voices—sometimes harmonious and sometimes raucous—are those who work in the spirit of Newman, the father of Vatican II, who wept on the steps of St Paul's London. Newman, in his affective and intellectual commitment to the truth, bequeaths

---

50. Francis, "Address."

us an image of the faithful theologian on the conversion path. His heart was not bitter but beat with a thoughtful fidelity, and he understood in argument and in affective gesture the needs of the heart in calling out to another. The heart that turns to the magisterium with obedience and respect is the same heart that centers itself in the person of Jesus Christ, fostering a disposition of adoration that grounds and motivates all other activity, including the theological task.

Bibliography

Ball, Jeffrey. "Laudato Si: An Environmental Watershed?" *Journal of Corporate Citizenship* 64 (2016) 33–36.

Balthasar, Hans Urs von. *The Office of Peter and the Structure of the Church*. Translated by Andrée Emery. San Francisco: Ignatius, 1986.

Campion, Edmund. *John Henry Newman: Friends, Allies, Bishops, Catholics*. Los Angeles: Dove Communications, 1987.

Coffy, Robert. "The Magisterium and Theology." In *Moral Theology*, edited by Charles Curran and Richard A. McCormick SJ, 3:206–22. New York: Paulist, 1982.

Committee on Doctrine. "Response to Observations by Sr. Elizabeth A. Johnson, CSJ, Regarding the Committee on Doctrine's Statement about the Book *Quest for the Living God*." In *When the Magisterium Intervenes: The Magisterium and Theologians in Today's Church*, edited by Richard R. Gaillardetz, 259–72. Adelaide: ATF, 2012.

Congar, Yves, OP. "A Brief History of the Forms of the Magisterium." In *Moral Theology*, edited by Charles Curran and Richard A. McCormick SJ, 3:314–31. New York: Paulist, 1982.

Curran, Charles. "*Humanae Vitae*: Fifty Years Later." *Theological Studies* 79, no. 3 (2018) 520–42.

Dorff, Mikayla. "A Comparative Analysis of the Reception of *Laudato Si'* by Progressive and Traditional Catholics." PhD diss., University of Nebraska. 2020. https://digitalcommons.unl.edu/cgi/viewcontent.cgi?article=1259&context=envstudtheses.

Dulles, Avery, SJ. "Criteria of Catholic Theology." *Communio* 22 (1995) 303–15.

———. *Newman*. London: Continuum, 2002.

———. "The Two Magisteria: An Interim Reflection." *Catholic Theological Society of America Proceedings* 35 (1980) 155–69.

"Editorial: The Guardian View on *Laudato Si'*, Pope Francis Calls for a Cultural Revolution." *Guardian*, June 18, 2015. https://www.theguardian.com/commentisfree/2015/jun/18/guardian-view-on-laudato-si-pope-francis-cultural-revolution.

Francis, Pope. "Address of His Holiness Pope Francis to Members of the International Theological Commission." Vatican, 29 Nov. 2019. http://www.vatican.va/content/francesco/en/speeches/2019/november/documents/papa-francesco_20191129_commissione-teologica.html.

———. "On Care for Our Common Home [*Laudato Si'*]." Vatican, 24 May 2015. https://www.vatican.va/content/francesco/en/encyclicals/documents/papa-francesco_20150524_enciclica-laudato-si.html.

———. "On Fraternity and Social Friendship [*Fratelli Tutti*]." Vatican, 3 Oct. 2020. http://www.vatican.va/content/francesco/en/encyclicals/documents/papa-francesco_20201003_enciclica-fratelli-tutti.html.

Gaillardetz, Richard R. *By What Authority? A Primer on Scripture, the Magisterium, and the Sense of the Faithful*. Collegeville, MN: Liturgical, 2003.

———. "Reflections on Key Ecclesiological Issues Raised in the Elizabeth Johnson Case." In *When the Magisterium Intervenes: The Magisterium and Theologians in Today's Church*, edited by Richard R. Gaillardetz, 276–94. Adelaide: ATF, 2012.

———. *Teaching with Authority: A Theology of the Magisterium in the Church*. Collegeville, MN: Liturgical, 1997.

———. *Witnesses to the Faith: Community, Infallibility, and the Ordinary Magisterium of the Bishops*. Mahwah, NJ: Paulist, 1992.

Goodchild, Philip. "Creation, Sin and Debt: A Response to the Papal Encyclical *Laudato Si'*." *Environmental Humanities* 8, no. 2 (2016) 270–76.

Gourlay, Thomas V., and Daniel Matthys, eds. *Nineteen Sixty-Eight: Culture and Counterculture; A Catholic Critique*. Eugene, OR: Pickwick, 2020.

International Theological Commission. "The Ecclesiastical Magisterium and Theology." Vatican, n.d. http://www.vatican.va/roman_curia/congregations/cfaith/cti_documents/rc_cti_1975_magistero-teologia_en.html.

John Paul II, Pope. *Man and Woman He Created Them: A Theology of the Body*. Translated by Michael Waldstein. Boston: Pauline, 2006.

———. *Veritatis Splendor: The Splendor of Truth*. Boston: St. Paul's, 1993.

Johnson Elizabeth, CSJ. "Statement of Elizabeth A. Johnson, CSJ." In *When the Magisterium Intervenes: The Magisterium and Theologians in Today's Church*, edited by Richard R. Gaillardetz, 273–75. Adelaide: ATF, 2012.

———. "To Speak Rightly of the Living God: Appendix." In *When the Magisterium Intervenes: The Magisterium and Theologians in Today's Church*, edited by Richard R. Gaillardetz, 252–58. Adelaide: ATF, 2012.

———. "To Speak Rightly of the Living God: Observations by Dr. Elizabeth A. Johnson, CSJ, on the Statement of the Committee on Doctrine of the United States Conference of Catholic Bishops about Her Book *Quest for the Living God: Mapping Frontiers in the Theology of God*." In *When the Magisterium Intervenes: The Magisterium and Theologians in Today's Church*, edited by Richard R. Gaillardetz, 213–51. Adelaide: ATF, 2012.

"*Laudato Si'* in Schools." Catholic Climate Movement. https://catholicclimatemovement.global/laudato-si-in-schools/.

Magliano, Tony. "'Laudato Si' Is Inspiration for Those Who Want to Be Part of the Solution." National Catholic Reporter, 22 June 2015. https://www.ncronline.org/blogs/making-difference/laudato-si-inspiration-those-who-want-be-part-solution.

Maguire, Daniel. *Moral Absolutes and the Magisterium*. Washington, DC: Corpus Papers, 1968.

Mannion, Gerard. "Magisterium as a Social Imaginary." In *When the Magisterium Intervenes: The Magisterium and Theologians in Today's Church*, edited by Richard R. Gaillardetz, 113–39. Adelaide: ATF, 2012.

McCallum, Malcolm L. "Perspective: Global Country-by-Country Response of Public Interest in the Environment to the Papal Encyclical, *Laudato Si*." *Biological Conservation* 235 (2019) 209–25.

Morse-Boycott, Desmond. *Lead, Kindly Light: Studies of the Saints and Heroes of the Oxford Movement*. New York: Macmillan, 1933.

Newman, John Henry. *Apologia pro Vita Sua*. London: Longmans, Green & Co., 1929.

———. *An Essay on the Development of Christian Doctrine*. New York: Cosimo Classics, 2007.

———. *Fifteen Sermons Preached before the University of Oxford between 1826 and 1843*, 293–324. New York: Longmans, Green & Co., 1909.

———. *Grammar of Assent*. Garden City, NY: Doubleday, 1958.

———. *Parochial and Plain Sermons*. London: Rivingtons, 1868.

Orsy, Ladislas, SJ. *The Church: Learning and Teaching: Magisterium, Assent, Dissent, Academic Freedom*. Wilmington, DE: Glazier, 1987.

Paul VI, Pope. "On the Regulation of Birth [*Humanae Vitae*]." Vatican, 25 July 1968. https://www.vatican.va/content/paul-vi/en/encyclicals/documents/hf_p-vi_enc_25071968_humanae-vitae.html.

Pell, George. "Yesterday's Council for Tomorrow's World." In *The Great Grace: Receiving Vatican II Today*, edited by Nigel Zimmermann, 1–18. London: Bloomsbury T&T Clark, 2015.

Ratzinger, Joseph, for Congregation for the Doctrine to the Faith. "Letter to Father Charles Curran." Vatican, 25 July 1986. http://www.vatican.va/roman_curia/congregations/cfaith/documents/rc_con_cfaith_doc_19860725_carlo-curran_en.html.

Schall, James V. *Another Sort of Learning: Selected Contrary Essays*. San Francisco: Ignatius, 1988.

Schillebeeckx, Edward, OP. *Vatican II: The Real Achievement*. Translated by H. J. J. Vaughan. London: Sheed & Ward, 1967.

Second Vatican Council. "Dogmatic Constitution on the Church [*Lumen Gentium*]." Vatican, 21 Nov. 1964. http://www.vatican.va/archive/hist_councils/ii_vatican_council/documents/vat-ii_const_19641121_lumen-gentium_en.html.

Sullivan, Francis, SJ. *Creative Fidelity: Weighing and Interpreting Documents of the Magisterium*. New York: Paulist, 1996.

———. *Magisterium: Teaching Authority in the Catholic Church*. Dublin: Gill and MacMillan, 1983.

Thornhill, John, SM. *Sign and Promise: A Theology of the Church for a Changing World*. London: Collins, 1988.

Trevor, Meriol. *Newman's Journey*. Huntington, IN: Our Sunday Visitor, 1985.

Trocholepczy, Bernhard. "Newman's Concept of *Realizing*." In *By Whose Authority? Newman, Manning and the Magisterium*, edited by Alan V. McClelland, 136–48. Bath, UK: Downside Abbey, 1996.

Walter, Alisson. "Secular Societies and Religious Communities Find Common Ground in 'Laudato Si.'" Earth Beat, 29 June 2015. https://www.ncronline.org/blogs/earthbeat/eco-catholic/secular-society-and-religious-communities-find-common-ground-laudato-si.

Ward, Wilfrid. *The Life of John Henry Cardinal Newman: Based on his Private Journals and Correspondence*. London: Longman, Greens & Co., 1912.

www.ingramcontent.com/pod-product-compliance
Lightning Source LLC
Chambersburg PA
CBHW021652230426
43668CB00008B/604